CELEBRATING EXCELLENCE
Canadian Women Athletes

CELEBRATING EXCELLENCE

Canadian Women Athletes

WENDY LONG

POLESTAR
BOOK PUBLISHERS

The publisher would like to thank the following for their financial support:
The Canada Council
The British Columbia Ministry of Small Business, Tourism and Culture
The Canadian Studies Program and the Book Publishers Industry Development Program of the Department of Canadian Heritage
Please see pages 9, 251 and 253 for further acknowledgements and credits.

Cover and interior layout and design by Jim Brennan
Editing by Suzanne Bastedo
Special thanks to Kim and D. for their work and support.
Printed in Canada

Canadian Cataloguing in Publication Data
Long, Wendy, 1958-
        Celebrating excellence
Includes bibliographical references
ISBN 1-896095-04-6
1. Women athletes—Canada—Biography. I. Title.
GV697.A1L66 1995   796'.092'271   C95-910722-3

Polestar Book Publishers
1011 Commercial Drive, Second Floor
Vancouver, BC
Canada V5L 3X1
(604) 251-9718

FRONT COVER PHOTOS (clockwise from the top):
Gail Greenough (on Jappeloup de Luze), Chantal Petitclerc, Anne Ottenbrite, Charmaine Crooks, Kate Pace, Silken Laumann.

CONTENTS

GYM DANDIES & COURT STARS

FIELDS & GREENS

TRAILBLAZERS

STATISTICS, ROSTERS, MEDALLISTS & AWARD WINNERS

Acknowledgements

A project of this magnitude can't possibly come together from the work of one individual. So many people contributed to this book via their support, suggestions and information that to mention them all would be a publication in itself.

However, credit is due to some folks who made a special effort to find phone numbers, to go through long forgotten files and memory banks, to put down work from already overloaded schedules to lend a hand in searching out and compiling information. Above all, thanks to all the athletes to whom this book is dedicated and without whose patience and willingness to be interviewed and questioned this project could never have been completed.

Thanks also to Allan Stewart of the Canadian Sports Hall of Fame for his guidance, suggestions and quick attention to queries and requests for background; and to work done by Cheryl McNeil and Loren Spagnuolo via the B.C. Sports Hall of Fame.

Crucial information was gained from files and archives from the national governing bodies of the sports represented, with some sport representatives having to go an extra mile by arranging interviews, tracking down athletes, confirming results and offering advice: Hugh Mitchener, Penny Joyce, Barb Koppe, Brenda Gorman, Gord Vincent, Tom McIllfaterick, Sara Waterton, Shirley Glauser, Audrey Ostrom, Linda Moore, Roch Pilon, Linda Hancock, Darcy Enick, Sylvia Doucette, Tom Johnson, Dave Johnson, Sheila Robertson, Marg McGregor and Diane Imrie.

Thanks also to colleagues Arv Olson and Lyndon Little for offering suggestions and support in their areas of sports writing expertise — golf and curling respectively; to Brian Pound for the use of his books and for his suggestions; to Ted Reynolds for his thoughts, enthusiasm and remembrances.

Staff at the Vancouver Public Library must be recognized for their quiet efficiency and assistance.

A special note of commendation goes to *Vancouver Sun* sports editor Brad Ziemer for his support and enthusiasm for the project and his understanding when work and book commitments clashed.

Years ago my parents, Helen and Ralph Long, instilled and promoted a work ethic that is crucial in attempting to put together a project of this intensity. Without that ethic the walls and pitfalls of the work would have been too overwhelming. Thanks to you both.

And to my partner Steve — through interviews and writing, research and rewriting you provided a steady supply of tea, muffins and cheerful moral support. I couldn't have done it without you.

Preface

The task seemed straightforward when the idea for this book came up in late 1993. In the initial stages we discussed the book's direction and decided it was to be a celebration of excellence achieved by Canadian women athletes in a variety of sports, with a focus on Canadian women who had won Olympic gold or a world championship.

The intent was to document not only what these women accomplished but also how they made it to the top — their struggles and successes, their fears and feelings as they improved and ascended their ladder of goals.

In a perfect world, conducting personal interviews with every athlete in the book would have been the ideal method of accumulating background and personal anecdotes. But writing this book while continuing my duties as a sportswriter for the *Vancouver Sun*, combined with limited resources for travel, required that some interviews be conducted via telephone and some information from sport groups and individuals be received by mail and fax. Yet, during the sixteen months it took to put this book together, it was helpful that many of the featured athletes who live in areas outside B.C. happened to be passing through the Vancouver area on holiday or on business and were most willing to be interviewed during their stay. In the end, I interviewed more than half of the featured athletes in person, another thirty per cent by phone and the remaining ten per cent a combination of the two.

The interviews began with a standard format — confirming results, checking birthplaces and birthdates; asking how the athlete became involved in the sport and what drove her to keep going — was she inspired by any individuals; was there a moment or event that caused her to question her participation or commitment and, if so, why did she keep going?

Through the interviews and research emerged some interesting parallels in the experiences of many of the women, regardless of their sport. Many were competent in several sports; most enjoyed family support for their athleticism and stayed involved in sport for life. Few were inspired to compete because of personal desire to become just like a sporting idol revered in youth. Indeed, most women could not name anyone they might have modelled themselves after, although the achievements of certain individuals in unrelated activities, such as Terry Fox or Rick Hansen, served as emotional inspiration for what the athletes would accomplish in their own sports.

What also became clear was that many of the women interviewed attained their greatest success only after enduring a considerable personal hardship, such as injury or disappointment, a pivotal and difficult moment in sport or life that would have been cause for many others to give up. It seemed that making the commitment to continue working on the sport was instrumental in then propelling the athlete not only through the difficult time but also to a higher plane of competitive excellence. In very few cases was the trip to the top remotely easy. The general public might believe that rower Silken Laumann was born with the proverbial oar in her hand but one of her greatest challenges upon entering the sport was learning how to keep the shell from tipping. Wrestler Christine Nordhagen had to separate her competitive self from the social individual who felt compelled to apologize each time she threw a rival to the mat. Figure skater Karen Magnussen suffered two fractured legs but recovered to become a world champion.

Initially, the task of compiling a list of athletes and sports seemed simple. But after poring over background files accumulated over years of working as a sportswriter, and once further research and requests to sport groups for more information uncovered more names, and interviews with athletes revealed still more stories and individuals, one thing became abundantly clear to me: a thorough celebration of the successes and achievements of Canadian women athletes would require a publication of encyclopedic proportions. So many Canadian women have done so much yet it is only in recent years that their accomplishments have come close to being noted with the same diligence and coverage as routinely given male athletes. A Saturday night television ritual highlighting a contest between two National Hockey League teams has made Canadian household names of even the most marginal stickhandlers, while Canadian women athletes have tended to toil in near anonymity until an Olympic Games or a world championship brings them into the sport pages and on the television screen for brief periods of time.

Some, like skater Barbara Ann Scott, skier Nancy Greene or basketball's Edmonton Grads, managed to capture the hearts of the people and remained popular long after their sporting achievements were accomplished. Others received attention for what seemed an instant, their names falling into obscurity as successive generations appreciated only the big names of their respective times.

"We were so much a part of Edmonton at that time, they have passed that feeling for us, that admiration and love, they've passed that on to their children," said Grad player Betty Bawden Bowen in assessing what it is that has kept the Grads so alive in the minds of not only the people of Edmonton but in the Canadian public.

"I can't tell you how many times I've gone to hand out awards or to make an appearance as part of the Grads and people come up and say: 'My mom, or my grandmother, told me all about the Grads.'"

Professional sports, and their subsequent widespread coverage on television, have served to bring role models and heroes to young men and boys right in the comfort of their own living rooms. With few professional sports other than golf and tennis open to women, and with media's preoccupation with professional sport, women have had fewer chances to see and appreciate what might be worthy heroes and role models for them. Word of mouth, the simple telling of a story, as Bowen notes, may be an ancient method of passing information but it can be highly effective. It is hoped the stories here might inspire, compel and move readers to appreciate the achievements of Canada's women athletes with the same vigour as one might celebrate the player who scores the game winner in a Stanley Cup playoff.

While this book primarily explores the lives and achievements of many Canadian women who have made it to the top of the Olympic or world championship podium, an effort has also been made to recognize those whose long-term commitment and participation made them integral players in their sports even if they never earned the title of world or Olympic champion. The most difficult task was paring the list down to a workable size — as it is the book is twice as large as originally envisioned — while ensuring the athletes and sports included represented an interesting cross section of sporting life without degenerating into an encyclopedic and arid array of facts, figures and names, names, names.

These are the stories of Canadian women who took on the challenge of finding out how good they could be in their chosen sports and persevered to become the best or, at least, as good as gold.

Wendy Long
May 1995

Introduction

An information sheet supplied by the Canadian Association for the Advancement of Women and Sport and Physical Activity notes that in 1500 BC women were taking part in the risky sport of bull jumping. Five hundred years later the women-only Herean Games took place in Greece and in 396 BC Princess Kyniska of Sparta became the first female Olympic champion by winning the chariot race.

That women have been competing in sports since early recorded history is not surprising in that humans are competitive creatures and seem to relish pitting one individual against another — whether it be in war, in politics, or in sport.

The ancient Greek notion of an Olympic Games — an event featuring competition in several sports drawing athletes from all regions of Greece — emerged again in 1896 as a celebration of athletic excellence featuring competitors from several countries and, eventually, separate Winter and Summer games. So many countries and athletes are now involved that Olympic organizers were working in 1995 to perhaps delete certain sports or to require a series of regional Olympic pre-selection events to choose fewer athletes to advance to the Olympics. Over the years individual sports such as track and field and alpine ski racing evolved their own world championships, giving competitors another major event to compete for in addition to the quadrennial Olympic competition. Access to the Olympic program was gained by sport groups lobbying, sometimes long and hard, and proving they had the necessary international infrastructure by playing successful hosts to World Cup and other world championship events.

While athletic participation has long been considered a necessary element of a boy's education, in many cultures it has been frowned upon for girls. As such, the bureaucratic framework of sport organization and subsequent athletic opportunity was largely a by-men/for-men situation. Or, if there were local opportunities for women in certain sports, those opportunities often did not extend past the provincial or regional level. For instance, a women's world curling championship did not exist until 1979 while the men had competed at the world level for years.

Recognition of athletes with a disability has also blossomed into the Paralympic Games — the Olympic Games equivalent for athletes with a disability. The first Paralympics were held in Rome in 1960 and since that time disabled athletes have begun to achieve a change in status in the general public eye. Initially it was perceived that sport was good for rehabilitation, and participation was a good social outlet.In the 1990s, athletes with a disability are being recognized for the work and talent integral in their achievements in what has become a fiercely competitive and varied international arena.

Sport Organizations and Governing Bodies

CAAWS — Canadian Association for the Advancement of Women and Sport and Physical Activity

CIAU — Canadian Inter-University Athletic Union

CONCACAF — Confederation of North, Central American and Caribbean Football

FINA — Federation Internationale de Natation Amateur/International Amateur Swimming Federation

FIS — Federation Internationale de Ski

FIFA — Federation Internationale de Football Association

IAAF — International Amateur Athletic Federation

IOC — International Olympic Committee

ISU — International Skating Union

LPGA — Ladies Professional Golf Association

NAIA — National Association of Intercollegiate Athletics

NBA — National Basketball Association

NCAA — National Collegiate Athletic Association

NHL — National Hockey League

IN THE SNOW

Alpine Skiing

On March 3, 1994, a gathering of historic proportion for Canadian sport unfolded at Pika's Restaurant atop Whistler Mountain in British Columbia. Eight world and Olympic champions took their places at a dais luncheon table in a cordoned-off area at the back of the noisy eatery. Cameras clicked, tape recorders whirred and skiing folk who were not part of the select group of media and invited guests for the occasion clustered around the lunch-area perimeter in an effort to catch a glimpse of the guests of honour — eight women whose collective achievements rank at the very pinnacle of Canadian sport endeavour and who also serve as personal examples of excellence in their respective generations of alpine ski racers.

Lucile Wheeler. Anne Heggtveit. Nancy Greene. Betsy Clifford. Kathy Kreiner. Gerry Sorensen. Kerrin Lee-Gartner. Kate Pace. All Canadian, all world or Olympic champions. All eight had never before been in the same room together prior to that week-long gathering that was part of the festivities for the Warsteiner World Cup downhills — the first women's World Cup races to be held at Whistler Mountain since 1975. Their coming together marked a long overdue celebration of Canadian women skiers who, despite their individual laurels, often took a back seat in the media and public imagination to the group of male downhillers who achieved worldwide acclaim for their verve and nerve in the late 1970s and early '80s — the Crazy Canucks.

Over five decades the individual exploits of Canadian women skiers consistently put them, and their country, at the top of the winner's podium at Olympic Games, world championships and World Cup races. As the secrets of nature, life and survival are passed from mothers to daughters, a silent and invisible torch of excellence passed from one Canadian woman ski racer to another.

As teammates or roommates, idols and friends, each played a part in the success of another. It all began in 1937 when a two-year-old girl skied across frozen Lac Ouimet near St. Jovite, Quebec, carrying messages from her mother at home to her father at the popular family lodge, the Gray Rocks Inn…

Good company: An historic gathering of champions at Whistler Mountain, March 1994. From left: Betsy Clifford, Anne Heggtveit, Kerrin Lee-Gartner, Lucile Wheeler, Kate Pace, Nancy Greene, Kathy Kreiner, Gerry Sorensen.

Lucile Wheeler

"I may have been the first Canadian to win an Olympic medal but I believe all of this goes back further," insisted Lucile Wheeler Vaughan. "I had people I looked up to — Rhoda and Rhona Wurtele never had the opportunity to win a medal but they did a lot for Canadian skiing. I learned a lot from them about sport and determination."

Lucile Wheeler's name, however, stands at the beginning of the international success story for Canadian women alpine ski racers. Born in 1935, she made Canadian sport history as the country's first skier to win a Winter Olympic medal, taking bronze in the 1956 women's Olympic downhill at Cortina, Italy. Two years later she was truly on top of the world, taking the giant slalom and downhill titles at the world championships at Badgastein, Austria. And, despite the national celebration that would come in 1980 when Ken Read became the first Canadian male to win the prestigious Hahnenkamm downhill at Kitzbuehel, Wheeler was the first Canadian ever to win the Hahnenkamm, taking the women's event in 1957.

"That was a big highlight in my life," she said. "Kitzbuehel was like my second home because my coach, Pepi Salvenmoser, came from there and it was always a big aim in my life to win there."

Skiing and competing were as natural as breathing to Lucile Wheeler. Her father had a great love for winter sport and had won a silver medal in the demonstration sport of dog-sledding at the 1932 Winter Olympics at Lake Placid. As the eldest of three children and the only daughter, Wheeler lived a healthy, active life that not only included skiing as soon as she could walk, but also swimming, hiking, horseback riding and other outdoor pursuits that were an integral part of her family's running the wilderness lodge.

Wheeler's ski racing career began when she turned ten years old. Herman Gadner, the ski school director at Gray Rocks, suggested to her father she be allowed to go in a double downhill event at Mont Tremblant. Racing against senior age racers, Wheeler finished a respectable seventh and the seed of a competitive ski racer was sown.

She won the national junior championship at age twelve and in 1950 was selected to compete for Canada at the world championships. It was then that she faced a frightening and difficult crossroad.

"I think I had almost gone too far, too quickly," she recalled. "I was very young, everyone else was much older and I felt I wanted some schooling and to be around peo-ple my own age. I kept my schooling going, I went to a boarding school in New Hampshire but because of my ski racing I was much more mature than the girls my age. I remember that was the time the seed was really planted for what I wanted to do in ski racing. I became very determined. Before, I was more overwhelmed. After that, I knew I had a purpose."

Gadner was killed in an avalanche and Wheeler's progress was later overseen by several coaches, the most influential being Ernie McCulloch. Wheeler credits him with cultivating her technical prowess — considered her biggest advantage against other rivals.

In 1952 Wheeler competed in the Winter Olympics in Oslo, Norway, finishing twenty-seventh in giant slalom and downhill and twenty-sixth in slalom. That same year she began training in Europe with Austrian master coach Salvenmoser, whom she credits with completing the racer package by honing her mental attitude and race focus.

"I stayed over in Europe to do a spring race series, skiing with the Austrians on a fun basis," noted Wheeler. "I watched how they always stayed alive on their skis, they never really stood still. I tried it and found it helped me. I had never done anything like footwork. If I climbed a slalom course I would try to climb it quickly, bouncy. If I was

Lucile Wheeler: Canada's first alpine skiing world champion.

waiting to go down the hill I would try to keep moving all the time."

Every winter thereafter Wheeler travelled to Europe to train with Salvenmoser and the move paid off in improvement, leading to her breakthrough performance at the Cortina Olympics. After being disqualified in the slalom she returned to finish sixth in the giant slalom. In the downhill she proved she had arrived, taking the bronze medal behind Swiss winner Madeleine Berthot.

"At the time Canadians were overjoyed a Canadian skier could win a bronze medal," she recalled years later. "Yet when the hockey team won a bronze medal — they were expected to win gold — it was almost a disaster."

A year later she recorded her incredible victory at Kitzbuehel and in 1958 was a gold medal favourite at the world championships at Badgastein. Despite nearly missing a turn when her vision of a gate flag was obscured by a crush of spectators, her finish line time proved fastest at the end of the day — despite her personal misgivings:

"My best friend, Mimi Seguin, was at the finish line and she came up to me and said: 'You won.' She was relieved that I had reached my goal but got upset with me because I wouldn't believe it. Finally she said: 'Go find out for yourself.' There were an awful lot of spectators in those days — TV wasn't as big as it was now — and there it was on the board."

In the giant slalom she was forced to use her coach's poles after losing hers in the heady hours following her downhill victory. She nearly lost one pole midway through the giant slalom run but recovered it and went on to win a second gold medal, announcing via her results that Canada had truly arrived on the international ski scene.

Natural talent aside, Wheeler was also a maverick in that she opted to race without goggles. She was one of the first racers to compete wearing contact lenses and found that her eyes tearing at the sides when she skied was preferable to enduring constantly fogging goggles.

"The whole process, training and competing in Europe, was in a way breaking a new frontier," she said. "Training, we had no idea how to dryland train. We didn't know how successful a lot of what we tried would be. We used to do a lot of running, mountain climbing — running up the mountain and down — skipping rope. One of the problems was that I almost came to a point where my legs were too strong. I needed to be more flexible."

Wheeler retired after her world championship victories and became busy on several fronts — raising two children, working as a journalist and broadcaster and, one of her favourite accomplishments, organizing a learn-to-ski program for youngsters.

"I'm an outdoors person," she stressed. "It still bothers me terribly if I have to be inside on a beautiful day. When we were younger we'd cross-country ski to the hill, then we would climb up that hill and ski down. That's how it all started."

Anne Heggtveit

ALPINE SKIING

Every person's life is sprinkled with moments that are remembered with vivid clarity and that serve as definitive events for what was and what might be. For Anne Heggtveit Hamilton, the respected status of Canadian women's ski racing on the international scene was confirmed and advanced not only by victory but also in a brief incident shared with Canadian teammate Lucile Wheeler and coach Pepi Salvenmoser on the Streif Course at Kitzbuehel, Austria. Both male and female racers were preparing to contest their respective divisions of the famed Hahnenkamm downhill.

"The women started a little bit lower down than the men so we had to go by the famous Mausfalle, literally a cliff that the guys ski into, pre-jump and then go down at seventy miles-per-hour. There was a catwalk that allowed the women to bypass that cliff and go down to the start. This one day, the whole Austrian women's team was lined up on the edge of this cliff looking down. We came along,

Lucile and I, and Pepi, who quickly took a look at the situation. The men's course was being prepared for their downhill. Pepi looked at us and just said, 'Go!' Lucile and I peeled off over the cliff and the whole Austrian team screamed and stood there in shock. That's what you call psyching the other group out. It was fun — we did it a few more times until the race committee put an end to it."

Born in 1939, four years after Lucile Wheeler, Anne Heggtveit quickly followed, and at times skied alongside, the trail of international excellence forged by her elder Canadian teammate. What Wheeler started Heggtveit confirmed and eventually advanced, becoming the first Canadian skier to win an Olympic gold medal, taking first place in the slalom at the 1960 Games at Squaw Valley. Both were protégés of coaches Ernie McCulloch and Pepi Salvenmoser. Both achieved success at unusually young ages and were forced to come to terms with that success before making their marks as older racers.

Anne Heggtveit: Going for gold at Squaw Valley.

And while Lucile Wheeler was the first Canadian woman to capture the imagination and hearts of European fans with her success, Heggtveit was proof that the country had many more good ski racers to contest the best of Europe.

"Lucile set a perfect example," said Heggtveit. "There was a lot of competition between us but we ended up being very good friends."

The rivalry and friendship began early in both careers.

"The first time I saw Anne, it was at a ski race called the Kate Smith Trophy at Lake Placid," said Wheeler. "It was a team of ten Canadian ladies and ten American ladies, competing against each other. I was on the team when I was eleven, very young compared with the other racers, and Anne came down to ski as a forerunner. She was only eight, very petite with lovely long blonde hair.

"We were alike in that we both started to have success very young, and we were very quiet. What was exceptional about Anne was her fantastic control over her edges. It was a natural control, something she was almost born with."

Indeed, wearing skis was like wearing shoes for Heggtveit,

who likely came by her natural feel for the boards by way of her father and uncle, both national cross-country ski champions. She began skiing at age two at Ottawa's Rockcliffe Park and five years later won the senior level combined and slalom Gatineau Zone titles, competing against racers much older than herself.

It was apparent early on that Heggtveit possessed a powerful competitive spirit to complement her natural talent.

"My brother, who was six years older than I, would often take me skiing," she recalled. "We'd park the car and have to cross-country ski in to where the lifts were. My objective was always to beat him, to get to the lifts first. My being competitive was pretty obvious at an early age."

At age fifteen Heggtveit proved she was an international calibre athlete, winning the giant slalom at the Holmenkollen Races at Opdal, Norway — the youngest skier to post a win at the prestigious event. A year later, however, in 1955, she suffered a broken leg in a training mishap at Mont Tremblant, giving her a challenge greater than any she so far had encountered on the slopes.

"That was the year before they started using release bindings," she said wryly. "Initially, I had some paralysis but I overcame it, feeling very fortunate to even be back walking. It took me about three years to get over it psychologically. It was a very painful injury."

Heggtveit returned to compete at the 1956 Olympics in Cortina, finishing twenty-second in the downhill and fifteenth in the combined. Four years later, and now the Canadian team leader with Wheeler in retirement, she enjoyed her finest day as a ski racer, winning the slalom gold medal by an astounding 3.3 seconds over silver medallist Betsy Snite of the United States. A magnificent first run gave Heggtveit the luxury of opting to take the second course a tad easier, although her margin of victory shows she couldn't have let up much. The slalom victory also secured her the world combined title, although it was not an official Olympic event at the time.

"When I look at the films I know at the time I felt relatively calm," she laughed. "But when I see film of my face in the starting gate I can't believe how keyed up and on edge I was for that second run."

Heggtveit retired after her Olympic victory. A career in promoting ski apparel followed, and in 1989 she earned her accounting degree.

She concedes that with her family skiing background there was little doubt she would take up the sport. Once on skis, her competitive spirit and natural talent eventually took her to the top of the world.

"If I hadn't been a skier I thought I might want to be a concert pianist," she said. "But you can't do everything."

Nancy Greene

The sun was just a promising glow emanating from behind the tall mass of mountain. The village below was coming alive with activity but it would be some time yet before the sun would spill over the 2,440-metre-high Blackcomb Peak and bathe the village side of the slope in sunshine. A short way up from the village a woman emerged from her car in the lower level of Blackcomb Mountain's upper parking lot. Two, perhaps three other vehicles were also parked and she smiled, knowing the vehicles and their owners who had already left them for the day. The woman quickly stepped into her skis and glided down the gentle incline to catch the Wizard Express chair, and then the Solar Coaster, to gain access to her favourite runs. When others gathered later in the upper parking lot, readying for a day's skiing, she was well on her way up, anticipating the rolls, terrain changes, and pristine snow her skis would touch first before anyone else that morning.

"This is the reward for becoming a good skier," she mused, still looking very much like the young woman whose face became recognized nationally in Canadian newspapers and on the burgeoning medium of television. "I wonder, when you're a shot putter, how do you motivate yourself? What do you do afterward, when you retire from competition? This is my reward."

Skiing and Nancy Greene Raine are probably the best combination to come together since someone plunked ice cream on apple pie. In Canada, her name is synonymous with alpine skiing, not only for her success in international competition, but also for her subsequent involvement in the tourism, development, promotion, and organizational aspects of the sport. Her face is one of the most recognized in the country. Her competitive record — World Cup and Olympic champion — remains one of the most celebrated in Canadian sport history. And her name conjures up images of a less complicated time, when television was just beginning to make big-time

heroes out of multi-dot images playing sports on a screen. Her ease under the media spotlight and her considerable success made her name and visage a Canadian household standard, indeed, a commodity. How else could newspapers get away with referring to her in headlines as "Our Nancy" and have virtually everyone in the country know the story subject without reading a line?

"She was, without a doubt, the number one woman skier at that time and probably one of the best ever," remembered longtime *Vancouver Sun* columnist Jim Kearney, who covered Greene's gold medal giant slalom victory at the 1968 Winter Olympics in Grenoble, France.

Nancy Greene, the second of six children, was born in Ottawa in 1943 but grew up in the B.C. interior community of Rossland. She learned to ski on Red Mountain, starting with a rope tied around her waist and a parent holding the end for safety because the mountain's slope was so steep.

"I took figure skating lessons for a while but to me there was no action, you'd stand around and one person would twirl, then the next," she said. "I wanted to just go around and around the rink, chasing the boys. I loved to skate and it was a big social thing in our teens. I should have played hockey but at the time they didn't have girls' hockey."

They had plenty of skiing however, and by age fourteen she was already making a national impact, finishing second behind her sister, Liz, at the national junior championships at Red Mountain. Two years later, in 1960, she was good enough to be considered as team alternate for the Olympic squad in Squaw Valley. But when she won the U.S. downhill championship prior to the Games, team officials opted to give her the vital experience of Olympic competition, putting another racer on the alternate list instead. At Squaw Valley, green-as-grass Greene roomed with Anne Heggtveit:

"As a sixteen-year-old rookie on the team, I couldn't believe it when I was assigned to room with Anne

Nancy Greene: Tiger on the slopes.

Heggtveit," she said. "She was one of my heroes and there I was rooming with her. She was a wonderful person, she gave me a lot of guidance and I was so proud to see her win at the Olympics. I was standing at the starting gate when Anne went down for her second run to clinch the gold medal and I can remember being so excited I hardly thought about the course. I just wanted to ski down and congratulate Anne."

Greene, who finished twenty-second in downhill, twenty-sixth in giant slalom and thirty-first in slalom at Squaw Valley, would often tell a tale about how important that rooming arrangement was for her career. After Heggtveit won her gold medal, Greene realized that champions didn't eat, drink or wash their laundry differently from anyone else. If Heggtveit could win Olympic gold, so could Nancy Greene.

She finished fifth in the 1962 world championship downhill then improved her Olympic performance to seventh in downhill, fifteenth in slalom and sixteenth in giant slalom at the 1964 Games in Innsbruck. Her big break came in 1967 when, just as she was finding her range and ability to be one of the best in the world, the World Cup ski circuit came in to being. Greene, whose tenacity earned her the nickname Tiger, won four of the first six races and took the inaugural women's World Cup title.

A year later in Grenoble, France, Greene was Canada's top hope for a medal and she didn't disappoint. Although she suffered personal disappointment by failing to win the downhill after applying the inappropriate wax to her skis, Greene improved to earn a silver medal in the slalom.

On February 15, 1968, Greene won gold. Worried that having too much time to think about the race might hamper her performance, coaches Verne Anderson and John Platt had devised a plan to keep her occupied until she was scheduled to come out of the gate. They took her to the teahouse at the top of the hill and engaged her in conversation until suddenly Anderson said," Oh my God, the race has started!" Greene went outside, jumped on her skis and went down the hill, arriving at the starting point just as Number Five was skiing out. She was Number Nine.

"I only had four minutes to wait and little time to think," she would say years later. "I only knew that (France's) Annie Famose was leading and I was sure I could beat her, so off I went."

Not only did Greene defeat Famose, but she skied as her nickname suggested, unleashing a ferocious run to win by a huge margin, 2.64 seconds.

"Afterwards Verne and John told me they planned it down to the nth degree because, two years earlier at the world championships in Portillo, I choked," she laughed.

All of Canada celebrated her gold medal win and more than one hundred thousand people wearing various shades of "Greene" jammed Vancouver streets for her post-Olympic victory parade. That same year Greene won her second World Cup overall title, then, with fourteen World Cup victories under her skis, announced her retirement.

Endorsements, television commentating, public relations work and marriage to ski coach Al Raine followed. In 1992, their son, Willy Raine, represented Canada at the Winter Olympics in Albertville, France. Thousands of children have also honed their skiing skills as members of the Nancy Greene Ski League.

The Raines went on to develop Blackcomb Mountain and the Nancy Greene Lodge at Whistler. In 1994, having sold the hotel in 1988 but continuing in an ambassadorial and public relations capacity for the hotel, Greene also served as race chair for the all-women committee organizing the women's World Cup downhill events at Whistler. The champions' reunion that was part of the race festivities was also her brainchild. In late 1994 Greene announced she had taken on a new project as director of skiing for Sun Peaks resort near Kamloops in the B.C. interior. Al was slated to join the management team at Sun Peaks to establish a resort association. Years after Grenoble and her retirement, skiing remains a passion, even at the most rudimentary level.

"I love going skiing with someone who's having trouble," Greene said. "I just love helping people get better at the sport."

But even more, she loves best the feeling of snow and mountain under her skis, and just letting those boards run.

Betsy Clifford

ALPINE SKIING

Two years after Nancy Greene won her Olympic gold medal and second World Cup title, a skier from Old Chelsea, Quebec, became the youngest ski racer ever to win a world championship, taking the women's giant slalom title on Valentine's Day, 1970, at the tender age of sixteen. Once again Canada was at the forefront of women's international ski racing, this time in the determined and at times volatile character of Betsy Clifford.

Betsy Clifford: Success on the slopes came quickly.

"Betsy Clifford was my roommate at the Olympics in Grenoble," Greene recalled. "It gave me goosebumps when two years later she won her gold medal at Val Gardena, Italy. I've never stopped thinking what a great race she had that day. She just went for broke."

Although her Canadian predecessors, Wheeler, Heggtveit and Greene, had achieved considerable, if not quite the same measure of, success at a similar age, Clifford's victory proved a welcome yet ultimately difficult triumph. At age sixteen, where do you go when you've already reached the top of the world? In turn, the media was accustomed to the easygoing manner of Nancy Greene and found Clifford at times more complex and difficult, prompting Clifford once to remind reporters tersely that she was not Nancy Greene, nor did she ski like her Rossland predecessor.

"When I was a kid, Anne Heggtveit was my idol. When Nancy came along *she* was my idol," Clifford noted years later. "In Grenoble she was twenty-four and I was fourteen so there was a real difference. Basically I just kept my mouth shut, hid in the background, kept my eyes open, listened, and watched how everything was done. But in a way I was way ahead of my time."

Betsy Clifford was born in Ottawa in 1953 and, like Wheeler, Heggtveit and Greene, came into a family where skiing was a dominant and at times consuming activity. Her father was a former national ski champion and responsible for the development of the Camp Fortune ski area near Ottawa. Her mother, who had a degree in health and physical education, taught her to ski and her father first coached her in the finer points of racing technique.

"I've spent my whole life skiing," said Clifford. "Every waking minute that I didn't have to go to school or eat was spent skiing and my body just developed that way. I think my body was made to be a skier — the way my legs are, my arms, my whole body, my muscle tone."

Her sturdy, compact frame and low centre of gravity indeed made for success at rounding gates and she had the raw, explosive talent in complement. By age twelve Clifford was already a national junior champion and two years later she made the considerable jump to the national team and international competition.

"I liked to watch the best in the world and figure out what they did differently and then try it myself and see if it made a difference or not," she explained. "In 1969 I watched the French girls train. They were so good and I wondered what they were doing differently. They went from start to finish in training runs, past the finish line, completely attacking the course. Every run. So I also figured you have to train like you race. You're not focused if you're cruising down standing up, so if you train like that in a race you're going to go off course or fall or give up. If you train 100 per cent you race 100 per cent."

Prior to the world championships in 1970 Clifford served notice she would be a skier to watch after finishing second in World Cup slalom events at Grindelwald, Switzerland and Badgastein, Austria. Her first international victory would come not in slalom, however, but in the world championship giant slalom.

"First, I fell in the downhill and hurt my ankle," she recalled. "Then I went in the slalom and came eighth so my only chance for a medal was in the giant slalom. I told my coach: 'I've got to win today, it's my only chance.' He said: 'You're not going to win today,' and I said: 'Go to hell.' I wasn't surprised I won, I had the capability to win and I felt I should have won because at the time I was really hot in slalom."

Naturally Clifford was expected to reproduce her success the following season on the World Cup circuit, which she did by winning two World Cup slalom races while tying for first in the World Cup slalom standings. Combined with her success, however, was evidence that the pressure and expectation of being a very young world champion was having a negative effect and for a time during the season she returned home while the national team continued to compete in Europe.

Disaster struck the following season when, just prior to the 1972 Olympics in Sapporo, Japan, Clifford broke both her heels in a training mishap and promptly retired. She was only eighteen.

"I was young. It was one of those things," she said. "But when I recovered I also realized I had a lot more to give, or get, so I came back. But I never really regained my excellence. I did well and all that but I didn't regain my slalom capability, which was my strength. I did one month of weight training and gained three inches of muscle all over my body but I lost 45 per cent flexibility, crucial to slalom skiing. I could do downhill all right, I was as strong as a bull but I couldn't move."

She did, however, win the slalom and giant slalom titles at the 1973 national championships. In 1974 she finished second in the world downhill championship at St. Moritz. At age twenty-two, after finishing twenty-second in giant slalom and in downhill at the Winter Olympics in Innsbruck, Austria, Clifford retired for good, although she still believed: "I could have done a lot better, been better."

When asked about an idol or coach who might have inspired her along the way, Clifford responded she always felt a kinship toward high jumper Debbie Brill.

"I have a lot of respect for her," she said. "She was a renegade, like me."

Kathy Kreiner

ALPINE SKIING

Nearly two decades later it would be known as The Zone, that special but elusive state sometimes enjoyed by athletes during a peak performance, a state of harmony and focus allowing the competitor to move without thinking, react without analyzing.

They didn't have a name for it at the 1976 Winter Olympics in Innsbruck, Austria, but they did have a sterling example of its existence — Canada's Kathy Kreiner.

"In a way, it was the most perfect skiing run that I ever had," she would recall years later. "I was most concentrated, and didn't lose focus all the way down. I didn't make mistakes. I was so focused and connected to what I was doing for that minute-and-a-half."

To be exact, her time for the Olympic giant slalom was 1 minute, 29.13 seconds. But what mattered on the day was that the eighteen-year-old from Timmins, Ontario, had sped down the giant slalom course from the much maligned Number One start position to take the gold medal, upsetting plans for a West German celebration of an Olympic gold medal hat-trick by Rosi Mittermaier.

The win made Kathy Kreiner the youngest Canadian skier to win an Olympic gold medal. The victory also capped a dream that began in Kreiner's back yard eight years earlier, after her father, a doctor with the ski team to the 1968 Olympics, returned with stories and home movies of Nancy Greene winning gold at Grenoble.

"I remember thinking then that I wanted to do that, stand on the podium and hear the national anthem played," she said. "I didn't know if I was capable but it was the start of the dream for me. I also decided when I was ten that I wanted to be in the Olympics although I didn't know what sport it would be. In the summertime I built a high jump pit in the back yard, and also did long jump, pretending I

Kathy Kreiner: Her gold medal run was perfect.

was getting ready for the Olympics."

Skiing was the obvious outlet for Kreiner's athletic enthusiasm. Her father was involved in developing the ski hill at Timmins and family weekends — Kreiner was the youngest of six children — were spent on the slopes. When the area's limited skiing became routine she took up racing at age seven for an extra challenge, determined to follow elder sister Laurie, who would also become a member of the Canadian ski team.

At age twelve, Kathy Kreiner was named to the Canadian espoir team, then two years later she was racing the World Cup circuit. At sixteen, she recorded her first and only World Cup victory in Pfronten, West Germany.

"I was pretty athletic and pretty big for my age," she said of her success as a young competitor. "In Grade 5, I was already five-foot-four. I probably wouldn't have done so well so young if I didn't have that size and strength. I had my sister, Laurie, too, and I was always trying to keep up with her. I wanted to do everything she did."

At Innsbruck in 1976 everything was coming up Rosi. The ski world in general and the German press in particular were convinced the Games would be the crowning glory for veteran Rosi Mittermaier. Going into the giant slalom, held on Friday the thirteenth, Mittermaier had already won the Olympic downhill and slalom and the press and fans virtually dismissed any chance that another skier could spoil the sweep.

"It was written up in the papers before the giant slalom that Rosi Mittermaier had won everything," laughed Kreiner. "And all the while I just said, 'No, she has not, they don't know it, but she hasn't .'"

Indeed, prior to the Olympics Kreiner left the national team to have some time on her own, using the solitude to develop what she thought was imperative mental toughness and focus.

"I decided: 'If I want to win, what do I want to think about in the starting gate and going down the hill?' I ran it over and over in my mind. When I got to the starting gate for the race I was really relaxed, I just knew that I was going to win."

The person drawing the Number One start position is considered at a disadvantage because the course often speeds up slightly after the initial few runners and the first competitor has no time gauge with which to compare and prepare herself. At the bottom, she waits in agony as racer after racer tries to beat her time. Mittermaier was a half-second faster than the Canadian midway down the slope but at the bottom the clock showed 1:29.25, twelve-hundredths of a second slower than Kreiner. At the end of the day Kreiner stood at the top of the podium, with Mittermaier

taking silver and France's Daniele Debernard the bronze medal. At the post-race news conference Kreiner was peppered with a variety of questions, the most inane being: "Sometimes when a young rising star defeats a champion they feel a sense of remorse. Do you feel like this after you prevented Rosi Mittermaier from winning three gold medals?"

Kreiner's reply: "I would have been very happy for Rosi to win three gold medals but I'm not unhappy to win one myself."

Nancy Greene was in the media centre watching the race, and years later described Kreiner's run: "Kathy had the finest touch on the snow of anyone I have ever seen. When she came out of that start gate onto the course there was a run that was true perfection. I don't think you could ever think of anything else to do on that run."

Achieving a goal that began as a dream eight years earlier, and experiencing the instant celebrity that comes with a gold medal victory, proved a hefty challenge for Kreiner. In 1977 she finished fourth in the World Cup giant slalom standings while earning second-, third- and fifth-place finishes. There was pressure for her to repeat her Olympian performance, and as the decade closed she became frustrated with what she felt was an increased emphasis on downhill racing in the team. Ironically, she finished second in a 1980 World Cup downhill at Val d'Isere, her final season on the circuit.

"I was so young when I won, it was pretty overwhelming and no one around me was prepared to deal with it," she said. "Sport psychology was just getting going in the '70s. There were books being written about it but it wasn't a recognized practice in sports. Now, most teams in Olympic sports have a sports psychologist working with them. Before, it was just left up to the individual to do something about it."

Kreiner followed her fascination with the mental side of sport, earning a Master of Science in sport psychology from the University of Ottawa. She went on to become an advisor to many teams in the mental approach to competition and conducted ski camps with a mental focus approach for the general public.

And no one can take away that perfect day on the slopes west of Innsbruck, when Kathy Kreiner was focused on winning an Olympic gold medal and the rest of the world, focused initially on Rosi Mittermaier, turned its attention on the teen from Timmins.

Gerry Sorensen

Gerry Sorensen Lenihan was the first Canadian woman to break what had become almost an expected pattern of international success. For her predecessors the story had been remarkably uniform — *Young Phenom Achieves International Success* was a headline that could have topped any account about Lucile Wheeler, Anne Heggtveit, Nancy Greene, Betsy Clifford and Kathy Kreiner.

Sorensen was different, in more ways than one. She didn't begin skiing until age eleven. She participated at national team training camps in her late teens but wasn't named to the Canadian national team for the World Cup until the then relatively late age of twenty-two. Clearly, a knee injury suffered during a team training camp in 1978 hampered her progress but Sorensen herself would later admit she wasn't in any hurry to test her skills against the world in Europe. An introspective and private individual, Sorensen did not hide her discomfort with the media attention and public relations commitments that by then had become an integral part of being a national team ski racer. She was the first of Canada's international women's champions to concentrate on one discipline — downhill. But, also unlike her predecessors who became skiers as soon as they were able to walk, Sorensen tried her hand at many athletic endeavours.

"When I was young I was always involved in sports and I think any sport, it doesn't matter what it is, makes you competitive," she stressed. "I wasn't all that serious about skiing until I made my first national team camp. I wasn't on a physical training program, I was just involved in sports and figured that was good enough, I could ski myself into shape no problem. It just came to me naturally. It wasn't until I started on a program and started to excel that I realized I had potential."

Gerry Sorensen was born in Kimberley, B.C., on October 15, 1958. Sorensen's life was not too much different from that of any young person in the interior of the province, except that she developed a love, and a knack, for skiing fast.

"I always skied because I loved to ski," she said. "Even when I first started ski racing and we'd have training, lots of times I would just take off and not even run gates. Those days kids liked to run gates, gates, gates all the time and I would just go skiing, take off from the group. I thought: To heck with these gates, I just want to go, so I did and the coaches always wondered where I went."

By the fall of 1978 Sorensen was named to the national

Gerry Sorensen: A natural athlete and world champion.

team training squad after finishing fourth in the previous season at the national championships and first overall in the west Nor-Am series. But torn cartilage in one knee suffered in a crash put an end to her season before it began. She returned to B.C. and may have abandoned her racing career had it not been for the B.C. team coach at that time, Glenn Wurtele, who provided the encouragement and support Sorensen needed to recover her confidence and competitive will.

By 1980 Sorensen had recovered and competed officially in her first year on the national team. Hers was a spectacular debut season. She finished fifth in a downhill at Megeve, France and then, starting from Number Thirty position just as West Germany's Irene Epple was giving her victory interviews, Sorensen streaked down the slope at Haus, Austria, to win her first World Cup downhill — the first downhill victory for a Canadian woman since Nancy Greene's 1968 victory at Aspen, Colorado.

A year later Sorensen won back-to-back downhills on a frighteningly icy course at Grindewald, Switzerland, then returned to Haus to race the downhill at the world alpine championships.

"I raced from Number Nine and I just remember hitting everything really well," she smiled. "When I got to the bottom the crowd was just roaring. I knew I had the fastest time but I knew there were racers starting behind me who could still win. That was the worst part, waiting at the bottom. As it turns out my closest competition came in part from my teammates — Laurie Graham finished third and Dianne Lehodey fifth. It was one of the best days ever in the history of Canadian ski racing. We partied big time."

After her sixth-place finish in the downhill at the 1984 Olympics in Sarajevo, Sorensen announced her retirement, ending her racing career with four World Cup victories and a world championship. Coach Currie Chapman attempted to change Sorensen's mind, believing she had the potential for more years of success but, at age twenty-six, Sorensen wanted to get on with her life.

"Skiing wasn't fun any more," she explained. "It got to the point that once you win you expect yourself to win and everyone expects you to win. If I came third in a race it was like something was wrong with me."

In 1982 Sorensen began a relationship with assistant coach Brendan Lenihan, who would eventually resign his position because romance between athlete and coach was a national team taboo. They married in 1984. (In contrast, only a few years later Kerrin Lee would marry assistant coach Max Gartner and the two were able to travel the World Cup circuit as husband and wife, athlete and coach.)

For her part, Sorensen had no regrets about leaving the circuit after a stellar four-year career. With hindsight and maturity, she was able to see that her discomfort with the media spotlight may have cost her exposure that could have resulted in more post-racing opportunities. But she also knew she could never have competed any other way.

"To a certain point I should have been more cooperative," she conceded. "But I was there to ski race, I looked at things differently. Now it's commercials, wearing headbands, there's big bucks in it and you have to do it. It's a job and they look at it more as a job. I didn't look at it as a job. I've always been a private person. That's the way I like it."

Kerrin Lee-Gartner

ALPINE SKIING

Kerrin Lee-Gartner: Her gold medal dream came true.

The skier tucked for all her might as she neared the finish line, looking to gain whatever milliseconds were left in her aching legs.

She sped under the banners and immediately looked at the board to her left as she braked her skis. From the depths of her crash helmet came a delighted cry, it was a sound of pure joy, emanating from the skier's very genes, forged with years of training every cell in her body toward that snowy, foggy February day.

"It's not so much that words can describe it," Kerrin Lee-Gartner would answer when asked to recount seeing she had posted the fastest time in the 1992 women's Olympic downhill at Meribel, France. "It was sheer fun, excitement, as much adrenaline as you could ever have. I put so much into that race, to win it was the most amazing feeling."

Some observers labelled Kerrin Lee-Gartner's downhill victory in the 1992 Winter Olympics a fluke. After all, the Canadian came into the race having never won a World Cup downhill. Others called it a feat long overdue, with injury hampering the Calgary resident's progress until she finally enjoyed the winning ingredients other rivals had already experienced — talent, experience, courage, and a little bit of luck.

Kerrin Lee was born September 21, 1966, in Trail, B.C. and grew up in Rossland, the same B.C. town that produced many a fine ski racer, including Nancy Greene. Indeed, her family lived on the same street as Greene's and stamped in her memory are occasional visits to the Greene residence where she would ogle the trophies and laurels earned by her famous neighbour.

"In a way, Nancy's success, and the fact that she came from the same town, gave me permission to dream that I could attain that same level, that something like that was achievable," recalled Lee-Gartner, one of five children. "I was also lucky to be raised in a family where we were all allowed, and encouraged, to dream big."

Kerrin Lee began skiing six months after her third birthday, tackling the formidable slope of Red Mountain that quickly measures the courage and ability of young skiers. By the 1983-84 season she was a member of the national alpine development group and a member of Canada's team to the world junior alpine championships, where she finished tenth in downhill. She raced in her first senior world championship in 1985 at Bormio, Italy, finishing twenty-ninth in giant slalom.

In December 1985 she suffered a major knee injury in a crash at Val d'Isere, France, putting an early end to the season. In all, Lee-Gartner's career injury tally would include five knee operations — three on her right knee and two on the left — including two reconstructions.

Her ability to recover from injury setbacks was matched by her courage on the hill. Early in her career, when Max Gartner was serving as an assistant coach, he marvelled at the young racer's tenacity. In time that racer would win his heart.

"One of her first years on the tour, we had a race at Megeve," he said. "It was foggy and snowing, and Kerrin was in the snow seed. They ran the snow seed, then the skiers in the top group. She was in third place and they decided to cancel the race. I thought: 'This girl has guts, she can hardly see but she just goes.' That is her strength."

(Author's note about snow seed: The lowest ranked skiers in the race are required to start first, rather than at the end, so that the track is packed sufficiently for the top seed racers in the event of snowfall.) Lee-Gartner finished fifteenth in downhill and eighth in combined at the 1988 Calgary Olympics, disappointed because a childhood dream of earning an Olympic medal had not materialized. She pressed on, only to meet disaster again at one hundred kilometers per hour in a 1989 downhill at Steamboat Springs, Colorado. That crash necessitated her second knee reconstruction. As she was transported off the hill by stretcher she told national downhill coach Don Lyon she would come back better than ever. Three months later she married Max Gartner, and despite all her past and future success on the slopes she would call her wedding day the happiest moment of her life.

Lee-Gartner returned to competition in 1990 and began establishing her trademark as a consistent skier who delighted in tough courses. It seemed only a matter of time before she would win her first World Cup race. The other top skiers on the circuit knew they couldn't celebrate a win until Lee-Gartner came down the hill. A year prior to the Olympics, racers gained a glimpse of the 1992 Olympic downhill course at a World Cup event in Meribel. Although bad weather forced cancellation of the race, training runs revealed the Roc de Fer course to be a tough, demanding slope. Several racers moaned it was too tough, others expressed feelings of fear. Lee-Gartner just pressed on.

"If you don't have that aggressiveness and all-out attitude, if you have a speed limit, you don't make it," said Don Lyon. "Kerrin never skied defensively. She was always on the offence, going hard at it. When conditions got harder, she got tougher."

The summer and fall training period leading up to the 1992 Winter Olympics in Albertville saw Lee-Gartner as a focused, determined athlete who devoted her entire being to training and preparing for the Games. Family and friends saw in her a new intensity and drive.

"Everything I did, all my training, all my focus, was directed toward that end," she said. "I had never been so focused in all my life."

On Saturday, February 15, 1992, Lee-Gartner's Olympic dream came true. Wearing start bib Number Twelve, she skied a courageous run down the Roc de Fer, her 1-minute, 52.55-second effort bettering the times of silver medallist Hilary Lindh of the United States and bronze medallist Veronika Wallinger of Austria. The win marked the first downhill Olympic gold medal ever won by a Canadian skier. Later she revealed to members of the Canadian press contingent that two years earlier she had had a dream which included a woman's voice announcing in French that Kerrin Lee-Gartner of Canada had won the *medaille d'or*.

"Too many times I've tried to be too perfect, too precise," she said after the win. "Today, I just wanted to look for speed."

The victory made Lee-Gartner a national celebrity. It also gave her some clout in convincing Alpine Canada to allow Max to travel with her as husband and personal coach, an issue so important to her she considered retiring. Alpine Canada relented and for another two seasons Lee-Gartner continued to represent Canada, still looking for the elusive World Cup win. It never came, although she would be close many times.

In February 1994 the ski world was stunned by the death

of Austrian racer Ulrike Maier, who crashed in a downhill at Garmisch, Germany. Lee-Gartner was particularly shaken by the tragedy, flying immediately to her parents' home in Tsawwassen, B.C., to reassess the rest of the season. Having planned to retire at the end of March anyway, Lee-Gartner conceded her confidence, courage and faith had been shattered by the incident and she needed time away from the circuit to come to grips with the tragedy and re-think her participation at the Winter Olympics in Lillehammer. A week later she returned to Europe and finished nineteenth in the Lillehammer Olympic downhill and eighth in super giant slalom. But during World Cup festivities at Whistler in March 1994, after finishing ninth in

the Whistler race, she announced officially her intent to retire from downhill racing. Kerrin Lee-Gartner's last World Cup race was a sixth-place effort on March 17, 1994, in a super giant slalom at the World Cup finals in Vail, Colorado. During her decade-long career she finished in the World Cup top five fourteen times, including second-place efforts in Switzerland, Vail and at Panorama, thirty-four times in the top ten and a hardy fifty-four results in the top fifteen.

"I would never trade anything I've done in this sport for anything else," she said at the end of her racing career. "It's allowed me to grow as a person, to see the hard times and the good times."

Kate Pace

ALPINE SKIING

In 1992 Kate Pace had planned to watch the television coverage of the opening ceremonies of the XVI Winter Olympic Games from Albertville, France. Instead, five minutes before the telecast she was going through a weight workout as part of her rehabilitation from a broken ankle suffered two weeks earlier — an injury that kept her out of those Games and out of the Olympic downhill race won by Canadian teammate Kerrin Lee-Gartner.

"I just couldn't do it, I couldn't watch the ceremonies," said Pace. "I trained for a couple of hours. I realized no matter how hard I wanted to be there, I wasn't going to be in those Olympics. I had something else to work on, getting back after my injury."

Much of Kate Pace's skiing career has been spent getting back to the slopes after injury, which is why it took her a little longer to establish herself as one of the world's best downhill racers after long serving notice she had the potential to be a top competitor.

Kate Pace was born in North Bay, Ontario, the third youngest of ten children born to Murray and Angela Pace. A natural athlete, she played volleyball, basketball and soccer on various school teams. She began skiing at age two and she displayed not only an aptitude for the sport but also a fierce side to her nature that she would later refine into competitive discipline.

"My next oldest brother was skiing already and he went in for lunch," she said of one of her earliest forays on skis. "My father decided he would put my brother's equipment on me and take me out. After the hour was over he said I had to go inside and give the equipment back to my brother. I was kicking and screaming because I wanted to stay out there.

"He sat me down on this bench, my feet were hanging over the side, and he went to take off my boots. I was so mad I reached down, grabbed his hand and bit him. He said he knew from that point on he'd have to get me my own equipment because I obviously loved the sport."

She loved it enough to persevere through some difficult times leading up to her 1993 world championship win. At age fifteen she qualified for the Canadian juvenile ski championships but broke a leg just prior to the competition. She was named to the national ski team in 1988 but spent part of that season on the sidelines with a knee injury. In 1991 she suffered another knee injury, then in 1992 the broken ankle kept her out of the Olympics.

Fate and potential finally came together in February 1993 when twenty-three-year-old Pace sped down the slope of Mount Kotakura at Shizukuishi, Japan, to win the world women's downhill championship — the first Canadian woman to win a world skiing title since Gerry Sorensen won the 1982 downhill title at Haus, Austria. The win wasn't without hardship, however. Two weeks before her victory, Pace, looking to take her first World Cup victory after wins in pre-race training runs, crashed through two fences in a downhill race at Haus. She suffered a broken left wrist in the mishap. Team doctors fitted her wrist with a special cast but her ability to push from the starting hut was severely curtailed as she was able to push only with her right hand — her left hand gripped a sawed-off ski pole used only to help with balance.

Weather problems delayed the women's world championship downhill race in Japan, allowing Pace extra time to work on her one-armed start. When race day arrived she quickly made up whatever time she lost at the top of the

Kate Pace: Weathered a storm of bad luck to become a world champion.

course, charging to her first major international victory in 1 minute, 27.38 seconds, with Norway's Astrid Loedemel finishing second and Austrian Anje Haas third. Pace concedes that she herself was one of the few people who didn't write her off as a medal candidate in Japan after her crash in Austria.

"When I broke my wrist two weeks before, I had won two training runs in that race and if I'd have won that race, who knows, I might not have won two weeks later," mused Pace. "That would have put a huge amount of pressure on me to win. Instead, I got the opportunity to say: 'It's like no one believes I can do this any more except me, and I'm going to go out and do it.' Kendra Kobelka (former national team skier) wrote me a card saying that it wouldn't be a season without a little adversity. I'd had adversity every season.

I never gave up because I knew there was a plan and a purpose for all of it," she said of her enormous well of patience and tenacity. "I couldn't push that purpose. I had to be patient and know my time was going to come."

Pace was labelled early in her career as a glider, someone who could generate enormous speeds in an aerodynamic tuck but vulnerable on courses requiring quick, high-speed turns. That label was accentuated after her world championship win in Japan, seen as a "glider's course." A month later she won the pre-Olympic downhill race at Hafjell, Norway, again on a course considered a veritable highway. The win was Pace's first World Cup downhill victory.

But early in the 1993-94 season Pace proved she could tackle the turns, winning a difficult downhill race at Tignes, France. She was among the medal favourites going into the downhill event for the 1994 Winter Olympics in Lillehammer, where a protest by many of the top women downhillers caused the women's Olympic downhill event to be moved from the easy slope at Hafjell to the more challenging piste at Kvitfjell, site of the men's downhill race.

A single but critical error on the course kept her off the medal podium and fifth in the Olympic event behind gold medallist Katja Seizinger of Germany. But Pace was disproving the notion that she was just a one-dimensional skier. By the end of the 1993-94 season Pace finished just behind Seizinger in the World Cup downhill standings after the two had battled for the championship all season. One of Pace's most striking traits is her ability and willingness to set and state goals. Leading up to the 1993 world championships, she wrote on a piece of paper her goal to win the world title and then taped the note to her exercise bike. A year later she replaced that message with a goal to win the Olympic gold medal and, just prior to the race in Norway, she stated bluntly to reporters that her goal was to win Olympic gold.

"Some people criticize me for that," she said of her ease in revealing and discussing goals. "They think it takes away from my goal, that it puts too much pressure on me. But if you don't believe in your goals — if you're not afraid to lay them out in front of everyone else — if you can't do that then you can't believe in them 100 per cent. If you're protecting them maybe you don't honestly believe in them. If I say it I hold myself accountable to training every day for that."

Laurie Graham

Laurie Graham never won an Olympic or world championship but she was probably the racer with the strongest shoulders. Following the 1984 retirement of Gerry Sorensen, Graham virtually carried the national women's alpine program through to the 1988 Winter Olympics in Calgary. She had help along the way with good results from teammates DeeDee Haight, Liisa Savijarvi, Karen Stemmle and Karen Percy, but for those four years much of the public and media attention was directed at Graham as Canada prepared to play host to the 1988 Games.

Born in 1960 in Inglewood, Ontario, Graham began skiing at age five, experiencing her first competition as a member of the Nancy Greene Ski League. She raced her first World Cup downhill in December 1977, placing twenty-second in the combined. That season she also won the national junior and senior overall titles.

Her first World Cup victory came in the first women's World Cup downhill to be contested in Canada, held March 5, 1983, at Mont Tremblant, Quebec. Sorensen was the favourite that day but Graham, then twenty-two, used the occasion to serve notice that Canada had yet another outstanding woman racer on the rise.

During the seasons leading up to the Calgary Olympics, Graham went on to win six World Cup races while establishing herself as one of the most consistent racers on the circuit. On February 18 at Nakiska, Graham finished fifth in the 1988 Olympic downhill, allowing a brief tear of disappointment to grace her face before she resumed the stoic yet outgoing persona so familiar to the nation's ski media. She retired at the end of that season.

"I'm proud of myself, of how well I did," she said after the Olympic downhill, a statement that also served to sum up her career. "I skied the best I possibly could. I have to be very proud of that."

Laurie Graham: A team leader.

Karen Percy

Karen Percy never won a World Cup race, a world championship or an Olympic gold medal yet when Canadians speak of their memories of playing host to the 1988 Winter Olympic Games in Calgary it is likely that the blonde dynamo from nearby Banff is high on their list of fond Games memories.

The summer before the Olympics Percy hiked up what would be the women's downhill course at Nakiska, about an hour's drive west of Calgary. She wanted to get a feel for every roll, every nuance of terrain. Several months later she made good in front of the partisan Alberta crowd, earning bronze medals in the Olympic downhill and super giant slalom and coming agonizingly close to a bronze hat-trick, finishing fourth in the combined after losing her grip on a pole in the slalom portion of the two-discipline event. Photographs of the smiling Canadian skier, hoisted upon the shoulders of her teammates, were flashed around the world, capturing for perpetuity one of the most endearing and popular images of those Games.

With the success of the Canadian male downhill skiers, specialization was a major tenet of the national alpine ski program. Percy, however, wanted to be an all-around racer in the spirit of her idol, Nancy Greene.

"I wanted to be a good skier, not just a fast skier," she recalled.

Percy's two medals from Calgary did, in fact, make her just the second Canadian to win more than one ski medal at an Olympics, the other being Greene in 1968. Percy went on to earn a downhill silver medal at the 1989 world championships at Vail, Colorado. The rigours of competition and public attention caused Percy's commitment to her sport to waver the following season and at age twenty-four, she announced her retirement, leaving the World Cup scene with career best second-place finishes at Zinal and Grindelwald, Switzerland. Soon after, in a royal wedding of Canadian sports, she married popular Edmonton Oiler defenceman Kevin Lowe.

Karen Percy: Two Olympic bronze medals.

Melanie Turgeon

ALPINE SKIING

A few days after the eight Canadian women Olympic and world champions said goodbye to each other and went their separate ways following their March 1994 reunion at Whistler, Melanie Turgeon of Quebec City was preparing to add her own page to the illustrious history of Canadian women skiers.

From March 10 to 14, 1994, seventeen-year-old Turgeon became the first female in the history of the world junior alpine ski championships to win a medal in all five disciplines. At the championships at Lake Placid, New York, she took gold medals in the combined (downhill and slalom) and giant slalom, silver in super giant slalom and bronze in slalom and downhill.

"I expected to be top-five in every event but not top-three in all events," she said in an Associated Press report after the championships. "I showed that you can do it. Coming from a small area in Quebec, it's possible."

Turgeon served notice in March 1993 that she was a rising star for the Canadian team when she finished ninth in her first World Cup downhill at Hafjell, Norway — the initial site for the 1994 women's Olympic downhill. (The race was later moved to nearby Kvitfjell because the top women racers felt the Hafjell slope was too easy.)

Turgeon continued to improve at the beginning of the 1993-94 season, finishing a respectable twenty-eighth in a

Melanie Turgeon: World junior sensation.

November World Cup giant slalom in Italy. Not bad for a junior racer who started sixty-second.

After Italy, coach Piotr Jelen remarked: "She has a real desire to succeed. I'm convinced it's just a matter of time before she breaks into the top group. She's very sure of herself."

A week later, in just her second career World Cup downhill, Turgeon improved again. She finished an astounding fifth in the season downhill opener at Tignes, France — a race won by Canadian teammate Kate Pace.

Lana Spreeman

Lana Spreeman's skiing style became evident the first time she put on a pair of boards at Alberta's Mount Norquay.

"I went straight down," she said of her first skiing experience as a Grade eight student. "I went to the top, [then] straight down, and hollered at everyone to get out of the way. That's what I was like. Was I looking for speed? No, I think it was more I didn't know how to stop."

Spreeman eventually learned how to stop, and more. But she didn't lose that zest for speeding down a hill and parlayed that enthusiasm into many international laurels. That her name remains largely unknown outside Calgary is because Spreeman is an amputee and made her name in a fourteen-year international career as a disabled skier with considerable ability. That career began in 1980 with a giant slalom gold medal at the Winter Paralympic Games in Geilo, Norway, and ended at the conclusion of a 1993-94 season that saw the thirty-eight-year-old racer take silver in slalom and bronze in super giant slalom, giant slalom and downhill at the Paralympics in Lillehammer.

Born in Olds, Alberta, Spreeman was five years old when she lost part of a leg in a farming accident. The mishap didn't curb her energy or love of sport. She went on to play basketball through junior and senior high school in addition to playing volleyball and competing in track and field.

Although she took up skiing at age fourteen, she didn't consider competition until several years later when she took a job as a lift operator at Sunshine Village ski area near Banff.

"I was always one for speed and racing," she said. "So I got into racing there. They used to have the disabled races there all the time and they were always after me to race. I didn't want to at the time but once they got me there I had fun, and that was the way it went."

Spreeman's initial reticence soon gave way as she found her passion for speed translated into results. After her initial success in Norway in 1980 she went on to finish third in the downhill at the 1982 world disabled ski championships and two years later earned silver medals in downhill and giant slalom at the Paralympics.

Lana Spreeman: Parlayed love for speed into a big career as one of the world's top disabled skiers.

"I'm not a good technical skier," she said when asked to assess her ability. "No, that's not my strong point. I am more of a speed, go-for-it type. I'm not scared."

At the 1986 world disabled championships Spreeman garnered a complete set of medals — gold in downhill, silver in giant slalom, bronze in slalom. The 1988 Paralympics saw her again take silver in downhill and giant slalom.

Her first big success in Norway remained a cherished moment.

"I think the first big win is always a special memory," she said. "1980 in Norway is one of my more special moments. Also, the first downhill I ever raced was in 1980 in France. That was an experience, that was probably my most fun race in terms of being scared and having a good time. I think I won that one, too."

A spate of injuries slowed Spreeman after 1988 — a severe left knee injury in 1989, torn thumb and right knee ligaments in 1990. But she returned to compete at the 1992 Paralympics in Tignes, France, and took home a silver medal from the slalom and super giant slalom and bronze in giant slalom and downhill.

After Lillehammer, Spreeman decided to stop competitive racing, although in early 1995 she conceded it was more of an adjustment than she expected. If she had one regret from a competitive career that offered more highs than lows, it was that she didn't win a gold medal in all four skiing disciplines — a small point in the grand scheme of things, she said.

"One of the reasons I love this sport is because it is an outdoor sport, it keeps you out and healthy in the winter," said Spreeman. "I find it very exhilarating. It's like kayaking. A lot of other sports are good physically but they don't give you the same kind of adrenaline rush."

Freestyle Skiing

No one knows for sure on what day freestyle skiing was born. Dates and stories vary in freestyle lore but it is safe to say that the sport, as the world watched it at the 1994 Winter Olympics in Lillehammer, Norway, had its beginning in the late 1960s and early 1970s. By then, the World Cup alpine ski circuit was well established and skiers such as Jean-Claude Killy, Gustavo Thoeni, Nancy Greene and Anne-Marie Proell were known worldwide for their prowess around gates or speeding downhill.

But in various parts of the world there were other skiers who believed skiing was more than just racing fast, that skiing could also be gymnastic, acrobatic and aesthetic. They spun on their skis, they flipped in the air — they were wild and different, and the media gave them the label "Hotdog Skiers." While this label acknowledged the daring, it also served to de-emphasize the skill required in freestyle skiing, and thus worked against establishing it as a serious sport.

By 1974 Vancouver's John Johnston founded the Canadian Freestyle Skiers Association and, as in other parts of the world, skiers committed to this new form of skiing and began organizing their own groups and competitions. A series of professional tours developed in North America and Europe and the sport attracted attention and sponsorship. But Johnston had greater hopes that one day the sport would be accepted into the Olympics. For that to happen it had to be designated an amateur sport. By 1979, after what was an understandable struggle between some professionals who enjoyed their livelihood and others who believed in an Olympic dream, the International Ski Federation (FIS), the world governing body for skiing, agreed to sanction freestyle. The first step to the Olympics had been made.

Johnston went on to lead the FIS freestyle committee and was a critical worker in the move to get freestyle into the Olympics. Right from the start Canadian freestylers made their mark as innovators and ambassadors of the sport. And, like their male counterparts, Canadian women quickly made their mark on both the professional, then amateur, circuits.

One of the first Canadian women to make her freestyle mark was Stephanie Sloan, who discovered the sport on a youthful sojourn in Europe.

Stephanie Sloan

"I'd been working in Geneva as an *au pair*, then went to Chamonix," explained Toronto-born Sloan, who had wanted to travel to Europe to learn French and earned her fare by working on a Canadian west coast fishing trawler.

"I got a job there working in kitchens. It was an amazing winter, lots of snow, lots of fun. I wanted to stay in Europe

Stephanie Sloan: A freestyle skiing pioneer.

separate events for men and women. At that time, when I started, it was strictly professional."

The sport offered a decent living for competitors such as Sloan, who went on to become a world professional champion. In addition to earning prize money and financial rewards from sponsors, she also gained modelling work on and off the slopes. The sport became established in Europe, but when Sloan returned to Canada in the 1977-78 season she discovered that events for women were barely organized or, as was usually the case, nonexistent. She became a vocal and powerful voice in the push to include women's events on North American freestyle programs and encouraged European women competitors to come to North America to give the women's events much needed numbers while increasing the international scope.

For Sloan, mogul skiing came naturally but aerials, while fun, required work. The ballet discipline proved most fascinating, however.

"I guess I spent the most time doing ballet," she said. "I found ballet to be one of the things that feels better to do than to watch, unless you watch the very best. To have music, to know what you're doing and to work on routines, it takes a lot of thought and effort. Skiing to music, you really do feel like you're dancing, you can become very fluid."

Sloan was one of the professionals who stayed with the sport through its transition to amateur, beginning with its official status in the International Ski Federation in 1979. In the 1979-80 season she won the World Cup combined title and finished third in the mogul standings in addition to taking the Grand Prix title. A year later she was third in moguls and second in combined. She opted to retire at the end of the 1980-81 season.

"I was skeptical, very skeptical at first, that it would work as an amateur sport because I grew up in the professional ranks," she said of the sport's transition. "It went through some difficult times. I'm really glad to see that it survived. You have to give Johnny Johnston credit for the vision he had. I remember in Germany he had a meeting and said we're going to change this sport to amateur. Most of us said you've got to be kidding, but he did it."

Sloan settled in Whistler. Her women-only camps became a popular institution at Whistler Mountain, as did her bump (mogul) clinics. Years later she was content knowing that she was not only a pivotal figure in the sport's development but also an important player in improving women's involvement in freestyle skiing.

And yes, along the way she did manage to learn French, the original reason for that first trip to Europe.

a little bit longer and needed to find a way to make ends meet. I saw this event, it was a Europa Cup freestyle event and there was one girl in it skiing against the men. I looked at her and thought: 'I can do that!' So I hooked up with a bunch of freestyle skiers and started training."

Sloan had grown up with a passion for skiing combined with an adventurous spirit and the two traits melded perfectly for her to take part in the new sport. In Norway she worked as a camp cook for freestylers, who were training on the glacier, in exchange for coaching. Various sponsors took notice of her and supported her through the next winter where she competed on the Europa Cup circuit against men because there were few women at that level of freestyle in 1975.

"I started winning the ballet. That made a lot of guys angry," she conceded. "There started to be more and more girls doing it, then the World Cup came on and they had

Lauralee Bowie

While Stephanie Sloan was learning the freestyle ropes in Europe, a compatriot who would be one of her top competitors in the late '70s and early '80s was gaining freestyle lessons from her brothers in Calgary. Rick and Darryl Bowie were among freestyle's pioneers in Canada so it was natural that their sister, Lauralee, would follow in their ski tracks.

"We grew up skiing. We raced," said Lauralee Bowie, who excelled as an aerial and combined skier. "Then my brothers got into freestyle skiing and I used to go to the competitions. I was maybe twelve or thirteen years old and I used to say: 'You guys are nuts, you're crazy.' But a few years later I was doing the same things. Then I took it back, they weren't that crazy.

"My success was very much through the push of my brothers. They were in the sport, they evolved the sport, they were successful in the sport and we became a very dynamic family."

Bowie's first victory came in 1977 at Mont Tremblant, Quebec. She recalled that earlier in the day a competitor was badly injured going off the aerial jump and the women, slated to compete next, gathered at the top looking less than willing to follow. Initially as reticent as the rest, Bowie went down the hill after some urging from her brothers and won the competition.

"You know what that taught me? That taught me that anybody can ski, anybody can be graceful and maybe spin on their skis and do tricks but not everyone can jump off a jump," she enthused. "That became my challenge and my goal. All the women, they were so scared, and I went out and did it. It became my excitement in freestyle skiing. Aerials were the hardest part of the sport."

Bowie went on to excel in both combined and aerials, winning a world championship on a pro circuit that was in the midst of its transition to amateur status. It was an exciting and exhilarating time.

"When I started it was professional and you got paid to compete and ski on the circuit," she said. "When I started there weren't a lot of women on the circuit. The sport was very individualized then. There were no team coaches, there was none of that. I had the experience because I had my two brothers as coaches and it was a team, the Bowie team."

Aside from sibling rivalry and brotherly assistance to spur her along, Bowie came into freestyle skiing as a former gymnast and a natural athlete who also liked to water ski, windsurf and play tennis. Her fondest memory was forged at Whistler Mountain at the end of the season in 1980. She needed a victory to clinch the World Cup aerials title.

"It came down to the last competition on the last jump," she smiled. "The last jump of the day, the last jump of the competition, the last jump of the year. My brother was giving me a play by play with hand signals for every girl who jumped before me. He would touch the back of his head and I'd know she'd touched with the back of her head; he would touch his hand and I'd know she'd put a hand down.

"At my turn, he pretended to walk his finger up the hill, ten fingers — ten steps. So I went up ten steps and did the jump. I did probably the highest back layout I'd ever done in my life. I felt like a bird. I felt I was up there five minutes and when I landed I knew I'd won — the day, the competition and the world championship. That was most exhilarating."

Lauralee Bowie went on to work in public relations and promotions and later developed a series of ski camps for women, mogul enthusiasts, and corporations which, in 1994, had expanded to not only several areas in Canada but also to California, Japan and France.

Lauralee Bowie: Joined her brothers on the freestyle circuit.

Marie-Claude Asselin

The transition from professional to amateur status initially took its toll on freestyle skiing as many experienced competitors who had been professional dropped off the circuit. Insiders call this time the "dark days" of freestyle — it had not become established enough yet as an amateur sport to attract much funding and organizers were still working at perfecting competition infrastructure within the International Ski Federation World Cup framework. The athletes who competed in the early 1980s came in without the support and notoriety of a professional network and still had to shrug off shreds of the "hotdog skier" label.

Marie-Claude Asselin was born in Montreal, but grew up in St. Agathe, Quebec, where she began skiing at age seven. She became intrigued with freestyle at age eleven when family friends who were involved in the sport introduced her to their summer training aid — a trampoline. A natural athlete who also competed at the provincial level in speedskating, Asselin was inspired by the acrobatics of freestyle and took it up in earnest, excelling particularly in aerials. She competed in her first event at age thirteen, went on to become a two-time national junior champion and in some events defeated older and more experienced athletes at the senior level.

Marie-Claude Asselin: Dominated aerials in her short career.

"They wouldn't allow me to go professional," she lamented. "I wanted to go professional at fifteen, I wanted to make money like everyone else. But I had to wait until I was eighteen. Their reason was that they wanted the sport to be in the Olympics, they wanted it to become amateur. When I turned eighteen there was no more professional. If I'd come in five or six years before, or ten years later…"

Few Canadian athletes have dominated their sport as did Asselin, who began her World Cup career in 1980-81 in outstanding fashion by finishing second in aerials and fourth in ballet in her first event. The next stop she improved dramatically, winning the combined, aerials, ballet and moguls at Tignes. By the end of the season she was hardly an unknown rookie on the circuit, although it took Canada some time to wake up and know the Quebec teen.

"Here in Quebec the publicity was pretty good, but outside Quebec it was infrequent. But because of that publicity people got to know me as an athlete and not as a hotdog skier. I started when that transition was being made, when people started respecting freestyle. I think in the '80s people started seeing us as freestyle skiers and athletes. Now, there is much more publicity and so the sport is better known. But some people did think we were crazy."

Marie-Claude Asselin enjoyed a brief but brilliant career on the World Cup freestyle circuit. In 1981 and 1982 she won the World Cup aerials and combined championship and in 1983 she took the aerials title, edged for the combined title by Switzerland's Conny Kissling. During her three-year stint on the circuit Asselin accumulated thirty-five World Cup victories — seventeen in aerials, one in moguls and seventeen in combined. To this day no Canadian woman has enjoyed such a record on the circuit.

"I was famous for three years and forgotten very quickly," said Asselin a decade after she retired. "Whereas Jean-Luc Brassard will not be forgotten because he has an Olympic medal. Sometimes you look back and wish you'd been born ten years later. But I don't regret it because I'm sure I helped the sport, as did Stephanie and Lauralee. We did what we could when we were there."

Asselin retired at the end of the 1982-83 season, and a decade later would still be ranked third on the all-time winning list for women freestyle skiers.

"Every year I had to do different jumps and it was getting harder," she said. "The older you get the more you realize that life is important. I wasn't the kind just to do a jump to try it. I'd do it on the trampoline, then the water ramp and then on the snow. I was starting to think: I'd won for three years in a row and I still had my body in one piece, so let's not push our luck."

Marie-Claude Asselin went on to gain her helicopter's licence and a degree in physical education. In late 1994, she and her son had recently moved to St. Adele, Quebec from James Bay where she had spent three years working as a teacher.

Meredith Gardner

FREESTYLE SKIING

By 1983 a concerted effort was being made by members of the International Ski Federation's freestyle committee to have the discipline included in the Winter Olympic Games. That year, FIS approved a plan to hold a freestyle world championship competition, slated for 1986. Conducting a formal, and successful, world championship would be considered a major step toward securing a future spot on the Olympic program. As the sport evolved through the mid-1980s, Canada would continue to be a leader in freestyle via success in competition and with athletes serving as innovators and educators. Marie-Claude Asselin had been part of an entity known as the Quebec Air Force, freestyle skiers from Quebec who made aerials their specialty and pleasure as the rest of the world looked on in amazement. When Asselin retired it was time for a younger group of individuals from other provinces to come forward, beginning the seed of what would eventually be known as the Canadian Air Force. One of these young skiers was Meredith Gardner of Oakville, Ontario.

"I was always a little, stocky kid," said Gardner. "I don't think I ever thought of myself as an athlete until I was on the national team for a year or two. I was involved in a lot of sports and I always did okay at them but I don't think there was ever one that I was incredible at. As a kid, and during my career, I was somebody who would crash, get up and go again. I was fearless when it came to doing those things."

As a youngster Gardner took part in gymnastics and diving and was a promising young ski racer. She discovered freestyle in 1972 when she saw several members of her ski club performing various flips and spins and she tried to emulate them. At age fourteen, after switching clubs and still developing as a ski racer, she decided to make a break to freestyle.

"The kids I'd skied with in freestyle were all independent and had a lot of personality," she explained. "I liked the atmosphere of freestyle, I loved the sport because it was artistic and acrobatic."

Meredith Gardner: Versatile freestyler started out as a ski racer.

Gardner was known as a combined skier but she was particularly adept at aerials. She won her first World Cup event in aerials at a late 1984 competition in Tignes. She went on to win the 1984-85 World Cup title in aerials and finish second in combined. A year later she finished third in aerials and fourth in combined at the first FIS-sanctioned freestyle world championships in Tignes. Shortly after, it was announced freestyle would be a demonstration sport at the Winter Olympics in Calgary and Gardner was already looking forward to taking part.

A crash at Lake Placid in 1987 destroyed her chances of making the Olympic team. Gardner missed the rest of the season, and the Olympic qualifying events, thanks to a shattered arm.

"If I'd been smart I wouldn't have jumped. I went into it not feeling well and afraid," she recalled. "But it was an

Olympic qualifier and I wanted to jump. I landed a twisting double and landed on my arm. I was rolling down the hill and could see my arm swinging backwards from the elbow. It was incredibly painful. I woke up in hospital and couldn't move my fingers. But even at that point I knew I wanted to go back and jump."

Gardner returned for the 1987-88 season and was in fine form, winning five aerial and three combined World Cup events to win her second World Cup aerials title while finishing second in the season's combined standings. But in an odd twist of fate, because she had missed qualifying due to her injury, Gardner served as a forerunner for aerials at the Calgary Games while teammate and rival Anna Fraser, who had won the Canadian aerials spot the previ-

ous season, was competing in the Olympics despite have recently suffered a knee injury.

"For the freestylers, it was our first Olympics. You could say it was just a demonstration event, but for us it was everything," said Gardner. "As it happened, I didn't get to compete but I was there forerunning. Being outside of it, I could see the amount of pressure and attention on those athletes as they got ready to jump. I looked around me and felt a sense of relief that I wasn't jumping. The pressure was just unbelievable."

Meredith Gardner retired in 1989, after finishing third in combined at the world championships in Hinderland-Oberjoch, with nineteen World Cup victories and seventy-nine medals earned in international competition.

Anna Fraser

Meredith Gardner wasn't the only Canadian woman freestyler to make a name for herself and her sport in the mid-1980s. While Lucie Barma became a consistent competitor in ballet, Vancouver freestyler Anna Fraser was also making her mark in aerials, a situation which created an interesting rivalry and incredible depth on the Canadian women's team.

"Everyone wanted there to be a rivalry and I'd be lying if I said there wasn't," said Fraser. "Meredith is my best friend and my best competitor. We were competitive, both of us are extremely competitive and we had to learn how to check that competitiveness. She had such a *joie de vivre* and I could get very, very serious. There were days I made her get up early to go out and train and there were days she made me get out and go dancing."

Anna Fraser began her competitive skiing career as a member of the Nancy Greene Ski League in B.C., although her main interest before taking up freestyle was gymnastics. Fraser discovered freestyle after her family moved to Ottawa. With her gymnastics background (she won the Ontario high school floor exercise championship), she was encouraged by members of her ski club to combine her two favourite sports. In 1981 she became convinced freestyle was her sport. She was a surprise winner in aerials at the Ontario championships and never looked back.

"I remember deciding I wasn't going to be satisfied with making the Ontario team," she recalled. "When I won aerials that day I remember thinking: I'm going to show you a lot more than this. That's when I really became committed."

Fraser spent her first full season on the national team in

Anna Fraser: Former gymnast found success in the air.

1984. When teammate Gardner won the World Cup aerials title for the 1984-85 season Fraser was making her presence felt, finishing third in the combined standings. In 1986

Fraser won the World Cup aerials title with victories at Lake Placid, New York, Mariazell, France, and Voss, Norway. She also finished third in the combined standings while taking a silver in combined and fourth in aerials at the first FIS-sanctioned world championships that year at Tignes.

While teammate Gardner was sidelined in 1987 with injuries, Fraser secured herself the only women's aerial spot on the Canadian team to the 1988 Olympics in Calgary, where freestyle was a demonstration sport. Fraser won the pre-Olympic aerials competition at Calgary Olympic Park in 1987 but by early 1988, she suffered a knee injury and had to work hard to recuperate in time for Calgary.

"When they chose the team I had more points because Meredith had been injured the year before," said Fraser. "That was a tough situation, it was tough for Meredith. I can't imagine how I would have felt."

Fraser finished fourth in the Olympic aerials, noting her biggest support in coping with the injury and the pressure of competing as a Canadian at the Calgary Olympics came from Gardner, who was forerunning at the Olympics and would go on to win the World Cup aerials title that season.

"When I won my first World Cup I didn't know what had hit me, I was in a daze for two weeks," mused Fraser. "But my most memorable moment was walking into the opening ceremonies in Calgary, no question. I was so proud to be wearing red and white. I'm a very patriotic person and I found it just incredible."

Fraser struggled to recuperate from the knee injury but was forced to retire in 1989. She remained involved in the sport, first promoting freestyle skiing youth programs around the country and eventually serving as a television commentator on the sport. As it happened, teammate Gardner also gained broadcasting work as a freestyle commentator.

Years later, Fraser conceded she had been part of an exciting time in her sport:

"I remember sitting on a chairlift with someone who was asking me about why I was in Maine and I explained I was there to compete in a freestyle competition. After we had gone through this whole conversation he looked at me and said: 'What do you compete in, the front crawl? Why are you on the ski hill?' He had absolutely no comprehension of what the sport was, and he was a skier. That was in 1981. Compare that to 1988 when someone would say: 'You're a freestyle skier? What event do you compete in?' To me, for that to happen in seven to eight years is phenomenal. People had become educated about the sport. We were no longer hotdoggers, we were athletes like any other athletes."

Katherina Kubenk

<u>FREESTYLE SKIING</u>

The Calgary Olympics proved the ideal forum to showcase freestyle skiing to the world. Shortly after the Calgary Games the International Olympic Committee approved freestyle skiing moguls as a full medal sport for the 1992 Winter Olympics in Albertville, France, with aerials and ballet added to the program as demonstration sports. At the 1994 Olympics in Lillehammer, aerials and moguls were presented as full medal sports.

In 1988, while veterans Anna Fraser and Meredith Gardner were winding down their careers in Calgary, another young athlete, Katherina Kubenk from St. Jacobs, Ontario, was beginning her climb to the top of the world championship podium. Kubenk joined the national freestyle ski team in 1989 after making the switch from figure skating to freestyle skiing nearly three years earlier. Gliding and jumping on the ice proved an ideal background for Kubenk to take into her new sport.

"Skating definitely helped me with everything," she said. "I had the muscles, the agility, the balance. Everything from skating went right in to skiing and if it wasn't for skating I definitely wouldn't be in this sport. I got so far so quickly just because of my background."

Kubenk had always enjoyed skiing, but figure skating had been a priority up until her mid teens. She discovered freestyle skiing and was thrilled to see she could perform some of her skating moves out on the snow wearing short skis.

"It was a funny switch because my mom would come to the ski hill and say let's go to skating practice and I'd say: 'Mom, look, I've got these short skis on, I'm doing ballet, can I skip skating today?' The first day it was cool, the next day, well... But I'm glad I made the switch. Figure skating for me wasn't going anywhere. I needed something new, something exciting. It was the age that we were all at, freestyle was new and it was exciting."

Kubenk's previous skating experience and dedication to hours of practice translated into quick competence in the three freestyle disciplines, making her an ideal candidate for the rigours of combined competition. In 1988 she finished second in aerials and third in combined at the national championships and that fall graduated to the national team and the World Cup circuit. In 1990 she won her first national championship in combined while that same year she finished third in the final World Cup standings for combined. She won her first World Cup combined event in January 1992, at Blackcomb Mountain in Whistler, B.C. and realized for the first time she had the potential to win a world championship.

"That was a shock. Suddenly it was possible," she said. "I got feedback for all my hard work, not just another progression up the ladder. For that day, at least, I was the best."

Kubenk continued to make inroads into the individual events, occasionally making finals in aerials, ballet and moguls at World Cup events. She capped off the 1992-93 season with a win in combined at the world championships in Altenmarkt, Austria, in addition to winning the World Cup combined title. Kubenk won the world title over Russia's Natalia Orekhova and American Kristean Porter. Leading the standings after ballet and moguls, she feared a hand touch in the aerials had cost her the world championship.

"Grant McDiarmid from Owens-Corning came running up to me. I was in the van changing my boots. He said: 'Katherina, you won.' I said: 'No, go check the scores.' I thought I had lost it. I needed a certain number of points and in my second jump I put my hand down so I didn't think I'd have them. Then the skier behind me had a bad jump as well, but I didn't see, I had left. I remember sitting in the van moping, thinking that in the last Worlds I was fifth, at least I was higher than that. Then Grant came with the news but it took a while for me to believe him."

Kubenk was a member of Canada's 1994 Olympic team to Lillehammer, Norway, where there was no combined competition, but she made the team as a moguls skier. She

Katherina Kubenk: Ex-figure skater turned potential into gold at the 1993 world championships in Austria.

finished sixteenth, injuring a knee, but recovered to compete in the 1994-95 season, where she finished third in combined at the world championships in La Clusaz, France.

Biathlon

Biathlon's origins, according to the 1994 information booklet published by the Canadian sport governing body, Biathlon Canada, go back more than four thousand years to when Norwegian hunters on wooden skis chased their prey through snowy woods. These days biathletes use cross-country skis and carry lightweight rifles. Biathlon requires athletes to ski a specified distance then stop at the designated shooting range, firing five shots at a mechanical target. Each target missed results in the athlete being penalized one minute.

It is a demanding discipline, requiring athletes to be strong and aerobically fit for the skiing portion yet, even as their hearts pound from the exertion of the skiing, they must steady hand, eye, and mind to aim the rifle.

Myriam Bedard

BIATHLON

Myriam Bedard left the shooting range believing she had no chance after missing the last two targets in the women's 7.5-kilometre biathlon at the 1994 Winter Olympic Games in Lillehammer, Norway.

Some would have said it wasn't the end of the world. After all, the twenty-four-year-old biathlete from Loretteville, Quebec, had days earlier made Canadian sport history by winning the women's 15-kilometre biathlon gold medal, becoming the first Canadian man or woman to win a gold medal in the difficult discipline that combines cross-country skiing and shooting.

But through her seven-year career in the sport Bedard had never been known to back down from a challenge, and she had endured many prior to that chilly Norwegian day. Strength and stubbornness had always been her allies and when she heard she was just sixteen seconds behind the leader with 2.5 kilometres of skiing remaining, she put both to good use in a determined bid to win her second medal.

"For me, I thought there was no chance with two penalties," stressed Bedard. "Then I realized I was not that far back so I kept going on my pace, giving everything."

After negotiating the last major hill she learned she was just seven seconds behind — with a kilometre remaining it still appeared a formidable deficit.

"I concentrated on technique, to glide as best as possible," she said. "Every step I was concentrating on my best and strongest way. The last kilometre to the finish line I had no more information, I finished as strong as I could, gave everything I had at every corner. When I looked at the

board I could not believe it."

Bedard's effort to the finish line at Bierkebeineren Ski Stadium will go down as one of the most memorable of the XVII Winter Olympic Games. She made up the sixteen-second deficit to win the 7.5-kilometre event in 26 minutes, 8.8 seconds, just 1.1 seconds ahead of Svetlana Parmygina of Belarus and 1.2 seconds better than Ukraine's Valentyna Tserbe.

Winning that second gold medal made Bedard the first Canadian woman to win two gold medals at a single Winter Olympic Games. It also supported her position as the world's best woman in biathlon and a Canadian sport celebrity even though biathlon is not a widely practised sport in Canada.

Circumstance brought Bedard into the sport at the age of fifteen when, as a cadet, she was asked by cadet friends to take part in a team biathlon competition. She possessed the necessary shooting skills but cross-country skiing was a new challenge.

"It was as if I were to bring you to an ice hockey rink, saying we need another player for one day," she laughed. "It was three men and they needed a woman for the team and they asked me. I was on rental skis, I was running on my skis, I didn't really know how to do it. It was just cadets, and it was more your strength than technique or skill that counted. I was not very good but I was better than some of the others. My team came in first."

Bedard started her athletic career as a figure skater, as did her older and younger sister, but by age twelve the expense caused her to hang up her skates. Her first foray into biathlon

Myriam Bedard: Made biathlon a household word in Canada.

ignited her interest in the sport and, buoyed by the initial success, she opted the next year to try biathlon in earnest. From 1987 to 1989 Bedard was a Canadian junior biathlon champion. In 1990 she won the Canadian senior championship over both 15 and 7.5 kilometres while also surprising the international biathlon world with a second place over 15 kilometres at a World Cup event in Austria, then taking eighth in the same distance at the 1990 world championships. By the end of the 1991 season she was ranked second overall in World Cup standings. In February 1992 she earned Canada's first Olympic medal in biathlon, taking bronze in the 15-kilometre event at Les Saisies, thirty-three kilometres from Albertville. The effort brought both satisfaction and frustration, however. In late 1991 Bedard had enlisted the help of a European coach in what she felt was a necessary move to help her to continue to compete at the same level as her European rivals. The move widened what was already a developing rift between Biathlon Canada and Bedard, an athletic example of Sinatra's song "My Way."

The rift continued through the Olympics as Bedard continued to prepare for competition her way. After she took the bronze medal, the media appeared to be more interested in her political leanings (was she competing for Que-

bec, or Canada, they asked) than in her accomplishment. At the end of the season she was suspended briefly by Biathlon Canada in a squabble over a contract concerning sponsorship and marketing opportunities.

The situation was eventually resolved and Bedard, still doing things her way, proved her method worked best by winning the gold medal in the 7.5-kilometre race at the 1993 world championships in Bulgaria. She took silver in the 15-kilometre race even though she skied over a rock and fell with one kilometre remaining.

Despite the emotional upheaval and controversy in 1992, she had no thoughts of giving up her sport in frustration: "After 1992 I thought: Why stop because I am having problems?" she said. "It was my plan in life to go to the 1994 and '98 Olympics."

Bedard is a clutch competitor, able to come through in major competitions. In her own way she has developed the ability to set a goal and achieve it even though some rough spots are encountered along the way. In the season leading up to the Lillehammer Olympics her results were mediocre, but there was no denying her excellence in Norway.

"If people had watched me the year before they would see I followed exactly the same plan for the world championships," she explained. "I was not too good at the beginning of the season. I came to the world championships and had a lot of success. Before the Olympics I told people there is nothing to worry about, I am following my plan. I knew what I was doing."

Indeed, Bedard moves as someone who has everything under control. After the 1993-94 season, which included a whirlwind of interview and appearance requests after the Olympics, Bedard and national teammate Jean Paquet were married. In May 1994, Bedard announced her pregnancy and her intent to compete in the world biathlon championships in February 1995.

In August 1994 Bedard proved her celebrity status was not limited to winter events. Looking fit and relaxed, with a bulky sweatshirt masking signs of impending motherhood, she was a surprise participant at the opening ceremonies for the XV Commonwealth Games in Victoria as bearer of the Queen's Baton. Bedard enjoyed a huge ovation as she entered the stadium wearing in-line skates and holding poles, taking a lap around Centennial Stadium as she might complete a summer training session on a mountain road, before presenting the ceremonial baton to Queen Elizabeth. Even in the pomp and ceremony Bedard performed her job her way — with great success. She gave birth in December 1994 and returned to compete on Canada's relay team at the 1995 Worlds, later winning the Canadian championship.

CON THE ICE

Figure Skating

The first world figure skating championship was held in 1896 but it was for men only. Women earned their own world event in 1906 and a year later the first world championship featuring men and women skaters was held. For all of its grace, figure skating demands strength, agility, speed and an artistic sense from its competitors in all disciplines — men's and women's singles, pairs and ice dance.

Barbara Ann Scott

FIGURE SKATING

Barbara Ann King's voice trembled slightly as she recalled the moment, slipping briefly back to the time when she was a nine-year-old girl. Like any youngster who meets her idol, the thrill of talking with figure skating great Sonja Henie had not abated with the passing of nearly sixty years.

"Oh, what a thrill to see this beautiful lady who I had read about, seen pictures of," she remembered. "I had gone to every one of her movies at least six times. There she was, with all of her costumes hanging there and all her show make-up on. She gave me a huge autographed picture. That is one of my great memories."

In Canada there are many people who grew up during and after the Second World War who likely harbour equally fond memories and continued admiration for an Ottawa figure skater who was their childhood idol. Petite and polite, with a debutante's charm, disciplined and dynamically athletic, Barbara Ann Scott captivated a country as few athletes had before, or have since. With her name comes more than just a remembrance that she was the first Canadian to win a figure skating world championship and Olympic gold medal. For just as Barbara Ann Scott skated with all the optimism and exuberance that is natural in a teenager's heart, so too did her accomplishments instill in a country a sense of optimism and hope after years of war and uncertainty.

Decades after her world championship wins in 1947 and 1948, and victory at the 1948 Winter Olympics at St. Moritz, Switzerland, Barbara Ann Scott would remain a special name in Canadian sport history, having earned a place in the minds of all who saw and admired her. Like a rare and beautiful piece of artwork, there was something about Barbara Ann Scott that touched the souls of Canadians.

"I think it was because it was after the war, when everything was down and gloomy and it was the first time a world or Olympic figure skating title came to Canada," she offered.

"I remember, when I went to Europe in 1947, going with the blessings of Canada, with lucky charms and telegrams. When I won I think it was something that was cheerful, something they could be happy about. I was kind of adopted as everybody's little girl, which was very sweet and kind."

Scott's childhood fascination with skating prompted her parents to join Ottawa's Minto Club, where they enrolled her in lessons. She showed natural talent immediately. In 1936, at age eight, she played Raggedy Ann in the club's annual follies, where in later shows she would appear as a raindrop and a powder puff. At nine her coach at the time, Otto Gold, arranged for her to meet Olympic champion and skating celebrity Henie while the Norwegian was performing in Montreal. The experience inspired Scott, who resolved to work even harder at her sport. At age eleven she became the youngest skater to win a Canadian junior championship.

Training eight hours a day, relishing the challenge of mastering the important school figures, Scott kept up her studies via tutor. For all the grace and gusto she displayed on the ice, even she had the occasional crisis of confidence.

"My mother insisted I keep on with my piano lessons," she recalled. "I had to play a recital every spring and I was almost sick, I was so nervous. She would say to me: 'But dear, you go out and skate in front of ten thousand people at the Minto Follies.' And I'd say: 'But they're away, they're not near me, I'm by myself out there.' The piano recital was just torture."

By 1947 Scott had won four national senior titles and, at the age of eighteen, charmed Europeans as she had charmed

Canadians, winning the European championship in Davos, Switzerland. The decision to compete at Davos allowed Scott to become acclimatized to training and competing outdoors. Her next stop was the world championships in Stockholm, Sweden, where she competed in -20F temperatures. During the school figures she worried that her ninety-eight-pound frame wouldn't make much of a dent on the stone-hard ice. She forgot about the cold in the free skating, earned two perfect sixes and became Canada's first figure skating world champion.

"For school figures you could wear warmer clothes and gloves or mittens," she said. "But for the free skating I had a little lamé dress and I couldn't wear gloves with it, it would look awful. Somehow, once you start you don't realize your hands are cold, you're thinking about what you're doing, you get on with it. They always say the good Lord doesn't send you any problems you can't overcome, so I just got on with it."

Scott returned to Canada a national hero and was feted at a huge celebration in Ottawa. She was presented with a yellow convertible which she returned soon after when told by International Olympic Committee president Avery Brundage that she would lose her amateur status, and Olympic eligibility, if she kept the car. To Canadians he appeared a veritable Grinch.

"People said he was a mean old man, but he was right," she insisted. "I gave the car back immediately. The next year, in St. Moritz, I met Mr. Brundage and he said: 'I suppose you hate me.' I said: 'Mr. Brundage, I'm eternally grateful to you because had you been a mean old man you would have waited until now, and then what could I do? You were kind enough to speak up immediately.'"

In January 1948, Scott travelled to Prague, Czechoslovakia, where she successfully defended her European championship as a prelude to the Winter Olympics in St. Moritz. The Olympic competition was complicated by ice problems — warm weather caused the ice to thaw, forcing postponement of school figures for two days. The ice was still soft and slow when competition finally began but Scott ended the day leading after figures. The free skate was contested February 6, on the same ice surface used for two morning hockey games. When the skaters arrived for warm-up they discovered the ice was riddled with holes, ruts and brittle spots. Scott and coach Sheldon Galbraith rearranged her routine to avoid the problem areas. She embraced the challenge and took seven of nine judges' first place votes to win the gold medal. The nineteen-year-old Canadian stood on the podium in a blizzard and clutched her gold medal, presented to her in a plain box, blinking back tears as "O Canada" was played.

Barbara Ann Scott: Captivated a generation of Canadians.

Scott completed the European sojourn with another victory in the world championships at Davos, then returned to another tumultuous reception in Ottawa. Soon after, she turned professional and joined the Hollywood Ice Revue. For six years she lived the high-profile, hectic life of an ice skating professional, although she was a self-confessed homebody who loathed living out of a wardrobe trunk. In 1954 Scott retired and settled in Chicago, where she still lived in 1994. Even then, requests for interviews and appearances were not uncommon. Scott remained as touched by the public's appreciation of her as she had been as a teenager.

"The kindness that people showed, and the interest, was so special," she said. "I wanted to do the best I could. That's something that worries me now. It seems a great many of the athletes figure: 'I won this, I'm doing this, my country's lucky to have me.'

"But it's the other way around. You represent your country and you should think of that first, and take great pride in that."

Petra Burka

As a child, Petra Burka didn't ponder what might have been had she first held a tennis racquet, or decided to take up competitive swimming, instead of putting on a pair of ice skates. Years later she noted the outcome might have been the same. If ever there was someone born to excel in sport it was Petra Burka.

"I had the kind of body that, if I decided to play tennis I would have been a good tennis player, if I'd tried another sport I would have been good at it," she noted. "I just had a natural ability. My body was built in such a way that I could handle anything."

As natural an athlete as she was, it was also natural that Amsterdam-born Burka would one day wear a pair of figure skates. Her mother, Ellen Burka, had been a Dutch national champion and, after the family moved to Canada in 1951, she took up coaching in the Toronto area. When Petra first donned skates at the age of seven her mother recognized immediately that her daughter had a knack for skating and decided to coach her through the various levels required for a youngster to become a competitive skater. By age fourteen Burka was national junior champion. A year later she was runner up at the Canadian senior championships and fourth at the world championships in Prague, Czechoslovakia, stunning the figure skating world that year by executing a triple Salchow to become the first woman to land a triple jump in competition. It was unheard of for women to execute triple jumps but, jumping being Burka's forté, she didn't see the accomplishment as unusual.

"It was very important how many double Axels you had in a program," she said. "I would have done more triples but at the time it was considered a no-no. Women didn't do triples. In practice, I did triple Lutzes. I tried it because I worked with Donald Jackson and he was working on triple Lutzes so I thought I would emulate him. But it just wasn't something people expected women to do."

Burka finished fifth at the 1963 world event and opted to work on her figures and grace to supplement her outstanding jumping and free skating ability. She improved to take the bronze medal at the 1964 Winter Olympics in Innsbruck behind winner and reigning world champion Sjoukje Dijkstra of the Netherlands.

At age seventeen Burka was poised to fulfill the promise she had shown so many years earlier when she first put on skates, and she embarked on a life far different from that of her peers.

"I probably sat at the table with all the people who didn't belong because I wasn't involved in any school activities," she said in assessing her school life, crammed between competitions. "You know, the table with all the rejects? I was never at school so I wasn't with the in crowd, I didn't know where to fit in. But it didn't bother me because I had a life in the rink and I had lots of friends through figure skating. I figured I could always make up for everything afterward."

In 1965, then eighteen, Petra Burka successfully executed another figure skating triple — winning the Canadian, North American and world championship. At the world event in Colorado Springs she thrilled the audience of five thousand spectators with a powerful free skating performance that made her the unanimous choice of the nine judges even though she slipped on her double flip near the end of her program.

According to an Associated Press report of her victory, "the new champion had woven so many

Petra Burka: Her athleticism changed figure skating.

difficult leaps and spins into her performance that the fall did little to mar it." The win made Burka the first Canadian woman to win a world figure skating title since Barbara Ann Scott won her second consecutive crown in 1948.

"I remember being very excited," she said, attempting to recall her victory nearly thirty years later. "I had won the figure portion which was mind-boggling because I'd been known as someone who didn't do good figures, although I always felt I was getting better and better. It was a good way to step into the free skating, which I remember as being a really good skate. When I realized I'd won I was almost stunned. I think it took six months to sink in."

Burka's road to the 1966 world championships in Davos, Switzerland, was less enjoyable. She won the 1966 national championship but suffered the ignominy, as reigning world champ, to have one judge award the free skating top mark to thirteen-year-old Karen Magnussen. At the time, such a move in the political world of figure skating was considered a damaging turn of events to Burka's aspirations of defending her world crown. She arrived in Switzerland to a swirl of intrigue and doubt even as the American team, seeing an opportunity, launched a campaign promoting Peggy Fleming.

Fleming won the world title and Burka finished third. Soon after, Burka signed a professional contract with Holiday on Ice, working in North America and Europe for three years before deciding she'd had quite enough of the gypsy life. Years later she was not bitter about the judge's decision in Peterborough but conceded its effect was devastating.

"It did affect me," she said. "Nowadays you go from third to first to fifth to second to whatever. In those days you went up and up and to be dropped like that, I felt very humiliated."

In 1994 Burka could be found at Toronto's Cricket Club coaching youngsters in the after-work hours from her job as a producer of television commercials. Just as her mother had advised years before, she had one rule she tried to instill in all of her protégés:

"Don't look at the marks," she said. "Just know how you're skating and try to be as good, if not better. That's how I managed to make it through all of those years. I wasn't thinking of winning, I was thinking of being the best I could be. It may sound corny but it's not."

Karen Magnussen

FIGURE SKATING

Karen Magnussen's voice rasped slightly, hoarse from a morning of teaching exuberant youngsters in the chilly rink at North Shore Winter Club in North Vancouver. But there was no hesitation when she discussed how she would like to be remembered as a figure skater.

"Being an all-around skater," she said. "Being good not just in figures but in free skating. That's why I won the Worlds, because I excelled in all those areas, not just one. I was a figure and free skater. There were either good jumpers or good spinners, good free skaters not so good at figures. That, I think, was quite an accomplishment, to be able to excel in all those areas of figure skating."

On March 1, 1973, in Bratislava, Czechoslovakia, Karen Magnussen used her command of figures and free skating to win the women's world championship. At that time skaters were judged in three phases of competition — the meticulous and technical compulsory figures, a short compulsory free skating program and a long free skating program.

The laurel was long in coming. Indeed, the world title might have been Magnussen's sooner had international skating officials acted earlier to alter an antiquated judging system that gave 50 per cent emphasis to basic figures. The rules were changed for 1973 to put less emphasis on figures which, while important, were viewed as being about as exciting as watching grass grow. A new element was added — a short free skating program with compulsory elements worth 20 per cent of the final total. The most entertaining and exciting element, the free skate, was worth 60 per cent. Although competent in figures, Magnussen and several other female skaters of the era were no match for Beatrix Schuba of Austria, who traced the stark lines with methodical brilliance but was an unspectacular free skater. The marking system allowed Schuba to accumulate such a hefty lead after figures that, as long as she skated competently in the free program, she could win over more versatile competitors.

Karen Magnussen's sojourn to the world championship began at age six, in an afternoon skate at Kerrisdale Arena on Vancouver's west side. While she and a friend honed their skills at one end of the rink, holding on to balance chairs, her mom and a friend casually chatted and skated around the rink.

"They turned around, looked up one end of the ice and

Karen Magnussen: Skating came naturally, like "ducks to water."

the chairs were at one end and the two of us were at the other," giggled Magnussen at the memory. "Not a care in the world. We just took off and from then on we never touched a chair again. My mom says it was like ducks to water. I just started skating."

Magnussen began formal training under Dr. Helmut May at Kerrisdale but later switched to the new North Shore Winter Club because it was closer to home. There she worked first with Eddie Rada and then Linda Brauckmann, who would oversee her progress to the world championship.

Magnussen won the Canadian junior championship at age twelve and moved to the senior ranks a year later, where she finished a credible fourth at the 1966 national championships to 1965 world champion Petra Burka. In 1967 she finished fourth in the North American championships and, in her first foray into international competition, twelfth at the world championships.

In 1968, just sixteen, Magnussen improved her international rank, taking seventh at the world championships and Grenoble Olympics behind winner Peggy Fleming of the

United States. A year later disaster struck — Magnussen suffered severe pain in both legs just prior to the world championships and it was discovered she had fractures in both limbs.

"I think I grew up a lot and realized how much I loved skating and that it could have been taken away from me," said Magnussen. "I came back appreciating it even more and being a lot more mature about how I trained. There was a lot of growing up in that period when I couldn't skate."

Magnussen came back in 1970, finishing fourth at the world championships in Yugoslavia. A year later Magnussen was third behind Schuba. At age eighteen she was already an international veteran with a different life from her teenage peers.

"I'd get about two weeks off in May and by the end I couldn't wait to get back on the ice," she said. "I was sick of going to movies and I'd be thinking: All they do is hang around, how boring! I was used to being busy and active and doing things. After two weeks I had enough of hanging around, to me it wasn't productive. I loved my friends but I was always ready to get back on the ice."

At the 1972 Olympics in Sapporo, Japan, and the world championships that same year in Calgary, Magnussen took silver medals behind Schuba. With Schuba announcing her retirement it was clear 1973 would be a battle between what media at the time dubbed the "two blonde beauties," Magnussen and American, Janet Lynn. In a curious but fitting farewell to amateur skating, Schuba performed a set of compulsory figures at the post-world event champions exhibition in Calgary.

By 1973 the American media machine was making much of the rivalry between Magnussen and Lynn. The ABC network drew the ire of Canadians when, in previewing Lynn's chances at the Bratislava worlds, a brief clip on Magnussen showcased the one fall she suffered at the Canadian championships.

In Bratislava, Magnussen refused to be intimidated or bothered by the incident. She was also clearly upset by Lynn's misfortunes in the compulsory free program, where she fell and lost crucial marks. But the Canadian relished her world championship victory secured by a strong final free skating performance. It was, as she said many years later, the skate of her life.

"It felt like my feet didn't touch the ice the whole time," she said of the Rachmaninov piano concerto program. "It was the most effortless performance I've ever had. I felt like Peter Pan, that I was on a cable and I literally felt like my feet never touched the ice. It was phenomenal."

Magnussen turned professional after her world victory, signing a contract with Ice Capades. In 1977 she began a new career as a coach. After several years in Boston, she moved to North Vancouver, where she continued coaching and developed her entrepreneurial side by opening Maggie's Muffins, a popular North Shore muffin and coffee shop.

In late 1994 she could be found again at North Shore Winter Club, overseeing the lessons of young skaters, coaching older competitors and teaching bantam A hockey players crucial technical points of putting blade to ice.

"I make them work pretty hard," she said of her work with the hockey youths. "But I can still do all of that stuff myself. That's a little perk. I can skate faster than every one of them."

Elizabeth Manley

FIGURE SKATING

Seconds before the end of her long program, the crowd witnessing Elizabeth Manley's performance was quietly hoping the diminutive Canadian wouldn't catch an edge and trip. For years Manley had shown potential to be one of the best, if not the best, figure skaters in the world. But as dynamic and exciting as her free skating could be, so too could it be hampered by nerves and, subsequently, mistakes.

But at the Olympic Saddledome in February 1988 spectators realized they were watching the Elizabeth Manley they knew would one day show up for a major event. And what timing! She was skating the performance of her life. When her routine finished Manley froze in the obligatory end-of-program pose then bent over, holding her face in her hands. Then she straightened and the face that emerged from her palms was radiant. Indeed, she had nailed five triple jumps and captivated the audience with an exuberant program to win the free skating portion of the competition and earn the Olympic silver medal behind gold medallist Katarina Witt of East Germany.

Throughout her career Manley had fought battles on and off the ice. Growing up she battled a weight problem, then depression, all the while knowing that her mother, who had been divorced from Manley's father since the skater was fifteen, struggled to pay what can be large training expenses for a talented young figure skater.

Ottawa's Manley won her first Canadian senior championship in 1985 and wound up ninth that year at the world championships. After finishing second at the 1986 nationals she improved to fifth at the world event in Geneva. In 1987, again as Canadian champion, she improved one spot to fourth place and, had it not been for her tendency to bow to pressure as she had shown in other events, she might have been considered more of a contender for the Calgary Olympics.

She was given a chance to earn a bronze medal but the media virtually ignored her while focusing on what was expected to be a showdown for the gold medal between defending Olympic champion Katarina Witt of East Germany and American Debi Thomas, the 1986 world champion.

Thomas was slightly ahead of Witt after the short program with Manley third. Then the unthinkable happened. Witt skated a theatrically impressive, but safe and technically mediocre performance. Thomas crumbled under the nerves that usually hampered Manley. The Canadian? Even though she had battled strep throat for the week leading up to the competition she gave no evidence in her performance that she had ever been sick a day in her life. She jumped. She smiled. She spun. She smiled. She conquered

Elizabeth Manley: Unleashed the performance of her life to take the silver medal at the Winter Olympics in Calgary.

her nerves and delighted judges, spectators and, most of all, herself.

Manley's free skating performance was given the best marks but her effort wasn't quite enough to topple Witt for the gold medal. She took the silver, an ecstatic figure clad in hot pink, while disappointed Thomas took the bronze.

At the 1988 world championships in Budapest Manley proved her Olympic medal was no fluke, again taking the silver. She then retired to the professional ranks, working first with Ice Capades then other touring groups. In early 1995 she was working again with Ice Capades as a feature performer in the show's production of Hansel and Gretel.

Ice Dance

Ice dance did not become an Olympic event until 1972. The event is less spectacular than pairs in that there are strict rules that regulate the brief time skaters can be apart in addition to rules about how high and in what way a male skater may lift his partner. Competition is judged in three separate stages — the compulsory dance, the original set pattern and the free dance. Timing, expression, unison, style and interpretation of music are all important as is use of skate edges and use of the entire ice surface.

Geraldine Fenton and William McLachlan were the first Canadians to win a world championship medal in ice dance. Their silver-medal effort came at the 1957 world championships at Colorado Springs, followed by another silver in 1958 and bronze in 1959. McLachlan also teamed with Virginia Thompson to take silver in 1960 and bronze in 1962. In 1964 Canadians Paulette Doan and Kenneth Ormsby took home the dance silver medal from the world championships in Dortmund, West Germany after earning the bronze in 1963 at Cortina.

Tracy Wilson & Rob McCall

They came from opposite ends of the country — she from Port Moody, British Columbia, and he from Dartmouth, Nova Scotia. They also brought distinctly opposite approaches to their sport. Tracy Wilson was a self-described jock most interested in technique. Rob McCall brought an artistic flair and delighted in the creative side of his sport. They came together in 1981, each looking for a skater to replace a retiring partner. Some observers wondered whether the mix was right but in no time there was little doubt that something special had been created.

Wilson and McCall won the 1982 national championship and finished a credible tenth at the world championships. A year later they improved to sixth at the world event and in 1984 wound up eighth at the Olympics and sixth at the world championships.

The duo had a flair for innovation right from the start. Some even said they were daring. They were also able to inject humour and fun, and a sense of exuberance, into their routines. In 1986 Wilson and McCall cracked the upper echelon of international ice dance by taking the bronze medal at the world championships in Geneva, Swit-

Tracy Wilson & Rob McCall: Fun and pizzazz were integral to their routines, and judges responded enthusiastically.

zerland. The accomplishment was heralded as a new era in Canadian ice dance and an important event at the international level, where Soviet and British skaters had tended to dominate the discipline.

Proving their result was no fluke, Wilson and McCall took home another bronze medal from the 1987 world event in Cincinnati. The Winter Olympics in Calgary proved an emotional and exciting point in their career, where in front of an ecstatic home country crowd they skated to Scott Joplin's "Maple Leaf Rag" to earn the bronze medal, the first Canadian ice dance team to earn an Olympic medal. Weeks later they wound up their amateur careers by earning another bronze at the world championships in Budapest, Hungary.

Shae-Lynn Bourne & Victor Kraatz

ICE DANCE

When Wilson and McCall retired they left a considerable void in Canadian ice dance that was not filled for quite some time. In 1994, however, it appeared Shae-Lynn Bourne and Victor Kraatz could be worthy successors. They too, came from different parts of the country — she from Chatham, Ontario, and he from Vancouver, B.C. They became national junior champions in 1992 and went on to win the national championship in 1993, 1994 and 1995.

They finished fourteenth in their first world championship try in 1993, then returned a year later to finish tenth at the Winter Olympics in Lillehammer and sixth at the 1994 world championships in Japan. Their rise up the international ladder has been surprisingly swift in a discipline that does not reward newcomers easily. But Bourne and Kraatz bring to ice dance some basics beloved by judges and technical purists — use of deep edges and impressive, difficult footwork. In addition, they exude a flair and energy that offsets some of the seriousness exuded by other dance duos. At the 1995 world championships in England Bourne and Kraatz again improved their world standing, finishing fourth.

Shae-Lynn Bourne & Victor Kraatz: Young dance duo earned favourable reviews in international competition.

Pairs

Men's and women's singles competitions at a figure skating championship are testament to what one individual can accomplish athletically, artistically and technically on the ice. While also a test of aesthetics and athletics, the pairs event serves also as a test of unity, nerve, communication, and cooperation between partners. The lifts and throws make the event spectacular and dangerous while moves like the death spiral require both grace and strength.

Just as Canadian women and men have served as innovators and inspirational performers in singles, so have the country's pairs earned respected spots on the world scene. While Canada's Barbara Ann Scott was charming spectators at the 1948 world championships in Davos, Switzerland, and the Winter Olympics in St. Moritz, compatriots Suzanne Morrow and Wallace Distelmeyer were making their mark in pairs, earning bronze medals in both the events. The pair also made Olympic figure skating history by becoming the first duo to perform the death spiral as it is performed today, with the woman's head so low it grazes the ice. In the space of nearly a decade, from 1953 to 1962, Canadian pairs skaters enjoyed considerable international success.

Frances Dafoe & Norris Bowden

Put two athletic and determined individuals together on the ice and you have the potential for something special. Frances Dafoe and Norris Bowden were both competent singles skaters who brought their powerful natures together to become the first Canadian pair to win a figure skating world championship, setting a standard of excellence for other young Canadian pairs skaters while making their mark on the international stage by introducing impressive lifts and jumps.

Bowden was a former Canadian men's singles champion who had teamed with Suzanne Morrow to win the national junior pairs title in 1945. He was also an academic and opted not to compete in the 1948 Olympics in order to pursue his studies. Dafoe had her singles career cut short in 1948 when she broke both her ankles. At the urging of coach Sheldon Galbraith, they came together and competed in dance events, winning the Canadian waltz title. The pairs

event provided the ultimate challenge, however, and the duo finished fifth at the 1952 Olympics in Oslo, Norway. A year later they finished second at the world championships in Davos, Switzerland, and in 1954 at Oslo they became the first Canadian pair to win a world figure skating championship.

They successfully defended their title a year later in Vienna even though they had to compete in a raging blizzard. Their energetic and innovative style made them popular with the crowd but somewhat suspect in the conservative ranks of the judges. The duo was favoured to take the gold medal at the Winter Olympics in Cortina d'Ampezzo, Italy. They skated their characteristic powerful performance in the Games but a slight slip by Dafoe going into a lift near the end of their performance was dealt with harshly by the judges and the Canadian duo took the silver medal behind Austrians Elisabeth Schwartz and Kurt Oppelt.

At the 1956 world championships in Garmisch-Partenkirchen, the duo skated an even better performance than they had at the Olympics, minus the slip by Dafoe, and they were still awarded second behind the Olympic champions from Austria. The spectators were irate and competitors and coaches from other countries were embarrassed and disappointed for the Canadian duo. In turn, Dafoe and Bowden were vocal in expressing what they felt was a lack of support from the Canadian figure skating officials, which landed them a suspension. They promptly retired, not the first nor the last individuals to be galled in a sport where politics in judging remains an integral component of competition.

Frances Dafoe & Norris Bowden: Audiences loved their exhuberant style.

Barbara Wagner & Robert Paul

PAIRS

While maintenance workers cleared the fruit and other debris that had been thrown on the ice after the judges released their marks for Canadians Frances Dafoe and Norris Bowden at the 1956 Olympics, Barbara Wagner and Robert Paul were warming up to skate the Olympic program that would put them sixth. They were the heirs apparent to Dafoe and Bowden and quickly took over the spotlight when the duo retired after the 1956 season.

Wagner was petite, energetic and outgoing. Paul was the tall, silent type. Opposites on and off the ice, they made the most successful figure skating pair in Canadian history. They skated separately as members of the Toronto Skating Club, coming together as a pair in 1952. Success was nearly instant — they came third in the 1953 Canadian junior championship. A year later they won the event and in 1955 finished second to Dafoe and Bowden at the Canadian championships.

In 1957 Wagner and Paul continued where Dafoe and Bowden had left off, winning the world championship in Colorado Springs. They dominated as few Canadians have at any time, in any sport, winning the world championship again in 1958, 1959 and 1960. It seemed that their opposite personalities proved the ideal combination on the ice and they charmed the audiences as much as they charmed the judges. While their predecessors had been the subject of controversy, Wagner and Paul appeared to be able to do no wrong, combining grace and technique in a package that was both aesthetic and proficient.

In 1960 the Olympics in Squaw Valley provided the only

Barbara Wagner & Robert Paul: Became the first Canadian pair to win an Olympic figure skating gold medal.

laurel that had not yet been attained by the Canadian pair. The sole glitch in their Olympic program came via the record player dispensing their music. Early in their routine the needle went for a screeching slide across the vinyl and, after a few minutes delay, the judges decided the Canadians would skate their program again. Every judge awarded them first place and they became the first Canadian pair to win an Olympic figure skating gold medal. After winning yet another world title in Vancouver, they turned professional and performed with Ice Capades until 1964. Wagner went on to coach while Paul turned to choreography.

Maria Jelinek & Otto Jelinek

PAIRS

When the 1995 Canadian figure skating championships were held in Halifax, one of the special events of the week was the induction of seven individuals into the Canadian Figure Skating Hall of Fame. Among the inductees were Maria and Otto Jelinek, who forty-four years earlier caught their first glimpse of Canada from the docks a short walk from where the Canadian championships were being held.

The Jelineks were born in Czechoslovakia and their parents were enthusiastic figure skating supporters. Communism forced the family to flee Czechoslovakia and, after pretending to take a vacation in Switzerland they arrived

in Halifax in 1951, eventually settling in Oakville, Ontario. Having shown interest and ability for figure skating while living in Prague, Maria and Otto continued working on their skating skills in Canada and won the 1955 national junior pair championship. Two years later, with Maria just fourteen and Otto seventeen, they finished third behind Wagner and Paul at the world championships in Colorado Springs. A year later the world results were the same, Wagner and Paul in first and the Jelineks third.

They suffered a setback in 1959, finishing fourth at the world championships and were also disappointed with their fourth-place finish at the 1960 Olympics at Squaw Valley.

Maria Jelinek & Otto Jelinek: Sister and brother fled Czechoslovakia with their family then returned to Prague to win the 1962 world championship in figure skating pairs.

pairs in the world. Anyone with a sense of romance could envision a storybook ending with the duo winning their first world championship in their home country. But the story turned sour when the world event was cancelled because the airplane carrying the American team crashed near Brussels. A twist of fate saved the Jelineks from being on board the flight as they had originally planned to take that plane but opted instead to take a different flight carrying the Canadian team.

A year later the world championships were held in Prague and the Jelineks thrilled their former compatriots by winning the gold medal. They retired after their world victory, then skated as professionals in Ice Capades. Maria Jelinek went on to become a travel agent, while Otto Jelinek became a member of parliament and a cabinet minister, including a stint as Canada's Minister of Sport.

But weeks later at the world championships in Vancouver they rebounded to take the silver medal behind the formidable Wagner and Paul, who then retired.

The 1961 world championships were to be held in Prague and the Jelineks were excited about the prospect of returning to their former country as one of the best figure skating

Barbara Underhill & Paul Martini

Just over two weeks prior to the 1984 world figure skating championships in Ottawa, Barbara Underhill and Paul Martini pondered hanging up their skates. A month earlier

Barbara Underhill & Paul Martini: From disappointment to triumph.

they had been among the favourites going into the pairs competition at the 1984 Winter Olympics in Sarajevo, Yugoslavia. A year earlier the Toronto duo had placed third at the world championships in Helsinki and many observers felt they deserved better. But instead of serving as their coronation event, the 1984 Olympic Games served instead to test the mettle of the Canadian pair.

Underhill and Martini became a competitive entity in 1977 after meeting at a summer skating school. They won the world junior championship in 1978 and took the Canadian senior title the following year. At the 1980 Olympics in Lake Placid they finished ninth, then finished the season with an eleventh place finish at the world championships. A year later they were seventh and, at the 1982 world event in Copenhagen they had inched up the world ladder to fourth. In 1983 they earned their spot on the podium, taking the bronze medal — the first world medal earned by a Canadian pair since 1964 when Debbi Wilkes and Gary Revell took bronze at Dortmund, West Germany.

In the early stages of the 1983-84 season Underhill was plagued by injury — first a shoulder separation, then a torn ankle ligament in January. Because the adage says bad luck comes in threes, Underhill's third bugaboo surfaced at the Olympics in Sarajevo, where an untimely tumble left the Canadian couple in seventh place. Their pride hurt as much as Underhill's ankle and their confidence evaporated with the world figure skating championships slated for just two weeks later in Ottawa. Underhill's physical comfort became of paramount concern and, for lack of anything new or better to try, she opted to skate on an old pair of boots she had abandoned in the fall. Comfort, then confidence, returned and the duo took second in the short pro-gram behind world and Olympic champions Elena Valova and Oleg Vasiliev of the Soviet Union.

Two days later, after being in the depths of despair some two weeks earlier, they were on top of the world. Underhill and Martini unleashed an outstanding long program in front of a partisan crowd of ten thousand at Ottawa's Civic Centre, out-skating their Soviet rivals to win the world championship.

The duo went on to skate professionally in addition to working as television figure skating commentators, armed with the knowledge of not only what it takes to be the best, but also what it feels like out there when things don't go as planned.

Isabelle Brasseur & Lloyd Eisler

PAIRS

Isabelle Brasseur managed to keep a smile on her face even though her teeth were clenched hard in pain. Cracked rib aside, she had been determined to compete at the 1994 world figure skating championships. Partner Lloyd Eisler tried to catch her as deftly and softly as he could but with the difficult lifts and twists the Canadian pair had made their trademark Brasseur was forced to endure consider-able pain in order to complete the manoeuvres.

They finished second at those world championships in Japan, their final competition before turning professional. It was a courageous end to an amateur career that saw both skaters mature as competitors and individuals making them popular and endearing figures in the minds of the public.

They came together in 1987. She was sixteen years old with skinny legs, weighing in at a scant ninety-six pounds. He was a veteran skater, already a bronze medallist at the 1985 world championships with Katherina Mathousek. He was outgoing, sometimes intense, while she was quiet, even demure. As opposites go they had elements that worked in their favour, but success would come when they could com-bine and adopt each other's characteristics. They finished ninth at the 1988 Olympics in Calgary then improved to take the silver medal at the 1990 world championships.

They earned silver again in 1991 and came into the 1992 Olympics as contenders for the gold medal. But it was not to be. They struggled and with each mistake their discom-fort became more apparent. Eisler's strength and enthusi-asm in the heat of competition at times resulted in Brasseur being thrown farther and faster than she anticipated. In turn, her confidence wavered with each mistake. By the end of the final they were both clearly disappointed and unhappy with their Olympic bronze medal. Weeks later

Isabelle Brasseur & Lloyd Eisler: Unafraid to push the limits.

they earned bronze at the 1992 world championships and appeared disillusioned. They pondered retirement but, with another Winter Olympics slated for Lillehammer, Norway in 1994, they decided to stay in the fray for two more years.

In November of 1992 Brasseur's father died. In her grief she became stronger, and in sharing her grief Eisler discovered composure and patience. The disappointment of 1992 also resulted in some self-examination and in 1993 they emerged a different pair — Brasseur exuding newfound confidence and control and Eisler some sensitivity and grace. They had, in a sense, exchanged some of their most prominent traits and nowhere was that more apparent than in 1993 at Prague, where they won the world championship with a program that was athletic, exciting and beautiful.

A year later their 1994 Olympic aspirations were confronted by the return of the formidable Russian duo Ekaterina Gordeeva and Sergei Grinkov. The Olympic competition proved one of the most exciting pairs events ever contested. At the end it was Gordeeva and Grinkov who won the gold medal, but in accepting their bronze medal the Canadians were content. Brasseur had been bothered at the Olympics by a rib injured in a fall but the duo refused to use the injury as an excuse.

She aggravated the injury again before the world championships in Japan and was told she shouldn't skate when an X-ray revealed a five-centimetre crack in the rib. She skated anyway, and at the end of their long program she could barely breathe because of the pain. The crowd saluted her effort with a standing ovation, as did her partner Lloyd Eisler by standing off to the side and applauding her grit.

They turned professional in the summer of 1994, having amassed in their eight-year amateur career as a pair five national championships, two Olympic bronze medals, and five world championship medals, including the 1993 gold.

Long Track Speedskating

Even a millennium ago the clever folk in Northern Europe were gliding on frozen ponds and lakes atop blades made from sharpened animal bones. Indeed, skating, just like skiing, had become a necessary mode of transportation for people who had to get around in the long, cold months of winter. Canada's first recorded speedskating race was contested on the St. Lawrence River in 1854. Forty years later Canada became the first non-European country to become a member of the International Skating Union (ISU).

Speedskating was a part of the first Winter Olympic Games in Chamonix in 1924, although it was a full medal sport only for men. Women's races were designated as demonstration events from 1932 until gaining full medal status at Squaw Valley in 1960. Until 1988, long track speedskating was the only discipline contested at the Olympics. In long track, pairs of skaters race around an oval and are required to swap lanes midway through each lap. Although racing in pairs, the skaters in fact race against the clock with the medallists being the three skaters who post the fastest times of the day.

It is unfortunate that Olympic officials took so long to recognize women's speedskating as an entity worthy of full medal status as early in the history of the Winter Olympics Canadian women proved speedy on skates.

Lela Brooks   SPEEDSKATING

Canada's first female speedskating star showed talent at a young age, no doubt helped by the fact that her parents had both been competitive racers. In 1925, after winning several Ontario and national age group titles, Toronto's Lela Brooks won the inaugural North American mass-start championship and rewrote several world records. She went on to win the world competition at St. John, New Brunswick, in 1926, another mass-start event, taking three of the four races.

As so many top competitors after her, Brooks may have been the dominant racer of her time but she was unable to repeat that calibre of performance at an Olympic Games. In 1932 at Lake Placid she set two world records in heats, finishing fourth in two races and falling in another. She qualified for the 1936 Olympics but opted to retire. It would be some time before another Canadian speedskater would even come close to equalling her results.

Lela Brooks: Rewrote several world records.

Jean Wilson: Illness cut short her career.

Jean Wilson

SPEEDSKATING

No one will ever know how good Toronto's Jean Wilson might have been had a muscular disease not taken her life at age twenty-three. At the 1932 Winter Olympics at Lake Placid, New York, with women's speedskating a demonstration event, she took the gold medal in the 500 metres. She set a world record in the heats of the 1,500 metres but had to settle for the silver medal in the final behind American Kit Klein. In the 1,000 metres Wilson fell and wound up sixth but Canadian teammate Hattie Donaldson was right there, taking silver in the event.

Wilson became ill upon returning from Lake Placid and never recovered. She died in 1933.

Susan Auch

LONG TRACK

When Susan Auch was two years old she was diagnosed as asthmatic and the doctor advised her parents to get her involved in sport to help strengthen her lungs. She became interested in speedskating when her brother took power skating lessons. In 1994 the Winnipeg speedskater earned a silver medal in the women's 500 metres at the Winter Olympics in Lillehammer, Norway. The feat made Auch only the second Canadian woman speedskater, in addition to Winnipeg's Cathy Priestner, to earn an Olympic long track speedskating medal since women's speedskating became a full-medal sport in 1960.

Auch, who initially tried short track speedskating then switched to long track in 1989, earned her first victory on the World Cup speedskating circuit by taking the gold medal in a 1995 event in Innsbruck, Austria. That race was particularly noteworthy in that she defeated five-time Olympic champion and venerable veteran Bonnie Blair.

In February of 1995 Auch thrilled a home country crowd in Calgary by again defeating Blair in the 500-metre race at a World Cup event at the Olympic Oval. A day later Blair triumphed in another 500-metre race, breaking her own world record to win in 38.69 seconds. Auch was a worthy second, finishing in 38.94, also under Blair's former world mark of 38.99.

A week later, at the world sprint championships in West Allis, Wisconsin, Auch took silver in one 500-metre event and bronze in the next day's 500-metre sprint to finish sixth overall behind American rival Blair, who swept the 500- and 1,000-metre races to take the overall world sprint title.

Susan Auch: The 1994-95 season saw her emerge as the main and formidable rival to venerable American Bonnie Blair.

Sylvia Burka: Speedy on skates and on the bike.

Sylvia Burka

LONG TRACK

It is enough that one athlete can say years later that she was a world champion and world record holder in one sport. Winnipeg's Sylvia Burka could say she was the best in one, and no slouch in another as she excelled first in long track speedskating and then cycling. She wasn't the first or the last athlete to compete successfully in both sports, but her attraction to cycling was based on more than just complementary muscle groups, fitness and seasonal compatibility of the two sports. In both, the athlete is solely accountable for her results.

"I didn't like team sports in school," said Burka (no relation to 1965 figure skating world champion Petra Burka).

"I must have learned early on that I didn't like to count on other people for what I did. Maybe I was a loner, I'm not sure. I went as far as playing baseball, only because I was a pitcher and my sister was a catcher and it was a fun thing to do. But all other sports I picked were individual sports."

Growing up in a family that encouraged physical activity and fitness, she began speedskating at age ten. As a youngster Burka lost her left eye after it was pierced by a shard of glass, but the accident didn't hamper her ability to take part in sports or compete. Although she was an active, athletic child when first introduced to speedskating as part of a school program, the sport didn't come to her as easily as others.

"I was not a talented speedskater," she noted. "My mother would be the first to say I was a horse on skates. I was terrible. I didn't win when I went in to it but I was so determined that I didn't want to come last. And I always enjoyed it, keeping fit."

Burka persevered and eventually the results started to come first at the club and then at the provincial level. She went on to win the Canadian juvenile championship and at age fifteen competed in her first world championship. At the 1970 event in Wisconsin, she finally realized she might have a niche in the sport.

"I was the youngest competitor there," said Burka, who finished in the top twenty-five in all four races. "I had to ask the way the seeds worked, I was up against someone who had been world champion the previous year and there I was, asking which side I'm supposed to cross over on. It became a joke through the years. But I certainly fell in love with skating at that point."

Burka made her first foray to Europe in 1971, again for the world championships and in 1972 made her Olympic debut at Sapporo, where she finished a credible eighth in the 1,000 metres. At the 1973 world junior championships in Holland, Burka made her international breakthrough, winning the title. That same year Burka set a world sprint point record and wound up the season with a fourth-place finish at the world championships in Oslo. The stage seemed set for an even better 1974 but what followed was a pattern that would characterize Burka's career — more ups and downs than a roller coaster.

"Just because it's a sport it doesn't mean you always enjoy this gradual climb," she said wryly. "I always did what I wasn't expected to do."

Burka wound up sixth at the 1974 world championships and in 1975 she was one of three Canadian skaters sent back to Canada from Europe in what was called a "disciplinary action" that was the result of a "personality conflict" between the skaters and coach Jorrit Jorritsma, a former Dutch national team coach and skater who had been brought over to coach the Canadians in 1974.

The problem was resolved by the fall of 1975, but the roller coaster wasn't on the up-swing just yet. Burka was a medal favourite for the 1976 Winter Olympics at Innsbruck but ended the Games with fourth in the 1,000

metres as her best result.

"I had been winning everything going up to the Olympics," she mused. "It was expectation, learning how to handle it. You're twenty-one years old, how do you know what you want? You're on the line with something that is so terribly important. My problem was going out like a shot and blowing up."

Two weeks later Burka became the first Canadian woman to win the ISU women's overall championship with an overall score of 184.840 points earned from finishing fifth in the 500 metres, third over 1,000, first over 1,500 and seventh over 3,000. Later she was third overall at the world sprint championships.

"I was expected to win at the Olympics," she continued. "And I didn't. But I went to the Worlds and won. In 1977 I was expected to win the Worlds, I was the reigning champion, and I didn't."

Burka was indeed favoured to win the 1977 world overall event at Keystone, Colorado, but that roller coaster of fate was on a downslide again. Burka lost her world title to Soviet skater Vera Bryndzey after hitting a soft spot in the ice and falling in the 3,000 metre race. Two weeks later the ride was more fun, with Burka winning the world sprint championship in Alkmaar, the Netherlands. The summer of 1977 saw Burka put to good use her cycling prowess, which she had begun to hone two years earlier after being bothered by an injury. Initially, cycling was supposed to help her recovery but she took it far beyond just turning the pedals. In 1977 Burka won the Canadian road race championship and finished fourth behind bronze medallist Karen Strong, also of Canada, in the women's pursuit at the world cycling championships in Venezuela. Burka went on to win twelve national cycling championships and in 1982 set a world indoor 1,000-metre cycling record. She stopped speedskating after the 1980 Olympics, where she finished seventh in the 1,000 metres.

In 1995 Burka was still skating, in a way. Although she gave up speedskating long ago and cycled a bit for fun, she had taken up in-line skating as a recreational pursuit. This time, the years of training having been ingrained in every cell of her body, she picked up the new form of skating easily — a lifetime of records and medals away from that girl whose first awkward efforts on ice resembled a horse on skates.

Cathy Priestner

Cathy Priestner spent the night before her 1976 Olympic speedskating competition as many other competitors had

before, and have since — visualizing the crowd and the noise so that she would be comfortable when it all became real the next day. The mind has a tendency to wander, however, and not always do as a nineteen-year-old might bid.

"So I visualized getting to the line and the gun going off, then I just went blank in my head," Cathy Priestner-Allinger laughed years later. "I thought: 'What am I doing? I have spent the last four years training laps, and laps, and laps, and have given up a normal life of school, all for forty seconds. It's not a game for an hour and a half, or a number of games that lead to a final. It's just one shot at it.' I remember thinking I must be nuts. Then I thought I'd better get refocused. The next day I got on the line and skated my race as well and as perfectly as I could. I crossed the line and the first thing I thought was: 'It was worth it, for forty seconds, it was worth it.'"

Cathy Priestner finished second in the women's 500-metre speedskating sprint at the 1976 Winter Olympics in Innsbruck, Austria, becoming the first Canadian woman to win an official Olympic speedskating medal. Forty-four years earlier Jean Wilson had taken gold in the 500 metres when women's speedskating was a demonstration event.

Priestner was born in Windsor, Ontario, grew up in Winnipeg, and eventually trained in Calgary. At nineteen, Priestner might have seemed young to earn such an important laurel as an Olympic medal, but she was a Canadian team veteran in Innsbruck, having joined the national team at age thirteen. In a six-year international career she became one of the world's best, finishing third overall in the 1975 world sprint championships with an individual win in the 500 metres, and ranked fifth at the 1975 world championships overall in Holland while also taking two silver medals at the 1975 world junior championships in Sweden.

She retired in 1976, likely well before her prime, but looking to get on with her life after a six-year international career and eight years in her sport. It all began when her family moved to Winnipeg. Her new friends at school were involved in speedskating and Priestner took up the sport, too.

"I was pretty athletic," she conceded. "At a young age I was skating at a high level. Maybe if I'd had time to develop in other sports I might have ended up in another sport, but speedskating was what I did. I was always technically so strong that it could compensate for a lot of other things. I was lucky I didn't have to spend hours and hours on technique."

Within a year of putting on the blades Priestner advanced

Cathy Priestner: Youngest member of national speedskating squad.

first to the provincial, then national level, where she won the national age group championship.

"Even at that time I don't think I ever thought Olympics or national team. I won it not having a clue what was out there."

She found out soon enough. Eighteen months after winning her first national title she competed at the world championships, gaining experience. A year later she took gold in the 500 metres at the Canada Games and at age fifteen earned her first Olympic experience, finishing a respectable fourteenth in the 500 metres and twenty-ninth in the 1,000 metres at the 1972 Games in Sapporo, Japan.

Four years later at Innsbruck, Priestner and elder teammate Sylvia Burka came into the Games as medal contenders. Priestner believed her best chance was in the 1,000 metres. The 500 metres was first, however, and Priestner was skating early in the competition in the fourth pairing. Her time of 43.12 seconds remained fastest for all of about three minutes, until American Sheila Young came along and skated a 42.76, ultimately good for the gold medal. After enduring many more skaters, Priestner's effort proved worthy of the silver medal, the first for Canada at those Winter Olympics. She quickly became the centre of Canadian media attention.

"At the time my stronger race was probably the 1,000 metres but I had to skate the 500 first," she said. "Winning the medal, I ended up having so much publicity, so much attention that I didn't go for a massage, a warm down or rest. When I went into the 1,000 the next day I wasn't as prepared as I should have been."

Priestner finished sixth in the 1,000 metres, with teammate Burka fourth and American Sheila Young again taking the gold medal. Priestner opted to retire. Prior to and during the Games she had come under some criticism from Jorrit Jorritsma, a coach from the Netherlands hired by the Canadian Speedskating Association. He told reporters he felt she didn't train hard enough even though he conceded she was a natural athlete. Also, in the months before the Games, Priestner had opted to remain in Canada to train while other Canadian speedskaters went to Europe. Her decision was unpopular with the coach.

As she noted nearly two decades later, she had been on the road as a competitor since she was thirteen, at times travelling and competing with teammates nearly old enough to be her parents.

"At the time, there wasn't really the support system there to continue," she said. "And I had an Olympic silver medal. I felt: I've done that, it's time to look at other things. I retired."

In late 1994 Cathy Priestner-Allinger was still very much involved in speedskating. For six years she had served as manager of the Olympic Oval for speedskating in Calgary and in December 1994 was named associate director of athletics at the University of Calgary.

Looking back, she said medalling in two races and fin-ishing fifth overall at the 1975 world championships was a "big accomplishment" and a big stretch for someone who largely made her name in the sprint events.

"The only thing that lingers a bit is knowing I was getting faster every time I skated," she said. "Each year I was getting better and better. I hadn't reached the top. I know I could have skated faster by competing longer. That would have been the only thing, could I have hung in there and been world champion?"

Short Track Speedskating

When short track speedskating was included as a demonstration sport for the 1988 Winter Olympics in Calgary, it was described as "roller derby on ice" because of the tight turns, speed and the physical jostling that can occur in races characterized by pack competition. At the time it was perceived as a new sport because long track speedskating had enjoyed Olympic status for a long time and tended to be the focus of media attention. But short track speedskating had been around for a long time, with North American competition dating back to the early 1900s. It was officially recognized by the International Skating Union in 1967 and enjoyed an explosion of public interest after its inclusion in the 1988 Calgary Olympics.

In 1992, short track speedskating became a full medal Olympic sport. Two years later, at the Winter Olympics in Norway, the sport aroused much controversy because of judges' decisions involving various crashes and collisions. A review of judging policy was called for so that the 1998 Olympic competition in Nagano, Japan, might enjoy less havoc.

Canada has long excelled in short track speedskating and in the 1980s two Canadian women, Sylvie Daigle and Nathalie Lambert, set the standard of excellence which other competitors attempt to attain.

Sylvie Daigle

SHORT TRACK

If anyone could live up to the label of "natural athlete", few could qualify better than Sylvie Daigle of Sherbrooke, Quebec. Who knows what might have happened had she chosen to concentrate on hockey, where she honed her skills playing on boys' teams; or in baseball, where she was a member of the Sherbrooke all-star team; or soccer, which she played through her mid-teens.

As fate would have it, however, Sylvie Daigle went on to make her mark as a speedskater. On smooth ice in long blades she excelled, particularly in the rough and exciting discipline of short track speedskating although she proved no slouch on the long track oval, either. From 1979, when she won three long track gold medals at the Canada Games in Manitoba, to the spring of 1994, when she retired after serving as a member of Canada's gold medal relay team at the world short track championships in England, Daigle amassed considerable success, including five world short track titles, an Olympic demonstration event gold and two silver medals, Olympic relay gold from 1992, several world records and many awards, including induction into the Canadian Amateur Sports Hall of Fame in 1991.

It all started with a misunderstanding. When Daigle was nine years old she went to her local arena in Sherbrooke, expecting to sign up for a girls' hockey program. She found speedskating instead.

"When I was young, what I loved to do was play hockey," she explained. "Every night after school I would play outside on the ice, on the street. I heard there was hockey for girls starting up so I went to the arena and there was no hockey, only people skating with those long blades. So I went to another arena, there was nothing. I went back to the first arena and said I was looking for hockey for girls. They said there's no hockey but there's speedskating, if you want to skate with us you can.

"I went out there with my hockey skates, we had some races and I almost beat them all. So they said: 'Do you want to come back next week?' It was very difficult at first, the blades are so long and you couldn't turn so much. I said in my head: 'I'm going to control those blades.'"

Daigle achieved early success in short track, winning her first of five overall short track world championships in 1979, at age seventeen. Like many national team counterparts and international competitors, including Gaetan Boucher and Bonnie Blair, Daigle initially skated short track more for fun while long track was considered the more serious discipline, particularly because it had been included in the Olympic program for decades.

Daigle finished nineteenth in the 500 metres at the 1980 Olympics in Lake Placid and two years later earned a career best ninth at the world championships. But short track continued to be her passion and preference and in 1983 she won her second overall world title, dominating her rivals by winning the 500-, 1,000-, 1,500-, and 3,000-metre events in addition to setting world records in the 500 and 1,000 metres.

"The Worlds in 1983, I remember being very, very strong," she responded when asked about a favourite event in her long career. "I felt I could do anything I wanted on the ice. I was very comfortable. Usually, the Worlds I won were not easy."

For a time Daigle opted to concentrate on long track and had some success, winning several national championships. But she was having problems with the muscles in her legs, finding the long straights of the long track oval particularly difficult. After some three years and two operations she returned to short track in 1987 and never looked back, making good with a gold and two silver medals in Calgary where the discipline was a demonstration event at the 1988 Olympics. From 1988 to 1990 she won three consecutive world short track championships.

"In long track, everybody is nervous but it's not the same kind of nerves," she noted. "You can say you're in your own corridor, by yourself and no one can get in your way. You know the only person who can beat you is you; if you don't do well it's your fault. That takes a lot of pressure off. When I went to short track the pressure was different, you have more because you are not alone. There are some things you cannot control — the others. That's very difficult to deal with."

Through the late 1980s and into the early '90s, Daigle was pushed by another talented skater from Quebec, Nathalie Lambert. Having a rival so close in ability training in the same province was motivation to train hard to stay on top.

"Nathalie was very determined. She was going to do everything she could to win," she said of Lambert. "She was somebody who liked to win. She worked hard. She said one day she could be the best and worked hard, very hard. And she did become the best. It's fun to have good competition in the country. The level of competition makes the sport better."

At the 1991 world event Lambert defeated Daigle for the overall championship. More difficult were the 1992 Winter Olympics in Albertville, where Daigle was favoured to win the 500 metres. By then, short track speedskating had advanced from demonstration to full medal status. But instead of enjoying victory Daigle endured disappointment. In the early round she locked blades with American Cathy Turner and slipped out of the race. She returned to join teammates Lambert, Annie Perrault and Angela Cutrone to defeat the Americans for the gold medal in the 3,000-metre relay but there remained some remorse for what might have been.

"When it happened, I couldn't believe it. I was very disappointed," she said. "I think I was the best that year at that distance. I should have been on the podium but it was not my time. I think my year was '92 — mentally and physically I was ready for Albertville."

In the spring of 1992 Daigle opted to take a year's sabbatical from her sport to begin studies as a medical student. But she returned to compete at the 1994 Winter Olympics in Lillehammer, where a decision by the International Olympic Committee to stagger Winter and Summer Games by two years gave winter sport competitors another quick chance for an Olympic experience. Daigle made the Olympic team and advanced to the semi-finals in the women's 1,000 metres at Lillehammer where she was disqualified by judges who deemed her responsible for a collision and subsequent crash that sent rivals into the boards.

The decision, indeed several decisions made by judges during the Olympic short track campaign which was punctuated by crashes and controversy, proved most unpopular with the crowd and the Canadians. Although Daigle returned to earn a relay silver medal with Lambert, Isabelle Charest and Christine Boudrias, it wasn't the Olympic exit most would have wished for a five-time world champion competing in her fifth, and final, Olympic Games.

In March 1994 Daigle closed out her career by contributing to Canada winning the world team championship in Ontario and the relay at the world championships in England. A few months after the Lillehammer disqualification, retired and returned to her medical studies, Daigle had in a sense come full circle. After devoting many years of her life to speedskating she had found time between medical classes to rediscover the sport that made it all happen in the first place — ice hockey.

Fleet Foursome: (left to right) Sylvie Daigle, Nathalie Lambert, Isabelle Charest, and Angela Cutrone.

Nathalie Lambert

Nathalie Lambert was the first to agree timing was important. She had defeated Canadian teammate Sylvie Daigle many times in short track speedskating competition but at a world championship, when a victory would count most, she was never quite able to match Daigle. In 1991 Lambert finally enjoyed her day in the sun. But she had to travel all the way to Sydney, Australia, where after a decade of competing she would become the overall world short track speedskating champion.

"It was a tough weekend," she recalled of the Sydney event. "I had been trying for so many years because I'd been second, third, fourth many times but I was never first. Then, it was up to the last race and it was between me and Sylvie and the one who beat the other would be the world champion, so it was a very stressful day. I was just glad it was over, and glad also that I finally was world champion after so many years. There was satisfaction, and relief."

Montreal's Lambert defeated Daigle in the final race of the event, the 3,000 metres, to win her first world title after first joining the Canadian national speedskating team in 1981. Like Daigle, she would dabble in both long and short track before eventually concentrating on short track in 1987. And, again like Daigle, she would secure a place in her sport as an athlete to be considered and feared at every major competition.

But unlike Daigle, Lambert was hardly athlete champion material when she first took up speedskating at age twelve.

"I was more into my friends, boys, playing outside," she said. "I got into speedskating because one of my girlfriends did it. It took me a few years. I had some qualities — I was very strong — but I had no technique and no coordination. And I was falling all the time. Sylvie (Daigle) is a natural, my boyfriend Frederic (national team member Frederic Blackburn) is a natural. If they did anything they'd be good at it right away. I wasn't like that."

Lambert's journey to the top of the world in her sport

was a gradual climb. She improved from one year to the next and was blessed with a capacity for hard work and a desire to improve. Initially she made her mark as a long track skater, joining the national team in 1981 after finishing fifth overall, at age seventeen, at the national long track championships. She conceded the travel and experiences were enjoyable parts of the sport but it wasn't until she failed to make the 1984 Canadian Olympic team that she decided to get more serious. She dominated the 1984 Canadian championships, finishing first overall and then second overall at the national short track championships that same year. The next eighteen months were busy as Lambert competed internationally, and with success, in both short and long track, including taking overall bronze medals at the 1984 and '85 world short track championships. In 1986 and '87 she improved to take the silver medal overall in the world event. She had to make a choice for the 1988 Olympics and, after skating in the 1987 short track Worlds, she was expected to remain in that discipline for the 1988 Winter Olympics in Calgary.

"That basically decided it for me," she said of the rest of her career, which would concentrate on short track. "The year before I was number one in Canada in long track. I think I could have done fairly well, I don't know if I would have had a medal."

Lambert took bronze in the 3,000-metre relay at Calgary. In 1989 she finished fifth overall to Daigle at the world championships and, in 1990, fourth overall to Daigle. The two were a formidable duo at any international event.

"She's good at pretty much every distance, and always a tough competitor," said Lambert when asked to assess Daigle. "She'd always give it 100 per cent. It took me many years to realize that I used to think she was so much ahead of me. She was good but I made her even better. In the last few years I realized she was as much worried by me as I could be by her."

After Lambert won the 1991 world championship over Daigle she finished sixth in the 500 metres at the 1992 Winter Olympics in Albertville, also taking home a relay gold medal. Considered better at slightly longer distances,

Lambert returned the next year to win the 1993 overall world championship with victories over 1,000, 1,500 and 3,000 metres and, at the pre-Olympic meet in Hamar, Norway, she dominated by winning the 500-, 1,000-, 1,500- and 3,000-metre events.

Although Daigle returned from a study sabbatical to compete at the 1994 Olympics in Norway, Lambert was by then considered the skater to beat. A nemesis from Daigle's past, Cathy Turner, also wreaked havoc with Lambert's Olympic aspirations. In their 500-metre quarter-final race Turner bumped Lambert. The Canadian sprawled to the ice while Turner, not disqualified for the incident, went on to win the gold medal for the 500 metres. Lambert returned to take silver in the 1,000 metres and in the relay, finishing her Olympic experience frustrated, as were many of her teammates who were also victims of crashes and collisions dealt with lethargically by the judges.

Lambert was known throughout her career as an athlete unafraid to speak her mind. "People have to realize Canadians had very bad luck," she said of the Lillehammer Olympic experience. "Falling and close passes are always going to be a part of the sport. It's frustrating but it's also the beauty of the sport. The only thing about Lillehammer was it was completely out of control. If the referees had done their job there would have been no problems. There would still have been falls but the thing that made the athletes frustrated was that they didn't do anything."

Lambert returned to help Canada win the 1994 world short track team championship. Two weeks later, at age thirty-one, she ended her competitive career by winning her third world overall short track championship at Guildford, England.

Lambert had not abandoned her sport, however. In late 1994, upon finishing classes in radio and television broadcasting, she was also coaching and training seven skaters. In retrospect, she conceded she had contributed to her sport's growth with her success while growing right along with it. In the future she may contribute still, as a coach, broadcaster, and former world champion unafraid to speak her mind if it will help her sport.

Ringette

It is fitting that a game invented by a Canadian should have Canada as its major player on the international scene.

Ringette was invented in 1963 by Sam Jacks of North Bay, Ontario, as a winter sport for girls and women. Basics required for the game include a patch of ice, skates, a rubber ring and a straight stick. The object of the game is simple — score by putting the rubber ring past the opposing team's goaltender. The team with the most points at the end of the game wins. Good skating, shooting and passing skills are essential in order to play the game at a high level.

Sam Jacks passed away in 1975 but his game flourished. As of 1995, Ringette Canada, the governing body for the sport in the country, noted some thirty thousand individuals were registered as playing the sport in Canada. Although originally devised as a sport for females, ringette had expanded its scope to include male players as well.

Since its inception in 1963, ringette has expanded to other countries, with six nations founding the International Ringette Federation in 1986. The first world ringette championships were held in 1990 in Gloucester, Ontario, with teams from the United States and Finland battling several Canadian squads. The final was an all-Canadian affair as Western Canada defeated Ontario 3-2 when Edmonton's Lisa Brown scored with just over a minute remaining to give her team the victory and the Sam Jacks Trophy.

Two years later the world championships moved to Helsinki, Finland, and once again the final came down to an all-Canadian tilt with Canada West winning 6-5 over Canada East. Lisa Brown and her sister, Cara, scored five of the six Canada West goals with Lisa Brown earning a hat trick on her third goal twenty-five seconds from the final buzzer. Finland took the bronze medal with a 13-1 victory over the United States.

In 1994, Minneapolis, Minnesota, played host to the world event and the results were proof the sport had grown in other parts of the world. This time, Finland took the gold medal with a 5-2 victory over Canada East with Canada West taking the bronze medal. The United States, Sweden and Russia finished fourth, fifth and sixth respectively. Canada East's Kim Poirier was named tournament Most Valuable Player.

The 1996 world tournament will be held in Stockholm, Sweden.

Making History: Canada West Ringette squad won the first world championship.

Hockey

At the end of the game scores of young girls waited for the players to sign autographs. On the ice the victors held a teammate aloft, clutching the bronze winner's trophy, as the partisan crowd of nearly nine thousand cheered. It was a scene that has become a familiar part of Canadian society, on a grander or more modest scale depending on the age and skill level of the players. Anywhere in the country winning a hockey championship is a big deal. But March 25, 1990, was a special day for followers and proponents of Canadian women's hockey. On the ice at Ottawa Civic Centre the Canadian women's national team defeated the United States 5-2 to win the first women's world ice hockey championship.

It didn't matter that their bright pink uniforms had attracted some derision or giggles, or that the game needed some development and parity on the international front, as the Canadians sailed past Japan 18-0 and West Germany 17-0. It was a beginning, a glorious and long-awaited beginning for thirty-seven-year-old Shirley Cameron of Edmonton. She was the oldest player on the team and never thought a world championship would come in her playing days. It was also a beginning for Geraldine Heaney, one of the stars of the final game who would go on to lead the Canadians to two more world championships.

Women had been playing hockey in Canada long before the 1990 world championships gave their brand of game some publicity and recognition. As far back as the late nineteenth century there are records of women playing the game, clad appropriately for the time in long skirts. But it wasn't until the 1960s that women's hockey began to become highly organized in Ontario, although it would take longer for the sport to develop in many of the other provinces. In 1982 the Female Hockey Council was organized by the Canadian Amateur Hockey Association and, that same year, the first Canadian women's national championships were held. For the record, Ontario's Agincourt Canadians defeated Alberta to win the inaugural Abby Hoffman Cup.

The first international women's tournament was held in Toronto in 1987. Six teams participated and the International Ice Hockey Federation moved to sanction a women's world championship for 1990. It was fitting that a country that has organized its Saturday nights around radio and television hockey broadcasts, that has embraced a sport into the national psyche, should not only play host to the first women's world hockey championship but also celebrate its team's historic victory in the event.

Two years later, the 1992 world women's championships were held in Tampere, Finland, and again Canada prevailed, shutting out the United States 8-0 in the final. By then the move was strong to have the women's game included on the program for the 1994 Winter Olympics in Lillehammer, Norway. Unsuccessful, the move gained momentum and ultimate success, with women's ice hockey slated to debut as a full medal sport at the 1998 Winter Olympics in Nagano, Japan.

Meanwhile, in 1994, Canada completed its world championship hat trick, spoiling the American dream of a distaff version of Miracle On Ice by defeating the United States 6-3 at the third world women's championship at Lake Placid, New York. The next world women's championships are slated for Kitchener, Ontario, in 1997, a deviation from the biennial format in order to serve as a selection event for teams to the 1998 Winter Olympics in Japan.

It wasn't that long ago that Canadian girls had little to aspire to in the way of hockey other than learning skills and enjoying the game at a club or local level. Now there are Olympics and world championships, worthy goals for any athlete. It is rare in any Canadian sport that an athlete can lay claim to having contributed to a team's victory in three world championships. Some of the following Canadian women have done just that.

Team Canada: Celebrates a 6-3 win over the United States in the final of the 1994 world women's ice hockey championships.

Manon Rheaume

Trailblazer. Role model. Rebel. Phenomenon. Celebrity. Oddity. Publicity Seeker.

Manon Rheaume has been called many things since she suited up to play her first league hockey game in 1977. She would prefer most of the labels used to describe her be forgotten, except a basic one that often gets buried under glitzier, more controversial titles — Goaltender.

"People ask: 'Do you play hockey for the money?'" bristled Rheaume. "For the publicity? I think: Are you crazy? I really love the sport. I have to get up early every morning, train hard. If I do it for the publicity, it's crazy. I enjoy doing it. I'm happy doing it. I find it hard when people say things like that."

Rheaume also knows the comments come with the territory — uncharted and wild country she forged by becoming the first woman to play in the prestigious Quebec International Peewee tournament in Quebec City; the first woman to play in an official game for a Canadian major

junior hockey team; the first woman to play in a National Hockey League game.

Her compass? A love of hockey coupled with determination, athleticism and a willingness to learn the nuances all good netminders must master. Her map? A largely blank piece of paper that she filled in along the way — a collection of dead-ends, exciting peaks and disappointing valleys she encountered and conquered, leaving a hint of a trail that others might follow.

Her sustenance? Love of family and friends, support of teammates and a fierce will that keeps her going with each smack of a puck blasted by a player who doesn't want her there, with each disparaging remark made by just about anyone who says she doesn't, and shouldn't, belong.

Manon Rheaume was born February 24, 1972, the middle child of three and the only daughter. Her earliest memories are of serving as goaltender to brothers' shots parlayed on a makeshift rink in the family backyard at Lac Beauport,

Manon Rheaume: A trailblazer who made history on ice as the first woman to play a National Hockey League game.

Quebec. She was good at many sports, including skiing, and even dabbled in figure skating, but from an early age the challenge of staring a breakaway forward in the eye and stopping a slapshot cold exerted the strongest pull of all.

"It's a great sport, a great feeling when you stop the puck, when you win a game," she said. "Sure, you also have lots of pressure. I love the speed, the action. For me the goal is always the same. I need to stop the puck, whether it's guys or girls shooting. Just stop the puck, whatever it takes."

Rheaume started her first game at age five, wearing white figure skates and playing for the team coached by her father, flanked by her teammate brothers and neighbourhood friends who were so accustomed to testing her netminding skills in street hockey and scrimmages they weren't surprised to see her between the pipes. Adults, particularly parents of other players, proved a different matter. Even as a youngster Rheaume, and her parents, would be criticized for her participation on boys' teams, taking the place of a budding NHLer when she would go nowhere. The reality was if she wanted to play hockey the only opportunity was to crack the lineup on a boys' squad. Rheaume resolved to go as far as she could in the sport.

She went farther than most people, except herself,

thought possible, netminding through atom, peewee and bantam AA levels until a decision not to invite her to midget AAA training camp forced her to quit the sport in frustration. She played on the Sherbrooke women's team in 1990-91, but the lure of challenges yet unmet proved too strong and she accepted an invitation to train with the Trois Rivières junior A team.

In fall 1991 she attended the Trois Rivières Draveurs training camp, becoming the team's third-string goalie while playing for Tier II Louisville. In November of that year she was called to dress for the Draveurs when their starter injured a collarbone. On November 26, 1991, with the Draveurs and Granby Bisons tied 5-5, nineteen-year-old Rheaume came off the bench at 12:28 of the second period to replace shell-shocked starter Jocelyn Thibault, who had earlier in the game enjoyed a 4-1 Draveurs lead. Rheaume let in three goals from twelve shots, and after seventeen minutes in the net she was forced to leave the game after being hit by a shot on the mask, a gash above her right eye, which required three stitches. The Draveurs lost the contest 10-6.

"My starting goalie wasn't playing well," Draveurs coach Gaston Drapeau told a Canadian Press reporter after the game. "She's the backup and I used her like I would any backup goalie. We don't look at her as a woman, we look at her as a goalie."

Her seventeen minutes of major junior experience earned Rheaume plenty of publicity but mixed reviews. Some observers felt the move was just a publicity stunt. They said the same when, after tending goal for the Canadian women's team that won the world women's hockey championship, Rheaume was invited to attend 1992 training camp for the NHL Tampa Bay Lightning. The howls of derision reached a crescendo when general manager Phil Esposito announced Rheaume would start in the September 23, 1992, exhibition game against the St. Louis Blues.

A woman, with just seventeen minutes game experience in major junior hockey, starting an NHL game? She hadn't paid her dues, she didn't belong, what a publicity stunt.

Rheaume saw the situation differently.

"I worked hard in training camp, why shouldn't I get a chance to show what I can do in a game situation?" she said. "Publicity stunt? That's a big risk. If I don't play well, perform well, they don't look very good. And do I turn down the chance, the challenge? No way!"

A standing ovation from the more than eight thousand spectators greeted her when she stepped on the ice, nervous beneath her mask but exuding quiet confidence to the outside world. She neatly blocked the first shot that came her way forty seconds into the game, then Blues' Jeff Brown scored at 2:21 with Brendan Shanahan scoring fourteen minutes later. The score was tied 2-2 at the end of the first period. Wendell Young took over the Lightning netminding duties for the next two periods, with St. Louis winning the contest 6-4.

"I was preparing myself for just a normal game," recalled Rheaume. "Everyone on the ice was playing for a job, trying to show what they could do. After the game I felt there were twenty pounds less on my shoulders. I knew I had done a good job."

Rheaume was signed to play and develop her skills in the Tampa Bay minor league system. She also had to cope with a flood of interview and appearance requests, including an offer for a pictorial feature from Playboy magazine. She declined.

Her professional hockey career in the Tampa Bay system took her to the Eastern Hockey League's Knoxville Cherokee. In February 1994 she was reassigned to the EHL Nashville Knights, which was a promotion of sorts in that she was the third-string netminder in Knoxville but would be the second goalie for the Knights. She finished the EHL season with a 5-0-1 record and a 3.64 goals against average.

Rheaume also returned to the national women's team in 1994 to contribute to another world championship win at Lake Placid, New York, looking ahead to compete for Canada at the 1998 Winter Olympics in Japan, where women's hockey will debut on the Olympic program. She also opted to continue working on her skills in the summer, signing with the New Jersey Rockin' Rollers of the Roller Hockey International league. In September 1994, she signed a contract with the Las Vegas Thunder of the International Hockey League.

"I am realistic. There are still ways I can improve," she said of playing as a professional. "You need to play a lot to make a team at that level. I'm playing, working on improving. My goal is just to go as far as I can in this game. That's all I've ever wanted."

Judy Diduck

Ask Judy Diduck for a best memory from the 1990 women's world hockey championships and her answer illustrates a distinct difference in the status of men's and women's hockey in Canada.

"It was extremely exciting. You just weren't expecting the people to respond to it, but they did," she enthused. "Ottawa came out in droves to watch. It was completely unexpected in that final game, coming out for the warm-up. The place was packed and going crazy and I thought: 'Holy Smokes, they've come to watch us?' It was a thrill, but you're not used to it. Maybe that illustrated a difference in female and male hockey. The guys expect the attention, the girls appreciate it."

Diduck came to hockey by way of developing as one of the top ringette players in Alberta while also excelling in school sports such as basketball, soccer and track. She was steered to ringette after trying to play organized hockey with her male peers, which included brother Gerald (who went on to play in the National Hockey League).

She began playing hockey at age nineteen and for a time juggled ringette and hockey. Working the puck, she was an integral member of the Edmonton Chimos, playing in every national championship since 1985. In 1990 she enjoyed what might be an athlete's dream season, although in retrospect the opportunity also caused some stress and fatigue. She was named to the Canadian women's team in the world hockey championships and to Team Alberta, which represented Canada at the world ringette championships. Scheduling allowed her to compete in both and at the end of the spring she was a world champion in both hockey and ringette.

"The Worlds were a huge deal. That was my first year of playing defence and I was just tickled to make the team," she said. "But having played ringette for so long I made it my priority. I also felt my chances were better to make that team than hockey, so once they told me I had made the hockey team I wondered about the scheduling and if I'd have to make a tough decision. Fortunately, it all worked out."

It is not uncommon for European players to try their fortunes in the NHL or for North American male pros to play in Europe. After the spring of 1990, at age twenty-four, Diduck wanted to expand her hockey experience and personal horizons and landed a spot with a Swiss women's team in Zurich. The squad won the Swiss women's championship that season and Diduck was able to travel and play her game — a situation male hockey players have enjoyed for years.

She says she and her brother engage in some natural sibling teasing about their hockey experiences but for the most part they are proud of each others' accomplishments.

Diduck is another national team veteran who hopes to gain a spot on the 1998 Olympic team. In addition to now offering travel experience and personal growth as a member of a team, the game itself offers many rewards and challenges.

"I love the challenges, being able to skate forward and back with a puck on your stick," she said. "Getting your individual skills down so you're not even thinking of what

you're doing technically, so you can see the game, play the game. And chemistry on a team is so important, it makes all the difference as to whether you can have a successful team or not."

Judy Diduck: Excelled in ringette and ice hockey.

Geraldine Heaney: Highlight star from the 1990 world women's ice hockey championships.

Geraldine Heaney

Geraldine Heaney is accustomed to being reminded she wears the same number as National Hockey League star Sergei Fedorov. But make no mistake who started wearing Number Ninety-One first.

"People say: 'You're wearing his number.'" noted Heaney, a Canadian women's national team veteran and longtime player for the Toronto Aeros. "But I've worn this number for twelve years. I had it way before him."

Heaney has established herself as one of the top women hockey players not only in Canada but also throughout the

world. A member of Canada's 1990, 1992 and 1994 world women's hockey championship teams, she was the leading item on many a sport highlight package in 1990 when her end-to-end rush and subsequent goal broke a 2-2 stalemate in the world championship final between Canada and the United States. The goal proved not only to be the game winner, but served to shift the momentum back to the Canadian team for what would ultimately be a 5-2 victory.

Many observers noted her effort was not unlike Bobby Orr's superb exhibition of speed and skill for a goal that won the Boston Bruins the 1970 Stanley Cup.

"It was so quick and I didn't really realize how it all happened until I watched it later on TV," said Heaney. "It was a great goal. I never expected it. It was a chance and I just jumped into the play and it all worked out well."

Heaney was born in Northern Ireland in 1967 but a year later her family moved to Canada. As she grew up she became immersed in whatever game was presented to her, playing soccer on a boys' team and making her contribution in school basketball and volleyball. She enjoyed team sports rather than individual competition but most of all she was intrigued by hockey. She began by playing the game with her brothers on outdoor rinks until her father, who coached minor hockey, found a girls' team for her to play on even though it was a long drive from the local rink.

"Every time you turn on the TV, it's on," she said when asked about her fascination with hockey. "It's a fast game, and I like fast games. Baseball, I wasn't really into because you stand around a lot. I also love skating. Hockey is quick, it's so fast compared to any other sport."

Heaney was twelve years old when she started playing for the Toronto Aeros and has worked her way up the competitive ladder, contributing to the team's six provincial championship victories. Initially a forward, for the past decade she has found her niche as an offensive defence player who also delights in making the perfect pass for a teammate to score.

At the 1990 women's world championship in Ottawa, Heaney scored two goals and had six assists in five games. She would have been sorely missed by the Canadian team if an administrative insight into her citizenship had not been discovered.

"For the first Worlds, I was only a landed immigrant and they weren't even going to let me play because someone didn't tell me I had to be a Canadian citizen," she said. "I'd been here all my life, I never thought twice about it. When the final cuts were coming they realized they'd made a mistake. Well, we rushed around and I got my citizenship two days before the deadline."

Like most of her current national teammates, Heaney hopes she will be a part of the 1998 Canadian women's team to the Winter Olympics in Nagano, Japan.

Her athleticism doesn't stop at the ice, however. Heaney was also a member of the Canadian women's team that won the 1992 women's roller hockey world championship in Germany. Heaney also enjoys playing Gaelic football — clearly the Irish part of her genes showing through.

"I like it better than soccer. It's a lot faster," she said. "You can use your hands, run with the ball, bounce it, kick it. You have to be in shape, the field's a lot bigger, probably one and a half times the size. There's probably more running at a quicker pace. If I try to go end to end in that game it's pretty tiring."

Angela James

"I'm aggressive. I hustle. I work hard and I'm pretty intense." Angela James' description of herself is likely similar to how others would describe her as they view her play on the ice. She has played forward on all three Canadian women's world hockey championship teams and led the national squad in scoring at the 1990 inaugural world event in Ottawa, registering eleven goals and two assists. Not bad for someone who at first didn't make the cut.

"The first world championship will always be important for me because initially I didn't make the team," said James, who plays for the Toronto Aeros. "They named fourteen people to the team and then said they wanted to look at me again. A week later they called and said 'you're on the team.'"

In the past, James' athleticism ensured she would be one of those kids picked first in neighbourhood games. She recalls being successful at just about every sport she attempted, recognizing that a strong competitive streak helped to push her along. Softball, soccer, field hockey and basketball were among her other sports but, growing up, she was like many other Canadian kids in that hockey held a special fascination.

"I think, living in Canada, Ontario especially, we had a lot of outdoor arenas. That's what we did for entertainment in the winter, otherwise we'd never get out of the house. Basically, that was our form of entertainment, playing shinny in the outdoor arenas. Sometimes we'd take over the street and the cars somehow had to get by. It was a big street. If not, we were playing hockey in the garage, or the courtyards."

James started playing senior level hockey at age fifteen. Back then there were no world championships or Olympic Games to aspire to. She is thrilled that new opportunities have opened for women in the game and is relieved that she came along at a time to enjoy hockey at such a crucial junction in its development for women. The 1998 Olympics in Nagano, Japan, are on her list of future projects — if she makes the team, of course.

"I'm concentrating on one thing at a time. For myself, I want to be in the top five. That's always been my goal as a

Angela James: Started out playing shinny in the streets.

player. If you're in the top five from year to year they're going to look at their top ten and take them back, so I aim for top five and try to be number one."

Hockey has become more than just a game for James, who works as a recreation coordinator at North York's Seneca College. She also is a certified referee and coach and runs an adult hockey school.

Spare time? Not surprisingly, that is utilized in another interesting athletic pursuit. In 1992, James was a member of the Canadian women's roller hockey team that won the gold medal at the world championships in 1992 and returned to take silver behind Spain at the 1994 event.

James says her best memory so far in her hockey career was being part of the Canadian team to win its third consecutive world championship at the 1994 event in Lake Placid.

"I really wanted a three-peat," she said. "Yes, I'd been on two other world teams but there was a lot of turnover so it didn't always feel like the same team. It was always something new to conquer because you had new people there as well. And you always want to be number one.

"Through my whole life — I've been playing hockey for more than twenty years — I've always been taught to be number one. I don't think I could ever stop wanting to win."

Stacy Wilson

In 1994, twenty-eight-year-old Stacy Wilson of Moncton, New Brunswick, contributed four goals and four assists to Canada's winning effort at the world women's hockey championships. The event marked her third appearance at a world championship in a national career that began in 1986 when she was the leading scorer at the senior nationals and named to the all-star team.

But it was a seemingly unrelated soccer game that began Wilson's hockey career in earnest. As a child she grew up in a neighbourhood with few other girl children so she fell right in with whatever game the boys were playing, including hockey. When they went to the local rink to register for organized hockey Wilson wanted to go too, and she received support from her family and from the coach. She was eight years old at the time and played with her male peers until the end of her bantam year, at about fourteen or fifteen. She didn't take up the game again until her second year of university.

"A few of us in second year at Acadia, were sitting at a soccer game and we decided we should have a girls' hockey team," she explained. "So we put a rec team together. The first year we played against Dalhousie and we lost, some-

thing like 18-1. We were so bad. But the next year we went to the nationals."

Wilson, who had also excelled in badminton as a youth, went on to teach physical education and science in addition to becoming one of the top women hockey players in the country. After competing in three women's world championships she conceded all three experiences were thrilling, although the 1994 event was particularly gratifying because friends and family drove from New Brunswick to watch her play and she rewarded their support by scoring a goal in the gold medal game. The first women's world event was also memorable because she participated in an important part of sport history.

"It was quite unbelievable," she said. "It seemed like you never heard anything about world championships for women until that year. It all seemed to happen so suddenly. It was hard to take everything in, I remember feeling very proud wearing the Canadian sweater. I didn't care that it was pink."

Wilson is also putting something back into her sport so that future female competitors from New Brunswick will have an organized system to hone their skills. In 1995 she served as a coach to the New Brunswick Canada Winter Games team and a month later led New Brunswick to the final of the national women's hockey championship.

"I am fortunate to have come along at this time. There are so many women who didn't have the chance," said Wilson. "Women have played the game for one hundred years but didn't have the opportunity to do what I do. Hopefully, I can give something back so that others can have the opportunity."

Wilson believes inclusion in the Winter Olympics will give women's hockey the necessary credibility and exposure that will prompt parents to enroll their daughters in the game. No longer a novelty, she sees women's hockey just getting bigger and bigger.

"I love it. It's a great game, a great sport. As you get older and train harder there are days when it's not so fun but that's the way with any sport. It's part of Canadian life, playing hockey in the wintertime."

Stacy Wilson: Eager to help other girls and young women to have the opportunity to play hockey.

Justine Blainey: Gets in the mix with a rival from the Aeros in her first bantam game for the East Enders in 1988.

Justine Blainey

Justine Blainey was just eleven years old when she discovered not all was fair and equitable in the sporting world.

She wanted to play hockey. She discovered that playing organized hockey for girls meant having to play with a team far from her home when her brother enjoyed the facilities at a nearby rink. She also discovered that, while her brother was able to play with his peers in a system highly organized and broken down into distinct age and ability levels, she was lumped in with female players far older and more mature in a system that also offered little in the way of competitive opportunities for players of varying abilities and desire.

Blainey made the girls' fourteen-and-under all-star team at age eleven, having been on skates for just a year. Believing she would have more fun and more opportunity to improve if she played and practised with her brother's Metro Toronto Hockey League team, Blainey was told that she couldn't play on the boys' team even though she had made the grade. She decided to do something about the inequity of her situation.

"I'm sure if I were the same eleven-year-old girl I would have started the whole thing again," she said years later. "At eleven years old you're more naive, you believe in fairness. Sometimes I think there's no way we're ever going to get everything to be fair in this world."

Blainey embarked on a four-year battle with the Ontario Hockey Association, a mission that went through five separate court battles in an effort to settle what she felt was her right to play on a boys' team so long as she had the skill, strength and ability to do so. Others, like Gail Cummings nearly a decade earlier, had challenged the system and failed. But by the mid-1980s Blainey's case struck a sensitive chord in the minds of the general public and the media. Blainey became known in households across Canada and her situation sparked many a dinner table discussion and argument.

Should a girl who had demonstrated the ability to make the grade on a boys' team be forced to play on a girls' team?

If the question sparked heated debate among families and friends, attempting to have it answered and settled in the courts proved a courageous and difficult move for Justine Blainey and her family.

"I didn't really realize at the time what it would entail to make a difference, to be able to get that right, to play at that level," she said. "Had I known, at that age I don't know if I would have been able to go through the struggle."

"During that time I heard insults, I had more fear of going out on the subway. In Grade 7, when the case was in full bloom with the media, I lost all my friends. By the time I was able to play it was a dream come true but I had lost quite a bit. During that whole time my brother, David, was my best friend and my biggest supporter."

In 1985 Blainey lost the first round of her battle when the Supreme Court of Ontario ruled as reasonable a section of that province's Human Rights Code discussing the right of athletic organizations to restrict participation to persons of the same sex. Six months later the Appeal Court of Ontario sided with Blainey. In June of 1987 the Supreme Court of Canada refused an appeal by the Ontario Hockey Association and later refused another petition by the OHA to hear the case. In late 1987 the Ontario Human Rights Commission ruled Blainey had been discriminated against because she had not been allowed to play boys' hockey, clearing the way for her to finally join her brothers' team.

She played with and against male players for nearly four years when, at age eighteen and at the midget level, she knew she wasn't big enough or strong enough to play junior and also knew she had academic as well as athletic aspirations. She enrolled at the University of Toronto and joined its outstanding women's hockey program while studying sciences and, later, psychology. In early 1995 she was pursuing a different path and wanted to become a chiropractor.

Although the two had never met, Blainey cheered goaltender Manon Rheaume's efforts to secure a spot in professional men's hockey, even though there are some people who believe Rheaume could do more for women's hockey by remaining in the women's game.

"There are some people who are opposed to what she has done," said Blainey. "I've always stuck up for her, even though she may not know it. Let her do what she wants to do, she has the right to make money if she wants to make money, to live her life the way she wants and to make her own decisions. Who are they to criticize her? It's given exposure for women in hockey. I think that's a positive thing, to have any advertising for women in sport — period."

Blainey's case caused her also to be in demand as a public speaker and over the years she has discussed her philosophy and hopes, not only for herself but for other women in sport, with school, university and community groups. She has since spoken out on other inequities she has seen in society, noting life would have been easier if she stayed quiet. But change doesn't happen if people don't speak up, even if the loudest, most persistent voice is from an eleven-year-old girl.

"I noticed very quickly the differences with what was offered me, and what was offered to the guys," she said of her initial hockey opportunities. "I just said that's not fair. I wasn't able to do what my brother was able to do. I think being so young and naive allowed me to do it, to come out and ask that question: It's not fair. How come? And what can we do about it?"

Curling

Canadian women curlers come close to being a dynasty in their sport. They haven't won every women's world championship but their names appear on the winner's list far more than any other, and those who didn't win were almost always runners-up.

It wasn't until 1961 that Canadian women curlers had the chance to compete at a national championship. Prior to that year women from western Canada took part in a western Canadian championship to choose the best from among B.C., Alberta, Saskatchewan and Manitoba rinks. In 1960 an eastern championship was also held, with the Ruth Smith rink from Quebec winning and going on to an east-west match against western champ Joyce McKee, who won the event.

The first women's national championship was played in Ottawa in 1961 with McKee's Saskatoon rink proving the best of the ten provincial representatives. While for years the Canadian men's champions could move on to a world championship, the national event was all Canadian women could aspire to until 1979, when the first women's world championship was held in Perth, Scotland. The B.C. rink of Lindsay Sparkes, Dawn Knowles, Robin Wilson and Lorraine Bowles won the women's national championship in 1979 and was among the rinks to play in that first world event. The Canadian champions came away with the bronze medal, with the Gaby Casanova rink of Switzerland making history as the first women's world champions.

Canada, considered a world curling power because of the depth of playing talent and public interest in the game, didn't have to wait long before honouring a world women's champion, however. In 1980 Regina's Marj Mitchell, Nancy Kerr, Shirley McKendry and Wendy Leach won the world title and brought it back to the most enthusiastic curling province in the country — Saskatchewan.

Marj Mitchell Rink

"Marj was one of the forerunners in having extremely good strategy," noted Nancy Kerr, who played third on Marj Mitchell's world championship rink from 1980. "She used to go and watch men curl and get an idea of how to build up ends instead of playing rock to rock. She spent extra time learning that. She was a disciplinarian, we got excellent leadership from Marj on our team."

Mitchell and Kerr had curled together for many years and were eventually joined by Leach and, in 1979, by McKendry who had just moved to Regina from Ontario and begun playing at the Callie Club.

"I was very fortunate to come in when I did," recalled McKendry, who played second. "I stepped right in and fortunately the mix was right. We were able to work together quickly."

Mitchell's Saskatchewan rink won the 1980 women's national championship by defeating Nova Scotia in the final after clawing back from losses in the first two games to win an eventual playoff berth in a tie breaker. Winning the Canadian championship meant a trip to the women's world

event in Perth, Scotland. A year before, the Lindsay Sparkes rink from B.C. had been favoured to win but came away with the bronze medal. Canada was again a favourite in 1980 but Sweden was the European favourite. The two rinks finished with 8-1 records in the round robin, with the Mitchell rink's only loss coming to the Swedes skipped by Elisabeth Hogstrom.

Like their 1979 counterparts, Mitchell's Canadian rink had several adjustments to make in their game for the different conditions they confronted in Scotland. The ice was different, the atmosphere was different.

"One of the big differences was the way people could come so close to you when you were playing," said McKendry. "There wasn't much to separate the spectators from the players and you could hear their comments. They could be very distracting and at times you had to work hard focusing on the game."

The Canadians dispatched Scotland 9-4 in the semi-final and advanced to meet Sweden again in the final. The two rinks battled back and forth and initially it appeared the Swedes would win the title when a simple draw into the house was all Hogstrom needed with her last rock. It appeared a perfect shot and, after some sweeping the Swedish third and lead raised their brushes in triumph as the rock came over the centre line of the house. But the Canadians weren't finished. As the Swedes celebrated, the rock kept moving and Kerr swept diligently as the rock came next to a Canadian team biter, with teammate Leach urging her on.

"I was on the ice, flat on my stomach," she laughed. "I was yelling to Nancy, sweep it out, sweep it out."

Kerr's effort forced the game into an extra end and Mitchell's rink came away with a 7-6 victory.

"When we got home, it was something I'll never forget," said Leach. "It was just wonderful, they put on a great reception. It was very, very special."

Marj Mitchell died of cancer in October 1983, just three years after her rink became the first Canadian women's team to win a world curling championship. She is remembered not only as the skip of a world team, but also as someone who gave much time and energy back to her sport.

"She was on the board of Callie, our home club, and was instrumental in organizing a large ladies' cashpiel," recalled Kerr. "At that time, there weren't any for women and there are quite a few now."

Marj Michell Rink: Skip Marj Mitchell (lower left) and Saskatchewan rinkmates Nancy Kerr, Shirley McKendry and Wendy Leach, 1980 women's world curling champions.

Connie Laliberte: Displays veteran's cool as Saskatchewan rival Sandra Peterson looks on at 1995 Scott Tournament of Hearts in Calgary.

Connie Laliberte Rink

Facing a tide of optimism surrounding the Canadian women's team's chances at the 1984 world curling championships in Perth, Scotland, Winnipeg's Connie Laliberte was trying to remember the old adages about pride going before a fall and not counting chickens before they're hatched.

"In 1984, the sense we got from the other teams was

that they were looking at us like we were going to win," she said. "Even the press assumed we were going to win and I thought: Wait a minute, we haven't even played a game yet, anything can happen."

The curling universe unfolded as expected that late March week in Scotland. Skip Laliberte, with her sisters Corinne

Peters and Janet Arnott, and veteran Chris More, finished the round robin portion of the tournament with an 8-1 win-loss record. They then put away a determined Norway rink 8-6 in the semi-final. In the final they cruised to a 10-0 win over the Swiss rink of Brigitte Kienast to win Canada's second world women's title in the brief history of the championships.

Perhaps the biggest surprise of the event was that Laliberte was only twenty-three years old, yet had shown patience and nerve beyond her years in skipping her rink to the world championship.

"It's something every curler dreams of during a curling career," she agreed a decade later. "To happen at such a young age, at times I wonder if I appreciated it as I should. Looking back on it, it's a tremendous thing to do at a young age. It wouldn't surprise me if even younger ones win it because kids start learning the game a lot younger now."

Laliberte began curling at age fifteen and five years later was a member of the Manitoba champion rink that went on to the Canadian championships. She played lead at the time, then switched to skipping. Laliberte felt she had a winning mix when veteran Chris More joined her rink. While Laliberte was certainly an emerging young talent in the game, More brought experience. She and sister Cathy Pidzarko were half of the Manitoba women's rink that won the national championship in 1978 and More joining the Laliberte group as third gave the rink a pivotal component — experience in what it takes to win a big event.

"Chris joined us in 1984," recalled Laliberte. "She came on board and we really lucked out. She brought a wealth of experience and that gave me the confidence I was looking for at that point. She contributed quite a bit to our success."

Nowhere was Laliberte's youth and relative inexperience tested more than in the 1984 Scott Tournament of Hearts in Charlottetown. Her rink lost its first two matches in the round robin then slowly regained confidence to make the playoff. She reeled off a pivotal shot in the last end of the semi-final to eliminate British Columbia, then unleashed a similar shot under pressure to defeat Colleen Jones of Halifax 5-4 and win the national title.

Jones later dubbed Laliberte "The Ice Queen." Quiet and rare to show emotion, Laliberte nevertheless possessed a competitive instinct that allowed her to make crucial shots under extreme pressure.

"I enjoy the challenge," she agreed. "I think I have always gone out to play the game as opposed to worrying about who we are playing."

In 1992 Laliberte again won the national championship, with Arnott returning and Laurie Allen and Cathy Gauthier rounding out the foursome, but it was Sweden's Elisabet Johnssen who took the women's world crown. In 1994 Laliberte came close again to earning a spot in the world event but the last rock delivered by Sandra Peterson gave her Saskatchewan rink a 5-3 win over Laliberte in that year's Scott Tournament of Hearts.

In 1995, however, Laliberte returned to defeat Alberta and advanced to the world championship in Brandon, Manitoba, but lost 6-5 to Sweden's Elisabet Gustafson in the final.

Linda Moore Rink

If anyone can attest to the depth of women's curling in Canada it is North Vancouver's Linda Moore, whose foursome struggled in the early 1980s just to advance through regional and provincial competition. They also struggled to find the right team mix. At times veteran Lindsay Sparkes skipped, other times Moore took control and Sparkes played third with Debbie Jones playing second to Laurie Carney's lead.

After nearly three years of close-but-not-quite results, the foursome won the 1984 B.C. championship in Kelowna and advanced to the Scott Tournament of Hearts in Charlottetown, P.E.I., where their aspirations ended in a tense semi-final contest that went into an extra end. The winner of that tussle, Connie Laliberte's Manitoba rink, went on to win the final and the 1984 world championship.

"We always did well but we had a number of runner-up results to show for our first two years together," said Moore. "Some people say being second is worse than being last because you are close enough to taste it but it is yanked away from you. When you're close, and you know you have a good team, it's frustrating."

It was natural that Moore and Sparkes would eventually join forces in competitive curling. Both curled as juniors out of North Shore Winter Club and, when Sparkes was looking for a rink to join after taking a year away from competition in 1980, Moore, Jones and Carney were looking for someone to complete a foursome. Sparkes' experience was welcomed and she eventually took over the skip duties while Moore played third. After the semi-final loss in 1984 Sparkes opted to play third and Moore once again took skip responsibilities.

Linda Moore: Skipped Canada to world championship and Olympic victories.

a 5-2 win over the Torrance foursome.

"We had a very interesting team," said Moore. "Laurie Carney was very quiet. You knew she'd always get the job done, you never doubted that. Our second, Debbie Jones Walker, she was the humorous one and full of energy. Lindsay was the stabilizing force, she did all the things a great third should do."

The foursome advanced to the national final again in 1986 but was defeated by the Marilyn Darte rink from St. Catharines. There was still a laurel to be chased, however. Curling was to be a demonstration event at the 1988 Olympics in Calgary. Carney opted to retire but Moore, Sparkes and Jones worked through the series of Olympic selection trials, joined by Penny Ryan. The foursome, and spare Patti Vande, earned the right to represent Canada and went on to win the gold medal in Calgary even though Moore was ill for much of the competitive week.

Afterward, the rink disbanded, leaving on a very high note. Moore went on to work as a curling commentator for The Sports Network and to serve as an administrator for Curl B.C. Years later she said she knew when the Olympic flame went out at the closing ceremonies in Calgary it also signalled the end of her competitive curling career.

For Lindsay Sparkes the extinguishing of the Olympic flame also marked the end of a national and international career that was nearly extinguished by doubt in 1979...

"When I took over we won nothing," Moore said ruefully. "We went into cashpiels galore and won nothing. The games were always close and, at that point, I was really struggling. But I kept looking back saying we lost to the eventual world champions in the national semi-finals . We stuck with it and finally the whole thing came together."

The Linda Moore rink sailed undefeated (10-0) through the 1985 Scott Tournament of Hearts championship in Winnipeg then carried the win streak to the world event in Jonkoping, Sweden. The streak was stopped at thirty consecutive victories with a 4-8 loss to Norway and a 3-8 loss to Scotland's Isobel Torrance in the final round robin games. But the Canadians recovered their winning way and advanced to the world final, where Moore's last rock secured

Lindsay Sparkes

F olks viewing the victory ceremony at the 1985 women's world curling championships in Jonkoping, Sweden, wouldn't have thought anything unusual about the four Canadian women who received the trophy in obvious celebration. Upon closer inspection, however, they would have noticed the cherished hardware wasn't held by skip and leader Linda Moore. Instead, it had been passed from Moore and her teammates to third Lindsay Sparkes.

It was a moment Sparkes would never forget.

"I had never let go of 1979, even though I had tried very hard," she explained. "When the girls gave me the trophy I remember standing there and — how silly it is in retrospect — I remember thinking this makes up for 1979, when we had let our country down. It was the exorcism of all that and that's what I'd been carrying around.

"The sensitivity they showed to let me hold that trophy, I think it just shows the depth on our team, the understanding and the friendship we had. It was really a celebration of effort."

Sparkes didn't celebrate in 1979. Instead, she pondered retirement after she and Canadian teammates Dawn Knowles, Robin Wilson and Lorraine Bowles returned from the first women's world championship in Perth, Scotland, as third-place finishers after being touted as favourites to win the first women's world title. The loss tormented Sparkes. She gave up curling for the 1980 season and pondered giving it up for good.

"It was an emotionally debilitating time for me," said Sparkes, who conceded she was not always comfortable in the role of skip. "People expected us to win. We were the

Canadian team. But the conditions were different in Scotland. The hacks were different, the aura of the event was quite different, the ice, we were overwhelmed by all the different languages. We couldn't adapt, we didn't know how to adapt."

Years before, Lindsay Davie was just another kid trying to become a figure skater at North Shore Winter Club. She switched to curling at age fifteen. Interestingly, the desire for precision and technique she experienced in skating seemed ideally suited for curling.

"The most enjoyable part of figure skating was the figures, I relished the technique, the execution, the precision," she said. "My parents curled and my brother curled but when I was younger I looked at curling and said: 'That's a stupid sport.' Then I started to look at it in a new light. Here was a sport where no one told you how you did, the scoreboard told you how you did. So I began curling and it just jumped up and grabbed me."

She took part in a mixed junior league at the club, enjoying some success at the local level and relishing the social life that came with the game. Those early junior years also provided her with an eventual world championship teammate when a young novice — Linda Moore — joined her foursome.

"Lindsay was my first skip," said Moore. "There I was in jeans, landing on two knees and she was my skip. She was so sweet. I was so horrible, I didn't have a clue."

Lindsay Davie went on to curl at University of B.C. as did Knowles and Robin Klassen (Wilson). They were joined by Bowles, another former North Shore junior. In 1976 they travelled to the national championships in Winnipeg and won the title which, at the time, was the biggest laurel available in Canadian women's curling.

Three years later Lindsay Sparkes — she had married Bernie Sparkes who had been a member of three Canadian men's teams to win the world championship — and her rink advanced again to the national championship, this time knowing the winner would move on to the first world championships for women in Scotland.

After Scotland, and her year away from competitive curling, Sparkes went back to the game and joined Linda Moore, Debbie Jones and Laurie Carney. The foursome enjoyed some success regionally, then advanced to the Scott nationals in 1984 and lost to Connie Laliberte in the semifinals. For a time Sparkes had skipped the foursome but after 1984 she opted to play third and Moore became the skip for good.

"It was after that game that I realized I wasn't a good leader for the team, that there were three people on that team who wanted badly to win the Canadians and to win

Elation: Canadian teammates Lindsay Sparkes (left), Penny Ryan and Debbie Jones celebrate Olympic victory in Calgary.

the Worlds and I knew I could not risk failing again at the Worlds as a skip. To do really well you have to stand on the brink and give it everything and if you fall over, well, that's what happens."

The Linda Moore rink went undefeated through regional, provincial and national competition in early 1985. After losing two games in the round robin they came back to win the world championship over Scotland in the final. Six years after considering permanent retirement Lindsay Sparkes finally enjoyed world victory many thought should have been hers in 1979.

Three years later Sparkes' career was capped by earning a gold medal with Moore, Jones and Penny Ryan at the 1988 Calgary Olympics, where curling was a demonstration sport. One of Sparkes' most memorable moments came at the closing ceremonies, when the athletes marched en masse carrying candles. A Soviet athlete had lit her candle prior to the procession and she marvelled at how two people from opposite ends of the earth could share such a brief but special moment.

Sparkes retired after the Olympics but has remained involved in curling as a coach and team leader. In early 1995 she was also working to obtain a master's degree in education while working as a primary school teacher. Too busy to play the game, she nevertheless was grateful for its lessons, both difficult and meaningful.

"The game's been a part of my life," she said. "The game was a teacher of life, that things don't always go the way you want them to but when they do you can really celebrate. I feel it strengthened me, and it provided me with wonderful friendships that I cherish."

Marilyn Darte Rink

"When we first started to curl our parents put us out on the ice and what was the curling attire? Ski pants. We wore ski pants and a sweater and a jacket and all this stuff and I just felt awful. Then, I threw my first rock down the ice and split my pants."

Marilyn Bodogh's first experience with curling attire resulted in her becoming a trendsetter of sorts in the 1980s while bringing a sense of entertainment to the sport. Not that Bodogh, her sister Christine Jurgenson, third Kathy McEdwards, and lead Jan Augustyn were competitive flakes. On the ice they were intense and volatile, displaying both disappointment and joy, depending on the shot. The team personality that was both outspoken and outgoing was accentuated by their competitive garb that would become their trademark. No ski pants or sweatsuits, thank you. The four curled in kilts, as Marilyn and Christine had for years.

Familiar faces in Ontario, the rest of Canada gained an appreciation for the flamboyant foursome from St. Catharines via coverage of the 1986 Scott Tournament of Hearts in London, Ontario, where by-then-married Marilyn Bodogh Darte skipped her foursome to win the national title 7-3 over defending and world champion Linda Moore. The partisan Ontario crowd was ecstatic as the victory marked the first Canadian title won by an Ontario women's rink.

"We were on a real high, we had so much confidence because we hardly lost a game," said Bodogh of the team's 10-1 record. "We were on an incredible roll. That takes chemistry within a team. We were confident, we had no fear, we had absolutely no fear. We played the game — we drew, we came around everything, we tapped everything. It was too aggressive for a lot of teams. That's what the style of the game is now, but we were kind of ahead of our time."

Four weeks later Bodogh and her teammates, clad in appropriate Canadian-red kilts, were in Kelowna, B.C., for the world championships. They confounded and confused their foreign opponents with their exuberance, going on to defeat Andrea Schopp's West German rink 12-5 in the final.

"I remember walking out on the ice in our final game and literally feeling the crowd and thinking: Yes, this is what curling should be every Friday night!", enthused Bodogh. "It was a tremendous feeling to have the crowd with you and we were making a lot of shots."

After winning the world title Bodogh challenged 1983 world men's champion Ed Werenich to a game. Televised on The Sports Network, the event was made a fundraiser for the Heart and Stroke Foundation of Ontario. Canadian curling's Battle of the Sexes proved entertaining if a bit lopsided as the Werenich rink won 10-2.

Marilyn Bodogh (Darte): Kilts and charisma brought new dimension to curling.

But the event proved what Bodogh had believed for years, that curling could be entertaining to those who knew little about the sport and that it didn't have to always be a serious game. Add a little pizzazz! Being a talented foursome didn't hurt, either.

The rink didn't duplicate its success in 1987, when they failed to make the playoffs at the Scott in Lethbridge. Eventually, Augustyn left the team and Jurgenson travelled west to B.C., where she was a member of the Marla Geiger rink that won the B.C. championship in 1995. Bodogh and McEdwards stayed put and their difficulty in advancing from regional play shows the incredible depth in Canadian women's curling at the provincial level. By 1995 Bodogh had amassed a frustrating career record of seven runner-up appearances at the Ontario championships.

"Seven times runner-up has been extremely hard to take," she conceded. "I know there are still a lot more shots left in me, hopefully a lot of good ones."

Pat Sanders Rink

CURLING

Pat Sanders and Louise Herlinveaux came to the 1987 Scott Tournament of Hearts with a national championship already to their credit. In 1985 they had joined Steve Skillings and Al Carlson to give B.C. the title in the Canadian mixed curling championships. They eventually combined their experience with two talented juniors, Georgina Hawkes and Deb Massullo, and it soon became apparent the mix was a success.

"My former team had been together so long we were burned out," explained Sanders. "So the two of us joined with Georgina and Deb, who had been juniors. They had been runners-up at the Canadian juniors so they had experience at the Canadian level."

The Victoria foursome earned the right to represent Canada at the 1987 world championships in Chicago by winning the Scott Tournament of Hearts in Lethbridge. During the round robin part of the competition, teams were bothered by ice problems that wreaked havoc with strategy and shot making. After recording six victories the Sanders rink stumbled with three consecutive losses, eventually finishing second with an 8-3 record.

But B.C. went on to the final, defeating Kathie Ellwood's rink from Manitoba 9-3 to advance to the world event in Chicago where, as in previous years, Canadians were expected to perform well. Going into the event Canada had enjoyed three consecutive world championship victories and Sanders was expected to earn the "four-peat."

"It was scary," recalled Sanders, who managed to combine curling with a demanding administration job with the B.C. government. "I felt like I had to win. There was this incredible pressure to win for Canada. And I could feel this

Pat Sanders: Learned to maintain focus under pressure.

incredible aura from other teams, they wanted so badly to win against Canada."

Sanders, a quiet counterpoint to her more lively teammates, had worked on the mental aspect of her game prior to the championships. Recognizing she had the technical prowess, she worked to maintain her focus at critical times in a game. The work paid off in Chicago, where mind games were becoming standard fare in international play.

"I remember at one point the other skip standing across from me. Normally you are supposed to stand behind," she said. "She was halfway into the house and she just stood and stared at me."

Mind games aside, the Canadian foursome survived some erratic play to finish 8-1 in the preliminary draw then advanced to the final with a 5-4 semi-final win over Switzerland. The final proved uneventful in that the West German rink of veteran Andrea Schopp appeared determined to give the Canadians as many chances as possible, giving the Canadians five in the first end in what would eventually be an easy 14-2 victory for the Sanders rink.

"Going into the semi-final was harder than the final," said Sanders. "That was the hardest game for us because people just expected we would be in the final. Once we got there, it wasn't nearly so difficult."

A year later the Sanders rink again went to the national championships where they lost to Heather Houston's Ontario rink. Later, Sanders mused she thought 1988 was the year her team should have taken it all because it was playing so well as a unit, whereas in 1987, when they went on to be the world's best, she felt they were still coming together as a unit.

In retrospect, however, she realized her rink had the talent early on.

"I think my team felt it early. I was too focused on making all my shots. I didn't realize until the end, when it was all over and with hindsight, how good a team it was.

"We all had strong personalities. We were catalysts for each other, we pushed each other to play to our potential."

Heather Houston Rink

Heather Houston: First Worlds were a learning experience.

What a difference a year makes. In the case of Heather Houston's rink from Thunder Bay, Ontario, twelve months meant the difference between losing and winning a world women's curling championship while finding out a lot about themselves in the process.

"In the space of a year there was a vast difference in the team," noted Houston. "We went to Glasgow in 1988 having won the Scott, the first Scott I'd ever skipped at after the first year I'd ever skipped. We were very scared, very tentative. It was a difficult time overseas for us, the first time in an international event for a number of us. It was quite an unsettling experience."

Houston and teammates Lorraine Lang, Diane Adams and Tracy Kennedy had only come together in the fall of 1987 and in early 1988 they surprised many observers by winning the Ontario championship over such notables as Marilyn Bodogh Darte, Anne Merklinger and Alison Goring in tricky ice conditions. With so much more experience in the field, Houston was virtually ignored until she won the final and a trip to Fredericton for the national championships.

"When it was all over, that was the first time a microphone came anywhere near me," she mused. "That was fine with me because I hadn't had much experience with the media. It was the beginning of what would be quite a learning experience."

The foursome had some early trouble in Fredericton then rallied to win several sudden death playoff matches, tie-breakers and, finally, the national championship over defending world champion Pat Sanders of Victoria. At the world event Houston's rink advanced to the final but lost to West Germany's Andrea Schopp, who had been knocking on the winning door for quite some time. Schopp had the experience and the Canadians returned home knowing they, too, had just been through a learning experience.

A year later, at the Scott Tournament in Kelowna, the Houston rink again had a slow start then rallied through tiebreakers to eventually defeat Manitoba's Chris More in the final, with Houston making the crucial shot in an extra end. From there, it was off to Milwaukee, Wisconsin, for a second chance at the world championship. Having gone through the event once before, the Canadians knew what to expect and were better prepared mentally and physically for what they knew would be a rigourous week.

"We were a different team going in," recalled Houston. "We understood what we had to be, how we had to be, what we had to do. We still understood there were all kinds of opportunities for it all to fail, but we had a much clearer idea of what was necessary."

The Canadians advanced through to the semi-final, and a meeting with 1988 nemesis Schopp. This time, they dispatched the West German veteran 8-3 for a final confrontation with Norway's Trine Trulsen. There was no succumbing to nerves and inexperience this time — the Thunder Bay foursome defeated the Norwegians 8-5 to become the fifth Canadian women's team in six years to win the world title.

"We were very committed to winning the world championship," said Houston, who juggled work as a graphics technician with the rigours of curling competition, practice and travel.

"The thought of being the only Canadian team to lose two world championships wasn't palatable. When we played Andrea Schopp in the semis there were many moments when it could have gone either way. Emotionally, it was probably tougher than the final because of the previous year."

Houston said in addition to experience, team members developed "total belief in each other" that contributed to the win. Recognizing a need to focus on the immediate task at hand rather than a win also helped them in difficult situations.

"The focus remained strong through the competition. But I remember thinking the joy of winning was rapidly overtaken with satisfaction and relief. To understand what it would take physically and mentally, ahead of time, made a big difference."

Sandra Peterson Rink

CURLING

Thirteen years after the Marj Mitchell foursome won the national and women's world championship, another Saskatchewan women's rink became the best in the country and the world. It is surprising it took so long, considering curling is a major activity in Saskatchewan. But while it was overdue that a rink from that province would show prominence, when that rink arrived it joined an elite women's curling club that included just one other rink as winners of two consecutive world women's championships. Until Sandra Peterson came along, Norway's Dordi Nordby rink was the only team to win two consecutive world titles, earning the trophy in 1990 and '91.

In 1993, skip Peterson, Jan Betker, Joan McCusker and lead Marcia Gudereit edged Manitoba 7-6 in the Scott Tournament of Hearts final in Brandon to win their first national championship. Betker had tasted some national success in 1984 as a member of Randy Woytowich's mixed national championship rink but the win in Brandon was like nothing any of the four had experienced before.

"We'd been to the Scott before and a lot of teams go with a goal of making the playoffs," said Peterson. "We really went to actually win the event, we had that in our minds. Once we did that it was one of the most exciting experiences of my life, winning the very first Canadian championship. Just because it's something you never, ever dream you're going to do."

A month later in Germany, Peterson's rink earned Canada its first world women's title since 1989 but it wasn't easy. The Canadians had lost two games in the round robin and went into the playoffs ranked third. They knocked off Sweden 10-7 in the semi-final and defeated Janet Strayer's German rink 5-3 to win the world title.

"The first one is the toughest," decided Peterson. "Because you don't know what you're going into, there's kind of a fear of the unknown. You don't know what the teams are going to be like, what the international play is going to

Sandra Peterson: Rushes to teammates Marcia Gudereit and Jan Betker after securing a last-rock victory over Manitoba in 1994.

be like. We had never curled in Europe before."

A year later curlers in Canada and the world had their sights set on the Peterson foursome as defending champions. The 1994 Scott final in Kitchener-Waterloo came down to a duel between former world champion Connie Laliberte and Peterson. Laliberte was leading 3-2 going into the tenth end. Victory rested finally on Peterson's last rock, which she delivered to knock a Manitoba rock from the button to earn a 5-3 victory.

"To play Connie Laliberte in the final was like a dream come true," praised Peterson. "She's such a great player. I've looked up to her ever since she won her first world championship. I can remember watching her win the Canadian championship in Halifax in 1992 and thinking: Wow, is she ever good. Then the next year it happened to us."

A year of appearances, pressure and public interest didn't seem to hinder the defending world women's champions when they travelled to Geneva for the 1994 world event. Canada dropped just one game in the round robin and went on to defeat the Christine Cannon rink from Scotland 5-3 to win their second consecutive world championship.

Peterson said the foursome's success came through a combination of hard work, commitment, and bringing together the best of their unique abilities.

"Marcia plays lead and she is quite quiet out there but when she does say something, you listen," said Peterson of the "team mix."

"Joan is like the cheerleader, that's her job. She's always upbeat, gung-ho to make a shot. She always has a positive attitude. Jan is about as intense as I am. We're really close to being at war out there. But she has a great sense of humour and is one of the funniest people I know."

As for Peterson, she grew up with curling and early on demonstrated a combination of competitiveness and ability to focus on the task.

Sandra Peterson

CURLING

Who knows what might have happened if Sandra Peterson had ended up wielding a hockey stick instead of a broom? One thing is sure — Canadian curling in the 1990s would have missed an exciting player who possessed ability to make the pivotal shot combined with a willingness to promote the game.

"I wanted to play hockey," recalled Peterson, who was born June 11, 1963, in Biggar, Saskatchewan. "I loved hockey but at that point we didn't have equipment in my family so I got into curling. And I was successful with it from the beginning. All my friends played and we worked really hard at it as kids. I spent a lot of time at the rink and played a lot of games and it just carried over.

"I probably started going to the rink when I was eight or nine, just hanging around and being a pest, tugging on Mom's jacket saying I want to go out there and throw. But I never really played any games until I was eleven or twelve."

Sandra Peterson took part in other sports as a youngster, notably volleyball, badminton and swimming. Whatever she attempted, she wanted to be the best. She recalled growing up with a peer group that was equally goal-oriented and ambitious, a "positive group of young people" who pushed each other to achieve, whether it was on report cards or in school sports.

So it was not, perhaps, too surprising that Regina skip Peterson and her teammates would go on to win two consecutive women's world curling championships. Commitment to the sport has been a pivotal part of the group's success and Peterson is as committed as they come. A former lifeguard instructor turned manager of a recreation centre, she has been described at times in media reports as "no nonsense" or even "acerbic." If she has appeared testy at times Peterson says the state is perfectly natural in a group of individuals who have worked hard to attain a goal and are bending their very will toward attaining it.

"I think that's the way the whole team is," she said. "It's business out there. When you're playing at a Scott or a world championship, it's business. It's something you just have to be ready for, you have to always be focused on what you're doing and you can't let your mind wander. If you do, you're going to find yourself on the bottom, looking up."

That said, however, she conceded she is hardly a placid figure on the ice.

"When you're making the shots you have to in order to win a championship like the Scott or the Worlds, you get fairly nervous," she said. "I'm really intense and I hate to lose. To me, that's just the worst feeling, to lose. That's not unlike probably 90 per cent of the population. I have a real desire, and it started when I was a kid, to do the best that I can and to be the best."

Life changed for Peterson and her teammates after they won their first world championship in 1993, and intensified following their second victory in 1994. Summer, once a quiet time, became filled with public appearances. The 1998 Winter Olympics in Nagano, Japan, will for the first time feature curling as a full-medal sport. Whether Peterson and her teammates can maintain their will to succeed that far into the future remains to be seen. There is no doubt, however, that Peterson harbours no regret about what might have been if someone had handed her a hockey stick.

"For me, curling is a lifestyle," she said. "It's something that has consumed most of my life over the last few years, and the team's life as well. A lot of the things I do now revolve around it, my holidays definitely revolve around it. And in our spare time, because of the various demands on us as a team, we do a lot of appearances and public speaking. It's a lifestyle for me, it's not just a game."

Sandra Peterson: Skipped her Regina-based rink to two consecutive world championships.

WINNING IN WATER

Swimming

Although humans are a land-based species, the need to be able to swim surfaced about the time someone drowned while fishing or when a canoe overturned. Competitive swimming is one of the glamour sports of the Olympic Games with races contested individually in freestyle, backstroke, butterfly and breaststroke or as a combination of all four. Marathon swimming is an adventurous offshoot of competitive swimming — indeed, in 1995 an international, open-water circuit was flourishing around the world. Swimmers who choose to test themselves in the open water of lakes and oceans discover there are additional challenges from those presented by a swimmer in the next lane of a pool — namely natural elements such as wind, waves or jellyfish.

Elaine Tanner

"I see myself as a dolphin," said Elaine Tanner as she regarded the ceramic dolphin on the table next to the window. Across the road a late fall storm was causing the ocean waves to rise and fall in explosions of shimmering pewter.

"The element of water gives me power, gives me control. I love being in the water, I love the feeling in the water. But I always hated getting in, and getting out."

Few Canadian swimmers have made waves in the international pool as did West Vancouver's Elaine Tanner in the 1960s. Nicknamed Mighty Mouse because of her compact build and tenacious approach, she accumulated an impressive array of medals and records that included seventeen national titles, seven British Empire Games medals, five Pan-American Games medals and three Olympic medals.

Hers is a story of a natural talent that first emerged in California, where her family lived for a time. Seven-year-old Elaine balked when her parents suggested she take swimming lessons at a nearby pool. She had paddled about on her own and felt she had become quite good without any help. But she relented and soon after, the swimming instructor advised her parents she had potential and should be enrolled in a formal club. Upon returning to the Vancouver area, Tanner joined the Dolphins Swim Club, training under the successful eye of coach Howard Firby.

By age thirteen Tanner was competing, and winning, at the national level. In 1966, just fifteen, she became a force internationally by unleashing an impressive week of swimming at the British Empire Games at Kingston, Jamaica. Going into the event, Tanner had set a world record for the 220-yard individual medley a month earlier and broken two American records in competition. But it was in Jamaica that she emerged as one of the world's best — winning gold in the 110- and 220-yard butterfly and 440-yard individual medley and joined Canadian teammates Jane Hughes, Marion Lay and Louise Kennedy to take the women's 4x110-yard relay in world record time. She also earned silver medals in the 110-yard backstroke events and 4x110-yard medley relay.

"Swimming was power, it was freedom," she said. "The water has freedom, it's like you're flying. It holds you, it's like you're in your own space. I like the feeling of being alone there with my own thoughts, in control of my body."

Tanner came home to attention and accolades and was named Canada's top athlete for 1966. In 1967, as a home country favourite, she splashed to two gold medals, two world records and three silver medals at the Pan-American Games in Winnipeg. The hours of training and commitment were paying huge dividends. In retrospect, Tanner didn't mind missing the social whirl that is usually an integral part of a teen's life.

"I never counted my medals and trophies because to me, once you've won then you've done it, you've accomplished it," she said. "I loved travelling, I loved the experience of travelling around the world as a teenager, meeting different people. I met the Queen, I dined with the prime minister. I met diplomats and celebrities, people a normal teenager would never get to meet. It was a different life and that's what I liked.

"But I tried to be a good person and tried never to

Elaine Tanner: Won four gold medals in her first international meet — the 1966 British Empire Games.

let it get to my head."

By 1968 Tanner was being touted as Canada's best hope for a gold medal at the Summer Olympic Games in Mexico City. For all the work her broad shoulders had done in previous years, even they couldn't handle the expectations of a nation and its demanding media. For all the laurels seventeen-year-old Mighty Mouse accumulated leading up to Mexico City, she would be labelled that year as the swimmer who should have won gold, and lost.

"I used to race it all over a million times," she said many years later. "Now, I don't. It doesn't matter any more. It's only a race. It's not your life. Life is much more important.

"But it was brutal. It was: Elaine Tanner lost the gold medal. Elaine Tanner let us down. It was hard. I tried to bury my feelings and ended up having to deal with them years later."

Tanner was expected to win gold in the 100-metre backstroke, with the pressure accentuated after Tanner set an Olympic record in the semi-finals. But American Kaye Hall, who had not beaten Tanner in more than twenty attempts, defeated the Canadian by a half second in the final. Newspaper accounts of the time relate how Tanner fled the pool complex after the race when she saw the crowd of television and print reporters waiting for her in the interview room.

"I don't remember anything that happened," she said. "You know how people have an accident and they don't remember? I don't remember getting my medal and I don't remember going into that press room. People say I never went there. I just seemed to disappear. It just seemed so much for a seventeen-year-old, it was too hard for me to bear."

Skier Nancy Greene, who had won Olympic gold some months before at Grenoble and was doing television work at the Summer Olympics, recalled vividly Tanner's pain:

"She climbed out of the pool and one of the journalists asked: 'Why did you lose, Elaine?' It was as if someone had smacked her in the face. Her face fell, she answered a few more questions, and you could see her start sobbing. If I'd been more experienced I would have turned and said: 'You said she was going to win. Why didn't you say the other swimmer was going to win? You spent the whole time telling them this Canadian was going to win and you forgot the competition. She swam her personal best, someone else swam faster. That's sport.'"

Tanner later earned a silver medal in the 200-metre backstroke, finishing second to American Pokey Watson. She also took home a bronze medal from the 4x100-metre relay team.

She retired in 1969 and married in 1971 after university studies in Edmonton and Calgary. She eventually settled with her husband in Prince George, where they would have two children. But peace eluded Tanner, who would be married and divorced twice by 1988, suffer the eating disorder anorexia nervosa and fail to find her niche after holding a myriad of jobs. She embarked on a personal healing sojourn of sorts into the United States, coaching, taking holistic counselling courses, writing a book. In 1994 she and husband John Watt moved to Victoria and, after years of attempting to deal with personal and imposed demons, Tanner set about helping others to deal with theirs by starting a holistic counselling practice.

What would she say to that seventeen-year-old girl who was deemed a failure for earning silver and bronze?

"If I could talk to her, I would be supportive and say the sun will shine the next day, you did your best and you're a winner," she decided. "Don't you let anybody tell you differently because it's how you feel inside, it's not how they think. No one will ever be in your shoes except you. So believe in yourself, and your own gut feelings."

Anne Ottenbrite

The din following the men's 400-metre individual medley had barely subsided around the outdoor pool at University of Southern California when it came time for the 1984 Olympic women's 200-metre breaststroke final to be contested.

Canada's Alex Baumann had just sent shivers through the eleven thousand spectators in general, and the Canadian contingent in particular, with his gold medal, world record performance in the medley final. The win made Baumann the first Canadian to win an Olympic swimming gold medal since Montreal's George Hodgson took gold at the 1912 Games in Stockholm with a world record win in the 1,500-metre freestyle and a victory in the 400-metre freestyle.

But the raising of the Canadian flag, and the unfolding of the country's swimming history, was not over for the day. Less than an hour after Baumann's brilliant effort, eighteen-year-old Anne Ottenbrite of Whitby, Ontario, splashed her way into Canadian sports history by winning the women's 200-metre breaststroke, becoming the first Canadian woman swimmer to win an Olympic gold medal.

"Going in to the race, I knew all that was there," Ottenbrite would remark a decade after her historic swim. "I knew no other woman had done it. I know Alex and Victor (Davis — men's 200-metre breaststroke gold medallist) kept saying it was really important for us to break this inferiority complex that Canadians have."

Canadian women swimmers have for a long time ranked among the best in the world but Olympic gold eluded some of the best — including medallists Leslie Cliff, Elaine Tanner and Nancy Garapick. Much has been written about the so-called Canadian inferiority complex but the term doesn't come into play where Ottenbrite is concerned. Going into the Games she came instead with the labels accident-prone, extroverted and talented.

Accident prone?

"I am extremely uncoordinated, I am a huge klutz on land, the whole list would go on and on," declared Ottenbrite, using as an example the day she walked through a glass door at the 1982 Commonwealth Games in Brisbane, Australia, sending shards of glass everywhere while suffering cuts on her head and hands.

More serious was the May 21, 1984, mishap — a month before the Olympic trials. Ottenbrite and teammate Julie Daignault were preparing for a night out in Montreal when Ottenbrite, seeing her friend was wearing high heels, kicked her left leg up onto a table to scrutinize the suitability of her running shoes. Her right knee rolled sideways at 90° to her thigh and her leg collapsed.

"I'm double-jointed all over," said Ottenbrite, known to delight teammates with exhibitions of her suppleness, including turning her feet backward while facing forward. "I looked at my knee and blacked out. Julie was laughing, she thought it was one of my party tricks and she said she had never seen that one before."

The knee was dislocated, keeping Ottenbrite out of the Olympic trials and necessitating a special ruling by the Canadian Amateur Swimming Association to name her as a provisional member of the team, based on her international standing and ability. Ottenbrite had to prove ability to compete at the team's pre-Olympic training camp prior to being named officially to the Olympic squad.

Extroverted?

"The world championships were my first international meet. I wasn't afraid of anything," she recalled. "That's the way I swam every international meet. I wasn't afraid of anybody. I'd be laughing and joking when people thought I should be freaking out. But that's the way I swam. I had to swim having fun, laughing and joking."

Talented. Anne Ottenbrite was born June 12, 1966, and honed her early swimming skills in the family's backyard swimming pool. Born with a love for water, she tried diving and synchronized swimming but settled on competitive swimming at the relatively late age of thirteen, an age when some young talents are making forays into the international level. By then her competitive, goal-setting personality was well established. At age ten Ottenbrite was captivated by television coverage of the 1976 Olympics in Montreal and one day declared: "That's what I'm going to do, I'm going to go to the Olympics and win a gold medal."

At the time she didn't know what her sport might be, but three years later competitive swimming seemed the perfect vehicle. Almost immediately she specialized in breaststroke, her supple joints causing her to adopt an unorthodox but effective kicking style. By 1981 she was Canada Games champion over 100 and 200 metres and in 1982 Ottenbrite took the Commonwealth Games gold medal in the 200-metre breaststroke and 4x100-metre medley relay, and silver in the 100-metre breaststroke.

In 1982 she also took on the world, finishing second in the 100-metre and third in the 200-metre breaststroke events at the world championships.

By 1983 Ottenbrite's odd kicking style became an international issue. She was disqualified in the 200-metre breaststroke at the 1983 Pan-American Games for what officials decided was an illegal "dolphin kick." Earlier in the year she had been disqualified at a three-country meet for the same problem.

"I came up high so the tops of my hands would break the surface of the water on the recovery and I would dive forward and the propulsion from my kick would cause what they would call a dolphin kick, my feet would break the surface of the water but that's where they would recover to the next kick," she explained. "It wasn't an up and down motion, but it did look strange.

"I still had to swim the 100 breaststroke and I thought they would disqualify me. The coaches said get in and try and fix it, we fixed it, I swam and won the event the next day. But I had to change my stroke and I had to think about it in my race, big time."

A year later Ottenbrite's biggest concern was having her knee recover sufficiently to compete in the Olympics. Her biggest disappointment was not being able to compete against the powerful East Germans when the Soviet Union led a boycott of Eastern Bloc nations from the Games, although in her mind she enjoyed some peace knowing she had defeated the East Germans at the European championships.

"They were scary, very male looking, but I was never intimidated," she said.

Ottenbrite said she was largely written off as an Olympic medal hopeful after she dislocated her knee. Much of the attention went to sixteen-year-old Japanese wunderkind Hiroki Nagasaki, who made her first Olympic team at age eleven but didn't travel to Moscow when her country boy-

Anne Ottenbrite: Churned to Olympic gold in Los Angeles.

cotted those Games after the Soviet Union's invasion of Afghanistan.

Years after deciding on swimming as her Olympic discipline, Ottenbrite imagined herself touching the wall and thrusting her arms in the air to celebrate victory. On July 30, 1984, she was able to do just that, putting away Nagasaki midway through the race and fending off challenges by American Susan Rapp and Belgium's Ingrid Lempereur to win the gold medal in 2 minutes, 30.38 seconds. On August 2, she returned to take the silver medal in the 100-metre breaststroke behind Holland's Petra Van Staveren, who took gold in an Olympic record 1:09.88.

"After I did my Olympic swim and accomplished my ultimate goal I swam at university but I wasn't swimming with any intensity," said Ottenbrite. "I am quite pleased I didn't have to go through plateaus — it would have been frustrating for me. This way, I was improving every time and getting closer and closer to my goal. I was pretty fortunate to have gone through the way I did, starting at a later age and still accomplishing stuff at a pretty young age."

Her ultimate goal accomplished a decade earlier, Ottenbrite had not turned her back on the sport in 1994. Working as a swim coach for the University of Guelph, she also served as honourary co-captain of Canada's swim team to the 1994 Commonwealth Games in Victoria — an energetic example of someone who wasn't afraid to state her goal, then went out and achieved it.

Leslie Cliff

Leslie Cliff took to swimming like a duck takes to water, even if she did give her family some anxious moments in the backyard pool.

"I can remember just loving it. I still think pools are neat," she said in remembering her initial forays into the pool, which began at about age three.

"They're blue, you go in the water and open your eyes and it's blue everywhere. We used to go around the pool, just grabbing the edge, before we knew how to swim. I remember letting go and just sinking to the bottom, thinking how beautiful it was. My Mom and her friend were sitting by the pool and her friend pulled me out with this look of horror on her face. And I thought: Why is she so upset?"

Years later Cliff would be dubbed Canada's most versatile swimmer, not only for her prowess in the individual medley but for her ability to compete in, and win, individual events. Her career continued through several years of summer club swimming with the Crescent Beach Swim Club. At age eleven, shortly after Dolphin Swim Club's Elaine Tanner turned the swimming world on its head with a superb meet at the 1966 British Empire Games in Jamaica, Cliff's coach suggested she join the Dolphins and train with Howard Firby. The connection was short-lived,

however, as Firby went on to work in Winnipeg and Deryk Snelling took over Dolphin coaching duties. Under his guidance Cliff blossomed, with the athletic talent she showed in basketball and volleyball at school carrying over into her being able to be competitive in all four swimming disciplines — freestyle, backstroke, butterfly and breaststroke.

"Versatile doesn't necessarily mean good, it just means diverse and I was," she said. "At the 1971 nationals I swam every event and made finals in all but the 100 breaststroke, and I think I won the 200 breaststroke. That's the way I did every meet, I would swim every event in every meet, for years."

Also in 1971 Cliff took three gold medals and a silver at the Pan-American Games in Cali, Colombia. At age sixteen the effort made her the youngest of thirty-seven individuals awarded the medal of service of the Order of Canada for that year. At the 1972 Olympics in Munich, Cliff broke her Canadian record to finish fifth in the 200-metre individual medley behind venerable Australian Shane Gould, who set a world record in taking the gold medal. Two days later Cliff smashed the existing world record but had to settle for silver in the 400 individual medley (where swimmers swim backstroke, butterfly, breaststroke and freestyle

Fleet Foursome: Canadian swimmers (left to right) Donna Marie Gurr, Jane Wright, Leslie Cliff and Angela Coughlan earned accolades after winning the women's 4x100-metre medley relay at the 1971 Pan-American Games in Cali, Colombia.

in one race) behind Australian Gail Neall, who chopped nearly two seconds off the world mark.

Two decades later she would remember the 1974 Commonwealth Games as one of the highlights of her career. Not only did she take gold in the 200 individual medley, she also lined up again with rival Neall in the 400 individual medley final, winning the race in a Commonwealth Games record time.

Throughout her career Cliff was dubbed by the media as a quiet individual, but her silence was more self-imposed than natural. Early in her career she was annoyed that a reporter had painted a negative picture of the regimented and focused life of an elite swimmer and she remained guarded thereafter in talking to the media. Years later, working as a portfolio manager in Vancouver, she expressed her concerns.

"I got turned off the press very early," she explained. "I read these articles about a young gymnast or skater or swimmer, a fourteen- or fifteen-year-old girl who works really hard in her sport and has given up her social life. The tone is negative — it's not normal or it's not good.

"Someone wrote an article like that about me and I was so mad. My attitude was: 'I am so lucky, I love to do this, I get to do this. I get to achieve at something I love to do.' This guy made it sound bad, that I was losing out somehow."

In 1975 Cliff was forced to withdraw from the Canadian Pan-American Games team training camp due to shoulder problems. She returned to compete at the Canadian Olympic trials the following year but finished fourth in the 400 IM, missing a spot on the team to Montreal. Prior to the meet she decided the season would be her last as an international competitor, although she went on to study and swim at Arizona State University where she contributed to the team winning two NCAA championships.

Years later, looking for an organized workout for fitness, Cliff began taking part in workouts with the Dolphins. Time indeed marches on for swimmers and she was amused at just how fast time had gone by.

"You know how you all take off in a line?" she mused. "I was at the end and there was this ten-year-old girl just in front of me. She turned around and said to me: 'I wrote a report on you in school. I got an A-plus.' Then she pushed off."

Phyllis Dewar

Phyllis Dewar of Moose Jaw, Saskatchewan, was Canada's first outstanding female freestyler in international competition. In 1934, at age eighteen, she ruled the pool at the second British Empire Games in London, winning gold in the 100 and 440-yard freestyle events. She also joined compatriots Florence Humble, Margaret Hutton and Irene Pirie to take gold in the 4x100-yard freestyle relay and Hutton and Phyllis Haslam to win the 3x100-yard medley re-

Phyllis Dewar: First Canadian woman to make a splash in international swimming.

lay. She made the Canadian team to the 1936 Olympics in Berlin but a severe bout of influenza did not allow her to compete to her potential. She returned to compete at the British Empire Games of 1938 in Sydney, Australia and anchored the Canadian women's team, which included Florence Humble, Dorothy Lyon and Noel Oxenbury, to a gold medal win in the 4x100-yard freestyle relay.

Marion Lay

Marion Lay: Has devoted her life to sport as a competitor, administrator and advocate for change and equality for women.

Marion Lay was Canada's Number-One-ranked woman freestyle swimmer from 1964 to 1968. Competing in her first Olympics at age fifteen, she finished fifth in the 100-metre freestyle at the 1964 Games in Tokyo behind great Australian swimmer Dawn Fraser. Two years later, serving as Canadian swim team captain to the British Empire-Commonwealth Games in Jamaica, she earned a gold medal in 100-yard freestyle and joined teammates Elaine Tanner, Jane Hughes and Louise Kennedy in setting a world record of 4:10.8 en route to taking gold in the 4x110-yard freestyle relay.

At the 1968 Olympics in Mexico City Lay finished fourth in the 100-metre freestyle, where the difference between gold and fourth was just half a second. Later, she and Canadian teammates Angela Coughlan, Marilyn Corson and Elaine Tanner churned to a bronze medal in the 4x100-metre freestyle relay.

Lay's career in sport didn't end when she retired from swimming after the Olympics. She went on to coach for a time and served as a CBC commentator for swimming. She also went on to become a founder of the Canadian Association for the Advancement of Women and Sport and Physical Activity (CAAWS) and its affiliated organization in British Columbia, Promotion Plus, in addition to working to promote and create gender equity and opportunities for women in sport.

Angela Coughlan

In the summer of 1968, fifteen-year-old Angela Coughlan of Burlington, Ontario, earned a spot on Canada's Olympic team to Mexico City by setting two Canadian records at the national championships in Winnipeg — one record being in the 400-metre freestyle where she chopped four seconds off the previous mark set by Elaine Tanner in 1967. That same year she set a world record of 18 minutes, 47. 8 seconds for 1,650 yards — just slightly less than 1,500 metres.

In addition to taking a bronze medal in the 4x100-metre freestyle relay at Mexico City, Coughlan also made the final in the 400 free, finishing seventh, and in the 800-metre freestyle, finishing sixth. At the 1970 Commonwealth Games she took gold in the 100-metre freestyle and silver in the 200 free, also earning silver and bronze in the relays.

Shannon Smith

Shannon Smith became the first Canadian woman freestyler to take an individual Olympic medal when, in front of a home country crowd at the 1976 Olympics in Montreal, she churned to a 400-metre freestyle bronze medal behind East German winner Petra Thumer, who won the race in world record time. The effort would earn the fourteen-year-old

New Westminster Hyack Swim Club swimmer the B.C. junior athlete of the year award for 1976 in addition to being named Canada's top female junior athlete for that year. She also finished sixth in the 800-metre freestyle at the Montreal Olympics, again behind Thumer who also won the race in world record time.

Shannon Smith: Freestyle bronze medallist at 1976 Olympics.

Allison Higson: At age thirteen she brought home two Commonwealth Games gold medals from Scotland.

Allison Higson

BREASTSTROKE

Allison Higson of Brampton, Ontario, picked up where Anne Ottenbrite left off in the breaststroke department. At age thirteen Higson delighted spectators, not to mention teammates and Canadian team officials, by winning the 100- and 200-metre breaststroke events at the 1986 Commonwealth Games at Edinburgh, Scotland, becoming the youngest swimmer to ever win a medal at those games. She also took home a silver from the 4x100 medley relay. Later that year Higson became the youngest swimmer to earn a medal at a world aquatic championship, taking bronze in the 200-metre breaststroke and just missing the podium with a fourth in the 100-metre event.

A year later, at the Pan Pacific championships, she won the 100-metre event and took silver in the 200-metre competition. Leading up to the 1988 Olympics in Seoul, Higson was the world's Number One ranked breaststroker over 200 metres after setting a world record in the distance at the Canadian Olympic trials, and was ranked second behind East German Silke Horner in the 100-metre event. In Seoul there was considerable pressure on her fifteen-year-old shoulders and Higson swam a Canadian and Commonwealth record in the 100-metre breast to finish fourth behind Tania Dangalokova of Bulgaria. In the 200-metre final she finished seventh, with her world record broken by Horner.

Donna-Marie Gurr

BACKSTROKE

Donna-Marie Gurr was just fourteen years old when she began to make her mark as the first of Canada's outstanding female backstrokers. Another member of what was an outstanding Canadian Dolphin Swim Club dynasty through the 1960s and '70s, Gurr burst on the scene in the summer of 1969 when she took five gold medals at the Canada Summer Games and earned the first of what would be four national backstroke titles. A year later, at the Commonwealth Games in Edinburgh, she took a silver and two bronze medals and improved to take three gold medals and a silver at the 1971 Pan-American Games at Cali, Colombia.

At the 1972 Summer Olympics in Munich Gurr churned to a bronze medal in the 200-metre backstroke, behind winner Melissa Belote of the United States who won the race in world record time. Earlier in the competition Gurr had been hampered by stomach problems and missed a chance in the 100-metre backstroke.

Two years later Gurr took a silver and a bronze medal at the Commonwealth Games in New Zealand and in 1976 was named to the Order of Canada.

Wendy Cook

BACKSTROKE

Wendy Cook played understudy at the 1972 Olympics when Dolphin teammate Donna-Marie Gurr came down with stomach trouble and was unable to make the final for the 100-metre backstroke. Cook, fifteen, posted a personal best in qualifying and went on to finish fifth in the event. A year later the Vancouver swimmer finished third behind world record holder Ulrike Richter, missing a silver medal by a fingernail, at the world aquatic championships in Belgrade, Yugoslavia. At the 1974 Commonwealth Games in New Zealand she edged teammate Gurr to take the 100-metre backstroke. A day later she broke the world 100-metre backstroke record in her leading leg for Canada's gold medal 4x100-metre medley relay team and returned again to take gold in the 200-metre back. The effort earned her the vote for Canada's top female athlete of that year, although rival Richter would later break the world mark Cook set at Christchurch. In 1975 Cook finished fourth at the World Aquatic Games in Colombia.

In 1976, by-then-married Wendy Cook Hogg continued to perform as one of Canada's top swimmers, earning five national championships that year. She led Canadian teammates Robin Corsiglia, Susan Sloan and Anne Jardin to a bronze medal in the 4x100-metre medley relay at the

Wendy Cook: Backstroker brought home a bevy of medals.

1976 Olympics in Montreal while finishing fourth and eighth in the 100- and 200-metre backstrokes.

Nancy Garapick

BACKSTROKE

Nancy Garapick was the next in line of Canada's top backstroke trio. Hindsight being what it is, and with revelations that came some fifteen years later about East Germany's precise administration of performance-enhancing drugs to athletes, it is worth wondering what might have happened differently on July 21, 1976. On that day,

East Germans Ulrike Richter and Birgit Treiber took gold and silver in the women's 100-metre backstroke at the Montreal Olympics, followed by Canadians Nancy Garapick in third, Wendy Cook Hogg in fourth and Cheryl Gibson in fifth. The same East German duo would go on to take gold and silver in the 200-metre backstroke with Garapick, a fourteen-year-old swimmer from Halifax, taking her second bronze medal.

Nancy Garapick leaped into the world swimming scene in 1975 when as a thirteen-year-old she broke the world 200-metre backstroke record and served notice as heir apparent to Wendy Cook's national domination of backstroke. In 1975 Garapick was no stranger to her East German rivals, having also taken a bronze medal in the 100 at the World Aquatic Games. In the 200 metres Garapick and Treiber waged a furious battle, with Treiber winning by an eyelash. Both went under the existing world record.

Garapick later opted to work on other strokes, taking a bronze medal as a member of Canada's 4x100-metre freestyle relay team at the 1978 world aquatic championships in Berlin. She earned two silver and three bronze medals at the 1979 Pan-American Games. Her Olympic aspirations were thwarted in 1980 not so much by the Canadian boycott of the Moscow event but by a broken arm suffered in a roller skating fall.

Nancy Garapick: Broke a world record at age thirteen.

Mary Stewart

Mary Stewart followed her elder sister, Helen, into the world of competitive swimming and it wasn't long before she was at the top. Stewart was as good an acrobat as she was a swimmer and at age nine began work as the bundle of energy beneath the costume as mascot for the Canadian Football League's B.C. Lions. By age twelve her dancing ability would win her a child's talent show at the Pacific National Exhibition and a trip to Hollywood.

Stewart would go on to become the top butterfly swimmer in the world, although she was no slouch in freestyle, either. At the 1960 Olympics in Rome the fourteen-year-old Vancouver

Mary Stewart: Receives one of her many swimming laurels from hockey legend Fred 'Cyclone' Taylor.

swimmer finished eighth in the 100-metre freestyle — laying a groundwork of experience for what was to come. In July 1961 she shattered the world record for the 110-yard butterfly, held previously by venerable Australian Dawn Fraser. Two months later she broke the world 100-metre butterfly mark and at the end of the year topped the annual Canadian Press poll as top female athlete for 1961.

She rewrote the 100-metre mark again in the summer of 1962 and in November of that year became the first Canadian female swimmer to win a British Empire Games medal in nearly thirty years, taking the 110-yard butterfly. She also took bronze in the 110-yard freestyle and silver in the relay, again earning top votes in the Canadian Press poll that December. Stewart took silver and bronze medals at the 1963 Pan-American Games and finished eighth in the 100-metre butterfly at the 1964 Olympics in Tokyo.

Wendy Quirk

Wendy Quirk: Set twenty-five Canadian records.

Wendy Quirk of Point Claire, Quebec, was another swimmer who excelled in butterfly and freestyle and in her national career from 1974 through 1980 she would set twenty-five Canadian senior and three Commonwealth records. At the 1974 Commonwealth Games she took a silver medal in the 400-metre freestyle and two years later finished fifth in the 200 butterfly and sixth in the 100 fly at the Montreal Olympics.

In 1978 Quirk won gold in front of a home country crowd at the 1978 Commonwealth Games in Edmonton while also earning silver in the 200 butterfly and bronze in the 100 freestyle. At the world aquatic championships that same year she took bronze in the 100 butterfly and 4x100-metre freestyle relay and fourth in the 200 butterfly. A year later Quirk took a bronze medal in the 400-metre freestyle at the Pan-American Games.

The 1980 Olympics should have capped what was an outstanding career. Quirk dominated the 1980 Canadian Olympic trials, winning four gold medals and a silver, but never had a chance to carry her outstanding form through to the Olympics as Canada boycotted the 1980 Games in Moscow to protest the Soviet Union's invasion of Afghanistan.

Cheryl Gibson

Cheryl Gibson parlayed what was also an outstanding ability in backstroke to become one of the best in the world in individual medley. At the 1976 Olympics in Montreal, Gibson, then seventeen, finished second with Canadian teammate Becky Smith third in the 400-metre individual medley. Winner Ulrike Tauber of East Germany smashed the world record by some six seconds but such performances might be viewed with some skepticism now as the reunification of West and East Germany in the 1990s brought with it news of systematic and widespread use of performance-enhancing drugs by East German athletes in the 1970s and '80s.

Gibson went on to earn gold in the 100-metre backstroke at the 1978 Commonwealth Games, also earning bronze in the 400 IM and 100-metre backstroke. That same year she swam a personal best en route to a bronze medal in the 100-metre backstroke at the world aquatic championships in Berlin. Gibson also swam a Canadian and Commonwealth record in taking bronze in the 200 backstroke after scratching from the 400 IM to concentrate on the backstroke event.

Gibson later took three silver medals at the 1979 Pan-American Games in San Juan,

Cheryl Gibson: A Versatile international competitor.

Puerto Rico. She was another swimmer affected by the Canadian boycott of the 1980 Olympics. At the 1982 Commonwealth Games, her final international competition,

Gibson took the silver medal in the 200-metre IM in a personal best time.

Joanne Mucz

Joanne Mucz won in the pool but the psychological aspect of victory was forged in the humid ready-room used to mobilize athletes for the next race.

"People win and lose races in that room," she said. "There are a lot of games that go on, you can hear the music people have on their headsets, and so many people had psyche-up music. That doesn't work for me because I'm psyched as it is, so tensed and focused. I need music that's fun, relaxing.

"I would look around the room and try to look into the eyes of the other girls and if I could see them look away, look down, see their legs shaking, or if they were frantically stretching, I knew they were too nervous. I didn't have to worry about them."

Whatever mental tactics she utilized in those pre-race moments, no one will argue that Mucz unleashed a most impressive week of performance at the 1992 Paralympic Games in Barcelona, Spain. The twenty-year-old commerce student from Winnipeg went into the Games as a world record holder, world champion and 1988 Paralympic gold medallist but had not recorded a personal best in some time.

She departed Spain with five gold medals and five world records. Rarely has a Canadian athlete come home so decorated from international competition. And never had Mucz, in eight years of competing internationally as a disabled swimmer, experienced such a time as an athlete.

"Barcelona was like no other games we had been to before because we were treated like elite athletes and the public was so behind it," enthused Mucz, who was born without feet or ankles. She honed her swimming skills with able-bodied teammates at the Manta Swim Club.

"I had never swam in front of so many people before. We were arriving for our heats and finals and you'd see the line up from the pool, all the way down toward the stadium. That's incredible. We were never at competitions where there's been that kind of response."

The 1992 Paralympic Games featured athletes from ninety-four countries and Mucz emerged as one of the biggest stars of the event, held September 3-14, 1992. She won gold in the 100-metre freestyle, 100-metre breaststroke, 200-metre individual medley, 400-metre freestyle and 100-metre butterfly, capping a swimming career that

Joanne Mucz: Dominated the 1992 Paralympics by winning five gold medals in a week of competition.

began seventeen years earlier when as a three-year-old she was enrolled in a YMCA children's swim and gym program.

At age nine she joined the Manta club because a close friend was a member. The coaches welcomed her and she quickly showed physical talent to overcome her disability.

"So many sports require your legs — running, jumping and balance — but with swimming what I didn't have with my legs I could make up with my upper body," she explained. "I could compensate for my disability in that sport. Initially, I don't think I paid too much attention to excelling, I was having so much fun."

Mucz showed enough potential to be chosen to the Canadian team to the 1984 Paralympics at Lake Placid, New York. She was just twelve years old and not expected to win a medal. But the experience gained and enthusiasm forged from participating set her up well for the 1988 Paralympics in Seoul. There, she earned gold, silver and bronze.

Mucz went on to compete against her able-bodied counterparts as a member of her school swim team and dominated the pool at the 1990 world championships and 1991 Stoke Mandeville World Games. Leading up to Barcelona, with commitments to university studies leaving less time to train, Mucz feared she was stuck in a plateau and might not improve upon some of her earlier times. Training at times was a personal struggle and she was unsure if the effort would be worth it.

Any doubts she had were laid to rest after she won her first and favourite event, the 400-metre freestyle.

"It was like a huge weight came off my shoulders because there was so much pressure for me to succeed... so I had attained a gold and I had set a world record," she said.

"After that, I just kept refocusing on the next event. I think the whole week kept feeding me more power, I was feeling more calm going into each race. I happened to peak at the time I was supposed to, and it was fun because I was confident, I was strong. The events weren't scaring me. They weren't a threat, they were an opportunity."

The 100-metre butterfly final was the most difficult for Mucz as it was set up as a showdown between the Canadian and her Australian rival Kelly Barnes. Both had battled in the same event at the 1990 world championships with Mucz winning by a fingernail.

It was in the pre-race hotbox that Mucz, relaxed and listening to music on her headphones, noticed her Australian rival was visibly nervous. Minutes later it was another gold medal for Canada.

"As soon as my last race was over my body crashed," laughed Mucz in discussing the mental and physical effort of winning her five gold medals. "Sometimes, I don't know how I did it."

Mucz was chosen Canadian team flagbearer for the closing ceremonies. When she returned to Canada she received more media and public interest than ever before, but it hardly compared with the deluge of personal appearance and endorsement requests that came the way of Calgary's Mark Tewksbury after he won the 100-metre backstroke gold medal at the 1992 Summer Olympics, also in Barcelona. While the profile of disabled sport grew considerably in the decade leading up to Barcelona, it clearly had a way to go before being considered equal with able-bodied events in the public and business psyche.

Mucz saw her achievements in Barcelona as another opportunity toward increasing public awareness of the commitment and ability of disabled athletes. She was thrilled to learn the 1994 Commonwealth Games in Victoria would include medal events for disabled athletes and was tempted for a time to come out of her post-Paralympic retirement for the chance to compete as a disabled athlete at a major games in her own country.

Mucz believes Barcelona will be looked upon as a turning point for disabled sport, where the Paralympic Games were truly embraced as an athletic event in its own right and the athletes honoured for their abilities. Looking back, she was proud to be a part of it.

"I think I closed a very important part of my life there," she said. " So many good things came from it. I was there through the evolution of disabled sports. It's really important to me that it remains an elite sport and gains the respect it deserves from people. Showing through example is sometimes the best way, and I could do that by competing."

Long Distance Swimming

Perhaps it's the climate. Maybe it's the food. Whatever the cause, Canada has produced many individuals whose pioneer spirit has at times captivated the entire country and the world. Wheelchair athlete Rick Hansen took his commitment to raising awareness and funding for spinal cord research around the world in his Man in Motion Tour. Mountaineer Sharon Wood became the first North American woman to climb Mount Everest.

Canadian women swimmers have also demonstrated and perpetuated that adventurous, courageous spirit. In open water, without the lane markers, clean chlorinated water and calm conditions found in public pools, Canadian women swimmers have set a standard of stamina and determination for the rest of the world to follow.

Winnie Roach Leuszler

In 1951, married and with three children, Winnie Leuszler became the first Canadian woman to swim the English Channel. She was born in 1926. Both her father and uncle had coached marathon swimmers and by age nine Winnie was showing a remarkable ability to swim long distances, winning her first medal in a 1.5 mile swim.

In 1951 she was picked as one of the top distance swimmers of the time when the *Daily Mail* newspaper in England was organizing a Channel swim, offering £1,000 to anyone successful in making the crossing from Calais to Dover. Leuszler took on the challenge and completed the task in 13 hours, 25 minutes. Near the end of the swim, she was on target to break the women's and men's records when a strong tide swept her far away from shore, forcing her to swim farther and longer than was necessary. When she returned to Canada she was fêted in a Toronto parade and presented with the keys to the city. Three years later she would play a part in an event that would captivate Canada and take a sixteen-year-old swimmer from virtual anonymity to national hero …

Winnie Roach Leuszler: First Canadian woman to conquer the English Channel.

Marilyn Bell

On September 9, 1994, a group of people gathered at the Canadian National Exhibition site in Toronto to celebrate the fortieth anniversary of a remarkable event. A fifty-six-year-old teacher from New Jersey, Marilyn Di Lascio, was the honoured guest at the ceremony. In 1954 she was Marilyn Bell, a sixteen-year-old long distance swimmer training with Gus Ryder of the Lakeshore Swimming Club. In the 20 hours and 59 minutes it took for her to swim across Lake Ontario, she went from being an unknown individual to a national hero who remains one of the most revered athletes in Canadian sports history.

It all began when the Canadian National Exhibition offered American swimmer Florence Chadwick $10,000 to make the swim from Youngstown, New York, to Toronto, landing at the exhibition grounds. Chadwick was considered the best marathon swimmer of the day. The offer didn't sit well with some members of the public and the swimming community. Why was an American being challenged to swim Lake Ontario? Were there no Canadians who could take part?

Earlier that year unheralded Bell had finished as first woman in a 25-mile marathon swimming event in Atlantic City. Although Chadwick's challenge to swim Lake On-

tario was between her and the CNE, Bell also decided to take the plunge, undertaking the swim "for the honour of Canada," despite not being eligible for the prize money. Winnie Roach Leuszler, who three years earlier became the first Canadian woman to conquer the English Channel, also decided to take on the challenge. The *Toronto Star* newspaper underwrote the expenses of the two challengers.

On September 8, 1954, Chadwick entered the deep, dark water off Youngstown at 11:00 p.m. Seven minutes later, Bell followed. Three miles into the swim Bell caught Chadwick, passing her in what was then fairly calm, 65°F water. As night passed to morning the water became increasingly choppy. The waves wreaked havoc on Chadwick and she became ill. After twelve miles, overcome with nausea and exhaustion, she was taken from the water.

Leuszler, meantime, was also beset with problems. Early in her swim she became separated from her pilot boat. She stopped swimming and returned to Youngstown, where she slept and began her swim again just after daylight. But by 5:00 p.m. on September 9 she, too, was pulled from the water, exhausted and suffering from severe cramps. She sent a message of support to Bell via radio.

Bell was soldiering on but clearly showing the wear of

her effort. At times glassy-eyed, unaware of her surroundings and listlessly clawing through the water, she was urged on by coach Ryder. By late afternoon she was challenged again by a stiff breeze and waves. She carried on. On land, as reports of her tenacity were relayed across Canada, a huge crowd gathered along the shoreline to witness an event

Marilyn Bell: Her swim across Lake Ontario transformed her overnight from just another teen to a Canadian hero.

that was almost storybook fare for its drama and emotion. At 8:06 p.m. Bell's swim ended with success as she clung to the breakwater near the exhibition grounds, 20 hours and 59 minutes after first entering the water. She was hauled into a rowboat and taken by ambulance to the Royal Oak Hotel where she was checked over by doctors. They found her tired, naturally, but were surprised to find her pulse normal despite the ordeal she had just completed. Although the distance from Youngstown to the breakwater was estimated at thirty-two miles, observers noted that Bell swam more than forty miles as winds forced her to zig-zag her way through choppy water. The next day she was guest of honour at a huge parade held at the CNE grounds and was deluged with endorsement offers and gifts.

A year later, Bell became the youngest swimmer to conquer the English Channel and in 1956 she swam the Strait of Juan de Fuca. Then, Bell gave up the rigours of marathon swimming, and embarked on a career as an elementary school teacher. Back problems would later pose a different challenge to her as she continued to swim for fun and fitness.

Although the exhaustion and pain of the ordeal left her quickly thanks to the resiliency of youth, Bell would relive the effort thousands of times via interviews and celebrations marking the historic event. Time and again she would relate the shiver she felt as eels clamped onto her skin, and how she dreaded most swimming in the cold, deep waters through the black night. And she often related a deep sense of personal honour for what was clearly unexpected and long standing admiration of her by the Canadian public.

Bell's accomplishments earned her entry into the Canadian Sports Hall of Fame which, in documenting her efforts, describes her as "the archetype of the Canadian girl."

Cindy Nicholas

Swimming the English Channel would be considered an ordeal for most people. In 1977, twenty-year-old Cindy Nicholas of Toronto — twenty-seven years to the day after Marilyn Bell plunged into the waters of Lake Ontario for her historic swim — became the first woman to accomplish a double crossing of the English Channel. Her round trip effort of 19 hours, 55 minutes, slashed an astonishing 10 hours, 5 minutes off the previous double crossing record set by American John Erikson in 1975.

Nicholas, who three years earlier had crossed Lake Ontario in 15 hours, 10 minutes, made her first English Channel crossing in 1975, arriving in Dover in 9 hours, 46 minutes. In 1976 she swam the Channel twice in the

space of two weeks.

When she left Dover to begin her two-way crossing in 1977 she had hoped to break the crossing record of 8 hours 56 minutes held by England's Wendy Brooke. But when she touched ground in France she was two minutes shy of the mark, coming in at 8 hours, 58 minutes. She then turned around and clocked 10 hours, 57 minutes for the return trip to Dover. The effort earned her Canada's female athlete of the year award for 1977. Nicholas, who would go on to forge a career as a lawyer, would swim the Channel nineteen times in her career, including three two-way crossings in 1981.

Vicki Keith: Marathon swimming's Madame Butterfly became the first to swim the English Channel using the butterfly stroke.

Cindy Nicholas: The first woman swimmer to complete the difficult double crossing of the English Channel.

Vicki Keith

LONG DISTANCE

Human nature being what it is, while Marilyn Bell's effort in 1954 was considered an outstanding achievement, it was only a matter of time before someone swam Lake Ontario both ways. Thirty-three years less a month after Bell completed her swim across Lake Ontario twenty-six-year-old Vicki Keith, a swimming instructor from Kingston, Ontario, completed her double crossing of Lake Ontario.

Keith was no stranger to marathon swimming. She was already in the Guinness Book of World Records for a 1985 effort that saw her swim butterfly for twelve miles in Lake Ontario; for a 129-hour, 45-minute swimming pool endurance record set in 1986; and for swimming forty-two miles nonstop in twenty-four hours.

In the summer of 1988 she continued her conquest of lakes. On August 31 she completed a summer-long quest to swim all five of the Great Lakes, finishing her swim of Lake Ontario at the eastern end of Toronto's harbour, swim-

ming much of the distance using the arduous butterfly stroke. Keith's Great Lakes effort was part of a fundraising effort to gain money for a Variety Village wheelchair-accessible pool for disabled youngsters. She would go on to raise hundreds of thousands of dollars for the charity in various distance swimming challenges. In 1988 alone she raised some $550,000.

In 1989 she became the first person to swim the English Channel using the butterfly stroke, reaching the French coast 23 hours, 33 minutes after leaving Dover in what was also a fundraising swim for the Variety Club. Earlier that year she swam butterfly for nearly thirteen and a half hours in swimming Sydney Harbour in Australia. Two hours into the swim she abandoned her protective shark net because she found the steel mesh restricted her stroke. In 1989 Keith also conquered California's Catalina Channel and the Strait of Juan de Fuca off Victoria, both times plowing through the water using the butterfly stroke.

Synchronized Swimming

Movie star Esther Williams brought her own brand of "fancy swimming" to the silver screen but synchronized swimming did not start with her choreographed routines in the pool. The sport began in the early 1900s and in Canada, the first compulsory figures competition took place in Montreal in 1925. A year later Frances Gale, a member of the Montreal Amateur Athletic Association, donated a trophy which would be given on an annual basis to the top competitor in Canada. Margaret Shearer would become Canada's first official synchro star, winning the Gale Trophy four years in a row.

The sport became a part of the Pan-American Games program in 1955, and in 1986 was included in the Commonwealth Games. It made its Olympic debut in 1984 with solo and duet events. At the 1996 Olympics in Atlanta, Georgia, the team event will be contested.

Canada has played an integral role in synchronized swimming, from development to coaching to organization and promotion. Canadian synchronized swimmers have enjoyed considerable success internationally and have served as innovators and ambassadors for the sport.

Helen Vanderburg

SYNCHRONIZED SWIMMING

Helen Vanderburg was fourteen when she discovered success and crisis of confidence can be intertwining entities. Rather than celebrating her national junior synchronized swimming championship she instead pondered her future.

"There was an incredible amount of pressure on me to win," she declared. "When I finished I remember going to Mary Ann Reeves, who was my coach at the time, and saying I was going to retire. I honestly thought I couldn't handle the pressure. To go on to seniors after that, I thought it was just too much, I didn't know if I wanted to do it.

"I do know my parents and Mary Ann were really good. No one at any point said I should or had to stay. I made the decision to go on, knowing what the pros and cons would be along the way."

The pros eventually outweighed the cons and in the 1970s Calgary's Vanderburg went on to become Canada's first international champion. Synchronized swimming was beginning to attract public and media attention as a move was afoot to include it in the Olympics.

Vanderburg began swimming at the local YMCA and, at age twelve, like many younger sisters who want to do what an older sister does, she followed her sister into synchronized swimming as a member of the Calgary Aquabelles. Success came immediately as the club's junior team won the national junior championship. For Vanderburg, the quick taste of success was an unexpected bonus for someone who as a youngster showed little athletic portent.

"I was quite weak and sickly as a child so they put me in swimming because they thought it would be good for me to develop some strength," she explained. "But when I hit puberty I grew up to be very strong. Initially I was thin and weak and it wasn't until I hit my teens that I became quite muscular. I don't think I'm a natural athlete but I do have a naturally strong body. I can work it hard and it doesn't get injured."

Strength became Vanderburg's trademark and it showed in her ability to perform as an Aquabelle and national team member and in her solo routines. By 1977 she was making an impact in international competition, finishing second in solo while taking gold with duet partner Michelle Calkins at the Pan Pacific championships. The Aquabelles also earned silver in the team event and at the end of the year Vanderburg and Calkins shared the Elaine Tanner Trophy as the top young female athletes in Canada.

For Vanderburg, the team event remained an important

and compelling part of competition.

"My focus was always the team," she said. "I always strongly believed in the team concept, working with eight people toward a goal. My goal was to be the strongest person on the team, and when I became the strongest person on the team that made me strongest in solo. But there are so many more dynamics in the team event, there are so many different variables."

In 1978 Vanderburg won the solo title at the world championships and also joined with Calkins to take the duet title. The competition was the highlight of her career and, in one sense, the end of a road she had decided to take when opting to stay in synchro during the uncertain days following her national junior championship win.

"That's where I broke the barrier, to win the first gold medal for Canada," she said. "My performance, in athletes' terms, was in flow state. Everything was one. But I was able to repeat performances like that again in my career."

Not content to rest on her world championship laurel, Vanderburg set out in 1979 to continue where she left off — winning. In a remarkable year she won not only the World Cup championship but also the Pan American Games and Pan Pacific championships. Calkins had retired after the 1978 season so Vanderburg teamed with Kelly Kryczka to also take the duet gold at the Pan Am and World Cup competitions.

Although synchronized swimming was to be part of the 1984 Olympic program, Vanderburg, having dominated her sport for two years, retired at the end of 1979 just before her twenty-first birthday, deciding to leave the hours of training to others in search of Olympic laurels.

Looking back, she believes her success was part of a crucial change in the evolution of synchronized swimming. She brought elements of power and strength into a sport characterized by grace.

Helen Vanderburg: Strength was her trademark.

"I changed the look of the solo event," she said in early 1995, just after teaching a fitness class at Heaven's Fitness in Calgary, a workout studio which she co-owns and serves as president.

"I went from doing the soft, graceful type of solo to doing a little bit of the bizarre, using music that was different, working on power and strength. My whole concept was that I wanted to lure the audience and the judges into my routine so that they just weren't watching it, they were a part of it."

Carolyn Waldo

SYNCHRONIZED SWIMMING

"Bringing the sport up a notch — that's what I'd like to be remembered for, bringing in different moves that are now standard," said Carolyn Waldo.

"I think I was more of a technical swimmer and the difficulty factor was definitely my strong point."

Carolyn Waldo of Beaconsfield, Quebec, virtually owned the sport of synchronized swimming in the mid 1980s. When she won the solo silver medal at the 1984 Olympics it marked the last time she would finish second at a synchronized swimming event until American rival Tracie Ruiz-

Conforto broke the streak at a pre-Olympic competition in Seoul, South Korea in June 1988. A swimmer of Waldo's calibre was just what her sport needed after it debuted at the 1984 Games in Los Angeles. Her long-term commitment and success allowed her name to become synonymous with the sport, which needed a name that would become familiar in the minds of the general public. Everyone loves a winner and Waldo proved most capable in that area, in addition to being willing and able to handle the media and public pressures that accompany a world champion.

Eager to promote her sport as more than just splashing, noseplugs and hair gel, Waldo often talked about the physical rigours of synchronized swimming. She was a natural athlete as a child and at times wondered what might have happened had she not been lured into synchro at age ten when a coach recognized her talent.

"As a kid growing up I was a real jock. I loved playing football, I liked volleyball, gymnastics, I loved running," she noted. "I was pretty fast in elementary school and then I went to synchro, which took up a lot of my time. I think I would have been a good athlete in other sports, but I didn't have time because I was doing synchro."

Waldo conceded she had the perfect build to excel in her sport. Slim, with a low bone mass, she floated easily and was able to lift her body high out of the water while using her natural strength to perform difficult and original moves.

Perhaps her most striking ability, one which set the tone for her 1988 Olympic routine, was being able to stay under water for long periods of time. Yet Waldo nearly drowned at age three after following her two older sisters into a lake. For years she was afraid to even put her face in the water, let alone submerge herself for a minute or more.

Even after her Olympic and world championship triumphs Waldo still treated the water with respect.

"Even when I was in my prime, when someone dunked me I would get really mad. I hate it. I can't stand it. Being a swimmer, it sounds kind of funny, you think I'd get used to it but it still really irritates me."

At age seventeen Waldo left friends and family to live and train in Calgary under national coach Debbie Muir. She enjoyed her first taste of international victory in 1981 when she was a member of Canada's gold medal team at the Pan Pacific championships and, a year later, she learned what a world title was all about by contributing to Canada's gold medal team performance at the world championships.

She won her first national solo championship in 1984 and never looked back, taking silver behind American Ruiz-Conforto at the Los Angeles Olympics. In 1985 she joined

Carolyn Waldo: Nearly drowned when she was a child but made staying under water for extraordinarily long periods her trademark.

forces with Calgary's Michelle Cameron and the two became the best synchro duet in the world. Indeed, it was at the 1985 FINA Cup that Waldo secured her place as the world's best, taking gold in the solo, duet, team and figures competitions. A year later she took gold in solo and figures and, with Cameron, won the duet at the world championships.

Waldo recalled being inspired for the rest of her career by a sad incident she confronted at the 1981 Pan Pacific championships.

"I'll never forget, it was my first big international competition and I heard Terry Fox had died. I was so upset. He was one of the biggest role models around. I felt if he could do what he did, then I had no right to complain about any problems I had."

Synchronized swimming proved to be just what a beleaguered Canada needed at the 1988 Olympics in Seoul. After sprinter Ben Johnson tested positive for steroids many Canadian team members had difficulty focusing on their tasks. Waldo, first in the solo and then the duet with Cameron, served up what the country desperately needed at the time — two Olympic gold medals.

"Honestly, it was such a blur," she said. "When you're at the Olympics you're so pumped, you have so much adrenaline going. I don't think I even remember the actual performance. I know it wasn't that hard, it wasn't as difficult as it normally was."

Retirement and various endorsements quickly followed Waldo's Olympic effort. Later, she challenged herself by taking work at the other end of the microphone, taking a job as a sportscaster for CJOH-TV in Ottawa.

"I don't consider myself special," she said when asked to assess her synchro career. "I've never graduated from university, so I look at anyone who has gone to university and who has a degree as special. I look at doctors as being special because they have skills — I have no idea how to save somebody. I happened to excel in one area but there are so many people who are successful in so many fields. What I did was such a small portion of what life's all about."

Sylvie Frechette

Sylvie Frechette laughed as she pondered how long it took for her to receive her Olympic gold medal.
"It was one year, four months and nine days," she quipped. "Well, maybe eight days depending on the time change."

Exact time aside, the consensus was that it was long overdue when Frechette ascended a special podium placed in the Montreal Forum at a gala ceremony on December 15, 1993. International Olympic Committee vice-president Richard Pound slipped the 1992 Olympic gold medal around Frechette's neck, a recorded version of "O Canada" was played. Finally, after a scoring error by a Brazilian judge cost Frechette the synchronized swimming gold medal at the 1992 Summer Olympics in Barcelona, the Canadian took her rightful place among Olympic champions. Already, she had secured a special spot in peoples' hearts around the world for exhibiting such grace under pressure.

"When they gave me that medal in Montreal, of course I cried," she said nine months later and a seeming lifetime away from that special night. "It was the end of my athletic career, it was the end of that chapter. I thought: Finally I won't talk about it, and I won't be so emotional about it, every hour of the day."

In the weeks leading up to the 1992 Olympics Frechette was one of Canada's top gold medal hopes for the Games. The twenty-five-year-old synchronized swimmer from Montreal had not lost a competition since June 1990, and in 1991 won the world championship with a world record 201.013 points that included seven perfect marks of 10. The battle for the Olympic gold medal was, on paper, between Frechette and American Kristen Babb. But Frechette arrived at the Games waging an even greater personal battle. One week before the opening ceremonies she came home to the condominium she shared with fiancé Sylvain Lake and discovered he had committed suicide.

A day later Frechette's coach, Julie Sauvé, released a statement on behalf of her protégé, saying Frechette would not comment on Lake's death and that her participation in the Games would "not be compromised."

Sylvie Frechette was born June 27, 1967. Early on her life was tinged with tragedy. Her father, René, was killed in a car accident nearly three months before her fourth birthday. Growing up, Frechette began her foray into aquatics as a competitive swimmer, but at age eight switched to synchronized swimming when, after swim practice, she became fascinated watching a group of girls who somehow seemed to float in the water even as they held their arms in

Sylvie Frechette: Grace under pressure.

the air. She abandoned the world of butterfly and freestyle for the unappreciated rigours of synchronized swimming.

History will show that Sylvie Frechette finished twenty-third out of twenty-four entries in duet at the 1979 national junior championships but two years later she improved to win in solo, duet and team, and in 1982 she again won in solo and team.

Frechette came to the sport with many traits that would contribute to her success, particularly her work ethic. While performing competent and clean routines, she struggled to attain the artistic and emotional brilliance that has become necessary for success at the international level. In conversation, she revealed it took a surprisingly long time for her to accept and appreciate her own talent.

"From the moment I began to compete I think people believed in me more than I did," she said. "I think the first time I realized who I was was at the world championships in 1991. It took me a long time. Over there in Australia I was so insecure, yet this was the moment to prove to the world what I could do. I did it, and I won by quite a lot. That's when I realized, 'Hey, you're good, You're not only winning, you're good at what you do.'

"But I was never 100 per cent confident, there was always something I could do better — I could always be stronger, more original, move faster."

Indeed, while Frechette had been criticized early in her career for lack of emotion and grace in her routines, she became an innovator in the sport by eventually combining a powerful artistry with her strong physical ability. Weight training was an integral part of her program and she exuded a confident and athletic presence on the deck prior to her routines.

If there was one thing that bothered her throughout her career, it was the lack of respect accorded her sport. Anyone who thinks it's all smiles and noseplugs should try it sometime.

"It's the muscular part that's the hardest," she explained. "You work nonstop. Even if your head is under the water, you support your whole body weight with two arms, you have to be in control of each and every muscle for three and a half minutes. Your arms burn so much it feels like they're on fire. So, on top of all that we have to hold our breath, then come out and smile. That's difficult, staying under the water, and many of us are very scared of it, staying under too long."

Frechette was unafraid to challenge the status quo. One of the hallmarks of synchronized swimming is the perpetual smile fixed on the competitor's face no matter how tired she is. In opting to perform to "Amazing Grace," Frechette's unsmiling yet serene countenance during the swim was the complete opposite to what spectators had come to expect in a synchro performance, yet it was perfect in light of the calm yet powerful melody.

And it was with amazing grace that Frechette arrived in Barcelona on July 23, determined to complete what she started nearly eighteen years earlier when she took up synchronized swimming. Aware of the tragedy of her fiancé's suicide and as if in appreciation of her determination to compete anyway, the normally aggressive array of sports journalists were uncharacteristically charitable, lobbing Frechette easy and vague questions. All too soon they had another big, if not tragic, Sylvie Frechette story on their hands. Frechette was tied with Babb after the preliminaries but lost that lead, and the gold medal, on August 5 when the Brazilian judge punched in the wrong score for Frechette's compulsory figures. The intended score would have put Frechette first; instead, she was fourth.

Once again Canada and the world watching the Olympics wondered just how much a person could take.

Frechette remained surprisingly stoic as the Canadian team launched a protest that was initially turned down. "I'm good under pressure," she said. "When life is tough, I fight." She fought. A day later she returned to win the solo final. The combined marks were good enough for the silver medal, while Babb took the gold.

After the Olympics Frechette had intended to retire and upon her return to Canada from Barcelona she began the difficult task of repairing her life and beginning a new one. The rigours of training were replaced by the rigours of public appearances and commitments, including her own television show. Frechette emerged as a brave and compassionate role model to many people, particularly young folk. And, one year, four months and eight or nine days later, rightfully received her Olympic gold.

In a surprise announcement on November 30, 1994, Frechette declared her intent to return to training, with the hope of making the Canadian team to the 1996 Summer Olympics in Atlanta, Georgia, where synchronized swimming will feature a team event instead of solo or duet competition.

Sharon Hambrook & Kelly Kryczka
SYNCHRONIZED SWIMMING DUETS

This Calgary-based duet became the first Canadian synchronized swimmers to win an Olympic medal when, on August 9, 1984, they finished second to the gold medal winning American pair of Candie Costie and Tracie Ruiz. Sharon Hambrook and Kelly Kryczka, the 1982 world duet champions and 1983 Pan American Games and Pan Pacific champions, were also integral members of the Canadian team that won the team gold at the 1982 world championships with Hambrook also taking first place in women's solo.

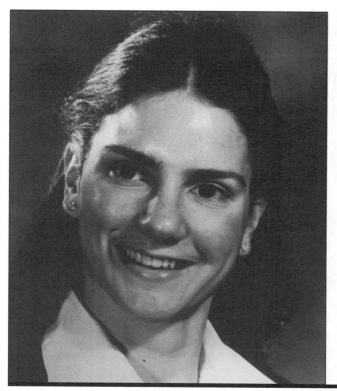

Kelly Kryczka (left) joined with **Sharon Hambrook** (right) to take duet silver at The Los Angeles Olympics.

Penny Vilagos & Vicky Vilagos

In 1980 at the Swiss Open this identical twin duet from Quebec became the first synchro duet to earn a perfect 10 score. They went on to contribute to Canada's 1982 world championship team victory and served as national team members from 1980 to 1985, opting to retire when they failed to make the Canadian Olympic team to the 1984 Olympics in Los Angeles.

They married and embarked on careers but in 1991, at age twenty-eight and having dabbled in masters competitions and in some international events, they confirmed a decision to make a comeback for the Summer Olympic Games in Barcelona, winning the duet at the 1992 Roma Synchro and Pero Canada Cup. They took the silver medal behind Americans Karen and Sarah Josephson in Barcelona.

The Canadian twins embarked again on what appeared to be retirement but in 1994, with the team event being the only synchronized swimming event slated for the 1996 Olympics in Atlanta, Georgia, they announced they would attempt to gain a spot on the Canadian team. Also coming out of retirement with eyes on Atlanta were former world champion Sylvie Frechette and 1990 Commonwealth

Games gold medallists Christine Larsen and Kathy Glen.

Penny & Vicky Vilagos: Came out of retirement to earn Olympic silver at the 1992 Games in Barcelona.

Michelle Cameron

Michelle Cameron: Joined with Carolyn Waldo to form international synchro's most dynamic duet.

It takes two to win an Olympic gold medal in synchronized swimming duet competition and Calgary's Michelle Cameron proved the perfect duet partner for Carolyn Waldo. The media tended to concentrate on Waldo because of her status as the world's top solo swimmer and Cameron never received the attention she deserved as a competitor in her own right. In addition to serving as a national team member for several years Cameron proved a competent solo swimmer as well, in particular taking the silver medal in solo and figures at the 1987 Moscow Invitational. Cameron retired following the duet gold medal victory at the 1988 Olympics in Seoul.

Diving

Women's diving was first introduced to the Olympics at Stockholm in 1912. Initially, only the 10-metre tower was contested but in 1920 at Antwerp the 3-metre springboard was added.

Doris Ogilvie was the first Canadian woman to earn a top-five finish in Olympic diving, taking fifth on the 3-metre board at the 1932 Olympics in Los Angeles. Two years earlier Canadians Pearl Stoneham and Helen McCormack had taken gold and silver respectively in the high dive at the first British Empire Games in Hamilton, Ontario.

Canadian women have dominated diving Commonwealth Games competition since the 1970s. Three times Canadian women divers have swept the medals — in 1974 Cindy Shatto took gold in the springboard with Beverley Boys and Teri York taking silver and bronze. Boys also took gold on the platform that year. In 1978, in front of a partisan crowd in Edmonton, Janet Nutter led a Canadian sweep by winning the springboard with Boys earning silver and Eniko Kiefer the bronze.

Another Canadian hat trick occurred at the 1994 Commonwealth Games, also in front of a partisan crowd in Victoria. Anne Montminy took the gold in the platform event with Paige Gordon earning silver and Myriam Boileau the bronze. Together, the threesome represented the next wave of young Canadian divers to carry on the tradition of excellence in women's diving.

Irene MacDonald

Canada's first Olympic diving medal came at the 1956 Summer Olympics in Melbourne, Australia. Two years earlier Toronto's Irene MacDonald had taken the bronze medal in springboard at the British Empire Games in Vancouver and in Melbourne she edged American rival Barbara Gilders for the bronze medal. At the 1958 British Empire Games at Cardiff, Wales, she took silver on the springboard. During her diving career MacDonald won fifteen national titles and six U.S. titles.

MacDonald's efforts in competition were matched by her commitment to her sport in retirement. For many years she served as a coach and administrator and became a familiar figure on television broadcasts of international diving events where her experience and insight served to inform a generation of Canadians about diving.

Irene MacDonald: Canada's first Olympic diving medallist.

Beverley Boys

Four Commonwealth Games teams. Three Pan-American Games teams. Three Canadian Olympic teams. Few Canadian athletes can look back on their careers and say they were the best in their country and one of the best in the world. Diver Beverley Boys maintained that standard for over a decade. Her successes included three gold medals, three silver medals and a bronze medal in Commonwealth Games competition, two silver and a bronze at the Pan-American Games and enough Canadian championships to fill a diving tank. Her three Olympic appearances included earning a fourth in platform and seventh on the 3-metre springboard in 1968 at Mexico City and fifth on the springboard at Munich.

But along with the laurels and attention came pressure to compete, to perform. In a sport where a long, lean body is not only an aesthetic plus but also useful when trying to enter the water as cleanly and quietly as possible, extra pounds can be a problem and sometimes Boys came under criticism for her at times sturdy frame. Lack of willpower? Perhaps, but years later she would put it down to a young person trying to find control of herself in a narrowly focused sporting world trying to control her.

"Diving was easy before it got complicated," she reflected. "Probably 1969 and '70 were my most successful and best years but it was the beginning of a power struggle. I didn't go through adolescence at fifteen or sixteen, I did it before Munich. But in 1969 and 1970 I won the U.S. nationals, a huge meet to win against all those Americans on their turf, I won in Russia that year, I won everything."

Boys grew up in Pickering, Ontario, in the kind of quiet, idyllic community that many people would love to know but never find. Dirt roads. One-room school. Country. She learned to swim in the family's backyard pool, later taking diving lessons at the pool that was part of the community golf course. When a neighbourhood friend began taking more serious diving lessons farther away, twelve-year-old Boys joined her so that the families could share the driving. Almost immediately she showed talent, winning small age-group competitions then working her way up the provincial and national ladder. She was just fifteen when she competed in her first British Empire (Commonwealth) Games in Jamaica, taking a silver medal on 3-metre and bronze on the 10-metre tower. Two years later she would make her Olympic debut and finish fourth on the tower.

Bev Boys: Top competitor for more than a decade.

ful and practical, Boys started an office cleaning service to make money to pay for travel costs and training camps.

By 1972 it was clear Boys had a good chance to take a medal at the Summer Olympics in Munich. Two months before the Games she won the prestigious Swedish Cup, defeating divers she would meet at the Olympics. But the life, the expectations and constant prodding that she had a little weight to lose somehow came to a head in that period before the Games. She gained more weight and the cycle of criticism about her size and subsequent lowering of her self esteem continued. She came fifth in Munich.

"Somebody told me the other day: 'you got a bad rap,'" she said years later. "But I was big. I was overweight. But there are reasons.

"I dove better than anyone in that event but I was big. I hated them (the judges), I thought they were horrible. I took it personally that they didn't like me. But they didn't have a personal vendetta against Bev Boys."

Boys retired after taking a silver medal at the 1978 Commonwealth Games in Edmonton. She eventually went on to live in the Vancouver area where for several years she operated a swimwear shop. She also became a diving judge — conceding she is just as critical about those half points as judges were to her — one of her international assignments being serving as a judge at the 1994 Commonwealth Games in Victoria.

At times anger welled again in her voice as she recalled her battle with her emotions, her surroundings and her weight as a competitor and the hurt that came when overweight sportswriters at times dubbed her a failure. Yet there are few Canadian athletes who could match her international record, her longevity or her tenacity.

"You know what meant more than anything?" she mused. "Being inducted into the (Canadian Sports) Hall of Fame. They judge you on the whole thing. One event is such a weird evaluation. The Olympic Games, I don't know. It's just two hours, not even a whole day. If it's the wrong two hours in your life or a bad biorhythm, look out."

"I wasn't very good in public school," Boys said wryly. "We had a one-room, then a two-room, school and I failed Grade 5. Once I started diving I had to do well in school or I was not allowed to travel, so it really turned my school around. Once I got to high school I was an honour student. My teacher, coming out of grade school, told my mother I should go to reform school, I shouldn't even go to high school."

Travel became an integral part of Boys' life. Most weekends she and several teammates and coach Don Webb travelled to Montreal to train on what was then the nearest available Olympic standard tower. She later moved to Winnipeg to train at the Pan-American Games pool. Resource-

Sylvie Bernier

Tension ran through the crowd like a train letting its whistle blow through a long tunnel — muffled but clearly intense. All around was that stifling, uneasy silence that permeates a diving facility when an athlete is about to leap into the air.

Kelly McCormick of the United States stood on the 3-metre springboard at the 1984 Olympic diving facility at

the University of Southern California and was on the verge of standing on the top of the Olympic podium. Daughter of four-time Olympic gold medallist Patricia McCormick, she needed just over seventy points on her last dive to overtake leader Sylvie Bernier of Canada and take gold of her own. The task was not insurmountable for the American, who came into the Olympic meet as second favourite on paper to China's Li Yihua, but was the crowd favourite.

Seconds later the scores went up for the American's effort on her back two-and-one-half somersault. Requiring 8.5s, she received mostly 8.0s to earn 67.20 points and the silver medal. As the results were announced twenty-year-old Bernier, of Ste-Foy, Quebec, hugged coach Donald Dion while he cried. Not only had Bernier won the gold medal but in doing so had become the first Canadian to win an Olympic diving event.

"My coach started crying, he could hardly speak," recalled Bernier. "It was a lot more emotional for everybody else because they had felt that pressure for two hours watching the competition and seeing the results after every round. It was pressure I would have felt had I known I was leading going into the fourth dive."

Bernier triumphed in that Olympic competition with 530.70 points. Her win also marked her personal victory over nerves that had compromised her exceptional talent in previous close situations. On a day when much of the amateur sport world was watching, Bernier chose to tune out that world, performing her dives and noting her scores then, wearing headphones blaring music from the movie *Flashdance*, quickly retreating from the deck. Between dives Bernier became lost in the music, which kept out announced scores from her rivals and muted crowd noise, and found her strength in the words.

"Everybody knew I was leading except me," she laughed. "That was something I did in the last two years after the world championships. I started listening to music and just concentrating on what I had to do instead of putting out so much energy worrying what anyone else was doing. At the Olympics the music from *Flashdance* was perfect — you know, take your passion, make it happen."

Sylvie Bernier was one of five children born to Raymond and Huguette Bernier, who instilled in all their children a sense of goal-setting and achievement and a love of sport. As a child she delighted in bouncing on the family trampoline but it wasn't until age nine, with eldest brother Marc-Andre already a member of a diving club, that she opted to give the sport a try. At the time she was suffering from asthma and the family doctor felt the activity would be good for her.

As it turned out, not only was it good for her but Bernier proved an adept study. Slender and bold, she won a regional championship at age eleven and even then served notice as one of the most exciting young divers in the country.

"I was diving for fun but a lot of people were starting to talk about me," conceded Bernier. "Where did she come from, was she doing gymnastics before?"

By age sixteen, Bernier was already taking part in senior

Sylvie Bernier: Conquered nerves to win Olympic gold.

competition, finishing a credible sixth in the Canadian Olympic trials for a team that ultimately would not make the trip to Moscow thanks to the boycott. A year later she was sixth at the FINA World Cup, and in 1982 took second at the Commonwealth Games and Fort Lauderdale International meet. That same year she took seventh at the world championships, conceding much later that she allowed nerves and other peoples' expectations to cloud what could have been a better performance.

"I always asked a lot of myself," she said. "I was aware of what the media was saying but I always tried to keep it aside, to remember my own personal goals instead of trying to achieve something that everyone expected me to do. When you start doing it for everyone else it's very hard."

By 1983 Bernier had become a major competitor on the international diving scene, finishing third at the FINA World Cup, the World University and Pan-American Games. In the year leading up to the Olympics she also won the three major competitions of the Can-Am-Mex series — Dive Canada, the Fort Lauderdale event and a meet in Acapulco. Although not as high profile as a major games, the events are important on the international diving calendar.

Bernier said lack of media interest in events on the diving circuit likely did her a favour leading up to the Los Angeles Olympics. Although one of the world's most consistent divers — she had finished in the top three in major meets 30 times — she was known as a diver vulnerable to pressure.

"Before the Olympics I never won a major competition, I won a lot of important competitions but people weren't aware of it, not like the world championships or Commonwealth Games or Pan-American Games but these competitions were very, very big in diving," noted Bernier. "It was a good thing for me."

Bernier conceded that, after spending much of the day trying to tune out her surroundings, it took her some time to appreciate her Olympic achievement when the event was over. Indeed, the end of the competition also marked the end of her competitive diving career.

"I had decided even before the competition it was going to be my last," she said. "I felt I had done everything I could. I wanted to go back to school full-time. It was easy to say after I had won. Maybe if I hadn't won. Well, it's hard to say. If I had kept going after the gold medal I would have had a lot of pressure, people expecting me to keep winning and I didn't want that because I always dove for myself. The day that you start to do it for everyone else, I thought

that wasn't right, either."

While Bernier was able to plan her retirement to coincide with the presentation of that Olympic gold medal, she had adjustments to make when she became a Canadian celebrity as a result of her achievement. Lively and articulate, she was much sought after as an interview guest and public speaker. In 1994, ten years after her Olympic triumph, she was juggling the demands of her two-child family with work as a sports commentator and host of a family television program, plus endorsement, business and public speaking commitments.

Diving?

"Once in a quiet while," she laughed. "When there's no one on the pool deck I just fool around. I miss the feeling of achieving something when you work so hard, but I don't miss the training. I'm happy with my life today. I'm happy I went through all of that when I was young, and I'm proud of what I did. I smile, I will always smile, when I think about that time."

Anne Montminy

DIVING

Anne Montminy: Thrilled home country crowd to win 10-metre gold medal at 1994 Commonwealth Games in Victoria.

Anne Montminy comes by her diving ability naturally, as both her father and her grandmother dove at the national level. A two-time age group national champion on the 3-metre board and tower winner at the 1992 Can-Am-Mex junior championships, Montminy challenged the Canadian Olympic Association when she was initially left off the team chosen for the 1992 Barcelona Olympics. After a brief court battle, a Quebec Superior Court judge decided that Montminy and another diver in fact did meet the qualifying criteria and ordered them placed on the team.

Montminy finished seventeenth in the Olympic tower event after a strong start, but the Olympic experience allowed her to handle pressure better in subsequent years. In 1993 she won the 10-metre tower event at the World University Games and followed that effort up with a victory, also on tower, at the world junior championships in London.

Montminy began the 1995 season ranked fifth in the world, winning the 10-metre tower event at the winter national championships in Montreal.

Paige Gordon

A former gymnast, Paige Gordon joined the Canadian national team in 1989 after becoming just the second diver to win all three events at the Canada Games. At age sixteen she took the tower bronze medal at the 1990 Commonwealth Games in New Zealand. In 1991 she earned the Elaine Tanner Award as Canada's top junior female athlete after posting several good international finishes, including silver at the 1991 Pan-American Games, a credible fourth in a major meet in Russia, and two silvers at the Bolzano International, featuring the top twenty-five female divers in the world. She was also named the most outstanding diver of that competition.

Although she had developed a reputation as a "pressure cooker diver," an uncharacteristic case of nerves appeared to get the better of her in the Olympic 10-metre competition. She started well then faded to finish sixteenth. A year later, however, she enjoyed much international success, winning the 10-metre at Dive Canada, at Vienna and at Bolzano, while finishing an outstanding fourth at the FINA World Cup in Beijing.

Paige Gordon: Former gymnast makes an international splash.

Medal Sweep: Gold medallist Anne Montminy (centre) and teammates Paige Gordon (left) and Myriam Boileau celebrate Canadian sweep of diving medals in women's 10-metre final at 1994 Commonwealth Games in Victoria.

Myriam Boileau

A tower age-group champion in 1994, Myriam Boileau also qualified for the 1994 Commonwealth Games, her first major international games. In 1990 she swept all three disciplines at the national age group championships in Montreal and three years later finished fourth at the world age group championships in London.

Boileau won her first senior national championship in 1994, taking the 10-metre winter national title in Quebec City, following that up with a promising seventh place in tower at the China Open. Following the medal ceremony at the Commonwealth Games Boileau, then sixteen, conceded she had been nervous competing in her first major games in front of a home country crowd. The experience served her well. In January 1995, Boileau, previously considered a tower specialist, edged Commonwealth Games double gold medallist Annie Pelletier to win the women's 3-metre title at the winter national championships.

Annie Pelletier

Annie Pelletier: Ended the 1994 competitive season with a world championship bronze medal.

A nnie Pelletier ended 1994 as Canada's top-ranked diver in world competition. A former gymnast who took up diving at age twelve, she finished the season with a bronze medal performance on the 1-metre board at the world aquatic championships in Rome, becoming the first Canadian to win a medal at the event since it began in 1973. She also took gold on the 1- and 3-metre boards at the Commonwealth Games in Victoria.

Pelletier came to the Commonwealth Games after enduring a turning point of sorts in March 1994. Although she won her third 1-metre national title at the winter national championships in Quebec City, she allowed nerves to take over her focus in the 3-metre event and finished fourteenth. One month later, after taking silver in the 1-metre and bronze in the 3-metre at Dive Canada, she conceded the result was a blessing in disguise.

"I'm a very emotional person and I let things bother me," she said. "After such a bad competition I had to do something, take control and see where I am going. Sometimes that is the way you learn best, you go one step back then take two steps forward."

Pelletier continued her fine 1994 form into 1995. Although upset by clubmate Myriam Boileau in the 3-metre event at the winter national championships, she so dominated the 1-metre event she could have bypassed her final dive and still won the competition.

WINNING ON WATER

Rowing

Watch closely the next time a rowing race is shown on television. At the finish line the winners will rarely erupt into a frenzy of celebration — more often than not they are trying not to be sick or trying to catch their breath. Such are the demands of the sport of rowing that the strength and endurance required to excel leave little energy left for frivolity at the end of a race.

Rowing is divided into sweep events, where individual competitors wield one oar on each side of the shell, or sculling, where one rower handles two oars, one affixed to each side of the shell. Competition involves racing alone, in pairs, or with four or eight to a shell.

Women's rowing was not included in the Summer Olympic program until the 1976 Games in Montreal. From then on Canada could be counted upon to field competent rowers who would be among the best in the world. But the country emerged as the best nation in women's rowing during a fourteen-month period in 1991 and 1992. At the world championships in 1991 Silken Laumann won the women's single sculls title; Marnie McBean and Kathleen Heddle took the pair; Jennifer Doey, Brenda Taylor, Jessica Monroe and Kirsten Barnes won the four; and McBean, Heddle, Doey, Taylor, Monroe, Barnes, Kelly Mahon and Megan Delehanty took the women's eight.

In 1992, at the Barcelona Olympics, Laumann returned from serious injury to take bronze in the single sculls while McBean and Heddle took gold in the pair. Taylor, Monroe and Barnes were joined by veteran Kay Worthington, who replaced injured Doey, to take gold in the four; the Canadian eight of McBean, Heddle, Taylor, Monroe, Barnes, Worthington, Delehanty and Shannon Crawford easily won gold to cap one of the most memorable weekends in Canadian sport history.

Silken Laumann

The calm, jade-green waters of Lake Banyoles provided a serene counterpoint to the fury being unleashed on a 2,000-metre stretch of shimmering surface. With just 250 metres left in the women's Olympic single sculls final, a tremendous battle was being waged for the bronze medal as Romanian Elisabeta Lipa and Belgium's Annelies Bredael appeared to have gold and silver in their respective grasps.

At the 1,500-metre mark American Anne Marden looked set to take the bronze medal when she passed Canadian Silken Laumann. But the Canadian had other ideas, refusing to yield as the final stage of the race swept the rowers past two bright, white boats filled with supporters and teammates. There were several Canadian flags draped from the railings.

"At that point your muscles are so heavy, screaming," Laumann would later recall. "But I had just come so far, with all the things I had overcome it was like a little flash in my mind: 'You've got to win a medal, I have to stay on that podium.' I was completely gone, yet something switched, something went crazy in my head. I just closed my eyes

and brought my stroke rate up again. I had to get those oars in as fast as I could."

As the finish line loomed spectators on that sunny, Spanish day were treated to one of those rare, precious moments that define what is good in sport — a beaten athlete who from the depths of her spirit finds untapped strength. They saw Laumann dig deep and fast with her blades, each stroke coming faster than the one before. Her shell moved even with the American's then leaped ahead just before the finish line. Olympic history would note Silken Laumann rallied to defeat two-time Olympic silver medallist Marden by one second to take the bronze medal.

After the Olympic race, coach Mike Spracklen was moved to note: "Winning isn't always about finishing first, is it? Sometimes it's about conquering yourself."

On May 16, 1992, Laumann was going through pre-race preparation for a regatta in Essen, Germany. Her shell was rammed by a German men's pair also preparing for their event. A shard from her broken shell sliced through her lower right calf, shearing the muscle away from the leg and fracturing the bone. Initial reports from German doctors predicted her 1992 Summer Olympic aspirations were over as was, perhaps, her rowing career.

But twenty-five days later at a news conference in Victoria, detailing the various surgeries and rehabilitation she had undergone, Laumann surprised reporters by saying her goal was still to make it to the Olympics. Then thirty-nine days after the mishap, Laumann declared her intent to row in the Summer Olympics at Barcelona.

Silken Laumann was born November 14, 1964, in Mississauga, Ontario. Her early athletic aspirations centred on middle distance running as a member of the Mississauga Track and Field Club. Her sister, Daniele, was a rower and Silken eventually followed into the gruelling world of strokes, shells and hard work.

"I got into a single and I tipped," she said of her first rowing experience at the Don Rowing Club. "Actually, I tipped pretty well non-stop all summer. Every time I'd think I was doing it right I'd tip. There must have been something good about it because I kept coming out and trying again. Finally things started getting better and I thought: This is just an incredible sport."

Success came quickly after that. In 1984, twenty-year-old Silken and twenty-three-year-old Daniele Laumann earned a bronze medal in double sculls at the Olympic Games in Los Angeles. The next year Silken emerged as a talent in the single shell, finishing fourth in single sculls at the world championships.

Laumann's career was threatened long before that May day in Essen. In the mid-1980s, she was hampered by severe back problems and some medical experts recommended that she retire. She worked through the problem, however, winning the single sculls gold medal at the 1987 Pan American Games and representing Canada at the 1988 Seoul Olympics, finishing seventh in double sculls with Kay Worthington.

Seoul represented another milestone of sorts. Disappointed and disgruntled with the state of Canadian rowing, Laumann almost quit.

"The big problem was more the politics in our sport," she recalled. "It was so terrible, the athletes weren't able to have any input into what happened. It led to a very negative team situation."

Changes were made in the following two years, with University of Western Ontario's head coach Al Morrow being named national women's coach in 1989. In 1990 British coach Mike Spracklen was hired to coach the national men's team, bringing with him a resumé that included eight men's world or Olympic champions. Spracklen's no-nonsense approach inspired Laumann immediately and she

Silken Laumann: Overcame adversity to take 1992 Olympic bronze medal in thrilling single sculls finish.

moved to Victoria from Ontario in 1990 to train with Spracklen.

"It was Mike coming to Canada that gave me confidence," she said. "There were a couple of things about him — he had an incredible track record and he was completely professional. It was obvious he was confident in his knowledge of the sport and really confident about what we needed to do, and down to earth about it."

In 1990 Laumann finished second in single sculls at the world championships. The following year she would take first place overall in the World Cup series standings in addition to defeating Romanian Elisabeta Lipa to win the world championship.

As the 1992 Summer Olympics drew near, Laumann's recovery and resolve to compete despite her injuries captivated Canadians as have few other Canadian sport stories. She began rowing again before she could walk. In preliminary rounds at the Olympic rowing venue at Lake Banyoles

Laumann showed much of her ability had returned, winning her heat and leading all the way in her semi-final race to advance to the August 2 final. But in the final it became clear that determination could not wholly compensate for precious days of endurance training lost to the accident.

"At the halfway point I was really having problems," said Laumann. "The pace was too fast. I remember going through thinking: My God, I'm not going to make it. I said to myself: Just pull twenty more strokes, I had to focus on something."

Lipa withstood a late charge by Bredael to take the gold, but it was Laumann's bronze medal effort that received most attention.

"Looking back, I realize I shut off whole areas of my life in order to be able to have the energy to focus on what I had to do," she said. "I couldn't let myself cry, get frustrated."

Laumann took a hiatus from competition in 1993, using the time to recover from her injury and to catch up on life away from the sport. In January 1994, Laumann returned to training, her sights set on the 1996 Olympics in Atlanta, Georgia, her more immediate goal being the 1994 world championships in Indianapolis. Disaster struck there, too, as Laumann, unaccustomed to a new starting system, was assessed two false starts in the final and was forced to withdraw from the race.

Laumann returned to compete at the 1995 Pan-American Games in Mar del Plata, Argentina, winning gold in single and quadruple sculls. Two days after the quad event it was revealed she tested positive for the stimulant pseudoephedrine, which had been part of a decongestant medication recommended by a Canadian team doctor and taken by Laumann in an effort to stop coughing the night before the quad race. The four Canadian rowers were stripped of their medals. The physician later noted he should have been more specific in recommending the medication to Laumann as there were two distinct types under the basic brand name — one allowed and one which contained the banned substance.

At a Victoria news conference following the positive test, Laumann expressed her intent to continue competing through the 1996 Olympics at Atlanta.

Kirsten Barnes

Kirsten Barnes began rowing in 1985 as a student at West Vancouver's Hillside secondary school. She joined the national rowing team in 1987, won a Pan-American Games gold medal in the pair with Kathleen Heddle, was a member of the gold medal four and eight at the 1991 world rowing championships, and won gold in the four without cox and eight with cox at the 1992 Olympics in Barcelona.

"To be honest, I started rowing because it was something I could do with a team, with my friends, as opposed to figure skating, which I had done for some time but it was an individual sport. It was after the summer of '85 I realized it was something I enjoyed doing. Rowing just naturally took over from skating.

"You always remember the good, but then you think: Wait a minute, what about February in 1992 when it was so cold, miserable and nothing was going well? The 1991 world championships were a real highlight. After 1991 we were trying to stay a step ahead of everyone else and we met the challenge of repeating. We had to prove it wasn't a fluke. Going into the Olympics we'd had a whole year with peoples' eyes on us. Our coach, Al Morrow, did a really good job reminding us you create your own pressure, don't worry about everyone watching. To me, that's what makes a real athlete, someone who can repeat good performance. We met that challenge."

Shannon Crawford

Shannon Crawford began rowing in 1985 after deciding to take a learn-to-row course at Toronto's Argonaut Club while working as an operating room nurse. She began competing at age twenty-four, joined the national team in 1991, won a gold medal as a member of the Canadian four at the 1991 Pan-American Games, travelled to the 1992 Summer Olympics as a team alternate, and was assigned to the eight when back problems forced Jennifer Doey to the sidelines.

"It's a bit of a romantic memory now, that being in synch with someone else or with seven other people. That perfect balance, coordination, knowing how the other bodies are going to be moving in the boat, and the feeling of power.

Simply The Best: Canadian rowers (from left) Kirsten Barnes, Shannon Crawford, Megan Delehanty, Brenda Taylor, Jennifer Doey, Marnie McBean, Kay Worthington, Jessica Monroe, Kathleen Heddle and coxswain Lesley Thompson (far right) celebrate their gold medal victory in women's eights final at 1992 Olympics in Barcelona.

It's really a wonderful feeling.

"One of my best memories comes from the first year I started rowing. I was in an eight, and it got split up into stern and bow fours for a fours race. I was in the bow group and we weren't expected to do very well because all the people with experience were in the stern. We won our heat. And then we won the final. I remember during the race promising myself I'd never do this again. But the euphoria afterward, I'll never forget that feeling, that delight. I wonder sometimes if I had not won that race in my first year of rowing if I would have continued.

"The Olympics were the highest point. I found it a really difficult time. I was put in the boat several days before the heat for the eight. I felt terrible for Jenny Doey because if anyone deserved success in rowing it was her. And there I was, replacing her because she had a bad back. I was the new kid in the boat and thought if we don't win this race, everyone will be looking at me. I was greatly relieved when it was over, successfully."

Megan Delehanty

Megan Delehanty starting rowing in her third year of undergraduate studies at the University of Alberta after years of track and field work in hurdles, sprints and long jump. She joined the national team in 1991, was a member of the women's eight that won gold at the 1991 world championships in Vienna and at the 1992 Olympics in Barcelona, and retired after the Olympics to work on her Ph.D. in microbiology at the University of British Columbia.

"I got into rowing pretty much by chance. I was in the weight room working out and a guy came up to me and asked if I'd be interested in trying a new sport he thought I might be good at. At that particular moment I was open to the possibility, so I tried it and fell in love with it.

"I remember the distinctiveness of the finals in 1991 and '92. At the world championships we came through in the last 500 metres to barely scrape by. In 1992 it was what you'd think of as the classic, perfect race. Everything went perfectly. It was a very unique experience. The two years that were primarily dedicated to rowing gave me a very different way of living. It was a learning experience, a very different period of my life because for most of the other years I'd been close to school. Also, things like struggling with injuries, you learn you are stronger than you thought you were.

"If I had to think of one special moment it would be watching the (Canadian) pair and the four win their races at the Olympics. For me, it was much more emotional than when we won in the eight."

Jennifer Doey

Jennifer Doey started rowing as a high school student in 1980, joined the national team in 1983, won gold as a member of the coxed four at the 1986 Commonwealth Games and bronze at the 1986 world championships. She was a double gold medallist at the 1991 world championships, in coxless four and eight with cox. Named to the 1992 Olympic team, she opted out of competition several days before racing started due to a lingering back injury. Later, longtime teammate Brenda Taylor gave one of her Olympic medals to Doey.

"I always liked to run and work out but I think I really loved the water. I grew up near the water and remember my mom canoeing. In Grade 10 I decided I didn't want to play volleyball. I was looking for another sport and tried rowing.

"The first time my back bothered me was in 1985 and I thought maybe I should think about other options. But I kept going, through '88 which was a disappointing time. I got home from the Olympics and thought maybe I was ready to quit but then decided I would keep going. Every year after that I'd come home and evaluate where I was, what was important to me. Every year rowing would come out on top and things started to work out better and better. As soon as you commit yourself to something, everything falls into place.

"In Barcelona, we went in for a couple of practices and my technique wasn't as sharp, I was having trouble getting my blade out of the water. Subconsciously I realized it had been too long, my back wasn't healing quickly enough. To be able to finally say no, I can't row, was a bit of a relief. There were times when I cried but I was able to think and grieve and deal with it all over there."

Kelly Mahon

Kelly Mahon began rowing as a high school student in 1983 and went on to compete for the University of Victoria. A finalist in single and doubles sculls at the 1987 world junior championships, she stroked the Canadian women's eight to the gold medal at the 1991 world championships in Vienna, was a gold medallist in quadruple sculls at the 1993 U.S. championships, double gold medallist at the 1993 World University Games (quadruple sculls, eight) and bronze medallist in straight four at the 1993 world championships.

"I was playing a lot of basketball and looking for something to do in the off season. In Grade 12 I had a tryout with the junior national basketball team and the junior national rowing team. I made the rowing team then got invited to another selection camp for the basketball team but it was too late.

"Whenever I think of being on the national team and racing with the national team I always think of sitting on the start line, looking across and seeing all these other high-calibre athletes, the best in the world. I can't believe I'm there with them and I'm considered one of them. That's the neatest feeling.

"I didn't make the 1992 Olympic team. There were two final races for the spare seat. I ended up losing by 1.067 seconds. That was probably the hardest moment. I still feel I'm not done because I missed that, that's why I've kept going. A lot of times I don't think of rowing as a sport but as a passion that I have. I row."

Kathleen Heddle & Marnie McBean

ROWING

If ever there was a case for opposites making a good team, Kathleen Heddle and Marnie McBean are a perfect example. The two combined Heddle's quiet strength with McBean's outgoing tenacity to become the best pair in women's heavyweight rowing in the early 1990s. After the 1992 Olympics the duo disbanded, with Heddle retiring and going to school and McBean opting to try her hand at single sculls, where she finished second at the 1993 world championships. When Silken Laumann edged McBean for Canada's only single sculls spot at the 1994 world championships, McBean called up Heddle and asked if she wanted to try to make the team in double sculls. Less than two months later the duo took the double sculls silver medal at the world event in Indianapolis and in 1995 they won the world championship in Finland.

Kathleen Heddle began rowing in 1985 with the University of B.C. team. She earned a gold medal in pairs with-out cox with Kirsten Barnes at the 1987 Pan American Games, was 1991 world champion in the pairs with Marnie McBean and a member of world champion Canadian women's eight with cox, and was a 1992 Olympic gold medallist in coxless pairs with McBean, and in women's eight. She retired in 1993 but came out of retirement in 1994 to take the silver medal with McBean at the world championships.

"I was quite old when I started rowing. I was going to UBC and it was flukey — I started rowing because I was recruited by the coach. He just tapped me on the shoulder at registration day and said: 'Why don't you come out for the rowing team?' I didn't know too much about it, but quite quickly I found I was quite good at it.

"I'd always wanted to be in the Olympics, maybe playing volleyball, but I didn't think I'd get a chance so late, I was almost twenty when I took up the sport. The hardest

Kathleen Heddle & Marnie McBean: Pair nonpareil.

thing for me was training when I wasn't improving. I always wanted to see improvement and if that didn't happen I'd get discouraged."

"My favourite racing memory was in the eight at the 1991 world championship. We had no idea how we'd do in the eight because we'd never raced it all together before. We were more than a boat length down on the Russians and we just got them at the finish."

Marnie McBean's first laurel came a year after she began to row, with a bronze medal in the pairs at the 1986 world junior championships. She was a silver medallist (pair) at the 1989 World University Games, a gold medallist at the 1991 world championships in pair (with Kathleen Heddle) and in Canadian women's eight, a double gold medallist in the same events at the 1992 Summer Olympics in Barcelona. She was a 1993 world championship silver medallist (single sculls), and won gold medal (quad sculls) and silver (single sculls) at the

1993 World University Games. She was also the 1994 World Cup series champion.

"In high school I played all sports. I was on the basketball team, the volleyball team, soccer team, cross country team. I wanted to try rowing and called up the Argonaut Rowing Club in Toronto. I went down Saturdays and Sundays, for two hours after my swimming lessons. I'd bike down to the club and row. I loved it right from the start. One of the things I've really enjoyed about rowing, about my career, was seeing how good I can get technically and how I can see if I can become best in the world not only in speed but also in technique."

"The problem is that the closer I get to what I think is perfect, the more I realize that there is still another big step to go. Sometimes in the wintertime you don't love it every day, but I still love coming down and working with the team and pushing myself. It's what makes me feel the best."

Jessica Monroe

ROWING

A former member of the False Creek women's dragon boat team, Jessica Monroe started rowing in the fall of 1988. Her older sister Joanell was also an elite rower and a member of the 1984 national Olympic team. Monroe made the national team in 1989, and was a member of the 1991 world champion, and 1992 Olympic, four and eight crews.

"With my older sister rowing I guess it was in the family. I liked to do dragon boating and kayaking and when I came home from dragon boating in Hong Kong I thought I'd like to try an Olympic sport so I got into rowing.

"My second year in rowing was the hardest. I rowed in a double with another woman and we tried to do the time standard and we did quite poorly, so poorly the coach wasn't going to give us a second chance. I realized what a fine line it was between making a team or not. I had to collect my thoughts and realize I had to work that much harder to make the team the next year."

"The 1991 world championships were so much fun, it was all new to me and quite unexpected."

Brenda Taylor

ROWING

A national team member since 1984, Brenda Taylor was a member of the Canadian women's four and eight crews that won at the 1991 world championships in Vienna, and took gold a year later in Barcelona. After the 1992 Summer Olympics Taylor gave national teammate Jennifer Doey one of her gold medals after Doey, also a member of the four and eight teams, bowed out of the Olympic competition due to back problems.

"Our coach Al Morrow would always tell us: 'You win a race by your preparation, your training, your mental focus, your level of fitness. All those things come together.' Jennifer did all those things. She was part of that four. You don't

win a race just on the day, you win it through the preparation and Jennifer was part of getting us there.

"When I was growing up I rode horses and when I went to university I had to sell them. Rowing, at that time especially, was something you could start later, not like some sports where you have to start young. It was outside, on the water and hard work — I like that.

"I remember best the 1991 world championships, especially the four. That was the first time we medalled and the first time we won, and we were the first boat that won. We came across the line and all I remember thinking was: We did it!"

Kay Worthington

K ay Worthington began rowing as a first-year student at Carleton University in Ottawa. She joined the national team in 1981 and competed in her first world championships that year, finishing fourth in the Canadian eight, and competed at the 1984 Olympics (fifth in eight) and 1988 Games in Seoul where she and partner Silken Laumann finished seventh in double sculls. Worthington was disillusioned with that Olympic experience and left rowing for a time, then came back in 1991. She was named to the Canadian Olympic team for 1992, and was a member of the gold medal-winning eight crew. She also replaced injured teammate Jennifer Doey in the four and won gold in that event.

"After Seoul I walked around with a black cloud on my head for eighteen months. I hated everybody, I hated everything. I'd done everything I could, I'd given up so much, given up law school. How could it be possible? I had never failed at anything before.

"Coming back was a risk, and that's where the huge reward came. There were some pretty dark days when I thought I would never row again. But I realized I wasn't getting beyond rowing and I had to do something about it. There was only one thing to do and it was to stare down my fear.

"In Barcelona it was clear Jenny's injury wouldn't let her be a part of it. Many times I'd been in a pressure situation where I wanted to be anywhere but where I was. I remember thinking that week that if I could be anywhere, this is where I would be. I chose to put myself in this pressure-filled situation. Bring them on, I have put everything in my life towards this.

"After the race, I stood on the dock and looked at the grandstand and saw my parents and my boyfriend. It came to me that this was what Seoul was all about. It's not about one race, it's the experience and what you learn from it.

"Now, I feel I have this piece of sunshine that I carry around. When things go wrong, on a bad day I can think: "Oh well, I'm a double Olympic gold medallist."

Tricia Smith & Betty Craig

W hen women's rowing was becoming accepted as an international event in the mid-1970s, two Canadians were among the first women to make their mark in the sport. Tricia Smith of Vancouver, B.C., and Betty Craig of Brockville, Ontario, in the pair and as members of crews in larger boats, set an early standard of excellence for Canadian women rowers aspiring to compete internationally. At the 1976 Summer Olympics in Montreal, the first Games to feature women's rowing, they finished fifth in the women's coxless pair behind the gold medallists from Bulgaria.

Canada opted to boycott the 1980 Olympics in Moscow but Smith and Craig returned to the Los Angeles Olympics four years later as members of Canada's 1984 team. There, they took the silver medal in the women's pair behind a Romanian duo. Between Montreal and Los Angeles both had accumulated many rowing laurels, including combining for a silver medal at the 1981 world championships and bronze at the 1982 and '83 world events.

Smith went on to compete in the 1988 Olympics. Upon retiring at the end of that season, she had competed in nine world championships from 1977 to 1987 and had earned

Tricia Smith & Betty Craig: Their success led Canadian women into a tradition of international rowing excellence.

six bronze and a silver at the world event, in addition to taking gold at the 1986 Commonwealth Games in the coxed four. When she was inducted into the B.C. Sports Hall of Fame in 1992, she was described as "Canada's Most Medalled Oarsperson."

Lightweight Teams

Rowing is divided into two weight classes — lightweight and heavyweight — and heavyweight has traditionally been given more attention and status. Women lightweight crews must average 125 pounds with the maximum being 130 pounds.

Like their heavyweight counterparts, Canadian women lightweight rowers have enjoyed much success at the international level even if their accomplishments have been less celebrated and documented. Women's lightweight rowing wasn't added to the international racing program until 1984. The discipline took another step in 1993 when the International Olympic committee approved a change to the 1996 Olympic program which would see women's lightweight double sculls added, replacing the women's heavyweight pair event. Male lightweight rowers were given two events — four without cox and men's lightweight double sculls — for the 1996 Games in Atlanta, Georgia, sparking cries of foul and "tokenism" from some lightweight supporters who wanted to see the women at least allowed the same number of events. Others observed one event was at least an improvement because until then women's lightweight rowing had never been included in the Olympics.

Heather Hattin & Janice Mason   LIGHTWEIGHT

This Canadian duo sculled to victory at the 1987 world championships near Copenhagen to earn the country's first world championship gold medal in women's lightweight rowing. They led from start to finish to win the lightweight double sculls final in 8 minutes, 36.60 seconds, some five seconds better than the silver medallists from Belgium.

Five years earlier Janice Mason had teamed with Lisa Wright to take bronze in the women's open double event at the world championships in Lucerne. Heather Hattin, meantime, was a silver medallist in the double with Marie-Claude Gaudet at the 1983 Pan-American Games and bronze medallist in single sculls at the 1986 Commonwealth Games.

Michelle Darvill   LIGHTWEIGHT

Michelle Darvill: Single sculls world Champion.

After finishing fourth in double sculls at the 1991 world championships and second with Colleen Miller in double sculls at the 1992 world lightweight and junior championships, Toronto-born Michelle Darvill took gold in the quad sculls at the 1993 World University Games and capped the season by winning the single sculls event at the 1993 world championships at Roudnice in the Czech Republic.

Colleen Miller & Wendy Wiebe

Winnipeg's Colleen Miller finished the 1994 season as one of the most decorated, and least known, rowers in Canada. In 1990 she was a member of the Canadian women's straight four crew (with Rachel Starr, Jill Blois and Diana Sinnige) that won gold at the world championships in Tasmania. In 1992 she took silver (with Michelle Darvill) in double sculls at the world lightweight championships in Montreal, then the following year teamed with Wendy Wiebe of St. Catharines, Ontario, to take the world championship in women's lightweight double sculls. In 1994 they handled the pressure that comes to every defending champion, again winning the double sculls title at that year's world event in Indianapolis.

In early 1995 the duo had relocated to Victoria to begin training for the 1996 Olympics in Atlanta, where women's lightweight rowing will be represented by a double sculls event. With selection trials and events slated through 1995, combined with the depth of talent in Canadian women's rowing, there is no guarantee that Wiebe and Miller will be the double sculls duo in Atlanta although, as two-time world champions, the seats in the shell are theirs to lose.

"I tried out for the heavyweight team in 1992 for the Olympics and I didn't make it," said Miller, who took up rowing in 1988 after years of competing as a swimmer.

"I almost quit after '92. It was hard because after I didn't make the team I had to make weight for the lightweight Worlds, which was really hard to do. I think getting through that period really helped me. I thought: Oh, well, I'll see how it goes this winter, I'll try again in 1993. I'm glad I stayed in there."

Miller and Wiebe were brought together in the double by a coaching decision some six weeks before the 1993 world championships, although they had competed as teammates for years. Wiebe was a member of the first Canadian women's lightweight team in 1984, bronze medallists in the eight at the lightweight world championships. She was a national team veteran with a single sculls bronze medal from the 1992 world championships and bronze from the 1990 world event among her laurels.

"We got along right from the start," said Wiebe, who took up rowing like many other high school students who have the sport at their doorstep in St. Catharines.

"Colleen is one of the best racers I know and that really helped me because I'm really consistent and a good trainer, doing the workouts and going faster. But I never felt really confident as a racer until the last two years that I've been with Colleen. She is a real racer."

Wiebe conceded in early 1995 she would like nothing better than to keep the partnership going through to the 1996 Olympics. But with just the women's lightweight double to be contested in Atlanta, there are many talented Canadian women lightweight rowers who want a seat in the boat.

"We probably have the top four or five lightweight women in the world right in Canada, so it's going to be really hard," she said. "Canada has always had a strong lightweight women's team."

Coxswain

Lesley Thompson

I only put up a fight once," declared Lesley Thompson of rowing's tradition of crew members throwing the coxswain off the dock into the water after a victory.

"That was when Prince Philip was there at the Commonwealth Games. Most of the time you think: Yeah, well, I might get thrown in, but this just caught me by surprise. They just grabbed me when we'd won and I remember thinking: Oh, no, I don't want to do this. But it's a tradition based on the fact that they've listened to this little pipsqueak and have had to take orders and, finally, they get revenge in the end."

Lesley Thompson has been thrown into lakes and canals all around the world in a coxswain career that began in 1978. Back then she was an injured gymnast, hobbling about on crutches in the gym at University of Western Ontario. A friend of a friend who was involved in rowing noted Thompson's lithe frame and, commenting that she probably wouldn't have anything else to do for the rest of the season, asked if she might want to serve as a coxswain for the rowing team.

"I thought: I don't like being cold, I don't like being outside, I really don't like being wet and I'm not keen on the water, but okay," recalled Thompson. "I went out and had the very good fortune of stepping into a situation that had a lot of very good women training at the university."

Since 1978 Thompson has been an integral component of some of Canada's most memorable rowing successes. A high school math and English teacher, she joined the national team program in 1980 and was named to Canada's Olympic rowing teams in 1980, '84, '88 and '92. She was in the shell when the Canadian women's four took silver at the 1984 Olympics in Los Angeles and, two years later, was thrown off the dock when the four won the gold at the Commonwealth Games in Edinburgh. She also joined the Canadian women's eight crew in a world championship win in 1991 and Olympic victory in 1992.

Observers may note that the coxswain appears to do nothing but sit in the boat and watch the rowers row. Contrary to lore they do not pound a drum and yell "Stroke!" What they do is provide a myriad of services for the rowers, who then can put mind wholly to task.

"You act as a coach in the boat and as a liaison between coach and athlete, and the reverse," explained Thompson, who weighs in at just under 100 pounds (45 kilos) on a 5-foot-3-inch frame (160 cm). "The main function is to steer the boat and in an eight that is somewhat difficult. In a race we also implement the race strategy, the race plan is something developed between the coach, the athletes and the coxswain.

"You tell them where other crews are in the race, you can be motivating, and you also correct technical things."

Thompson is as committed to her fitness as the rowers are to theirs. She runs, she cycles and rows, aware that the lighter she is the easier it is for the rowers to have her in the boat. Training also produces a bond between herself and the athletes, who respect her for working to be the best she can be physically.

After so many events and so many races, is there one that stands out?

"The 1991 world championships," she said without hesitation. "When you win the Worlds for the first time, it's a goal you've been striving to attain for so long. We had never won before. We came into Vienna and just dominated the field in the small boats. Then we got into the big boat, which we'd only practised in about thirteen times.

"At one point we were so far behind. If I'd told them how far behind I think they'd have given up. It's not supposed to be physically possible to be that far behind and still win."

STROKE! Canadian women's eight in action: (from left) Kirsten Barnes, Brenda Taylor, Megan Delehanty, Shannon Crawford, Marnie McBean, Kay Worthington, Jessica Monroe, Kathleen Heddle, and coxswain Lesley Thompson.

Sailboarding

Caroll-Ann Alie

Caroll-Ann Alie of Gracefield, Quebec, spent many of her early years taking part in sport, ski racing in particular. So as an athlete and someone driven by an interest in physical fitness it was with some surprise that she discovered an activity she wasn't able to master almost immediately. That sport would become her passion, taking her to many exotic places and to the top of the world as a three-time world champion in a sport known by the general public as windsurfing or sailboarding.

"Every sport I'd picked up I'd been able to do, no problem," she said. "This one, I couldn't and I hated it because of that. I said I never want to do this sport again."

That was in 1978 when her sister received a sailboard as a gift and Alie was eager to try the new toy. Despite her initial frustration, Alie began to get the hang of manoeuvering what was essentially a basic board with a sail.

In 1980 Alie and her sister competed in the national championships. Again the experience proved challenging even though Alie was accustomed to competition as a promising ski racer in her youth and teen years.

"My sister knew a bit about sailing and about racing and I knew nothing. I didn't know there would be a gun and we had to start together. I didn't have a clue. By the second race I started to clue in quite quickly and eventually I finished sixth.

"I thought: Wow, I wasn't born to be a ski racing champion, maybe I can be a windsurfing champion. I think, from ski racing, I did know how to perform, to compete. A lot of those kinds of skills carry over from one sport to another."

Four years later Alie made good on the idea of being a windsurfing champion. At the windsurfer women's world championship in Perth, Australia, Alie surprised others, but not herself, by winning the world championship. When landing in Perth she felt an immediate affinity for the Western Australia city and a stirring in her heart that she was going to win the competition.

A year later, in Spain, that stirring returned but this time it was the confidence enjoyed by a twenty-five-year-old world champion. Alie won her second world championship on the Mistral board, one of several types of boards used in divisions of boardsailing.

Caroll-Ann Alie: Was hooked by challenge to master sailboard.

For a time, she turned professional. Although men's windsurfing was made part of the Olympic program in 1984, women's windsurfing, like many other women's sports, was later in coming into the Olympic fold. After 1985, with no suggestion that women's windsurfing would be included at the Olympics in the near future, certainly not for Seoul in 1988, Alie tried the professional route. There she had some success, although in the end she found it more expensive than worthwhile.

She returned to the amateur ranks and, in 1988, proceeded to win her third world title, taking the Mistral title at the International Yacht Racing Union (IYRU) world women's championships in Brazil. It couldn't get much better — she won every race and came home loaded with trophies given not only to the overall winner but also to the winner of each race.

"It was the performance of my life, for sure," she said. "I don't think I'll ever see that again."

Alie didn't have a chance to defend her laurels in 1989, after catching a virus that left her unable to compete for some time. In the interim, she spent time earning a master's degree in nutrition and exercise physiology from the University of Michigan. In 1990 she competed again in the IYRU world championship and finished eighteenth, improving the next year to win the Canadian, U.S. and North American championships, finishing eleventh in the IYRU Lechner women's world event to end the season ranked fourth in the world.

In 1992 women's sailboarding would finally make its Olympic debut with the Lechner designated the Olympic board for Barcelona. But Alie's Olympic aspirations sank quickly when she suffered a severe bout of food poisoning. The disappointment prompted her to continue on even though the Olympics initially seemed the perfect place to end her long career.

"I was hoping to do well at Barcelona but I got very sick," she said. "I didn't want to end it on that note, so I decided to continue a bit and see what happens."

By early 1995, with the Summer Games in Atlanta just eighteen months away, Alie's Olympic aspirations were renewed and intact. While trying to forge a career as a dietitian, she was also sailing better than she had in some time. At the Miami Olympic Classes International regatta in February 1995, Alie showed she was still among the best in the world, finishing third in the women's Mistral class behind France's Anne Francois and 1992 Olympic bronze medallist Doreen Devries. The effort earned Alie a spot on the Canadian team to the 1995 Pan-American Games in Argentina, where she was a gold medallist. At age thirty-four, a decade older than many of her competitors, she could see no reason to retire when her experience and continued fitness could only help her on the water.

"I grew up as an athlete," she explained. "I started snow skiing and racing when I was six years old and did it until I was sixteen. So I was always really fit. I always ran, I was always playing outside. I was also good about stretching and flexibility and I think I've built strong bones, strong muscles, strong tendons. At thirty-four I can see the benefits of working on fitness and proper nutrition."

Besides, in competing on Mistral, her favourite by far over the larger and more finicky Lechner board, she feels at home — a far cry from those first and frustrating awkward days in 1978.

"I have such a good feel on these boards, it's become an extension of my toes and my fingers. It's so easy, you're hooked in and you just ride."

Sailing

The 470 craft is a tricky vessel in that it is quick and agile but requires considerable skill and coordination on the part of the two sailing crew members. Canada has produced two women's crews who have gone on to become the best in the world at handling the 470.

Karen Johnson & Gail Johnson SAILING

Karen and Gail Johnson, sisters from Toronto, are light in weight but they became heavyweights in the 470 division both nationally and internationally. In 1984 they won every race at the Canadian women's championships and finished third at the International Yacht Racing Union women's world championship. A year later they finished second at the IYRU event after competing in the 470 world championships at Marina di Carrara, Italy. There, they finished fifth in the final race to land twenty-fourth overall of eighty boats and first in the women's division to become the official world champions in the 470 class for 1985.

"We gained a lot of respect there among all the sailors, not just the women sailors," said Karen Johnson. "That made it extra special."

The duo went on to win the 470 Class at the 1986 Goodwill Games and finished eleventh in the class at the Seoul

Karen & Gail Johnson: Sailing sisters gained respect with 1985 world championship.

Olympics. In a discipline where size counts, particularly in heavy winds and rough water, their small size was no advantage in the turbulent conditions in South Korea.

The sister duo went separate ways in 1989 but in the fall of 1994, with Gail having eventually followed her elder sister to Vancouver, they sailed together again as part of a five-member crew at the Canadian women's match racing championships, finishing second. In 1995 Karen Johnson served as team leader for the Canadian yachting team to the Pan-American Games in Argentina.

Judy Lugar & Morag McLean SAILING

Judy Lugar and Morag McLean of Halifax enjoyed their own success in the 470 even as sisters Karen and Gail Johnson were winning the gold medal at the 1986 Goodwill Games in the Soviet Union. A rivalry had begun to develop between the two crews, with both looking ahead to represent Canada at the 1988 Olympics in Seoul, where the 470 class for women would be contested for the first time.

The Halifax duo competed in the 1985 world women's championships in France and came in second to last, which Lugar would describe years later as "a most humbling experience." But a year later in Spain the duo's fortunes reversed dramatically for the world championships. Initially, they had trouble with their boat and lamented that the calm waters did not suit their ability. The day before the first race the wind came up, delighting Lugar and McLean and frustrating their rivals with difficult conditions that played to the Canadians' strengths. At the end of the competition they were the new world champions.

"We were just used to the breeze, and other people were wiping out," laughed Lugar. "At one point I asked Morag: 'Where is everybody? What's wrong with them? Maybe we are going the wrong way.'

"It was a pinch-me kind of competition, where things just go really well."

As fate would have it, the Johnson sisters earned the right to represent Canada at the 1988 Olympics and Lugar was chosen as team alternate. While other competitors lamented the tough, tricky conditions Lugar lamented that she and McLean weren't competing — the rougher the weather the better they sailed.

The duo retired from competition in 1991.

Judy Lugar & Morag McLean: Excelled in tough conditions.

Tine Moberg-Parker: Norway's loss was Canada's gain.

Tine Moberg-Parker

SAILING

Tine Moberg-Parker is a new name to watch in Canadian sailing although to Canadian competitors she is well-known. Married to a Canadian, she competed for her native Norway until 1992 when she gained her release from the Norwegian Sailing Federation in order to begin competing as a member of the Canadian sailing team in 1993. As a competitor for Norway she put herself among the best in the world as a Europe Class sailor, winning the overall World Cup title from 1990-92 and in 1991 winning the world title in Los Angeles.

In July 1994, competing in her first world championship as a Canadian team member, Tine Moberg-Parker took the silver medal, stamping herself as a contender for a medal at the 1996 Summer Olympics in Atlanta, Georgia.

Water Skiing

Pat Messner

WATER SKIING

The boat does all the work.

That, at least to the uninitiated, is how the sport of water skiing appears. Pat Messner is living proof of not only the successes that can be enjoyed in water skiing but also the physical toll the sport can take on a body. In early 1995 she underwent a hip replacement operation to remedy lingering effects from a fractured and dislocated hip suffered in 1972. Through the 1970s and into the '80s she would compete despite back problems and surgeries to repair dislocations in both shoulders.

"I guess I'm paying for it now," she said in 1995. "But even now, I wouldn't have changed anything. I had a goal right from the beginning."

Messner's goal from the first time she made a solo run at age five was to become the best in the world in a sport that receives little attention in Canada. She came by her prowess honestly, however, as her father had been a water skiing champion in Austria before emigrating to Ontario. Messner began swimming at age two and her ease in picking up the rudiments of dog paddle revealed an athletic ability that might have translated into success in other sports had she chosen to put her energy in other areas. But early on Messner discovered she also possessed a competitive streak, particularly where her two older brothers were concerned, and she did her best to not only try to beat them in water skiing, but to beat her father as well.

By age fourteen Messner was an Ontario provincial champion and a year later took bronze at the Canada Summer Games. Throughout her career she would win some fifteen national titles and forty-five Ontario titles, but her best years began in 1972. Water skiing was a demonstration sport at the 1972 Summer Olympics in Munich and eighteen-year-old Messner picked up a bronze medal in the slalom. Off that result she had to be considered a favourite for a medal at the 1973 world championships but injuries kept her off the water that year.

Fully recovered in 1975, she took the bronze medal at the world championships and, two years later, earned a silver in slalom at the 1977 world event in Italy.

"I almost stopped after I got that second," she said. "I guess I was frustrated, I figured I should have had first in that tournament. But then I found out the next world championships

Pat Messner: Has a complete set of world championship medals.

were going to be in Canada and I figured that was as good a place as any to try to win. That's why I stayed on."

Messner came into the 1979 world event in Toronto having won the prestigious U.S. Masters Invitational in slalom while picking up a bronze medal in tricks. Fully recovered from two shoulder operations, she weathered the pressure of being a hometown favourite and won the world slalom title.

"I used to dream about it. From a very young age, I'd have dreams about what it would be like to win a world championship," she mused. "The dream I had turned out to be exactly what it was like on the day."

Messner, as talented a musician as she was a water skier,

retired in 1981. As she noted years later, it was time to explore other things in life after spending so much time on the water.

"My initial goal was to become a world champion and once that was accomplished, with all I had given to get there, I thought: How much better would it be to get there more than once?" she explained. "It didn't seem logical to me. At that point I was twenty-five already, considered old by competitive standards."

She went on to work as a paramedic before the physical rigours of the job became too much for her body that had already endured much in the way of injury. In 1995 Messner was working as a teacher and looking forward to getting back on the water in a recreational way.

"No more tricks or jumps," she said. "This hip has to last me a long time. But I still want to get up there on one ski."

Kim de Macedo

Kim de Macedo: Came home from Singapore with a world championship.

There is a saying that notes as one door closes another door opens. Kim de Macedo thought the door had slammed shut in her face when she was left off Canada's team to the 1993 world water skiing championships in Singapore.

She went on to win the prestigious U.S. Open championship, the victory buoying what had been shaken confidence. Upon returning home to Shawnigan Lake on Vancouver Island, she received a phone call: One of the Canadian team members had been injured in training. Could she get on a plane as soon as possible?

Not only did she arrive in Singapore in time to compete, de Macedo won the world jump championship and finished sec-

ond overall in also leading the team to the gold medal.

"Winning the U.S. Open did a lot for my confidence," she said. "I felt bad about not making the team, I felt like a bit of a failure. It was a kind of roller coaster season because I'd had some really good results to that point and some really bad ones. Then I didn't make the team. Then I made the team. Then I won. I felt I should have been there anyway although it almost didn't happen."

Kim de Macedo's road to the world title in Singapore began at age three when she started skiing on Shawnigan Lake. Her father was a competitive water skier and de Macedo's earliest memories are of hanging around the dock and playing in the water.

"My mom said my brother and sister and I were all fearless, we'd just jump in off the end of the dock and we didn't care, we'd just float around," laughed de Macedo. "I grew up skiing from the time I was three years old, with my friends, with my Dad and his friends. By the time I was ten I was better than half of Dad's friends and he used to be so proud."

De Macedo went on at age eighteen to win the 1988 world junior championship in slalom while taking second in tricks and third in jumps. She harboured a desire to win the overall title more than any other. She came a step closer to that goal in 1994 by taking the overall title at the Pan-Am championships.

Her advice to anyone who thinks her sport is easy? Try it.

"If anything we're working against the boat. What people don't realize is we just don't stand up behind a boat. It takes a lot of strength and stamina, doing the tricks is hardly easy and in the jumps a mistake can mean injury."

De Macedo started her 1995 season by winning an event in Australia before travelling to Argentina where she would earn gold in team, silver medals in tricks and jumps and a bronze in slalom at the Pan-American Games.

As in many sports, competitors at the highest level make it look easy.

"You do get into a bit of a groove," conceded de Macedo. "You get into that zone now and again and it feels like all you have to do is stand there and everything works. That's usually at the end of the season after you've been skiing hard. But you're thinking on every trick, working on every buoy."

Judy McClintock & Susi Graham

WATER SKIING

Judy McClintock and Susi Graham have served as outstanding members of Canada's national water ski team. Their names are largely unknown because the sport is not as high profile in Canada as it is elsewhere.

In 1994 Graham rewrote her own world record in slalom in addition to winning the slalom event at the U.S. Open championship. A bronze medallist in slalom at the 1993 world championships in Singapore, Graham also won the world professional women's slalom title in 1993 and 1989.

Susi Graham: Slalom world record holder.

Judy McClintock Messer: National team veteran and 1985 world tricks champion.

McClintock won the tricks competition and finished second overall at the 1985 world championships. She maintained her outstanding ability through the birth of three children, finishing third overall at the 1991 and '93 world championships.

RIDING HIGH

Cycling

Women's cycling was not included in the Summer Olympic program until 1984, although women had for many years competed at the world championship level. Even so, the Olympic cycling program for women was limited, featuring just one event — the 80-kilometre road race won by American Connie Carpenter-Phinney. The 1988 Olympics expanded the program by one event, adding a women's sprint event on the track in addition to the road race. By 1992 the program had again expanded by one event, to include a women's road race and two track events, the sprint and pursuit.

Karen Strong

In 1977 a twenty-three-year-old cyclist from St. Catharines, Ontario, became the first Canadian in nearly eighty years to earn a medal at the world cycling championships. At San Cristobal, Venezuela, Strong out-finished Canadian teammate Sylvia Burka to take the bronze medal race in the women's pursuit after losing in the semi-finals to eventual silver medallist Ann Riemersma of the Netherlands.

In 1980 Strong returned to take a world championship silver medal in the 3,000-metre pursuit and eighth in the road race. Two years later she just missed a medal, finishing fourth again in the pursuit. She retired from competition in 1984 after a decade-long career as a competitive cyclist that saw her win more than 30 national titles. In 1989 Strong embarked on what would be a four-year career as coach of the Canadian women's road team.

Karen Strong: Became first Canadian cyclist to earn a world championship medal in nearly eighty years.

Kelly-Ann Way

The *maillot jaune*, the yellow jersey, is considered the symbol of excellence in cycling's road racing, a coveted prize celebrating the leader of the prestigious Tour de France road race. The women's Tour de France, more correctly known as the Tour de France Feminin, also awards the race leader with a yellow jersey at the end of each day and in 1989 Kelly-Ann Way of Windsor, Ontario, became the first Canadian woman to wear the coveted jersey. She would wind up finishing tenth overall in the event.

Way, who didn't make the Canadian Olympic team in 1984, had her first success at the women's tour that year by winning a stage of the gruelling event, also finishing fourteenth in the 3,000-metre individual pursuit at the world championships.

During her career Way would earn twelve national championship medals and a bronze medal in the pursuit at the Commonwealth Games in New Zealand. At the 1992 Olympics in Barcelona she was the only Canadian woman cyclist to compete on both road and track.

Kelly-Ann Way: Wore coveted yellow jersey.

Tanya Dubnicoff: Born to race.

Tanya Dubnicoff

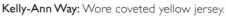

Confident. Enterprising. Self-motivated. Tanya Dubnicoff displayed early in life qualities that would make her a world champion.

"I was very energetic and outgoing," she said. "If I wanted something done, I did it. When I was four years old I took the training wheels off my bike. My Dad wasn't home to do it so I did it myself and away I went down the driveway."

There is no hiding, no opportunity to reconsider strategy, no second chance once a match sprint cycling race begins on the track. Often referred to in cliché terms as a game of cat and mouse, the event simply puts one rider against another on the banked oval in a test of speed and tactics. The initial stage of the event has both riders pedalling slowly around the track, one following the other, with the race suddenly erupting in a furious sprint. The element of surprise is paramount, yet to be left behind, to be caught unaware, is disastrous.

Winnipeg's Tanya Dubnicoff suits the event and the event suits Dubnicoff. Blunt and forthright in conversation, aggressive and unyielding on the bike, at age twenty-three she became the 1993 world match sprint champion, just five years after taking up the sport. The effort also made her the first Canadian woman to win a cycling world championship.

"I think I was born for this sport," she said when assessing the physical and mental traits necessary for success in her discipline. "It's a very individual sport, not like any other sport, and that's why I like it. You need a certain personality, a certain amount of physical ability, a great amount of mental ability to do well in this sport and I think I have all three of those areas covered to be one of the best."

Dubnicoff was born in Winnipeg and through her rise up the national and international cycling ranks she chose to reside and train there despite that city's long, and at times arduous, winters. Through her youth and early teens she competed on the BMX circuit, later playing baseball and ringette. As a general arts student at University of Manitoba she played centre for the Lady Bisons ice hockey team.

While her school interests leaned toward sport rather than academics, Dubnicoff conceded that even in high school she was more comfortable working out on her own.

"I never participated much in school sports," she conceded. "I did the odd year of volleyball, basketball and field hockey, I hung around the gym all the time but I never really did become part of any major team around the school. I did things outside of school."

One of those things turned out to be cycling, which she did as a matter of course as her mode of transportation to school or work, even after her competitive BMX days were long over. One day she phoned her local cycling association inquiring about how she might learn about racing and was invited to try a few training sessions.

"That was relatively easy," she said. "From there, we went on the velodrome and once I was on the track I was hooked."

Success came almost immediately. In 1990, after winning her first major race, the Winnipeg Grand Prix, twenty-year-old Dubnicoff took two silver medals at the Western Canada Games held in her home city, and a silver medal at the Coors Pro-Am Classic in Minneapolis. It was there that she had her first inkling she could be a force in the sport.

"I was racing against the 1988 Olympic gold medallist," she said. "I didn't win, but I was right there and I thought: Gee, this is pretty good, this is exciting. That drove me to train even harder the next year, and the year after that."

The next year saw Dubnicoff continue to improve after her promising Minneapolis finish. She took the sprint gold medal at the Pan-American Games in Cuba and, a year later, finished a credible sixth at the Summer Olympics in Barcelona.

But 1993 marked her year to take on the world. Dubnicoff finished first in the World Cup standings then travelled to Hamar, Norway, for the world championships. Defending world champion and Olympic bronze medallist Ingrid Haringa of the Netherlands advanced to the final, as did Dubnicoff. The Canadian rider took the world title from Haringa in two straight heats and was probably the least surprised of all that she was now world champion.

"I'd been in the sport for five years, to me that was a long time," she said of news reports that had her rocketing from complete unknown to champion virtually overnight.

"I think they were surprised that I'd won, but I did it. That's what it all comes down to, you put in the hard work and you're rewarded for it."

Hard work?

"Sometimes it's not the most fun thing in the world," stressed Dubnicoff, who once took to speeding laps in an underground parking garage when the Winnipeg winter was too hostile for outdoor training.

"It's all the sacrifice you put into it, that you have to do to be Number One. I miss weddings, birthdays, I'm away from home a lot. I miss a lot of things that I would like to do but sometimes that's the price you have to pay. No matter what you do, if you want to be president of a company, you have to make sacrifices to become Number One."

Being a world champion also brought its own brand of pressures and expectation. In Dubnicoff's case, her sterling 1993 year was followed by a consistent but at times frustrating 1994. She finished second overall in the World Cup but finished out of the medals at the world championships in Sicily. Yet she capped off the season with a memorable home country ride at the Commonwealth Games in Victoria, where she outclassed seventeen-year-old Australian Michelle Ferris in two straight heats in the best of three final to take the gold medal on a hot, August night in front of a decidedly partisan Canadian crowd.

In the spring of 1995 Dubnicoff continued her winning ways, taking the women's sprint gold medal at the Pan-American Games in Argentina. A vacation and fall respite from training allowed her to look back and assess her performance at the 1994 world championships:

"I was concentrating on too much negativity," she explained. "I went into the world championships thinking I'm defending world champion, I have to not lose, which is a no-no. You don't think you're not going to lose, you think of who your next competitor is, who your next victim is, whose butt you're going to kick next. That's what you should be thinking about."

No doubt it will be uppermost in Dubnicoff's mind leading up to 1996, as she assesses each rival she meets on the track, pondering the best moment for her to put power to pedal.

"Each race I do or finish is a bit more experience that makes me a better rider, so that, hopefully, I can be as good as gold."

Alison Sydor

Alison Sydor was able to laugh at the memory years later. At the time the situation was anything but funny. "I definitely had a bit of a career crisis at the 1990 Commonwealth Games," she said.

"On the track I was far back in anything I did. In the road race I came off the start line, I was pedalling, but it was so hard to move the bike. I was getting dropped just off the start line thinking: I know I'm nervous but I didn't know I was this nervous. Before we hit the first hill I was already about 200 metres behind. I looked back and saw my wheel rubbing against the frame. I got off and fixed it and by then everyone was gone. So I rode the whole race by myself, off the back.

"It was one of those absolutely, unexplainable situations.

I don't know why I kept riding. It was very humiliating — my mom was there, friends were there in Auckland and I'm thinking: Here I am, dead last. So I guess whatever was driving me then just kept me going."

Sydor kept going, all right. Humiliating as that experience was, she enjoyed the fruits of paying those difficult dues when, on September 17, 1994, she won the women's cross-country title at the world mountain bike championships in Vail, Colorado. The victory supported Sydor's tenure as one of the best cyclists in the world, on or off-road, and proved wrong all who disapproved years earlier when the Canadian rider opted to add the increasingly popular mountain bike circuit to her racing schedule.

At the time, North Vancouver's Sydor was seen as a maverick whose performance would surely be compromised by commitment to two different cycling disciplines. But there was common sense in her decision — mountain bike racing was a new, exciting sport with sponsors looking to become involved. Women's road cycling in Canada has not enjoyed the same opportunities as the men's event and, except for a brief two years when Team Kahlua Canada was an entity and Sydor one of the team members, Canada's female cyclists have had to depend on government funding, help from individual sponsors or regular jobs to finance their racing.

Sydor's decision to ride two disciplines proved positive almost immediately. In 1991 she led the prestigious Tour de l'Aude women's cycling stage race for a gruelling six days, then returned to Europe later that year to take the bronze medal in the women's road race at the world cycling championships. Off road, she surprised with a victory at a World Cup mountain bike race in Switzerland, later finishing fifth at the 1991 world mountain bike championships in Italy. Her exploits that year earned her Best All-Around Athlete laurels from *Velo-News*, the influential cycling magazine.

Sydor's success prompted more Canadian riders to try the off-road circuit, or interchange the two disciplines. For Sydor, the success was all part of a notion she developed as a young girl.

"My interest in sports and the outdoors really defined who I was, basically determining all the things that I did with my time whether it was at school or working for parks and recreation," said Sydor, who was born in Edmonton. "I always envied people who were professional athletes. What better job could you have than being a professional athlete? The Olympics were an actual dream when I started cycling but my ultimate dream was: Wouldn't it be the coolest thing to make your living from a sport?"

Cycling was just one of many activities Sydor took part

Alison Sydor: Made a name for herself on both road and trail.

in as she was growing up in Alberta. She worked in outdoor recreation camps from the age of thirteen, and through school she played basketball, volleyball and field hockey. A competent but not exceptional athlete in those sports, she came close to finding her athletic niche when she finished third, and top junior, in the 1986 Alberta triathlon championships. Sydor enjoyed the cycling component of the swim-bike-run event most of all, and after moving to Victoria to earn her biochemistry degree she joined a cycling club. She finished last in her first race, against male competitors, but then enjoyed success, winning three gold medals at the 1987 Western Canada Summer Games, finishing first overall in the Coors Cascade Classic road race in the United States and finishing second in the national team time trial and road race championships.

By the end of 1993 Sydor's performance confirmed she had done the right thing. Although tinged with some disappointment, including a twelfth-place finish at the 1992 Summer Olympic road race, her resumé showed that she had scored three World Cup mountain bike wins, eight stage wins in various international road events, a second in cross-country at the 1992 world mountain bike championships and third in the 1991 world road race championships.

The 1994 season saw Sydor still juggling two cycling disciplines, taking first place in a World Cup mountain bike race in Italy. After suffering subsequent disappointing results on the circuit she came home and worked on her road skills, winning the national road championship in

Edmonton then travelling with the national team to race the women's Tour de France before dropping out with a knee problem after eight stages. Tour officials were outraged when the Canadian entered a mountain bike race a few days later and finished second, saying Sydor feigned injury. Sydor responded that weeks of competing on the mountain bike circuit had left her with a fitness level different from her teammates who had many more road miles under their tires. To have competed further in the demanding stage race would have invited physical disaster just as the Victoria Commonwealth Games were approaching.

At the Games Sydor put her dismal 1990 performance in Auckland behind, taking a silver medal in the team time trial with teammates Lesley Tomlinson, Clara Hughes and Anne Samplonius and a bronze in the road race behind winner Kathy Watt of Australia and silver medallist Linda Jackson of Canada.

A month later, back on her mountain bike, Sydor won the 22.3-mile women's world cross-country race in Vail, defeating second-place rider Susan DeMattei of the United States by more than three minutes.

Sydor credits her success in both disciplines with being able to stay calm and assess opponents' weaknesses in pressure situations. Brute strength, while sometimes necessary, is not what wins races.

"Everybody has this perception that mountain bike is kamikaze but for me it is riding an edge," she continued.

"The uphill is a real physical part and the downhill, you're trying to get down as fast as you can but not losing all the time you gained going up, you want to be in one piece. It doesn't pay if you end up in the bushes. The idea is to ride on the edge of your abilities and not cross that edge. If you go over, it will catch up later. I'm more calculating, I'm not willing to crash, I value my skin."

That patient, calculating side to her personality is evident in another critical aspect of her sport — bike maintenance.

"I love to work on my bike, making it lighter, making it better. I spend a lot of time doing that in the winter. It does seem to be a fairly unique trait, not just with women racers but also with men, a lot of them take what they've got and go. I like my bike to be absolutely perfect, a little rattle will drive me crazy."

Alison Sydor ended her 1994 season on top of the world in Vail, Colorado, not exactly where she envisioned herself four years earlier when she was toiling behind the pack at the Commonwealth Games in Auckland. She continued her good form early in 1995, winning mountain bike gold at the Pan-American Games.

"All the hard work eventually pays off," she said. "You have to really believe that one day it will. I've seen many times that when something goes wrong, if you can deal with it and find a way to turn it around you'll reach something higher."

Equestrian

This unique sport combines the individual talents of two distinct athletes. While some might believe the rider is just along to watch the scenery, both horse and rider must be fit and be able to react quickly in whatever activity they are involved: from the grace and artistry of dressage to the endurance and bravery in cross-country to the timing and precision demanded in show jumping.

Gail Greenough

Gail Greenough conceded the situation was rather like seeing one's spouse getting cozy with another person.

"It was a little disconcerting," she said. "You spend a lot of time together, build up a bond. It's a bit like a marriage. Watching, on one hand you hope they have a rail down, and on the other hand you hope they don't."

Greenough was recalling her feelings watching three of the world's top show jump riders take her horse, Mr. T, over fences at the 1986 World Show Jumping Championships at Aachen, West Germany. On the last day of the event, July 13, the top four competitors took part in the championship final, riding a round on their own horses then switching mounts for a tough test of riding skill — taking the other three finalists' horses over the course, with horse and rider getting to know each other in a brief, three-minute warm-up over two fences.

The final four featured a dramatic cast that might have made an excellent script for a movie had *National Velvet* not cornered the market on equine-related films. Britain's Nick Skelton, the 1985 World Cup winner, and his horse, Raffles Apollo, were thought to have a slight edge over American Conrad Homfeld and Abdullah, 1984 Olympic silver medallists in the individual show jumping event and gold medallists in the team final. French veteran Pierre Durand, bronze medallist at the 1985 World Cup, and the great Jappeloup were a tremendous pair but slightly suspect because in similar competitions Durand had no trouble riding his own horse but had problems adjusting to competitors' mounts.

There was also Edmonton's Greenough, who had rallied from twenty-fourth on the first day of competition to ride Mr. T through two clear rounds the next day, advancing to fifth place. The top-twenty riders then took part in a qualifying round to determine the final four, with Greenough again perfect over the fences, with just one small time fault, to finish third behind Durand and Homfeld.

That the Canadian had even advanced that far was considered a surprise. At twenty-six she was riding against international veterans in the world event, including Canadian team captain Ian Millar and his venerable mount, Big Ben. The odds were also against her as no woman, and no Canadian, had ever made it to the final four in the quadrennial world championship.

Gail Greenough was born into a sports-minded Edmonton family on March 7, 1960, the youngest of three children and the only daughter. Athleticism and commitment were in her genes. Her father, Greg, played for the Regina Pats junior hockey team and her mother, Audrey, was an energetic volunteer worker for many city charities. Early in life Greenough was afflicted with that horse-crazy bug that seems to hit many young girls.

"I was just another one of those little girls who loved horses," said Greenough. "My girlfriend, Kim Kowaluk, and I used to jump cracks on the sidewalks with our bikes, pretending we were jumping on horses. My Dad was probably hoping to have an athlete in the family, maybe a hockey player. Then I came along and did something completely different."

She and Kowaluk spent every weekend riding rental horses. At age fourteen Greenough acquired her first horse

Mr. T and Gail Greenough: A formidable combination.

at an auction. She described the young, gray beast's lineage as "Heinz 57, a bit of everything." An inexperienced horse coupled with a young, relatively inexperienced owner proved difficult and the steed ended up making a career as a lead pony at the racetrack. Other mounts followed, included an Arab that died tragically in a fire. Greenough, who by her late teens was immersed in riding, also managed to study art at Foothills College in California and later enrolled at the University of Alberta.

Greenough met Mr. T in 1983 after purchasing another horse from Pinon Farms in New Mexico. The farm owner was National Basketball Association Phoenix Suns' owner Richard Bloch. Greenough came to realize that she and the new horse were not a good match and approached Bloch and American national team rider Robert Ridland, who was helping Bloch organize the business while riding some of his horses, about a switch. Ridland said there was one horse she might be interested in, a dark bay with an engaging white blaze, who had just come from Europe, although they weren't sure what he could do.

"The first thing I look at in a horse is the eye," explained Greenough. "Mr. T had a big, round, beautiful dark eye, but with a bit of a glint to it. Horses need a little mental toughness and you could see that in his eye instantly. I liked his body type, and conformation-wise he was built to jump.

"But horses are like people — sometimes you get along with them, sometimes you don't. They pick their people as much as we pick them."

By 1986 it was clear the two were a match made in equestrian heaven, having recorded two wins and a second in the Canadian team's three world championship qualifiers. But a twenty-first place at the World Cup in Sweden three months before the world championships indicated that perhaps the July world event would be good experience, but little more, for the young Canadian rider.

More than sixty thousand spectators, including Britain's Princess Anne, gathered to watch the world final four at Aachen's Reitstadion on July 13, 1986. By the end of the day 'perfect' would go along with the title 'world champion' earned by Greenough, who recorded clear rounds on all four horses to become the first woman, first Canadian and youngest rider to win the world title, and only the third competitor ever to record no faults in the final.

Roses rained down on the young Canadian, whose modest 5-foot 3-inch stature seemed dwarfed by some of the obstacles she had just cleared. The West German crowd appeared nearly as pleased by her victory as by one of their own.

"I had watched a lot of videos on the horses and tried to visualize what they would feel like and compare them to horses I had ridden previously, which worked very well," said Greenough. "You needed to do a lot of homework before you went on. I was lucky the horses did resemble some I had ridden in the past."

In one afternoon Greenough became a national and international celebrity, as did Mr. T, receiving floods of mail and requests for appearances. The duo later returned to West Germany, winning a Grand Prix in Stuttgart.

But reality became as sobering as their world championship win was intoxicating. A year after the victory Mr. T was beset with physical ailments, particularly recurrent hoof problems. In June 1991, just six weeks after announcing Mr. T was on a comeback after eighteen months in recovery from a stifle injury, Greenough announced that the fifteen-year-old gelding had been humanely destroyed after suffering an intestinal problem that caused him to lose 350 pounds.

"It was lymphosarcoma, cancer of the intestine," Greenough recalled. "It was the worst time, the worst thing that could happen. It was very sad."

After missing an attempt to make the Canadian Olympic team, Greenough sold her horses and retired from international competition in 1992. She travelled the world conducting clinics and promoting her video and the Gail Greenough saddle.

1988 Olympic Dressage Team

While Olympic officials were huddling over a positive drug test from a Canadian sprinter in what would unfold as the scandal of the 1988 Summer Olympics in Seoul, one of the most compelling and positive Canadian team stories from those Games was being played out.

On Sunday, September 25, 1988, the Canadian dressage team beat the odds and tradition by taking the bronze medal in the Olympic team dressage competition. In a sport dominated by German, Dutch, and other European riders, the Canadian team of Hamilton's Cindy Ishoy and her steed Dynasty, Eva-Maria Pracht of Cedar Valley, Ontario, and Emirage, Saskatoon's Gina Smith and Malte, and the Toronto duo of Ashley Nicoll and Reipo posted a mild upset in taking the bronze medal with 3,969 points behind gold medal winner West Germany (4,302) and Switzerland (4,164).

Going in to the Olympics, the Canadian dressage team was probably the strongest ever, even without venerable veteran Christilot Boylen, but as in other judged sports, sometimes the benefit of the doubt goes to the better known, more experienced team or individual and in dressage that often means a European squad. Ishoy, a World Cup silver medallist and fourth-place finisher at the 1987 world championships, led the foursome in summer qualifying for the Canadian Olympic team. Pracht edged out her own daughter for an Olympic berth. Smith brought experience from living and training in West Germany and Nicoll, at twenty-four, brought considerable ability despite her youth.

The bronze medal marked the first ever Olympic medal for a Canadian dressage team. Ishoy also finished fourth in the individual standings followed by Smith in twelfth and Nicoll sixteenth.

As the best three out of four scores were taken in the team competition, Pracht's effort was the one not counted for the Canadian team but hers was a particularly moving story. At age fifty-one she became the oldest woman to win an Olympic medal. Watching her on the podium were her daughter, Martina, and her father, Dr. Josef Neckermann,

Gina Smith: She and steed Malte travelled from Saskatchewan to Seoul.

Cindy Ishoy: Continued in international competition with Dakar, a half-brother to Dynasty.

who as a rider for West Germany was a member of his country's Olympic gold medal dressage teams in 1964 at Tokyo and in 1968 in Mexico City.

There was considerable celebration in Canadian equestrian circles, but a year later the Olympic postscript for Ishoy turned to tragedy. The future looked promising for Ishoy and her brilliant beast, Dynasty, for the 1989 World Cup, but in the summer of 1989 Dynasty died following a severe bout of the equine bellyache known as colic.

By 1990 Ishoy had found another steed and a suitable successor to Dynasty — his half-brother, Dakar. The duo finished eleventh at the 1992 World Cup and Ishoy repre-

sented Canada at the 1992 Barcelona Olympics, finishing tenth in the team competition which included Martina Pracht, riding for Canada on her mother's Olympic bronze medal horse, Emirage.

A year later, Ishoy and the more experienced Dakar returned to international competition, taking the Grand Prix at the prestigious annual dressage event at Devon, Pennsylvania. In 1994 the duo again dominated the event, sweeping the freestyle and Grand Prix while fueling Canada to a second place finish. Earlier in the year they contributed to Canada's tenth place team dressage finish at the World Equestrian Games in the Netherlands.

Eva-Marie Pracht: Carried on a family tradition of excellence in Seoul.

Ashley Nicoll: Finished 16th in Seoul astride Reipo to help Canada gain bronze medal.

Christilot Boylen

Christilot Boylen and dressage go together like hockey and Wayne Gretzky. The latter may be much better known to Canadians but Boylen has been a dressage pioneer in Canada ever since she competed in her first Olympics at Tokyo at age seventeen astride her horse, Bonheur. They finished twenty-first while the only other Canadians entered, Inez Fischer-Credo and steed Gordina, finished eighteenth.

Born April 12, 1947, in Java, Indonesia, Boylen has led an intriguing life that includes acting work as a youngster on CBC television, a side career as an author, being a mother of two children and, of course, an international reputation as Canada's top dressage rider. Since her Olympic debut in Tokyo, Boylen, who moved to Germany in 1987 after living for years just outside Toronto, has six Olympics to her resumé, her best finish being seventh in the individual competition at the 1976 Olympics in Montreal. She has been named to seven Canadian Olympic teams, missing out on the 1980 Games in Moscow when Canada boycotted the event.

Her resumé also includes five gold, a silver and a bronze medal in Pan-American Games competition. Equestrian events are often highly competitive at these Games because of the military equestrian tradition in Mexico and several South American countries.

Boylen's one major missing laurel is an Olympic medal. In 1988 she was not part of the Canadian team that took bronze in Seoul because her top horse at the time, Epernay, had been sold and her other horse, Leonardo, was owned by Austrian interests and a Canadian Olympic team horse must be Canadian owned. In 1992 she returned to the Ol-

Christilot Boylen: From Java to Germany, she remains Canada's most experienced dressage rider.

ympic fray on her nine-year-old chestnut gelding, Biraldo, finishing twelfth in the individual dressage competition.

Three-Day Event Team

It was, by many accounts, one of the biggest upsets registered by an international Canadian team. Most Canadians never heard about it even though the team's victory received considerable play in Europe.

The three-day event is the horse world's triathlon, with horse and rider expected to compete in three distinctly different disciplines. Dressage is equine gymnastics, with horse and rider working together to perform an intricate set of moves that are both precise and beautiful. The next day the dignity of dressage gives way to the gruelling cross coun-

try and steeplechase, where courage and stamina of both horse and rider are tested over roads and tracks in addition to negotiating a cross-country and steeplechase course. On day three the horse and rider combinations who successfully make it through the previous day's rigours, and the mandatory morning vet check, advance to the final leg of the competition — show jumping.

In September 1978, the Canadian three-day event team survived searing heat and three days of international competition to win the world three-day event team championship at the Kentucky Horse Park in Lexington, Kentucky. As news reports of the time would tell, the Canadian squad of Liz Ashton from Orangeville, Ontario, Juliet Graham Bishop of Calgary, Saskatoon's Cathy Wedge and Mark Ishoy of Woodbridge, Ontario, were unsure just how they would fare as the team had been beset by injuries to their equine partners prior to the event. Ashton eventually had to loan Wedge her second-string horse, fifteen-year-old Abracadabra, when both Wedge's steeds came up lame. It was expected the British, American and West German riders would battle for supremacy.

Ranked fifth after the dressage, the Canadian team was the only squad to record all members finishing the second day cross-country and steeplechase. The difficult, second-day conditions eliminated some of the world's top horse and rider combinations while the Canadian horses appeared fittest and best able to handle the heat. At the end of the day Canada's strong cross-country performance put the squad in the lead and the foursome clinched the world championship the next day, finishing the stadium jumping with 436.6 points. The West Germans were second, one hundred points behind, followed by the Americans.

Ishoy registered the top Canadian performance, finishing eighth overall aboard Law and Order with Juliet Graham Bishop and her horse, Sumatra, ninth. Ashton and her

Liz Ashton & Sunrise: Helped Canadian three-day event team make a considerable splash at the world championships.

mount, Sunrise, were eleventh and Wedge and Abracadabra, a former show jumper, placed twenty-third.

Horse Racing

Thoroughbred racing has long been called the Sport of Kings because it has been a favourite of royalty and the very rich and only those with sufficient funds were able to participate. In addition there was, and in some quarters still is, a notion that only men could serve as jockeys because only they possessed the required strength to control a thousand-pound beast running at full speed. Anyone who watched legendary jockey Bill Shoemaker quietly and softly urge a mount to the finish line knows brute strength is just one aspect to the game, and since the 1960s women have slowly entered the North American jockey ranks, although they are still grossly outnumbered.

Valerie Thompson

HORSE RACING

In 1980 a ninety-seven-pound dynamo from Port Colborne, Ontario, made Canadian racing history by winning the fall meet at Greenwood racetrack en route to becoming Canada's top apprentice, or rookie, jockey with 89 victories gained that year.

The feat earned the jockey a Sovereign Award for top apprentice rider of 1980. The Sovereign Awards are Canada's highest honour in horse racing and are awarded annually to the best trainers, riders and racehorses in the land. The 1980 award for the country's best apprentice was

Valerie Thompson: Canada's top apprentice jockey in 1980.

unique in that it marked the first time a woman jockey received the honour. If you'd told Valerie Thompson five years earlier she would be honoured in such a way she'd have said you were crazy.

"I had nothing to do with horses. I was a hockey-crazed little girl," she laughed. "I was a goaltender and I just lived for hockey. I played with the boys but with all that gear on no one knew I was a little girl. Then, a town next to Port Colborne was having a little girls' team start up so I joined that. Then, after a year or so I also started playing with the guys again. You know how you go to an arena, there would be open skate time where people would rent the ice. They'd see me in my equipment and say: Hey, we need someone to shoot pucks at."

Thompson's athletic youth was otherwise unremarkable in that she took part in the usual neighbourhood ball games and showed some talent as a sprinter before her small stature was no match for the long-striding bodies of her still-growing peers. She discovered the racetrack by accident. At age sixteen a double date to the beach became a double date to Woodbine racetrack and diminutive Thompson was taken immediately with the excitement of racing.

She gained a job "walking hots" for trainer Frank Passero and eventually worked her way into exercise riding. She earned her first victory in her third race in May 1980, aboard Big Gypsy.

"He had a habit of getting out on the turn, towards the quarter pole. For some reason he just wanted no part of the race," she said of Big Gypsy. "And he'd just bolt to the outside fence. Well, we were on the lead with this other horse, head to head, I got halfway around the turn and my horse started to bolt. I took a bigger hold of him but this horse was going wider and wider, I was not quite in the middle of the track but I was way out there. All these horses started passing me so I gave him his head and let him bolt. Boy, did he fly, on the outside fence!"

Thompson was not afraid to take chances or be aggressive but at times crossed that fine line, earning suspensions on three occasions that year. But it takes a special breed of individual to sit atop a powerful thoroughbred running at some thirty miles per hour. Possessing the nerve to find the strategic holes in the pack is as important as being able to think quickly in a dangerous situation. Sometimes the scenario is one and the same.

One of Thompson's most memorable rides in her apprentice year came aboard Northern Mystic on the turf at Woodbine. The pre-race instructions were simple. The horse, a "massive animal," had to make a move from off the pace.

"When this horse wants to run you'd better have a place for him to go or he's going to run right over the top of the other horses," she recalled.

The race initially set up as it should, with Thompson and Northern Mystic trailing the field with tiring horses, who had gone out too fast, slowing down directly in front. Thompson debated her next move — to wait a few seconds longer or start moving Northern Mystic around the pack.

"It was too late, he took hold of the bit and said the show is on. But I was stuck, nowhere to go, and this horse was rolling. I remembered the guy who taught me how to ride, Jackie Robinson, he said when you're waiting for a hole to open don't make any noise, just sit there. So I was very quiet.

"Where the horses cross the dirt there's a little space where the hedge stops and I ducked through. Robin Platts was there on No Connection but I squeezed through. We won by half a length."

Thompson, a hard worker who did not mind putting in the seven-day work weeks to hone her craft, did not enjoy the same success that seemed to come so easily in 1980 and, understandably, her confidence at times wavered. After two more years of riding in Ontario, she travelled to the United States, riding at various tracks in several states. She suffered a bad spill in Virginia in 1987, shattering an arm and breaking six ribs and a foot. She returned home to recuperate and, perhaps more annoying than the convalescence was realizing that her arm would heal but would likely never withstand the force of a puck hitting it. Sadly, she realized she would not play goaltender again.

Thompson went on to settle in New Hampshire, where she galloped horses at Rockingham Park. In the winter of 1995, she was making the trek to Boston's Suffolk Downs to gallop horses, having decided to take a break from race riding in 1993. Two years later she still craved the exhilaration that comes in riding a winner.

"It's a tough sport for anybody, no matter who you are, a man or a woman," she said when asked if she might have had an easier time in her career had she been a man. "It's dog eat dog, it's business. People at the top have to work even harder to stay there. It's a very tough business, no business for the weak at all. In how many sports are you chased by an ambulance?"

Dance Smartly

If only she could talk.

If she could, it is a tossup how Dance Smartly might answer a reporter's query as to her most memorable moment as an equine athlete. Was it when she showed her heels to the best colts in the land and ran away with the prestigious Queen's Plate? Or maybe it was when she took on a strong international field of runners, including 1990 Breeders' Cup Juvenile winner Fly So Free and Grade 1 winner Jackie Wackie, to win the Molson Million?

Perhaps, in an afternoon gossip session in the broodmare pasture, she will regale her stablemates with memories of Churchill Downs in Kentucky, where under the shadow of the venerable twin spires she became the first Canadian horse to win a Breeders' Cup race en route to becoming the richest female racehorse of all time.

Dance Smartly was born April 5, 1988, to the mare Classy N Smart, herself a former Canadian champion three-year-old filly. Her sire, Danzig, had already proven himself as an outstanding sire of runners as had his sire, the great Northern Dancer. Clearly her pedigree stamped Dance Smartly as a runner on paper for owner-breeder Ernie Samuel and Sam-Son Farms. But in racing, a fancy piece of paper isn't worth much if there isn't talent and heart to go with it.

Dance Smartly made her racing debut on July 7, 1990, at Woodbine, defeating a group of non-winners by an easy 3 1/2 lengths. She stepped up into allowance company and again won comfortably. She finished second in her next start, a stakes race, then returned to win her division of the Natalma Stakes, her first start on grass.

Dance Smartly and Sam-Son stablemate Wilderness Song were then sent to Belmont Park to race in the Breeders' Cup Juvenile Fillies, where they dueled for much of the 1 1/16-mile race before they were overhauled by unbeaten Meadow Star and Private Treasure. Her third-place finish at Belmont Park secured Dance Smartly the Canadian two-year-old filly championship for 1990.

It was in 1991 that Dance Smartly blossomed into one of the top racehorses of her time and one of the best ever

foaled in Canada. Her coronation began on July 7, 1991, when she romped over a field of nine rivals, include runner up and stablemate Wilderness Song, in the 11/4-mile Queen's Plate at Woodbine.

"She's a lovely filly," enthused owner Samuel after her outstanding Queen's Plate win. "You won't find a filly with a better disposition than she has. I know fillies are supposed to be temperamental but nothing bothers her."

Three weeks later Dance Smartly won the second jewel in the Canadian Triple Crown, taking the Prince of Wales Stakes by a handy two lengths as the overwhelming favourite.

On August 18, 1991, she became the first filly to sweep the Canadian Triple Crown, dominating her male rivals to win the 1 1/2 mile Breeders' Stakes on the turf at Woodbine by eight lengths. When a top international field came calling a month later in the Molson Million, she again bettered the boys by taking command at the head of the stretch to win the 1 1/8-mile test by two lengths.

Those accomplishments alone might have been enough to clinch Canadian horse-of-the-year honours for the talented daughter of Danzig but the world was waiting at Churchill Downs for the 1991 Breeders' Cup. Owner Samuel and trainer Jim Day, a member of Canada's 1968 gold medal show jumping team at the Summer Olympics in Mexico City, considered entering the talented filly against the boys in the $3 million Breeders' Cup Classic but opted finally to pit her against the best distaff (female) runners of the day in the $1 million Breeders' Cup Distaff.

She didn't disappoint. Jockey Pat Day kept her just behind the leaders then urged her to the lead as the field entered the stretch. She cocked her head briefly toward the grandstand as she cruised to the wire, with Versailles Treaty and rider Angel Cordero making a brave but unsuccessful bid behind. At the wire Dance Smartly was 1 1/2 lengths ahead, and on top of the world. Her Breeder's Cup winnings propelled her past the great Lady's Secret into the world's all-time leading money-winning filly or mare.

Dance Smartly: Retired as the richest female racehorse of all time.

"Magic, it's magic," was all Samuel could say. "She is just a wonderful filly, she is very special."

Dance Smartly went on to be named Canada's Horse of the Year for 1991 and was also honoured with an Eclipse Award as the top filly in North America for that year.

Dance Smartly was retired in 1992 when ankle problems did not allow her to race back to her 1991 form. She retired as the richest Canadian bred and female racehorse of all time with earnings of $3,263,835.

TRACK, FIELD & MORE

Track Field & More

Some of Canada's most glorious track and field moments were never witnessed by average Canadians. Had television been invented by then, Canadians could have watched the heroics emanating from the 1928 Summer Olympics in Amsterdam and the 1932 Games in Los Angeles, and they would have witnessed two of the most successful Games for Canada in track and field. Women took part in athletics for the first time in 1928 and the Canadian team of Ethel Smith, Florence Bell, Myrtle Cook, Bobbie Rosenfeld, Jean Thompson and Ethel Catherwood were a small but dominant force in the limited track and field events for women at the time.

Ethel Catherwood
TRACK & FIELD

E thel Catherwood was called "The Saskatoon Lily" but she was no shrinking violet in the high jump. Indeed, through 1992 in Barcelona she remained the only Canadian woman to win an individual gold medal at the Summer Olympics. She burst onto the international scene in 1926 by setting a world record leap of 1.586 metres (5 feet, 2 7/16 inches). Broken by a South African jumper in 1927, Catherwood reclaimed the world mark in 1928 with a 1.6-metre leap although prior to the Olympics that mark would be rewritten to 1.61 by Dutch jumper Carolina Gusolf.

At the 1928 Olympics in Amsterdam much ado was made about Catherwood's tall and graceful beauty. She won the high jump with a leap of 1.59 metres and upon returning home was feted in both Toronto and Saskatoon. Her high jump career appeared to end shortly thereafter when she and her sister moved to the United States.

Ethel Catherwood: Remains the only Canadian woman to win an individual gold medal in Olympic track and field competition.

Bobbie Rosenfeld
TRACK & FIELD

B obbie Rosenfeld was born in Russia but came to Canada with her family while she was still a baby. Her given name was Fanny but she was known throughout her career in several sports as Bobbie. As early as 1921 she was Canada's top-ranked female sprinter and by 1925 she was listed as Number One over 220 yards, and in long jump, shot put, and discus.

On July 31, 1928, she became the first Canadian woman to win an Olympic track and field medal, taking silver while teammate Ethel Smith earned bronze in the 100-metre final. The race was won by American Elizabeth Robinson and at the finish the competitors appeared to hit the line all together, making for a difficult judge's decision. Myrtle Cook, who came into the Olympics as Canada's No.1-ranked sprinter over 60 and 100 yards, had also been favoured to take a medal but was disqualified from the 100-metre final after posting two false starts.

Rosenfeld returned on August 2 to run the 800 metres

with teammate Jean Thompson. Accounts of the time relate she was in the race more to spur on Thompson than with a chance for a medal herself as she hadn't trained for the distance. At the time, the distance sparked controversy in some quarters because many people believed 800 metres was too long a distance to be run safely by women. At the end, Thompson finished fourth in the race, followed by Rosenfeld in fifth. Several women did collapse in exhaustion after the race and, although men often did the same thing at the end of their races, there was such a commotion following the 1928 women's race that the 800 metres was not included in the Olympic program again until 1960 in Rome.

Rosenfeld returned to the track to contribute to Canada's victory in the 4x100-metre relay. With her ability in throwing and jumping events it must be wondered how she might have fared if a pentathlon or heptathlon competition had been available at the time.

But Rosenfeld made her mark in more than just track and field. She was inducted into the Canadian Sports Hall of Fame not just for her achievements in track and field but as an all-around athlete who excelled in many disciplines. She was an excellent tennis player, winning the Toronto Grass Court championship; she played ice hockey and often noted it was her favourite sport; she played basketball and was a key player on several Ontario championship teams; she also made her mark as one of the country's top softball players. In 1949 Rosenfeld was named Canada's woman athlete of the half century.

Arthritis began to bother Rosenfeld in 1929 and a few years later she was forced to give up competitive sports. She became a sportswriter in Toronto and continued the job through 1966 when poor health forced her to retire. She died on November 14, 1969.

Bobbie Rosenfeld: Canada's woman athlete of the half century.

Myrtle Cook: Anchored the Canadian team to a world record and gold medal at the 1928 Olympics.

Myrtle Cook

Myrtle Cook rebounded from her disappointing disqualification in the 100 metres to anchor the Canadian women's 4x100-metre relay team to a gold medal in a world record

48.4 seconds. She went on to set world records over 60 and 100 yards through 1929 and 1930. Like Rosenfeld, she went on to become a sportswriter and also excelled in other sports, particularly tennis. In her early days of sportswriting she noted that a young sprinter from Montreal — Hilda Strike — would emerge as Canada's next top sprinter, and the next Olympics proved her right.

The 1932 Olympic Track & Field Team

Team Spirit: Canadian women's team to the 1932 Olympics in Los Angeles: (from left) Lillian Palmer, Aileen Meagher, Mary Vanderbilt, Betty Taylor, Alda Wilson, Hilda Strike, Mary Frizzell, Mildred Frizzell.

The 1932 Olympics in Los Angeles saw Canadian women earn three medals in track and field, and one of them was Montreal's Hilda Strike, who took the silver medal in the 100 metres. She posted the same time, 11.9 seconds, as Poland's Stanislawa Walasiewicz, more commonly known in America as Stella Walsh, but judges deemed the Polish runner had won by a half stride.

Strike also anchored the Canadian women's 4x100-metre relay of teammates Mildred Frizzell, Lillian Palmer and Mary Frizzell. Canada led up to the final baton pass but miscommunication between Mary Frizzell and Strike made for a slow exchange and at the wire the Americans won by one-tenth of a second in 46.9 seconds, erasing the world record set four years earlier by the Canadian women's Olympic relay team.

Canada's Eva Dawes went on to earn a bronze medal in women's high jump in what was an exciting battle between two Americans for the gold medal. Jean Shiley and venerable Mildred (Babe) Didrikson tied for the gold in a world record 1.657 metres.

FROM 1936 TO 1984 CANADIAN WOMEN relay runners would achieve most of the country's success in Olympic track and field. While Betty Taylor would take a bronze medal in hurdles at the 1936 Games in Berlin, it would be forty-eight years before another Canadian woman would earn an individual track and field medal at the Olympics.

In 1984 Canada accumulated two relay medals in addition to the bronze medal earned by Lynn Williams in the 3,000 metres. Angela Bailey, who would go on to hold the Canadian 100-metre record, teenager France Gareau, Marita Payne and Angella Taylor took the silver medal behind the Americans in the 4x100-metre event. In the 4x400-metre relay Charmaine Crooks, Marita Payne, Molly Killingbeck and Jillian Richardson finished second, also behind the Americans.

Charmaine Crooks

Charmaine Crooks laughed when reminded she was named to her first Olympic team in 1980. In 1996 she hopes to be named to her fifth Olympic team when Canada competes at the XXVI Olympics in Atlanta, Georgia.

"It seems so long ago, and yet it seems like yesterday," she said in early 1995. "I can't believe I've been doing this sport at a high level for almost sixteen years. It just blows my mind. But time flies when you're having fun. It's amazing, some of the changes I've seen through those years, just in the whole philosophy of sport, the people, even entire countries have changed."

It is considered an achievement for any athlete to compete in five Olympic Games. In track and field the statistic is particularly impressive as it remains the most competitive and widely participated-in sport in the Olympics. As a competitor, Crooks has made her name in two events — the physically and technically difficult 400 metres and the 800 metres.

Born in Jamaica and one of nine children, Crooks moved to Canada with her family when she was six years old. She started competing at age ten and in 1979, at age seventeen, was national junior champion over 400 metres and silver medallist over 200 metres in addition to winning the national 400-metre championship.

"I'm not that coordinated, I have trouble hitting a golf ball," she laughed. "When I was younger I always wanted to be a ballerina — that's SO funny! I was always calling up ballet schools. But it was expensive and in a family of nine kids you can't do everything. So running was an easy thing, and I liked it. My legs were just as long when I was 10 years old as they are now."

Although named to the 1980 Canadian Olympic team at age eighteen, Crooks and other Canadian athletes did not compete at the Moscow event, which Canada boycotted. Two years later, competing for University of Texas-El Paso while studying psychology, she finished second in the 400 at the NCAA (National Collegiate Athletic Association) championships and a year later won the one-lap event at the Pan-American Games in record time.

At the 1984 Olympics in Los Angeles she finished seventh in the 400 metres in personal best time and was part of the Canadian team to earn a silver medal in the 4x400-metre relay.

"It takes years of preparation for that one moment," she decided years later. "What I remember most was when they put the medal around my neck. I remember the stadium,

Charmaine Crooks: National record holder and first Canadian woman to run 800 metres in under two minutes.

the excitement, but sharing it with your teammates is a highlight. It's not just yourself, it's four people."

Crooks was not content with just developing herself as an athlete. In addition to earning her psychology degree she worked as a model and singer. After leaving the Toronto area for Vancouver in 1989, she supported herself first by selling photocopiers, then by working in television and public relations.

In 1989, under the guidance of national middle distance coach Dr. Doug Clement, Crooks worked to extend her speed in the highly competitive and tactical 800 metres. Less than a year later she was the first Canadian woman to run 800 metres in under two minutes with her 1:58.52 remaining a national record through 1994.

"The 800 is a very physical race," she explained. "Sometimes I'll finish and I've got bloody legs after being hit by spikes. There is chaos, people elbowing. Middle distance running can be a contact sport."

Through her athletic and professional commitments Crooks also finds time to fulfill what is a dedicated social conscience. In late 1994 she was named to the board of directors of the Canadian Centre for Drug-Free Sport while also serving as a motivational speaker for several programs.

After missing the 1993 season due to injury Crooks returned at age thirty-two to take a silver medal in the 1994

Commonwealth Games 800 metres. At the time she was asked if she pondered retirement but with the 1995 world track and field championships and 1996 Olympics looming, she was looking forward to running her best yet.

"Why retire, especially after a year when you've had an injury, and when you're just getting back into it," she said. "I always planned on staying through 1996. I was named to the 1980 Olympic team. This is my drive for five."

Diane Jones Konihowski

Diane Jones Konihowski: Weathered the pressure of home country favourite at 1978 Commonwealth Games.

The crowd was getting restless.

Some eight thousand spectators had gathered outside Edmonton's Commonwealth Stadium, waiting to be admitted to the August 6, 1978, afternoon session of track and field for the XI Commonwealth Games. Fifteen minutes after they should have been settled in their seats the gates remained locked, while folks who had morning session tickets were enjoying a long stint for their money.

The confusion came because on the field one of the most memorable days in Canadian track and field history was

unfolding. Edmonton's Diane Jones Konihowski was leading the pentathlon. The morning session, which was to have ended at the conclusion of the pentathlon high jump, had extended into the afternoon as Konihowski was enjoying an outstanding time over the bar, eventually leaping a Games record and personal best 1.88 metres.

Hours later the ticket holders' indignation was replaced by glee and goodwill that swept the stadium and the entire country. Konihowski won the five-event pentathlon with a Games record 4,768 points, earning her the world's Number One ranking for 1978. She won four of the five disciplines and took second in the final event, the 800 metres, finishing a commanding 546 points ahead of silver medallist Susan Mapstone of England.

"It was in my new city, my new home — we had just moved to Edmonton the year before," she remembered. "It was great — the sky was blue, the sun was shining, the Queen gave me my gold medal. The script was written and everything went smoothly, there were no hitches. The whole day was perfect."

Pentathlon must have been created especially for Diane Jones, who as a youngster growing up in Saskatchewan became immersed in as many activities as possible. A love of sport combined with a need for variety made the five-event pentathlon, which has since given way to the seven-event heptathlon, an ideal challenge.

"I always wanted to do a lot of things," she laughed. "I wasn't a very good spectator. I couldn't watch, I had to be doing things. It wasn't unusual for me to go to a track meet and enter eleven events. In the long run I think it made me a better athlete.

"Multi-event athletes are a different breed. They have to keep their level of motivation going, whereas if you run, say, 100 metres, it's over in about eleven seconds. In multi-events the focus has to be there all day, you have to have the ability to put a bad performance behind you and get on immediately with the next; or take a really good performance and control your enthusiasm in order to stay focused for the next event."

Born in 1951, Diane Jones joined her first track club in 1964 and by 1967 was named to Canada's junior national team. She trained in Saskatoon with coach Lyle Sanderson, devoting time to track and field but also developing tremendous skill as a volleyball player. She would play the sport through much of her years at University of Saskatchewan, her need for variety and challenge extending beyond the rigours of training for the five pentathlon events — 100-metre hurdles, shot put, high jump, long jump and 200 (later changed to 800) metres.

A promising athletic career was put on hold in 1971 when Jones reached a personal crossroads. To her surprise and chagrin, she wasn't named to the 1971 team to the Pan-American Games. She was frustrated, gained weight, and began to look "more like a shot putter." With some advice and support from John Konihowski, with whom she had developed a friendship at the 1969 Canada Games, she made some decisions.

"I dropped the weight, got serious and from there I never looked back, I didn't quit," she said. "It was good for me, not making that team. You need those reality jolts to tell you it isn't so easy. If you want to go to the Olympics you'd better do something about it. John helped me through it, he was with me every step of the way."

A year later Jones was at the Olympics in Munich, finishing a credible tenth. Jones came away from the 1972 Games knowing she must improve, but believing that the women who had won medals there could be beaten if she worked hard enough.

A year later at the World University Games she earned a bronze medal. At the 1974 Commonwealth Games in Christchurch she was expected to give 1972 Olympic gold medallist Mary Peters of Great Britain a battle for the gold. But two months before the games, still playing volleyball, Jones severely injured her left ankle. She arrived in New Zealand having done little hurdling or high jump training since the previous summer. She finished eighth.

She recovered, taking gold at the 1975 Pan-American Games while being touted as a medal threat for the 1976 Olympics in Montreal. The pre-Olympic process proved to be another learning experience. She moved to California to train but interrupted her regimen to make frequent trips to Canada to promote the Olympics.

"I was so unfocused, I had given so much to promote the Games that by the time I got to Montreal, well, I knew it was trouble," she said. "I felt horrible, I thought: I'm not prepared for this. The edge was taken off me, I wasn't mean."

There was a wistfulness to her voice when she talked about the Montreal Games: "During the competition, I knew I could have won a medal, it was up for grabs." Indeed, after four of the five events only seventy points separated the top seven competitors, with Jones fourth. But the 200 metres decided the gold medal winner and in the end it was East German Siegrun Siegl first with 4,745 points and Jones sixth at 4,582.

Knowing the Commonwealth Games would be held in Edmonton two years later, Jones vowed to focus all her effort on the competition.

"I came sixth in Montreal, very respectable, but I knew deep down I could have won a medal. I learned from that, so I was a more controlled person going into 1978. I gave of myself, but in a smarter way. I made sure I was prepared."

In 1977 she married John Konihowski, who by then was making his athletic career as a player for the Canadian Football League's Edmonton Eskimos. They moved to Edmonton, and she quickly became one of the most sought-after 1978 Commonwealth Games athletes. She was Canada's top pentathlete whose marriage to a professional athlete, wholesome public image and status as one of the best in her sport garnered much media attention.

Despite the tremendous pressure, Diane Jones Konihowski didn't disappoint, winning the event with a record performance and receiving the gold medal from Queen Elizabeth in front of family and a hometown crowd. It was a day that seemed scripted by fate, it was so perfect. Perhaps the only frustrating sidebar to the day was that her total, 4,768 points, would have won her the gold medal two years earlier in Montreal.

In 1980, when form indicated she probably would have stood on the Olympic podium, Diane Jones Konihowski was among the Canadian medal hopefuls forced to miss the Olympics when Canada boycotted the Games in Moscow. Four years later she pondered competing in Los Angeles, boycotted by the Eastern Bloc, then decided against it, effectively putting an end to her career.

Although her victory in Edmonton proved to inspire an entire nation, Diane Jones Konihowski's athletic career spanned an important and sensitive time in sport for women. Always willing and happy to speak with the media, her capable and commanding presence made her a powerful role model to young women discovering the joys and lessons of sport.

"I just did what I wanted to do," she explained. "And I feel my two daughters can do anything they want to do in the world of sports if they have the passion, the desire and are willing to discipline themselves. At that time, I felt that way, too — and nobody ever told me otherwise."

Ljiljana Ljubisic

Every time Ljiljana Ljubisic steps into the throwing circle at a track and field meet she wages a tremendous battle — not necessarily against other rivals, for she is quick to note that she focuses mightily on her performance rather than on what others are doing.

There is a more fierce confrontation. Every time Ljubisic competes she fights her instinct for survival, knowing she must somehow ignore the warnings and cautions that scream through her mind and body.

"In most sports you've got to be fast, quick, explosive, moving forward," she explained. "If I make a quick move I whack my shins on the coffee table, if I drop my keys and bend down I can split my forehead on the side of a table. I have a million reinforcements every single day to not move fast. Then, I go into a circle and I have to move quickly, be explosive, move forward. The inhibition in the mind holds you back, that programming is so heavy. That is a constant battle."

Ljubisic is completely blind, having lost her dwindling sight in 1990 after a series of corneal transplants proved unsuccessful. Born December 17, 1960, she began to lose her vision at eighteen months when her family was living in Yugoslavia and she was given improper medication for an illness.

Since 1984 Ljubisic has been one of Canada's premier disabled athletes, first as a Paralympic Games silver medallist and World Cup champion on the Canadian goalball (team handball for the visually impaired) team. Her accomplishments in sport were worlds away from the life Ljubisic endured as a visually impaired teenager growing up in the suburbs near Vancouver. Her eyes were highly sensitive to light and her peers not always sensitive to her plight. In reminiscing about those days shortly after her world championship victory in 1994, Ljubisic was blunt in her assessment of the time.

"There were a lot of difficult times," she said, describing unseen feet that would trip her, or unseen hands that would shove her down stairs.

"I had dark glasses, I read my book with my nose. I was 5-foot-10 in Grade 8, a skinny beanpole kid with tears always running down, eyes swollen and red. On a sunny or cloudy day you've got an umbrella and a baseball cap and dark glasses and your hand is still up there trying to shield your eyes. It doesn't take much more than that to be the class geek."

Tall and with the genetic predisposition to athleticism — her mother was a world-class rower and her father a basketball and water polo player — Ljubisic yearned inwardly to take part in sport but, except for a brief dabbling in school track and field, she worked instead to "build a brick wall around me as thick as Fort Knox, to protect myself from everybody and everything."

University proved a different story. Her classmates accepted her visual impairment and Ljubisic's confidence soared as she gained a social life along with her psychology studies. In 1983 a friend encouraged her to play goalball. She discovered she was not only athletic, but competitive. After earning a silver medal as a member of the Canadian goalball team to the 1984 Paralympics, she took up throwing and by 1986 earned her first international medal, a bronze in discus at the 1986 world track and field championships for disabled athletes.

At the 1988 Paralympic Games in Seoul, South Korea, Ljubisic took a bronze in the shot put, even as her sight deteriorated despite surgery. Two years later she earned her first world championship in her class in discus, and a bronze medal in the shot put at the

Ljiljana Ljubisic: Found her niche in sport and went on to set world records.

world championships in the Netherlands.

After five corneal transplants, she also lost her remaining sight.

"It was truly the one time I felt I had lost hope," she said. "It was such a scary, falling-down-a-bottomless-pit kind of feeling. Once I got home I didn't know what colour my pants were. You know the layout of the house but if you take a one degree sharper turn you wrap yourself around the banister."

Ljubisic persevered, enjoying one of the finest times in her life in 1992 when she set a world record in discus by more than two metres en route to winning a gold medal at the Paralympic Games in Barcelona, also taking silver in shot put. She pondered retirement, but came back in 1993, exceeding her previous world record by another two metres for a 35.14-metre effort, also setting a shot put world mark of 11.18 metres.

In 1994, Berlin offered new challenges. Recovering from back problems suffered in a May car accident and adjusting to a change in coaches, Ljubisic had just two meets under her feet when she went to Germany for the world championships. Her B1, or completely blind, category had been eliminated and she was competing against partially sighted competitors in the B2 class.

In shot put she took the silver medal behind world record holder Jodi Willis of Australia. In discus, Ljubisic was bothered by an unexplained delay that resulted in her not gaining a complete warm-up. Her practice efforts were dismal and as she prepared to compete she attempted to regain the feeling she enjoyed in training sessions where she knew she was throwing well.

"I don't know what happened," she shrugged. "I just concentrated on what I had to do, focused on the process and not on the outcome and my first throw just flew. As my coach talked me out of the circle I asked how I'd thrown and she said 32.33 metres, a really good start. Then thirty seconds later they're announcing a world record of 35.88."

Ljubisic plans to compete through the 1996 Paralympics in Atlanta, Georgia, when she will be nearly thirty-six years old. Through sports and competition she has attained experiences she never thought possible when she was that "little grey mouse who tried to become invisible" in high school. Yet her accomplishment is tinged with some regret she didn't take up discus and shot put earlier. She ponders what levels she might have attained with youth and technique.

But there is also immense satisfaction in making the difficult decision not to retire after the 1992 Paralympics.

"I'm a far more mature athlete than in Barcelona," she said. "I've grown up. When I walk into a competition now my heart rate isn't at 250 beats a minute. I certainly have butterflies but now they're flying in formation instead of in chaos."

Through the years Ljubisic has become known as much for her athletic ability as for her willingness to speak strongly on issues related to disabled athletes and women in sport. By her own admission she is "honest, sometimes tactless," with an affinity for that proverbial bull in a china shop.

There is passion when she talks about her sport, losing her sight and not being able to see a world record throw. She knows she is the best in the world, even if she can't see it.

"To see that little red flag out there and see the discus land beyond it, what a thrill that would be," she mused. "You can throw a lousy throw and you can throw a wonderful throw and they can feel the same. Sometimes I wish I knew how far it was, to see how far it was. That's what turned me on to discus. I could still see. I threw the discus, not very well, but I saw the sun glinting off the metal. I saw this shiny thing flying farther away. I loved the feeling, the sight of it, the feeling of finesse and flight."

Debbie Brill

Debbie Brill clasped her long legs at the shins, resting her chin on bent knees while in her mind she returned to her early days as an athlete.

"In my first international meet I was fifteen years old, this skinny stick girl, jumping backwards. Nobody had seen me before. It was in Stockholm and they laughed their faces off. I was so shy, I was in tears. I came last and jumped terribly. I didn't ever think I could be comfortable in that situation."

For much of her two-decade career as a high jumper Brill never did become quite comfortable, or happy, with certain aspects of her athletic status. The media attention, public adoration, expectation and politics that have become an integral part of international sport worked at odds with all the things she loved about sport — the challenge and, most of all, the sheer joy of leaping cleanly over a high bar.

"For me, it wasn't just high jumping to win medals," she explained. "It was always much more. It was the kind of freedom you get, a sense of freedom of movement and expression. You have to move smoothly, in one piece, and have all parts working together. So when you put it all together it's an extraordinary feeling, the most wonderful feeling."

Debbie Brill: Her Brill Bend changed the high jump forever.

It was a feeling Debbie Brill discovered early in life. Born in Mission, B.C., on March 10, 1953, one of five children, she tried her first high jump at age nine in a sand pit in South Otter school in Aldergrove. By 1967 she had developed an unorthodox style of getting over the bar — running up to it then twisting through take-off so that her head, then arched back and legs, flipped over the barrier.

Brill's style was decidedly odd but the technique, combined with her athletic talent and suitably tall, lean build, resulted in quick success. By 1968 she was competing internationally for Canada utilizing her Brill Bend, just as American Dick Fosbury was surprising crowds with his backbend jump, the Fosbury Flop. Indeed, Fosbury won the high jump gold medal at the 1968 Olympics and is often credited with introducing the new technique. But it is clear Brill was equally responsible for changing the sport of high jumping forever.

"I realize now just how exceptionally talented I was in high jumping," she reflected. "I walked into a void. There was nobody in North America jumping more than 5' 9" when I started and that was so low. I just flew right by it. I didn't even realize it, but within three years of jumping I was already in the top few of the world, even though I didn't know what that meant."

At age seventeen, by then under the tutelage of coach Lionel Pugh, Brill won the women's high jump at the 1970 Commonwealth Games with a leap of 1.78 metres (5 feet 10 inches), receiving the gold medal from Queen Elizabeth. Earlier that year she had cleared 1.83 metres, or six

feet. In 1971 she took the gold medal at the Pan-American Games in Colombia and great things were being expected of her for the 1972 Olympics in Munich. Clearly, while the joy of jumping was still there, the attention, adulation and expectation was starting to get to Brill, who also by then had begun to try some of the popular hallucinatory drugs making the rounds of her generation at the time. Later, she would candidly admit to their use, enhancing what was becoming a public image of her as a "black sheep," causing some folk to condemn her for not living up to the squeaky clean image they had expected, even created, of her.

"People said they wanted their daughters to be like me and I'd think: You're crazy, you don't know anything about me. Why would you suspend your judgement because I can jump high? It is a terrible thing for people to do, and at the same time I felt I had to live up to those things. I had a continual war, and the rebellious side tended to be the side that said no way. It was a rebellion against what I was being cast as."

The 1972 Olympics in Munich proved a turning point for Brill, who finished eighth after contemplating dropping out when terrorists killed a group of Israeli athletes. She was disillusioned with the politics and excess of the Olympics, which had initially been created with a much different, more hopeful, and encouraging spirit in mind.

She disappeared from competition, working as a waitress, travelling, doing whatever made her happy. But Brill returned to competition in 1975, earning a spot on the 1976 Olympic team. Going into Montreal she was touted as a medal prospect, but she never made it to the final, failing to advance from the qualifying round after three misses at 5 feet 8 inches.

Choke. Unfocused. Unprepared. Uncommitted. Erratic. Too much pot. The labels and accusations rained down on Brill like a West Coast squall and she deflected them like a sturdy raincoat. At times her performance was inconsistent but in the years following she would continue to compete as one of the best: third at the 1977 World Cup, gold medallist at the 1978 Commonwealth Games, first at the 1979 World Cup and first, with a Canadian record 1.97 (6 feet 51/2 inches), at the 1980 Olympic Alternative competition held in Switzerland after Canada boycotted the Moscow Olympics. Ironically, the Olympic gold medal was awarded in Moscow to Italian Sara Simeoni, whose winning jump of 1.97 was an Olympic record.

Brill concedes the embarrassing debacle in Montreal might have caused some athletes to quit. When asked why she didn't, she explained what many people had already come to know that within her was a resolve and a strength to do her will and no one else's, even if they might not agree with her decision. At the time, the only person who could make Debbie Brill quit was Debbie Brill, despite laughing fans in Stockholm, or Montreal.

"Many athletes I competed with didn't make it because they couldn't get through fear — fear of being in front of large crowds, fear of losing," she said. "I had, from the time I can remember, an ability to withdraw and move into this strong-willed, centred place inside and just stay there."

When she held a news conference in 1981 most people thought it was to discuss her retirement. Instead, she told reporters she was pregnant. There were no plans to marry the father. Her son was born in the late summer of 1981.

Debbie Brill would then enjoy one of the finest moments in her athletic career. Surprisingly thin, with just 125 pounds clinging to her tall frame, she leaped a world indoor record 1.99 metres on January 24, 1982, less than five months after the birth of her son. Tired, indeed exhausted from setting an American indoor record of 1.96

metres in Los Angeles the night before, she marvelled at the hidden well of strength. She went on to win the Commonwealth Games gold medal in Brisbane. Her baby travelled with her to Brisbane.

In retrospect, Brill believes she competed too soon after pregnancy. She would suffer several problems in the ensuing years, particularly Achilles tendon woes and back problems. She finished fifth at the 1984 Los Angeles Olympics but by 1988, when she enrolled in psychology courses at Simon Fraser University, she quietly said goodbye to her competitive career.

Coaching, studying, marriage, and raising three children have filled her days, but in February 1995 Brill made a quiet comeback just short of her forty-second birthday. At the U.S. Masters indoor track and field championship she shattered the world women's master (over age 35) high jump record. She leaped 1.72 metres before a slight injury forced her to stop, and noted that the experience was the most fun she'd had in sport in some time.

Lynn Williams

Once women's track and field became a part of the 1928 Olympic program it took several decades for officials to approve what is now a far more extensive, but still incomplete, array of events for women. After several women competitors collapsed after the 800 metres in Amsterdam, women did not have the opportunity to run the two-lap event again until the 1960 Games in Rome. The 1,500-metre race finally opened to women at Munich in 1972. Women had more options again in 1984 when the 3,000 metres and marathon were included in the program for the XXIII Summer Olympics in Los Angeles. For the record, American Joan Benoit won the first women's Olympic marathon. But it was the 3,000 metres that captured the attention of the world because it brought together two of the best woman distance runners of the time in Mary Decker Slaney and Zola Budd. It also served to introduce a Canadian runner who was relatively unknown until that day, August 10, 1984 — Lynn Williams.

THERE WERE THREE LAPS remaining but Lynn Williams lost her concentration for an instant.

"I remember hearing the crowd booing, it was deafening," she recalled. "I remember thinking: Wait, this is the Olympic final, what's happening here?"

What had happened seconds before, initially sent the

Lynn Williams: Former competitive swimmer found her niche on the track as a middle distance runner.

crowd of eighty-five thousand spectators at Los Angeles Coliseum into stunned silence. On the side of the track lay American favourite Mary Decker Slaney. On the track, Zola Budd was running like a scared rabbit, her bare feet and legs bloodied by track spikes. With just over three laps remaining in the women's 3,000-metre Olympic final, spectators who had expected a battle between Budd and Slaney for the gold medal witnessed instead a human traffic jam. Budd and Slaney were out in front, stalked by Britain's Wendy Sly and Romania's Maricica Puica. Slaney attempted to pass Budd on the inside. They bumped, then bumped again. Suddenly their legs tangled and in an instant Slaney fell to the infield.

"I was maybe two steps back. We were doubled up in all the lanes," continued Williams. "It all happened so fast, it happened before anybody really knew it. After it happened a lot of us still expected her (Slaney) to eventually come up beside us again."

When Canada's Williams lined up that day for the women's 3,000-metre final she thought she had a good chance at a medal even though to observers outside Canada she was just one of the bodies in the group expected to be led by Budd and Slaney, with Puica and Sly touted as strong challengers. But three months earlier Williams had, at least in her own mind and that of coach Thelma Wright, arrived in the international big time when in a training race she smashed her personal 3,000-metre best by 11 seconds and recorded a most respectable 8 minutes, 42 seconds for the distance.

At age twenty-four Lynn Williams had for some time demonstrated talent and considerable potential but injury had stalled her just when she looked ready to unleash a breakthrough performance. She came into Los Angeles with a bronze medal from the 1983 World University Games and a tenth-place finish in the 3,000 metres behind winner Slaney at the first world track and field championships, held in 1983 at Helsinki.

Born July 11, 1960, in Regina, Saskatchewan, Lynn Kanuka honed her athletic skills as a competitive swimmer before quitting at age fourteen. She took up jogging for fitness and was recruited for her school's cross country team. In her first meet she defeated experienced athletes who belonged to a track club. She went on to compete provincially, then nationally.

"I liked doing sports but I always had another side to me, I was the one on the team bus knitting stuff," she mused. "I was the social coordinator in high school. I was never an executive type but I loved organizing the dances and always had an active social life. I felt this need to be well-rounded."

Brief university stints in Regina and Saskatoon followed high school until she realized a year-round training climate was what she needed to realize her running potential. She applied to many American institutions and was offered a scholarship to San Diego State University. She met national distance runner Paul Williams and in a relationship made in athletics heaven, the two married and settled in Vancouver.

"San Diego was where things took off for me, but I was injured every summer," said Williams, the reigning Canadian champion over 3,000 metres going into Los Angeles. "I never did much on the Canadian scene during that time."

After August 10, 1984, the entire country knew her name. Williams finished second, just behind Slaney, in the Olympic semi-final and secretly felt she had a medal chance. Meantime, the media was focusing on Slaney and Budd. Slaney came in as a double gold medallist from the 1983 world championships. The only laurel missing was Olympic gold. Budd, a quiet teenager from South Africa, ran barefoot. Her country was banned from the Olympic program because of its apartheid policy but, because her grandfather was British, Budd was allowed to change her citizenship and compete for Great Britain. The seventeen-year-old came into the Olympics as the unofficial world record holder in the 5,000 metres (the mark was made when she was a South African citizen), having broken Slaney's world mark by some seven seconds. Theirs was to be a battle for supremacy.

But with 1,300 metres remaining in the race, Slaney lay sprawled on the infield while Budd, confused and upset by the incident and subsequent crowd uproar, took the lead. She could not hold off Sly and eventual gold medallist Puica. In the end, she finished seventh. Meanwhile, Williams was running the race of her young career.

"After the incident everyone lost their focus and Zola took the lead," she said. "I remember passing one person and, feeling pretty good, I thought I could catch the next one. I looked ahead and saw Zola was fading. I thought: 'If she starts to die I only have to get in front of Cindy Bremser and I'll have a medal.'"

Williams edged American Bremser for the bronze medal, finishing in 8:42.14. She was met by Diane Clement, the Canadian team manager and a former Olympic sprinter.

"I remember Diane hanging on to me saying: 'Do you realize what you've done? There hasn't been a Canadian woman to win a track and field medal for decades!'"

Anyone who thought Williams' achievement was a fluke would think otherwise in successive years. In 1985 she finished third on the Grand Prix circuit while rewriting national records over 1,500, 3,000 and 5,000 metres — despite a stress fracture problem that kept her running in the pool and cycling that spring as part of a rehabilitation program. She also won several important road races.

In 1986 her laurels included victory in the 3,000 metres at the Commonwealth Games. By then, her face was familiar to many Canadians as was the determined and powerful presence she exuded as a runner despite being just 5 feet tall and weighing 105 pounds.

"I feel like I'm some kind of Dr. Jekyll and Mr. Hyde. It's very weird," she laughed. "There's 90 per cent of me that is this laid back, homebody, non-competitive person. And that's where I've surprised myself. Every once in a while I'd see myself running on TV or in a photograph and I'd think: 'Is that me?'"

Williams' ability to focus on a task was illustrated superbly at the 1988 Olympics in Seoul where the Canadian team was mired in the fallout of the Ben Johnson steroid scandal. She finished fifth in the 1,500 metres and eighth over 3,000 metres. Both she and Paul pondered retirement after the Seoul debacle, but in 1989 she was back, finishing third at the world cross country championships in Norway. Elite runners will tell you the event is the toughest race in the world and, despite all her other laurels, Williams relished that race the most.

"It was a glorious, sunny day," she said. "I remember feeling fantastic while I was racing."

A stress fracture kept Williams out of the 1990 Commonwealth Games in Auckland. In 1991, suffering another injury and weary of the recovery process, Lynn Williams retired, possessing still the 1,500- and 3,000-metre national records she set in 1985 and, of course, the Olympic bronze medal.

Angela Chalmers

TRACK & FIELD

In June 1978 the fourth annual Manitoba high school provincial B track meet was highlighted by three outstanding performances from an unknown runner who had recently moved from British Columbia.

The fourteen-year-old surprised observers by shattering the junior girls' 1,500-metre record of 5 minutes, 10.7 seconds, winning the race in 4:57.1. A day later she set records en route to winning the 400 and 800 metres.

Some sixteen years later few people at Centennial Stadium in Victoria didn't know her name. As host country favourite and defending Commonwealth Games champion in the 3,000 metres, all eyes were on thirty-year-old Angela Chalmers as she swept past Kenyan pacesetters, Jelagat Cheruiyot and Eunice Sagero, just 1,000 metres into the race. She ran the rest of the race alone, engulfed in the din of stamping feet that followed her sure strides around the oval. Chalmers crossed the finish line in a Canadian and Commonwealth Games record 8 minutes, 32.17 seconds, 13 seconds ahead of Canadian teammate and race runner-up Robyn Meagher.

The victory marked the latest in many laurels that had come Chalmers' way since she dominated the junior girls' field in Shilo, Manitoba, so many years before. The win also marked a high point in an athletic journey that had taken Chalmers to high and low places in her own heart.

"I'm pretty sure I started competing at age nine, but it gets to be like ancient history," Chalmers laughed in the fall of 1994.

"I had always been running, I was always trying to race somebody. I ran to school. I ran home. I remember being

Angela Chalmers: Thrills hometown crowd in Victoria with runaway victory in the 3,000 metres at the 1994 Commonwealth Games at Centennial Stadium.

picked to compete at the B.C. elementary championships in Richmond and I had to pick three events, so I picked high jump, the 400 and the 1,500 metres. I bombed in the high jump, was third in the 400 and first in the 1,500. I still have those medals."

Angela Chalmers was born in Brandon, Manitoba, but called many places home as her parents were posted to various Armed Forces bases. For several years the family lived in Nanaimo on Vancouver Island and it was there Chalmers remembers acquiring a zest for running and competition. Being one of nine children meant having to work hard to stand out in the outside games and round-the-block relay races. Her seven brothers all played hockey and keeping up with them, and at times beating them, helped sow the competitive seed that would later blossom in international venues around the world.

Following her unheralded success as a Manitoba high school junior Chalmers was named to the national junior team. At age sixteen she dropped out of the sport for a time, not so much because of pressure, although she conceded that with her early success pressure was present, but because she had reached a time in life when struggles with her parents for power and independence were paramount. As for most teens, that combative time in life passed and by age seventeen Chalmers was once again national junior champion.

"I learned it was a way of identifying myself within my family and getting attention from parents," recalled Chalmers of her athletic success as a teenager. "It was my identity, but too much at one time, too much to bear. I had big fallings out with my father when I was in my teens and a lot of it was related to that. I had to learn and grow as a runner."

Chalmers' father died in 1984 and for several years after, during her stint as a dietetics student and runner at Northern Arizona University and as a Canadian national team athlete, she struggled with his death and the sudden end of an important relationship in her life. The one thing that remained constant was her running and she enjoyed gradual improvement — earning a bronze medal in the 3,000 metres at the 1985 World University Games and silver at the same distance at the 1987 Pan-American Games.

Like many members of Canada's 1988 Olympic team, Chalmers' enthusiasm was drained by the Ben Johnson steroid scandal in Seoul, where she finished fourteenth in the 3,000 metres and seventeenth over 1,500 metres. The next year she suffered from anemia and spent much of her time attempting to regain her strength.

So it was that Chalmers, then twenty-six and relatively unknown, earned a spot on the Canadian team to the 1990 Commonwealth Games in Auckland. In less than a week she was the talk of the Games, winning the 3,000 and 1,500 metres and defeating, among others, British stars Yvonne Murray and Liz McColgan. After years of competent results but relative obscurity, Angela Chalmers had arrived at a point she had always seemed destined to meet.

"Wynn (coach Wynn Gmitroski) says I inherited all the right things from my mother and all the right things from my father — I'm put together to run," she decided years later. "I know, just looking at my body, it's not made for looking like a glamour queen or a gymnast. This is a runner. When I run, when I'm really healthy, nothing compares."

Later in 1990 Chalmers went on to win her second national 1,500-metre title but the year ended with as much difficulty as it had begun with success. Chalmers came down with mononucleosis and her marriage broke down. She moved to Victoria and quietly began to rebuild her life and her health. By 1992 Chalmers was back, winning the 1,500 metres and finishing second over 3,000 at the Canadian Olympic trials. Then, on a brilliant, humid August night in Barcelona, Chalmers brought it all together, outracing Ireland's Sonia O'Sullivan for the bronze medal in the women's 3,000-metre final to become one of just a handful of Canadian women athletes to win an individual Olympic medal in track and field.

In the cramped, sweltering post-race interview area a tearful Chalmers dedicated the medal to her deceased father, declaring "I wanted to prove to him I could do it." A day later Chalmers came down with a cold and lost a chance for a possible medal performance in the 1,500 metres, but she had secured her status as one of the top women middle distance runners in the world. After Barcelona she appeared to have put many of her personal demons behind her and embarked on a new path that not only had her enjoying athletics as never before, but also dedicated to enjoying life and exploring her Sioux heritage, which she gained from her mother.

"In Barcelona there was a lot wrapped up with my father," she said in the summer of 1994. "Now, I have to let that go and I have to find different reasons to run. It's more of a mission to try and run faster than I ever have before. I'm at a point in my career where I'm learning about myself and about my potential, mentally and physically."

Chalmers finished the 1994 season ranked third in the world over 3,000 metres. She conceded she has taken her running to a new dimension, exploring her abilities with confidence and desire she once thought impossible.

"I feel more relaxed and able to enjoy my sport because

I'm tuning in to what is most important," she said.

"What is most important for me now is knowing that I am happy. I used to go along, thinking that when I get from A to B there will be something else in my life to make me happy, looking for the future while trying to live in the present. Now, if there's a good moment in the day I try to stop myself and say: 'Angela, this is a great thing happening right now, let's absorb it a bit.'"

Chantal Petitclerc

Ontario's Hilda May Torok Binns was the first Canadian woman wheelchair athlete to excel in international competition, winning gold in swimming and track and field at the 1968 Stoke Mandeville Games in Tel Aviv. Since that time athletic opportunities have burgeoned for athletes with disabilities.

Where Binns started, other athletes followed and Canada continues to be an international leader in both women's and men's disabled sport, including track and field.

"EVEN WHEN I WAS a kid I had a vision of doing something, and I don't think that changed. Maybe I'm doing some-thing different from what I would have done. But I had a very positive attitude before my accident and that's why I could take it so well."

Chantal Petitclerc was twelve years old when a heavy barn door fell on her, breaking her back and causing spinal cord injury that would leave her a paraplegic. A decade later she would be regarded as one of the top athletes in her field — wheelchair racing — and as someone with considerable ability, rather than by the moniker "disabled."

"I was just a normal kid," she said in 1995 shortly after finishing fifth in the wheelchair division of the Los Angeles marathon. "I was always playing outside but I wasn't committed to one sport. I liked sports, but no more or less than any other kid."

Her athleticism emerged after the accident. Because Petitclerc couldn't take part in many of the physical education class programs, her school's physical education teacher, Gaston Jacques, offered to help her swim at the local pool three days a week over lunch hour. For five years the duo worked together in the pool with the teacher learning as much as his pupil about what was possible.

The lessons not only helped Petitclerc regain physical strength but they also did wonders for her confidence.

"My phys ed teacher was very athletic himself and he was a very good model for me,"

Chantal Petitclerc: Wheelchair racing is pure sport.

recalled Petitclerc. "He really believed in what I could do. He didn't have a clue about how I should swim, being in a wheelchair. But he tried stuff and that was very important to me, learning and trying to do something again. During that time I also learned the discipline of training."

After high school Petitclerc advanced in 1987 to the CEGEP at Ste-Foy, Quebec, and found the local pool times didn't always jibe with her classes. She took up weight training and a coach there suggested she try working with some wheelchair athletes in Quebec City. In 1988 she competed in her first race, the Nabob Challenge in Sherbrooke, and won.

"They decided to send me to Edmonton for the Canadian nationals and I ended up finishing second," she said. "That was very good for me. Once you do that you start thinking: If I can do that after eight months of training, I can do a lot more next year.

"I also think I made a good impression. Everybody was saying how natural my technique was and that I had good potential. So right away I started wondering how good I could be."

By 1990, at age twenty, Petitclerc found she could be among the best in the world, finishing second in the 800 metres and marathon and fifth in the 1,500 metres at the World Games for the Physically Disabled in the Netherlands. A year later, at the 1991 World Track and Field championships in Tokyo where able-bodied athletes such as Carl Lewis and Mike Powell achieved celebrated world records, Petitclerc was among the group of wheelchair athletes invited to compete. She finished third in the 800 metres. A year later, at the Paralympic Games in Barcelona, she took home bronze medals from the 200 and the 800 metres.

Still improving, she went on to the first world athletic championships for athletes with a disability, held in 1994 in Berlin. There, she won gold in the 200 and the 400 metres and finished third in the 800.

In savoring the memory of that achievement Petitclerc noted not only her improvement but that of others involved in her sport. When she first began there was a smattering of outstanding individuals in international competition. She has seen the fields becoming bigger and more competitive.

"I don't consider wheelchair racing a handicapped or disabled sport," she said. "I consider it a pure sport. I see the chair as a bike. I think really the sport belongs to the Olympic movement. In Canada, anyone can do wheelchair racing. If you want to buy a chair, you just buy one. It's just a sport you do in a racing chair."

In 1994 Petiticlerc completed a stint at the University of Alberta in Edmonton, where she studied history. She moved back to Quebec and, in addition to training, began work as an announcer for lottery television broadcasts. Since 1991 she has trained with coach Peter Eriksson and plans to compete through the year 2000.

"The reason I don't stop is that I have the feeling I haven't reached my goal," she declared. "It's a question of seeing how far I can go. To me, it's more than sport. It's a way to test and exceed my limits. Trying to achieve a goal is a long process of learning about yourself. A race is a race, but you also learn about who you are."

Linda Hamilton

At age forty-four, Linda Hamilton thought about retiring once the Berlin 1994 world championships for athletes with a disability were over.

She finished fourth by an eyelash in the 100 and the 200 metres and fifth in the 400 metres. No medals, but sometimes gold, silver and bronze mean little in the overall scheme.

"I did a personal best time in two of my events, the 200 and the 400, so I was just thrilled," she recounted. "I was going to retire but it was so positive, a great meet. I gave everything I had and was so close I thought I've got to come back and give this another shot. My times are better than they were in '88 and I'm faster now than I ever was."

Hamilton, of St. Catharines, Ontario, was a competent and competitive age-class road runner prior to an accident that changed her life in February 1984. She was hit by a car while cycling. A week after her accident, despite some paralysis, many broken bones and leg amputation, she began her journey back to fitness by attempting to lift a half-pound intravenous bag over her head. In June, an amputee and in a regular wheelchair, she took part in her first road race since the accident.

"It took me over an hour to do five miles," she recalled. "At the time I was actually planning to run again. I figured if Terry Fox could do it...but I didn't realize the extent of my injuries."

Hamilton went on to play some wheelchair basketball and a teammate suggested she try racing on the track. She took part in her first meet in 1986 and went on to compete at the regional level and in the United States, by then using a racing wheelchair. It was an exhilarating learning experience, one which Hamilton mastered quickly. In two years she was in Seoul, South Korea, competing for Canada at the Paralympic Games.

Linda Hamilton: Times keep improving.

"It happened so quickly for me," said Hamilton, an elementary school teacher. "I remember being at a regional track meet, doing events and saying things like: 'Is this good?' I didn't know what was good. There I was, a rookie, I didn't know if I was good or not. At the time I did a few throwing events and I remember that everyone was very supportive."

Hamilton took silver in the 400 and the 800 metres at the Seoul Paralympics and bronze in the 100, 200 and 1,500. Two years later, at the World Games in the Netherlands she became a double world champion in her class, taking gold in the 100 metres in addition to taking silver over 200 and 400 metres and bronze in the 800. A subsequent change in classification put Hamilton in with a bigger group of athletes and she finished seventh and eighth in the 200 and 100 metres at the 1992 Paralympic Games in Barcelona. Improving and just missing two medals in a photo finish in a more competitive class in the Berlin meet led her to believe that, at age forty-four, she wasn't through yet.

Hamilton now looks ahead to the 1996 Paralympics in Atlanta, Georgia, where she hopes to improve her individual performance again and to be part of the Canadian relay team. Although she concentrates on shorter distances, that situation may change if she winds up her track career in Atlanta.

"I am going to do a marathon when my track career is finished," she said. "After '96, that will be a goal."

Diane Rakiecki

TRACK & FIELD

In 1983 Kelowna's Diane Rakiecki became the first Canadian woman wheelchair athlete to complete a marathon, finishing the Vancouver Interna-tional Marathon in 3 hours, 3 minutes. Who knows what her time might have been had her chair's wheel not fallen off less than a mile from the finish line, forcing Rakiecki to wait until a spectator could grab proper tools from a car trunk and help her re-attach the wheel.

In 1977 Rakiecki, then fifteen, was injured in a highway car crash that killed her father. Her spinal cord was severed in the ordeal and she became a paraplegic. She competed in her first national wheelchair championship in 1979 and won the 200 metres. In 1984 she was a member of the Canadian Olympic wheelchair relay team that won gold in the 4x100-metre relay and she also took silver in the 800 metres. She went on to establish national records over 100, 400, 800 and 1,500 metres and in 1987 won the 800 metres at the world track and field championships in Rome.

Rakiecki was named to the Canadian Paralympic team to Seoul in 1988, but injuries forced her to retire from wheelchair racing prior to the Games. She took up basketball and in 1992 was a member of Canada's gold medal-winning women's wheelchair basketball team at the Paralympic Games in Barcelona.

Diane Rakiecki: Marathon pioneer.

Triathlon

Triathlon is a sport relatively new to the international scene although for years people interested in fitness were doing their own brand of triathlon via cross training — combining swimming, cycling and running for overall fitness. Recognizing that combining all three elements could create an exciting event and a challenging athletic test, some enterprising folks in California began organizing swim-bike-run races and word of the new sport quickly spread. In the late 1970s and early 1980s the first stars of the sport began to emerge via an incredible endurance test held in Kona, Hawaii, and known as The Ironman. Participants were required to swim 2.4 miles, cycle 112 miles and run the standard marathon distance of 26.2 miles.

Not surprisingly, there were endless human interest stories about the endurance event that took most of the day under the tropical sun. The one that captured the imagination of many North Americans and people around the world as news clips were beamed all over, was the dramatic 1982 finish in the Ironman women's division. Exhausted, Julie Moss struggled to reach the finish line, at one time so determined she continued her quest for the line by crawling on hands and knees. Then, with victory just yards away, Moss was passed by Kathleen McCartney.

Recognizing that the day-long event proved too great a challenge in terms of training time and commitment for average working people, race organizers began putting together shorter events. In time, two classes of triathlete would emerge — those who would excel at the longer Ironman distance and others who relished what would eventually be standardized as Olympic or short-course distance — a 1.5-kilometre swim, a 40-kilometre cycle and 10-kilometre run. A few athletes would demonstrate considerable ability in both.

Triathlon made inroads into the established sport community by serving as a demonstration event at the 1990 Commonwealth Games and, later, on the official program of the 1995 Pan-American Games in Argentina. With Australia, a major triathlon nation, playing host to the 2000 Summer Olympics in Sydney, the sport will almost certainly be included on the Olympic program for the first time.

The first Canadians to make an impact in triathlon in the early 1980s did so not only because of their athletic ability, but also because spectators were often puzzled as to just who was who.

Sylviane Puntous & Patricia Puntous   TRIATHLON

Triathlon is a sport which features an unusually high number of twins who have gained success at the international level. Among the top competitors on the women's side are Australia's Michellie and Gabrielle Jones and Americans Joan and Joy Hansen. Canada's triathlete twins, Sylviane and Patricia Puntous, were among the early celebrities of triathlon. In 1983, known as The Puntous Twins From Montreal, the twenty-two-year-olds finished first and second in the women's division of Hawaii's Ironman. Sylviane won the event in a women's record 10 hours, 43 minutes, 39 seconds, while Patricia was second at 10:49:45. In the past, the two had been known to finish races together, joining hands at the finish area, but Patricia suffered a flat tire in the cycling portion and lost contact with her sister. In 1984 they again finished first and second, with Sylviane taking first place in record time.

The twins became celebrities in a burgeoning sport that would make names such as Scott Tinley, Dave Scott and Mark Allen familiar in North America. For a time they trained in the United States then opted to move to Kelowna, B.C., an outdoors-minded community in a region that had embraced the sport of triathlon.

In 1986 Patricia broke the Ironman tape first in a record 9:47:49 but officials later disqualified her because she was charged with drafting off a rival in the cycling portion. (Author's note: Drafting, a term used in cycling, motor sports and track and field, refers to one athlete following closely behind an opponent so that wind resistance falls solely on the athlete in front, and the athlete behind is swept along in an air pocket.) Sylviane finished second in that race and a year later would finish second again to New Zealand's Erin Baker.

The duo also excelled in short course, among their laurels being Sylviane's victory in the 1989 Canadian short course championships in Calgary, finishing the season ranked third in the world by the International Federation of Elite Triathletes, and Patricia's victory, with Sylviane second, at the 1989 Reebok World Triathlon in Toronto.

The pair also extended their ability to road racing and became a familiar and successful presence in running events in Canada and the United States.

Dynamic Duo: Patricia Puntous (right) finishes just ahead of sister Sylviane in California Bud Light Triathlon.

Carol Montgomery: A world class competitor in two sports.

Carol Montgomery

When triathlon was a developing event there were cynical sportswriters who labelled the sport as something swimmers, cyclists or runners did when they couldn't make it to the top in their individual discipline. While the sport did attract individuals who had competed in one or more of those events, it took some time for the triathlon to emerge as an athletic entity on its own.

North Vancouver's Carol Montgomery has proven she can do all three, or just one. In the late spring of 1994 she arrived at Town Centre Stadium in Coquitlam, B.C., with the same goal as many other Canadian women distance runners competing at the Harry Jerome Track Classic — to finish as top Canadian and ensure a team berth for the Commonwealth Games in Victoria. Montgomery's presence added extra interest to the women's 10,000-metre race because she came in known as one of the top female triathletes in the world — she was ranked second behind Australia's Michellie Jones. Running was her strongest discipline of the triathlon events but how would the twenty-eight-year-old competitor fare in just her second 10-kilometre race on the track? Her first foray came a month earlier in California and she dropped out of the race.

But Montgomery surprised many observers, except herself and coach Jerry Tighe, and finished third in the race behind Switzerland's Daria Nauer and Australia's Krishna Stanton in 32 minutes, 26.7 seconds, to qualify for the Commonwealth Games team. Earlier that year, after qualifying for the Canadian team with a fifth place finish at the national championships in Vancouver, Montgomery was top Canadian at the world cross country championships in Budapest, finishing thirty-second.

Carol Montgomery was a competent high school distance runner whose promise was compromised by injuries. Always a keen cyclist, she added swimming to her athletic repertoire and the combination made for a fitter, stronger and less injury-prone athlete. She quickly made her name as a triathlete, first on what was then an extensive national circuit and then on the International World Cup circuit. In 1990 she finished second to home country favourite Erin Baker at the Commonwealth Games in New Zealand, where triathlon was a demonstration sport. She was again a fast-closing second to Baker at the 1990 world championships.

A year later she confirmed her status as one of the top triathletes in the world, winning several major events including races at St. Croix, in San José and in Texas. Ironically, her most disappointing finish that year came at the 1991 world championships in Australia, where compatriot Jo-Anne Ritchie was the winner while Montgomery finished sixth.

Montgomery's Commonwealth Games aspirations did not go as planned. A runner stepped on her heel midway through the 10,000-metre race and, feeling her Achilles tendon tightening with some urgency, she dropped out, knowing that to keep running might risk serious injury.

After the race she acknowledged she was not through with what had been a successful foray into the track and field world. "I'll be back," she said when asked of her future plans. Indeed, in early 1995 Montgomery continued her track explorations, earning a silver medal in the 10,000 metres and bronze over 5,000 metres at the Pan-American Games in Argentina.

Jo-Anne Ritchie

TRIATHLON

"I'm extremely competitive," Jo-Anne Ritchie answered when asked to assess herself as an athlete. "But I think people misread me and I don't appear the competitor that I am."

Being a thirty-one-year-old mother of two doesn't preclude an individual from becoming an elite athlete, but it does make the logistics of training and competing that much more complicated. So it wasn't surprising that Canada's Jo-Anne Ritchie wasn't foremost in peoples' minds when they pondered who might win the women's division of the 1991 world short course triathlon championship at Surfer's Paradise in Australia. They were looking at another Canadian, Carol Montgomery, or France's Isabelle Mouthon, Australian favourite Michellie Jones, or American Karen Smyers as more probable and well known candidates for victory than a competitor from Kelowna, B.C.

Ritchie came into the Australian event with far fewer races under her feet than many other competitors. Most of the races she had competed in were Canadian events, hardly making her a household word to triathlon fans around the world. She had finished fourth in the prestigious Chicago Sun-Times triathlon earlier in the season but no one was prepared for her smart, and stirring, performance in Australia.

New Zealand's Ann Keat was first out of the water after the 1.5-kilometre swim, but the first ten competitors emerged from the waves with just seconds between them, making a quick change to the bike that much more crucial

for each. Ritchie, a competitive swimmer as a teen, was part of that main group.

Perhaps inspired by the partisan Australian crowd, Aussie Bianca Van Woesik sped to the lead in the early going of the 40-kilometre cycle portion of the race. Ritchie was close behind and surprised when some of the better known athletes failed to make their presence known.

"The Australian took off on the bike and no one went after her," she explained. "It bothered me to let her go so far ahead. So I decided to go get her, no one else did."

After forty kilometres, Van Woesik and Ritchie were still dueling for the lead. In the transition area Ritchie was surprised at how fresh she felt going in to the final leg, the 10-kilometre run. She passed her Australian rival with two kilometres remaining in the event and won the world championship in 2 hours, 02 minutes and 04 seconds. In second place was compatriot Terri Smith-Ross, of Cochrane, Alberta, at 2:02:11 with Michellie Jones third at 2:02:50.

"It was a real thrill, the adrenaline was pumping, and I was in shock," said Ritchie of crossing the finish line alone and unthreatened by rivals. "I was very proud. To come down that finish chute, surrounded by all the flags, that's a feeling that's unmatchable. But it did shock me."

Ritchie's victory was labelled a surprise, an upset. But it could be looked upon instead as proof that immersing oneself in a sport and training incessantly are not necessarily paths to success. Ritchie made the most of what she had in terms of time, energy, resources and support, and combined it all with natural athleticism and strength buoyed by a competitive streak that didn't emerge until sometime in her twenties.

She was a swimmer until age fifteen when friends and social life outweighed whatever athletic aspirations she might have harboured. Sport remained fun but she did not feel compelled to work on her personal fitness until two events changed her approach. One occurred in 1979 when she was a commerce student at Simon Fraser University.

"I was jogging and I hated it," she said. "I was playing basketball at the time. We were sent on these fitness runs, which I just despised. I wasn't into fitness at all. I remember it was raining and I was feeling cranky. Then, Terry Fox ran by."

Watching the one-legged runner, who would go on to inspire Canadians with his Marathon of Hope for cancer research, inspired Ritchie. Later, like many other North Americans, she became interested in improving her fitness after watching the popular Jane Fonda workout videos. She entered her first triathlon in 1983 and finished fifth. A year later she won a major triathlon in Kauai.

But Ritchie didn't embrace the notion of being a full-time athlete pursuing sponsorship and opportunities throughout the world. She married, she worked, and later juggled training with the responsibilities of raising children. In 1991, the logistics of being able to leave her family to compete in Australia presented a challenge, as did being as well-prepared as possible to warrant the trip.

"It had taken so much to get there, so many things had to happen at home," she noted. "For the race the year before, I had made a stupid change to my bike the night before. This time I wanted to make sure I didn't have a mental breakdown or a mechanical breakdown that resulted in not giving it 100 per cent."

Ritchie arrived in Australia six days before the race. Unlike many of the prominent competitors, who spent their time doing interviews and resting, Ritchie seized the opportunity to do "all the tourist stuff" in addition to making her own pre-race preparations. She was determined to enjoy the experience. After all, she had come a long way.

"I'm sure from a sport psychologist point of view I'd be interesting because for some reason, I don't know exactly why, I had absolutely no expectations for that race," she said. "I think it was because in 1990 I came in very fit and I had expectations and it all fell apart on me. And it was such a big decision for me to go. I had a two-year-old and a four-year-old and I wasn't prepared to leave them for the amount of time that I should. I had real guilt feelings about that.

"Then, when I was there, I was just happy to be in Aus-

Jo-Anne Ritchie: Finished on top Down Under.

tralia and I wasn't thinking at all about the race. In retrospect, I realize I was in very good shape. I had been injury-free for a long spell and to me that was a huge key. The course was my type of course and the way the race played out, it played into my strengths."

In 1992 Ritchie defended her world title against 120 other women at the world event in Muskoka, Ontario. Ritchie and Michellie Jones duelled for much of the cycling portion but the Aussie eventually drew away, winning the event in 2:02:08 followed by Ritchie in second at 2:03:22. That same year Ritchie won her second consecutive Canadian triathlon championship, finished second overall in the

International Triathlon Union (ITU) World Cup triathlon series and second in the Chicago Sun-Times triathlon.

Knowing that she simply couldn't spend all day training, Ritchie ensured that whatever training time she had available was given to tough, quality workouts. Her natural athletic ability and all-around fitness also showed when she finished first in her age group at the world indoor rowing championships in 1992. That year she also found time to contribute to her team's second place finish in the pro-

vincial senior B women's basketball championships.

In the fall of 1994 Ritchie gave birth to her third child. Pondering what the future might hold for her as an athlete, she also conceded she was looking ahead in other directions.

"There are other things that interest me too," she said, conceding her life was already quite full with a new baby and two youngsters to oversee. "I'd like to take a French class, and these days I'd like to stay awake long enough to be able to read the whole paper."

Modern Pentathlon

Some people believe modern pentathlon is an outdated, antiquated activity which no longer belongs in the Olympics. Others cherish it as a sporting slice of history which required soldiers to be able to ride a horse, to run, to swim, to wield a sword and shoot a gun.

Lynn Chornobrywy

MODERN PENTATHLON

Lynn Chornobrywy doesn't remember too many details of her first event at the 1983 world modern pentathlon championships in Gotheburg, Sweden. There was a set of jumps and a small, dappled grey horse which she was supposed to guide over the obstacles. She does remember her relief at the end of the discipline, after she and the steed had paired for a competent effort, taking down just one rail on the course and earning Canada 1,060 points in the first of five modern pentathlon disciplines.

Chornobrywy, just a few days shy of her twenty-first birthday, went on to win the world modern pentathlon championship that week with a world record 5,328 points, defeating favoured Anne Ahlgren of Sweden by 130 points. In reflecting on her victory more than a decade later she conceded her win came not so much from conquering a lifelong fear of falling from a horse, but from learning to manage that particular fear, and others.

"I knew the horse I had was good. I was riding last or second to last and I watched him in other rounds," said Chornobrywy (pronounced Shorno-bree). "I basically knew all I had to do was stay on, the rest of it would take care of itself. Stay with the horse and you'll be okay."

It is odd that someone with a fear of falling from the back of a horse should take up a sport like modern pen-

tathlon, where riding, fencing, swimming, shooting and running make up the sport's five disciplines. The sport is rooted in military tradition and scope, with each competitor looked upon as a soldier whose task is to deliver a message. In order to complete the task the soldier must ride an unfamiliar horse, and along the way the individual's ability to defend him or herself is tested, first in a sword duel then via pistol marksmanship. Eventually the soldier is required to swim across a body of water, then run to complete the mission.

"Modern pentathlon is not an easy sport, and it's something you don't realize takes a long time," Chornobrywy explained. "You look at it and think: Wow, anybody can shoot a gun. Fencing is the same, you make a hit. In riding, it's a matter of getting the horse over the jump. It's not until you find out there are fears within yourself that you have to overcome, that's what makes it difficult. In riding, it was falling. I think it was because I fell when I was younger. Maybe subconsciously that fall when I was younger triggered something that wouldn't let me fall again."

Lynn Chornobrywy was born in Ottawa on September 16, 1960, but grew up just outside Montreal in the community of Baie d'Urfe. At about age two she fell, hitting her head and suffering subsequent symptoms of dyslexia and problems with her coordination. Her parents immediately enrolled her in a variety of activities to improve her coordination — swimming, ballet, gymnastics, soccer.

It became evident early on that Chornobrywy had a solitary side, that she preferred individual sports to team activities, yet enjoyed testing herself in a variety of athletic disciplines. At age thirteen she followed her brother, Denis, into modern pentathlon after a brief stint as a competitive swimmer.

"Swimming twice a day in the pool every day didn't appeal to me," she said. "With modern pentathlon, even though you're working hard, it doesn't seem so bad because it's all different. That was appealing, something different every day of the week. It was also fun because there was a good group of people. It made it fun socially for me."

Indeed, high school was difficult for Chornobrywy because as a teen she was extremely shy and soft-spoken. Sport, she conceded, gave her "a good place to hide" while allowing her to gain confidence in her own way, by training, competing and travelling. Some may see that experience as negative, concentrating on sport instead of academics and the social whirl that is high school, but as Chornobrywy aptly noted, she saw her experiences as far more beneficial than those she would gain by "smoking dope on a Saturday night with your friends."

Her first competition was an inauspicious beginning — she fell off her horse and earned zero points for the ride. But by 1977 she was competing at the national level and in 1980 finished a credible thirteenth in that year's World Cup. A year later, at the world championships, she was eleventh. Hoping to crack the top ten at the 1982 world championships, Chornobrywy instead endured the humiliation of falling off the horse in the show jumping discipline, firing three shots into the dirt in the pistol portion and finishing a disappointed twenty-eighth.

It was no wonder people were surprised when a year later, Chornobrywy not only won a major meet in Denmark earlier in the season, but also upset favoured Ahlgren to win the 1983 world championship. Her Swedish rival had fared so poorly in the shooting that the Canadian, a competent runner and sitting in second place going into the final event, knew she had to defeat Ahlgren by four seconds in the cross-country run to win the world championship.

The 2,000-metre cross country event was held as a halftime race during a major soccer match, with the women modern pentathlete contenders finishing in the stadium. Just 500 metres into the run Chornobrywy breezed past the struggling Swede to gain the lead, entering the stadium as a runaway winner, watching her larger-than-life figure on the screen as her legs moved her toward the finish line

and the world title.

It was, as Chornobrywy described later in her quiet, understated manner, a satisfying achievement. But she relishes more those feelings she enjoyed in performing well in each discipline. Riding presented its own difficult challenge, fencing another obstacle as she pushed herself to be aggressive while fighting back the urge to say "Sorry" every time she scored a hit. Shooting, swimming and running offered her a chance to withdraw to what was a special place inside her competitive soul.

"You go into this little room inside your brain and you're happy," explained Chornobrywy. "Nothing else exists there — you've got the motions down. In swimming, you just make sure you don't crash into the wall, make sure you go back and forth. With shooting, it's just you and this gun and it's almost Zen-like, it's really incredible when you get

Lynn Chornobrywy: Conquered fear of falling.

inside yourself and it's peaceful, calm, serene. Running, too, you get to the point where you don't feel your legs hitting the ground. You don't realize what you're doing physically. It's a repetitive motion. You're so in control of the outer part and inside are feeling so incredibly happy. That's probably what keeps you going, too."

Chornobrywy retired in 1985 and makes her home in the Fraser Valley just outside Vancouver. Raising three children offers a different set of challenges from the five she faced in modern pentathlon, an event which remains popular in Europe but still has a meagre following in Canada despite Chornobrywy's success. Some say it is an outdated discipline and have called for its removal from the Olympic program.

Lynn Chornobrywy sees the sport as having provided a shy, young person with some of life's most valuable lessons.

"I don't see it being anything but fond memories," she said. "Now, I realize I am the way I am because of that. It isn't the things you do on Saturday night, it's the ups and downs that you learn to conquer and face. I know I'm going to survive. Inside myself, I am capable of anything, anytime, because of my involvement in sport. It's a never-say-die attitude. If it doesn't work out today it doesn't mean that it won't tomorrow."

GYM DANDIES & COURT STARS

Gymnastics

The ancient Greeks were intensely interested in gymnastics as a means of promoting fitness, discipline and athletic artistry. Gymnastics are one of the most popular of Olympic sports. In the athlete, strength, balance and coordination must be combined with technique and artistry. While in some circles tumbling and trampolining come under the umbrella of gymnastics, two of the most popular branches of gymnastics are artistic gymnastics and rhythmic gymnastics.

Artistic Gymnastics

Artistic gymnastics for women were introduced to the Olympics in 1928 in the form of a team competition combining scores from each apparatus. Individual competition on each apparatus — the floor, balance beam, vault, and uneven bars — and an all-around competition became part of the program in Helsinki in 1952.

Traditionally, the former Soviet Union dominated the sport until it broke down into many republics in the early 1990s. Canada has yet to win a medal in Olympic artistic gymnastics competition.

Ernestine Russell Weaver

ARTISTIC GYMNASTICS

Ernestine Russel Weaver was Canada's first prominent female gymnast. In the 1950s she virtually owned the sport of gymnastics in Canada and was the first Canadian woman to achieve success internationally. In an elite career that spanned from 1954 to 1960 the gymnast from Windsor, Ontario, won five senior national championships, three American championships and, at the 1959 Pan-American Games in Chicago, took gold medals in all four individual events and gold in the all-around competition.

She also competed at the 1956 and 1960 Olympic Games. Russell wound up her competitive gymnastics career after the 1960 Games but years later resurfaced in a different capacity. She coached gymnastics at Clarion State in Pennsylvania, leading the school to the national title in 1976. She later moved on to the University of Florida and for more than a decade coached the Gator squad to become one of the best in the United States. Not forgetting her Canadian roots, Weaver began recruiting Canadian gymnasts to the Florida institution and many Canadians, including Elfi Schlegel, Tracy Wilson and Anita Botnen, became integral members of what was a highly successful gymnastics program.

"These girls are going through the same struggle I went through," Weaver said in 1991 while discussing the greater popularity and opportunities for gymnastics in the United States as compared with Canada.

"Gymnastics was what I excelled at but it never would have given me the opportunity to go to college in Canada. Here, they get an education and they compete."

In 1993 Weaver moved again, taking her gymnastics knowledge to the University of Nevada-Las Vegas.

Ernestine Russell Weaver: Two-time Olympian.

Elfi Schlegel: Competed in four world championships.

Elfi Schlegel

ARTISTIC GYMNASTICS

Elfi Schlegel of Etobicoke, Ontario, spent seven years as a member of Canada's gymnastics team — a long time in a sport where being nineteen years old is considered old, at least in international circles. She was a senior national champion in 1978 and was a home country favourite at the Commonwealth Games in Edmonton where she led the Canadian team to the gold medal and also won the individual competition. She also took a bronze medal at the 1979 Pan-American Games and was named to the 1980 Canadian

Olympic team, which stayed at home due to boycott.

Schlegel competed in four world championships and was a team bronze medallist at the 1983 World University Games where she just missed medals by finishing fourth in beam, uneven bars and the floor. After studying broadcasting and communications at the University of Florida she combined her sport and her degree by embarking on a career as a television sportscaster.

Stella Umeh

ARTISTIC GYMNASTICS

Stella Umeh of Mississauga, Ontario, began competing at age six and enjoyed her first taste of elite success when she won the 1988 national all-around championship

at age thirteen. Eighteen months later, having not made the Canadian team to the Commonwealth Games, Umeh made the long trip to Auckland after all, to replace an in-

Stella Umeh: Vaults to victory at 1994 Commonwealth Games.

jured teammate. The trip was worthwhile as the Canadians won the team gold medal.

By 1992 Umeh had established herself not only as the top gymnast in Canada but had also cracked that rarefied world top ten group by finishing fifth in beam, eighth in vault and ninth on the floor at the world championships — the best results ever recorded by a Canadian female gymnast.

In 1993 she maintained that status by winning the uneven bars and finishing fourth all-around at the World Gymnastics challenge in addition to finishing eighth in floor exercises at the world championships.

In front of a home country crowd at the 1994 Commonwealth Games in Victoria Umeh, by then nineteen, won the individual all-around and vault competitions.

Rhythmic Gymnastics

In recent years, particularly with its inclusion on the Olympic program beginning in 1984, rhythmic gymnastics have become another popular form of gymnastics. As in artistic gymnastics, competitors from the former Soviet Union and eastern bloc countries have been most successful in the sport. Canada's Lori Fung made national sport history in 1984 by winning the rhythmic gymnastics gold medal at the Olympic Games in Los Angeles.

Lori Fung

RHYTHMIC GYMNASTICS

The problem was basic — on a sultry California summer day no one was going to turn off the air conditioning even though it was wreaking havoc with the ribbon routines of Olympic rhythmic gymnastics competitors.

In practice, Canada's Lori Fung saw how the air blast gave the colourful satin tendril a mind of its own. Necessity being the mother of invention, the Vancouver gymnast changed her routine. Immediately.

"My final routine, the one that secured the gold medal, was my hoop routine but everyone remembers it as the ribbon routine because I was the only who had finished without it wrapped in a knot around my throat," she laughed.

"Everyone was saying: 'Oh, well, the air conditioning, we'll just have to deal with it, accept it. I decided in the change room I wasn't going to accept it. I wanted a 9.7 and I wasn't going to accept 8.5 just because the air conditioning might create problems. So I completely changed my routine. I stayed on one side of the floor because the wind was going just one way. In the warm-up if you had the ribbon on your right side it would tangle, so I did everything on the other side."

Going into the evening final program, Fung was tied for third behind Romania's Doina Staiculescu, who enjoyed such a commanding lead she appeared destined to take gold unless disaster struck. It did, when the Romanian attempted to perform her ribbon program and was confounded when the air conditioning caused it to twist and turn with as much reliability as a leash with a puppy on the end.

When the medals were awarded, twenty-one-year-old Fung took the gold medal with a combined total 57.950 points for her hoop, ball, clubs and ribbon routines. Staiculescu, whose points had won her the hoop, ball and clubs routines, had dropped to ninth in ribbon and finished second, just behind Fung, at 57.900. West Germany's Regina Weber was third at 57.700.

It was an emotional evening — Staiculescu wept for what might have been while Fung smiled and cried as "O Canada" was played in the medal ceremony.

"I remember standing on deck with the hoop, watching the ribbon go around her back, around her neck, on the floor," said Fung. "I was in shock. She came off in tears and, while I thought it was terrible, I wondered suddenly: Where am I in the standings? All I knew was I was somewhere in there, in the top five."

Lori Fung's road to the podium in Los Angeles began on the road outside her East Vancouver home.

"I was energetic and I loved to perform," she said. "I was always roller skating and bike riding and didn't want to come in to eat dinner because it interrupted my play. I liked to roller skate under the street lamp of Eighth Avenue. I used to pretend I was performing. I'd make up routines on the road. Cars would wheel around the corner and I'd be doing my arabesque."

Fung took part in artistic gymnastics as a youngster, idolizing Russian gymnast Olga Korbut, but didn't take up rhythmics until age fourteen when she joined the Rhythmika Club under coach Mall Vesik. Rhythmics became an instant passion, although her commitment was tested when she went through her level one exam and discovered everyone else at the same level was eight years old. A year later she had made the huge jump to level six and went to national championships in New Brunswick, where she finished eleventh. A year later she made the national team.

Fung, an outstanding student, immersed herself in her sport and took her final year of high school via correspondence. While competing in Japan at age seventeen she realized her sport had far more prominence and support in

Lori Fung: First Olympic champion in rhythmic gymnastics.

other areas of the world. Deciding that to be the best you had to train with the best, she approached her parents about the possibility of training in Bulgaria. They relented, agreeing to pay for the excursion. Fung made the arrangements herself.

"I had only been on a plane a few times. I got off in Sofia, my first time in an eastern bloc country and this man came up to me and said: 'Canada?' I had Canadian emblems plastered all over me, and I said: 'Yes!' He grabbed my suitcase and went out to a van. I got into this van, we were driving, and he didn't speak a word of English. I thought I could end up being lost forever. The man could be an axe murderer. I got a little panicky. It turned out he was the training centre's ballet master."

Fung trained with the Bulgarians for four weeks. For a time she also worked with Japanese coach Yukiki Morumona. Fung was, as national coach Liliana Dimitrova once noted, like a sponge, trying to soak up as much as she could from as many sources as possible. In 1981 Fung finished thirtieth overall at the world championships in Munich, West Germany, the highest placing by a North American. A year later she won her first Canadian senior title, finished twelfth at a major event in Japan, then finished second all-around at the prestigious Four Continents competition, winning the clubs event while taking the silver in ribbon.

In a short time Fung had gone a long way.

"I didn't have natural flexibility, I didn't have the best leg line or strength, but I had the determination and performance," she said in assessing her abilities. "People said I would play a lot *with* the audience, not play to the audience. I used to make eye contact with people and try to make them laugh or cry."

In 1983, with only the top fifty gymnasts allowed to qualify for the Olympics, Fung finished twenty-third overall at the world championships after winning a pre-world competition in Switzerland.

The 1984 Los Angeles Olympics were marred by the boycott of most eastern bloc countries. But with Romania's Staiculescu and Alina Dragan there, in addition to Spain's Marta Canton and Yugoslavia's Milena Reljin, Fung's gold medal still registered as a tremendous achievement. In Olympic history she will be remembered as the first gold medallist in rhythmic gymnastics.

"The only thing I was sad about on that day was for Doina," she said. "I trained with her in Romania and I knew how important it was for her, and the pressure that was on her. I felt mixed emotions."

Fung surprised people by opting to continue competing instead of resting on her Olympic laurels. In 1985 she finished ninth in the world championships, the only western gymnast to crack the top ten among the Bulgarian, Romanian, Soviet Union and East German competitors. In 1986 she finished seventh at the World Cup of rhythmic gymnastics in Tokyo and won the Four Continents meet in Australia. Her Olympic gold medal had also brought endorsement and modelling opportunities and when she wasn't travelling to competition Fung was working in Los Angeles.

"I was being pulled in all areas," she conceded. "It was becoming increasingly difficult."

In 1987 Fung's plans to compete at the 1988 Olympics in Seoul were threatened when she injured her neck in a training fall which forced her to spend the night in a Vancouver hospital spinal cord unit. She later suffered bouts of extreme fatigue, diagnosed as Epstein-Barr syndrome, and she retired before the '88 Games.

Fung took up coaching and at the Commonwealth Games in 1994 could be found overseeing protégé and national champion Camille Martens in addition to coaching many young hopefuls as members of the Vancouver Rhythmic Sportive Gymnastics Club.

Mary Fuzesi: Earned four gold medals at the 1990 Commonwealth Games.

Madonna Gimotea: Enjoyed a top-five World Cup finish.

Mary Fuzesi

Mary Fuzesi of Thornhill, Ontario, became Canada's top rhythmic gymnast after Lori Fung. At age thirteen, as the youngest member of Canada's team to the 1987 Pan-American Games in Indianapolis, Fuzesi showed remarkable maturity for a young competitor. Despite being hampered by a back injury, she earned a silver medal in clubs and a bronze in the hoop and ribbon. A national all-around champion in 1986, Fuzesi went on to win the all-around competition at the prestigious Four Continents competition and to finish tenth overall at the Seoul Olympics. A year later she finished ninth all-around at the world championships and in 1990 won four gold medals at the Commonwealth Games in Auckland.

Madonna Gimotea

Madonna Gimotea of Maple, Ontario, succeeded Mary Fuzesi as Canada's top rhythmic gymnast going into the 1992 Barcelona Olympics. A strong technical competitor, Gimotea started rhythmic gymnastics at age six and joined the national team in 1987. A Commonwealth Games gold medallist in the ball at the 1990 and '94 competitions, she enjoyed her best result in 1992 with a fifth-place all-around finish at the World Cup. In 1991 she succeeded Fuzesi by winning the national all-around championship.

Camille Martens

Camille Martens became interested in rhythmic gymnastics after watching Lori Fung win the gold medal on television. Several years later Fung would become Martens' coach and the young athlete from Vernon, B.C., would eventually move to the Vancouver area to train with Fung and her club based at the University of B.C.. Martens' climb up the competitive ladder began in 1990 when she earned gold and bronze medals to finish fifth overall at the Pan-Am junior championships. That same year Martens also finished fifth in the junior category at the Four Continents meet.

By 1994 Martens had established herself as the top rhythmic gymnast in the country, winning the national championship and going on to earn a gold and four silver medals at the 1994 Commonwealth Games. Martens also finished third overall, taking gold in clubs, silver in ribbon and bronze in the hoop at the Four Continents competition in Seoul. She finished the 1994 season ranked twentieth in the world.

Camille Martens: Protégée of Olympic gold medallist Lori Fung.

Basketball

The Edmonton Grads

Women's basketball wasn't introduced to the Olympic program until the 1976 Summer Games in Montreal. It could be argued that the move came thirty-six years too late to include the finest women's basketball team ever produced in Canada. If there is one laurel missing among the myriad records and achievements recorded by the Edmonton Grads, it is an Olympic gold medal.

Had television been around to offer as much exposure to the Edmonton Grads as it does now to the National Basketball Association, Noel MacDonald and Margaret MacBurney might be as familiar in households as Michael Jordan or Charles Barkley. The Grads' dynasty began in 1915 and continued through to 1940 when the team was disbanded. During that time the team played 522 games, winning 502, while inspiring a generation of Canadians weathering war, then depression, and war again.

"We're absolutely amazed that we're still being honoured in various ways," mused Betty Bawden Bowen in 1995. For many years, Bowen has overseen the memorabilia and information which is still being requested by researchers and individuals interested in the team.

"I don't know why that is. Our fans were very loyal. It was a small city at the time. It is remarkable that that affection has carried on."

The Grads team had its beginnings in 1912 when John Percy Page came from Ontario to teach at Edmonton's McDougall Commercial High School. Two years later he began coaching the girls' team at the school and the squad went on to win the city championship. In 1915 the graduating players were reluctant to give up the camaraderie that had forged such a successful team, so Page organized the Edmonton Commercial Graduates Basketball Club, from which the players would become simply known as The Grads. The success continued as the squad won the 1915 Alberta championship, continuing to win every provincial title except the 1921 laurel.

Page also ensured the club had a feeder system to provide new athletes to replace retiring players, starting with Page's tutelage as basketball coach at the school and moving up to an intermediate team called The Gradettes. It was, as Kay MacRitchie noted, a phenomenon that attracted the interest of every female teen in Edmonton.

"It was something that every girl in Edmonton who played basketball wanted to do," said MacRitchie, who played on the Gradettes and began practicing with the Grads when she was sixteen, eventually joining the team just before her seventeenth birthday to play the final two seasons in the team's history. "They wanted to make The Grads. When I came up I think I just wanted to play and didn't think about the history of the team. That didn't sink in until it was all over."

Clearly the best of western Canadian women's basketball, the Grads won the first Canadian championship when it was inaugurated in 1922 and never lost the event through 1940. In 1923 they made their first foray into international competition, playing an international series against the Cleveland Favorites. The series was supported by the Underwood Typewriter company and the Underwood Trophy became the coveted prize in what would become a North-American-wide series dominated so much by the Grads that they were given the trophy as a permanent keepsake after they disbanded in 1940.

The Grads did enjoy Olympic experience of a kind in that they took part in exhibition tournaments organized as part of the 1924, 1928, 1932 and 1936 Olympics. They didn't lose a game throughout all four tournaments.

The team enjoyed the contribution of exceptional athletes, but Page's contribution was also obvious in the way his athletes conducted themselves on and off the court.

"One thing Mr. Page did instill in all the girls was a great deal of discipline," noted MacRitchie. "After a game we didn't go out and have a brew or anything. I don't drink to this day. There was a real camaraderie and a real caring among all the girls. That's continued on over the years. I've played on other teams since then and I've never run into a group that was as close-knit as we were. And he knit us together."

Dot Johnson Sherlock was a member of the Grad squad that won the first Canadian championship in 1922. She played for six years as a forward and remembers Page as a disciplinarian who wasn't always appreciated by rival coaches, who thought his playing style old-fashioned.

"Some of the coaches didn't think he was up-to-date with his plays but he got the results," she laughed. "I don't know if

Edmonton Grads: 1940 World Champion squad (from top left) Mabel Munton, Jean Williamson, coach J.P. Page, Winnie Gallen, Kay MacRitchie. Bottom left: Betty Bawden, Helen Northup, Etta Dann, Sophie Brown.

you'd say he was severe, he was fair but you had to toe the line."

Of the many talented players who wore the Grads' black and gold, Noel MacDonald became the best known and remains the only Grad to be inducted into the Canadian Sports Hall of Fame. In a career that spanned 1933 to 1939, MacDonald scored 1,874 points but also demonstrated superb ability as a defensive player. When she was inducted into the Hall in 1971 she demonstrated the close-knit nature of the team by accepting the honour only on behalf of the team. Gladys Fry, a sterling centre who upon retirement was replaced by Noel MacDonald, also suited up in 170 Grad games while Elsie Beenie played in 168. MacBurney was another Grad stalwart who played a large number of games for that time — she appeared in the black and gold 182 times from 1926 to 1936. In 1931 she established a free-throw world record by scoring on 61 consecutive tries. Over her ten-year career she averaged 12.6 points per game.

The Grads disbanded in 1940 when World War II necessitated that the Royal Canadian Air Force take over the team's arena. The Grads played in one exhibition game for charity but by the war's end the team had scattered, with players moving on to other lives or other squads. Page, for example, went on to become a member of the Alberta legislature and served as that province's lieutenant governor from 1959 to 1966.

But the Grads' legacy didn't disappear. In 1995 half of the thirty-eight women who played for the team were living throughout Canada and the United States, with many still being called upon to appear as honoured guests at high school, university and national competitions. The last full reunion of the squad came in 1987 in conjunction with the making of the film *Shooting Stars* which honoured the Grads' achievements as the best basketball team ever to play for Canada.

Achievements of the Edmonton Commercial Graduates:

- Over 25 years the Grads played 522 games, winning 502 (nine of those games were played against men's teams — they won seven)
- Enjoyed two consecutive winning streaks of 147 and 78 games.
- Outscored opponents with an all-time average of 48 to 20. Biggest point spread in an official game was against Alberta University in 1934, where the score was 136 to 16.
- Grads' Margaret MacBurney earned a world record for free throws in 1931, scoring on 61 consecutive tries.
- Won the first Canadian title in 1922 and never lost a national series.
- Played exhibition matches as part of the 1924, 1928, 1932 and 1936 Olympics, winning all 27 matches played.
- Travelled more than 125,000 miles to compete.

Wheelchair Basketball Team

Canada's seventy-five medals at the 1992 Summer Paralympic Games in Spain earned seventh place overall in the standings. Among the twenty-eight gold medals won by Canadian disabled athletes at the Games, one earned on the second last day of competition was testament to the old sport adage which says that on any given day anybody can win.

The Canadian women's wheelchair basketball team was ranked fourth coming into the Games. Two years earlier the squad had stamped itself as a medal contender by taking bronze at the world championships. Advancing to the semi-finals from round robin play, the gritty Canadians edged the favoured team from the Netherlands 46-43 to advance to the final against the defending champions from the United States. Clearly the underdog, the Canadian women frustrated the Americans with superb defence. At the final buzzer Canada was the best, winning 35-26 after holding their rivals off the scoreboard for the final five minutes of the game.

"I think we felt that the teams were properly ranked above us," remarked team head coach Tim Frick. "We felt we were close enough that on any given day we could actually beat those particular teams. With a bit of luck I suppose it just happened to be that given day. However, luck is usually a byproduct of hard work and the team members leading in to Barcelona worked as hard as was humanly possible."

Frick noted the organization of the Canadian women's wheelchair basketball league prior to 1990 helped set a standard of competitive opportunity necessary for Canadian women wheelchair basketball players to begin to succeed in the international game. The success didn't end in Barcelona.

Two years later, the Canadian women's team, with a smattering of new faces replacing retired teammates from Barcelona, proved the 1992 Paralympic victory was no fluke. At the world wheelchair basketball championships in Aylesbury, England, the Canadians added a world title to the Paralympic gold medal.

Frick said his team in 1994 was even better prepared physically than it was in 1992, and was tougher mentally. During a pivotal point in the tournament the Canadians were not faring well against the Dutch and appeared on the verge of elimination. Then Linda Kutrowski launched a left-handed hook shot — what Frick described as a "hope shot"

Back Row standing left to right: Kristine Godziuk (Team Physio), Tim Frick (Head Coach), Barb Griffin (Assistant Coach), Paul Zachau (Team Manager). Second Row left to right: Judie Millard, Kelly Krywa, Chantal Benoit, Linda Kutrowski, Lori Radke, Renee LeDrew. Front Row left to right: Kendra Ohama, Jennifer Krempien, Marni Abbott, Tammy Cunnington, Tracey Ferguson.

— from the top of the key as the clock was running down. The ball went in, the Canadians laughed at their good fortune, then went on to win the game. From there, said Frick, they never looked back.

Canada met the United States again in the final and responded with a 45-34 victory, led by an eighteen-point effort from Chantal Benoit. Renee LeDrew and Kutrowski scored eleven and eight points respectively to be named to the tournament all-star team.

"I think every time you have a success it's a unique experience," said Frick. "Barcelona was the time they proved if they worked hard enough and believed in themselves they could accomplish something. The world championship in 1994 was a confirmation of that work ethic."

Chantal Benoit

BASKETBALL

The twelve thousand spectators who had just witnessed Canada's 35-26 victory over the United States in Paralympic wheelchair basketball were clearly perplexed and surprised when coaches lifted thirty-one-year-old Chantal Benoit to the basketball net and the Canadian player proceeded to cut the net down.

Benoit and her teammates knew exactly what she was doing. The moment had been in their minds for a long time and, finally, it was being played out for real.

"Two years before Barcelona that was the big goal inside the team, to win that gold medal," Benoit explained.

"We worked very hard to make that dream come true. Often the coach would talk about visualization, to see ourselves cut the net in victory after the game. In Spain, people were really surprised and wondering what was going on. For our team, it was like the dream came true. This was it, this was the reality and we have the net for a reminder."

Chantal Benoit played an integral role in that 1992 Paralympic Game victory, the first major international win by the Canadian women's wheelchair basketball team. She led the team in scoring, notching eighteen points in the final against the United States and also netting twenty in the team's pivotal 46-43 semi-final victory over the Netherlands.

Two years after Barcelona, Benoit again led the Canadian women's wheelchair basketball team to victory at the world championships in England, where Canada downed the United States 45-34. The win marked a high point in a decade of wheelchair basketball competition for Benoit, who calls Beloeil, Quebec, home.

Her national team wheelchair basketball career began in 1984, a year after she took part in a selection camp. Until age eighteen Benoit had competed as a national level diver. Cancer developed in her left leg and subsequent amputation put an end to aspirations in that sport. Benoit began looking for different competitive opportunities. She fell in love with wheelchair basketball after watching a demonstration game in 1980.

"Before, I'd always competed in individual sports, so

Chantal Benoit: Prolific scorer on offence.

when I saw wheelchair basketball I liked the challenge of trying to control the ball," she said. "I also saw a difference between playing a team sport and individual sport. I learned a lot in team sport about how I act off the court, with family and friends."

Benoit's first major tournament was the 1984 Paralympic Games, where the Canadian women finished fourth. Two years later she contributed to the Canadian team's silver medal performance at the Pan-American Games in Puerto Rico. As Canada improved its international standing in the game, earning a bronze medal at the 1990 Gold Cup, so, too, was Benoit making a greater impact in her sport. She became known as the "Michael Jordan" of women's wheelchair basketball because of her considerable offensive ability. But when asked about her approach she prefers to talk about the team and the unity and confidence that began to blossom with the 1990 bronze medal.

"That was a big thing for us," she said. "We started to believe we had a lot of talent on the team and we've got to develop that structure. The coach believed in us and just tried to put the program ahead and the women's team became pretty strong.

"In Barcelona the unity within our team was indescribable. Everybody had a role, everybody played that role and I'd never seen that before. The spirit of the team was big-time strong."

In 1994, Benoit was studying honours sociology in Ottawa. She will be nearly thirty-six years old when the Paralympic Games are held in Atlanta, Georgia, in 1996. She believes she still has ways to improve her game and

has no plans to stop in the near future.

"I still have so much to learn," she stressed. "That's what I like in this sport, you always have things to work on. For now I will put in everything I can toward the Atlanta Games. But I don't expect to stop. I will keep going. How long? I don't know but in the year 2000 the Paralympics are in Australia and I would enjoy being a part of that."

Jodi Evans

BASKETBALL

Jodi Evans: Caused a stir at Oxford.

The 1993 version of the annual Oxford-Cambridge varsity men's basketball game received more attention than usual for a game that is hardly a major sport in Brit-

ain. A quick look in the program at the list of names under Oxford Men was the clue — who was Jodi Evans and wasn't she in the wrong game?

No. Jodi Evans of Calgary, a member of the Canadian women's basketball team and the top woman university basketball player in the country for 1991, was attending Oxford as a Rhodes Scholar in management studies. Evans had joined the Canadian national team in 1988 and was an outstanding player for the University of Calgary in CIAU (Canadian Inter-University Athletic Union) competition.

She often practised with the Oxford men's team because, basketball hardly being a national pastime there, she could gain more competitive experience with them than she could working out with the women's squad. When it came time for the annual Oxford-Cambridge dustup, Evans was approached to play on the men's team, despite howls of protest from the British University Sports Federation.

As the Federation wasn't the organization in control of the match, Evans was allowed to go ahead and play. She played sixteen minutes of the forty-minute game and netted four points but it wasn't enough to save Oxford from going down 86-64 to Cambridge. Time and again the Oxford side fumbled the ball to the delight of their opponents.

Reviews of Evans' play noted she was most capable in setting up plays despite the physical turmoil under the hoop.

IT MAY BE THAT CANADA will never again field a basketball team like the Edmonton Grads. The sport of basketball has grown tremendously since the Grads' heyday and it is rare now that a club team represents a nation in international competition. Instead, the top players from across the country are chosen to form a national team to represent the country at international events. Canada has never won a world women's basketball championship or a medal in women's basketball at the Olympics, although Canadian teams have been competitive and have consistently ranked in the top ten in the world.

Through the 1970s and '80s, two players in particular were key contributors to Canada's international basketball efforts and were an integral part of the team's international success...

Sylvia Sweeney: Most Valuable Player at 1979 world championships.

Bev Smith: A long and illustrious international career.

Sylvia Sweeney

BASKETBALL

Sylvia Sweeney was voted Most Valuable Player at the 1979 world championships in Seoul, South Korea, and was a member of the Canadian women's team at the 1976 Olympics in Montreal.

She joined the Canadian national team in 1974 and for a decade was a major force in Canadian women's basketball. She was selected as Canadian team flag bearer for the 1979 Pan-American Games in Mexico, where the women's basketball team earned a bronze medal, and also contributed to Canada's bronze medal performance at the 1979 World

Student Games in Mexico and to Canada's fourth-place finish at the 1984 Olympics.

She went on to become a television sportscaster, eventually moving into current affairs and production, remaining active in basketball as a member of the organizing committee for the 1994 men's world championships and as a director of the Toronto Raptors.

In February 1995 she was named assistant chef de mission of Canada's team to the 1996 Summer Olympics in Atlanta, Georgia.

Bev Smith

BASKETBALL

Bev Smith grew up in the scenic British Columbia town of Salmon Arm, where she first made her mark as a playmaker and scoring ace while serving as a member of her high school basketball team. At age eighteen she joined the Canadian national team and in 1979 was selected to the tournament all-star team at the world championships

in Seoul after contributing to Canada's bronze medal finish there.

Smith was also a member of the 1984 Olympic team, which finished fourth in Los Angeles, in addition to serving on two Pan-American and two World University Games teams. Smith also played at the University of Oregon from

1978 to 1982 where she was selected All-American.

She has also taken advantage of playing opportunities in Europe where the popularity of the sport has allowed for the formation of a professional women's game. After play-ing for a time in Italy, Smith returned to Canada for a brief stint as coach at the University of B.C. but, still smitten by the challenge of playing the game, later returned to com-petition on the national team and in Europe.

University of Winnipeg Wesmen

BASKETBALL

Winnipeg Wesmen: Share the 88 game record for consecutive wins with the UCLA Bruins.

The University of Winnipeg Wesmen women's basket-ball team hadn't lost a game since October 24, 1992. On December 2, 1994, some two years and six weeks since they began their winning streak with a 73-57 victory over University of Alberta, the Wesmen had won two CIAU na-tional championships and were poised to make North American collegiate history in looking for an eighty-ninth consecutive win.

Twenty-one years earlier the UCLA Bruins won eighty-eight straight games in men's NCAA (National Collegiate Athletic Association) basketball competition, setting a col-legiate benchmark that appeared difficult to equal. The Wesmen tied that mark on November 25, 1994, with an 89-57 victory over cross-town rivals, University of Mani-toba Bisons. The two were to meet again in the pivotal game a week later.

The Wesmen, known for finishing stronger than they started, had a 39-26 lead at the half. Resolute, the Bisons refused to give up and their pressure was perhaps respon-sible for the Wesmen starting to lose concentration in the second half. The score was tied 62-62 when the Bisons' Lorissa Crellin drove to the hoop with less than five sec-onds remaining and netted the game winner, 64-62.

The record of consecutive winning games remains at eighty-eight, and will be shared by the University of Win-nipeg Wesmen and the UCLA Bruins until another team comes along to take it away.

Tennis

Tennis was one of many sports where Canada's Bobbie Rosenfeld achieved success during her remarkable athletic career. Claire Lovett excelled in tennis in addition to badminton, as did Dorothy Walton.

But as money and sponsorship made tennis one of the few professional sports open to women, it became apparent women who hoped to achieve international success had to do so by concentrating on tennis, and the wonderful years of the all-around athlete, of which Canada had many, came to a close.

Canada has never produced a winner of a women's tennis Grand Slam event or Federation Cup, but several Canadian women have gone on to compete at a high level on the women's circuit. In the 1970s Toronto's Jane O'Hara parlayed early success as a national junior champion into status as an integral member of six Canadian Federation Cup squads, where she would amass a 7-6 record in Federation Cup play. In 1975 she was ranked Canada's top woman singles player.

Marjorie Blackwood also achieved considerable success nationally, ranked number one in Canada in 1977, '78 and '79. She advanced to the third round at Wimbledon in 1982 and contributed as a player on six Canadian Federation Cup teams. In 1983 she served as team captain for Canada's Federation Cup squad and as team coach in 1987.

Carling Bassett

TENNIS

C arling Bassett remains the only Canadian woman to crack the singles top ten on the Women's Tennis Association rankings list. Daughter of former Canadian Davis Cup team member John H. Bassett, Bassett was ten years old when her father took her to Nick Bollettieri's tennis academy in Florida. Success came quickly. Bassett won the United States under-twelve clay court title and became the first Canadian to win the Orange Bowl junior international competition. At age fifteen she was the youngest competitor at the 1983 Wimbledon tournament and unleashed a most credible showing, advancing to the fourth round in a year that would see her earning the Bobbie Rosenfeld award as Canada's top female athlete. A year later her laurels would include reaching the semi-finals of the U.S. Open.

By 1985 Bassett had climbed as high as Number Eight on the rankings computer, again earning the Bobbie Rosenfeld award for that year. From 1982 through '86 she was the top-ranked woman tennis player in Canada. Following marriage and the birth of her first child, Bassett returned to competition in 1988. At the Seoul Olympics that year she joined Jill Hetherington to finish fifth in women's doubles.

Carling Bassett: Advanced into the Top Ten.

Jill Hetherington

Jill Hetherington: From junior sensation to top doubles player.

Jill Hetherington of Peterborough, Ontario, has made her name as Canada's premier woman doubles player. Her career began in earnest in 1982 when, as a five-time Canadian junior champion, she arrived at the Nick Bollettieri tennis academy in Florida to train prior to competing for the University of Florida. In 1983 she took gold medals in women's and mixed doubles at the World University Games in Edmonton.

By 1986 she was making her mark internationally with American doubles partner Patty Fendick, becoming the first Canadian to advance to the Wimbledon semi-finals. In 1987 she joined with Helen Kelesi to upset the favoured Russian duo of Larissa Savchenko and Svetlana Parkhomenko 6-4, 6-3, to advance to the Federation Cup quarter-finals, where Canada met Czechoslovakia. After splitting singles matches the Czech doubles team of Hana Mandlikova and Helena Sukova defeated Hetherington and Kelesi 7-6, 6-2.

A year later Hetherington contributed to Canada's best finish ever in Federation Cup play as the team advanced to the semi-finals where they were stopped 3-0 by the Czechs.

Hetherington also took part in the 1988 Olympics in Seoul. That year she also won her first professional tournament title in singles, defeating American Katrina Adams to take the Virginia Slims of Wellington. A highlight for the year was Hetherington and Fendick advancing to the final of the U.S. Open after a thrilling contest that saw them defeat Steffi Graf and Gabriela Sabatini in the doubles semi-final 6-4, 7-6 (7-1). Earlier in the week they had downed Chris Evert and Wendy Turnbull in quarter-final action.

Hetherington's aspirations to become the first Canadian to win a Grand Slam title were not to be, however, as she and Fendick were defeated 6-4, 6-1, in the U.S. Open final by Americans Gigi Fernandez and Robin White.

A year later Hetherington and Fendick would also reach the finals of another Grand Slam tournament, the Australian Open, but also left the court as runners-up. Later, Hetherington would team with another American, Kathy Rinaldi, where in addition to winning several tournaments they would advance to the semi-finals of the 1993 Australian Open and the quarter-finals at Wimbledon. In 1995 Hetherington advanced to her third Grand Slam final but came short of victory, reaching the mixed doubles final at the French Open with playing partner John De Jager of South Africa.

Hetherington has also worked to put something back into her sport, serving on the World Tennis Association drug testing and Special Olympics committees.

Sonya Jeyaseelan

At age eighteen, this player from North Vancouver ended the 1994 season as Canada's top "up and comer" in the tennis world, although her competitive resumé reads as long as some veterans' accomplishments. In September of 1994 she won her first professional tournament, taking the $25,000 SunLife Challenger with a 6-2, 5-2 win over American Janet Lee.

Sonya Jeyaseelan won her first major title in 1989, taking the Canadian indoor under-fourteen title. From there she would go on to become Canada's top junior female player, winning the under-eighteen singles title at the 1991 SunLife nationals while taking the singles hardware at the 1993 Canadian Junior International — the first Canadian junior to win the singles title in thirteen years.

Jeyaseelan secured herself a spot as one of the top junior players in the game when, in December 1993, she advanced to the final of the forty-seventh annual Orange Bowl international tournament. Jeyaseelan was seeded fourth in the event and lost in the final to Spain's Angeles Montolio.

Sonya Jeyaseelan: Considerable success in junior ranks.

Helen Kelesi: They called her Hurricane Helen.

Helen Kelesi

TENNIS

Helen Kelesi earned the nickname Hurricane Helen for her volatile and explosive style of play, a style which earned her a career best WTA (Women's Tennis Association) ranking of thirteenth during the 1989-90 season. A Canadian under-fourteen and under-eighteen champion at age thirteen, Kelesi turned pro in 1985 at age fifteen and in only her second professional tournament she stunned the tennis world by defeating Czech star Helena Sukova to ad-

vance to the final at Monticello. Kelesi finished that season ranked 48th in the world.

She reached the quarter-finals of the French Open in 1988 and '89 and was ranked Canada's number one woman singles player from 1987 through 1991, winning four consecutive national titles from '87 to 1990. She also competed for Canada at the 1988 and '92 Olympics in addition to being an integral member of several Federation Cup teams.

Badminton

Badminton suffers from an erroneous reputation in North America, where too many movies have depicted genteel Victorian women gently batting the bird about for so-called exercise. In other parts of the world, such as Asia, New Zealand, Australia and Britain, badminton is not considered a gentle game but a fierce challenge of speed and tactics. In Malaysia, for example, badminton players receive as much honour and attention as football or hockey players in North America.

Canadian women have enjoyed international success in badminton despite the limited attention it receives in North America. Before there was a world championship the All-England competition was considered the pinnacle of international badminton competition. The sport was not included on the Olympic program until 1988, where it was a demonstration event. In 1992 badminton became a full-medal sport at the Summer Olympics in Barcelona.

Three women who excelled in many sports — Dorothy Walton, Claire Lovett and Marjory Shedd — were the first Canadian women to make a considerable mark in the badminton ranks:

Dorothy Walton   BADMINTON

Dorothy Walton epitomized the all-around Canadian woman athlete that was so prevalent in the 1920s and '30s. Born in Swift Current, Saskatchewan, she excelled in track and field, tennis, basketball and hockey. While studying economics at the University of Saskatchewan she showed astounding versatility, competing in fourteen varsity athletic programs.

But it was in racquet sports that she went on to make her mark — first in tennis where she won more than fifty local, provincial and regional titles from 1924 to 1931. At the time she also played badminton and enjoyed some success. Her athletic career was put on hold for a time when she married in 1931 and while she worked on a masters thesis. From 1934 onwards, badminton would be her main sport.

By 1939 Walton was clearly the best woman badminton player in North America, having won national singles and doubles titles and many events in the United States. She travelled to England with an eye on finding a greater challenge — playing in the prestigious All-England tournament. She dominated competition in a warm-up tournament and breezed past competition in the early rounds of the All-England. She dispatched the defending champion in the semifinals and won the championship with an 11-4, 11-5 victory.

Walton's athletic aspirations were stalled as World War II wore on. She took her energy and assertiveness into the public court, becoming a consumer activist with the same gusto she displayed in becoming one of Canada's top woman athletes of the first half century.

Claire Lovett   BADMINTON

Claire Lovett followed where Walton was forced to end at the start of the war. Born in Saskatchewan but later living in Vancouver, she dominated tennis play at the Vancouver Lawn Tennis and Badminton Club, winning some sixteen titles out of the club. She won the national women's singles and doubles badminton championships in 1947 and '48 while also serving as a member of Canada's Uber Cup team — badminton's version of the Federation Cup.

It didn't seem to matter whether she had a tennis or badminton racquet in her hand. In 1966 she won the national singles tennis title and would go on to compete, and succeed, as a master level competitor, winning national and United States masters championships

Lovett also played ice hockey and baseball and was an outstanding bowler.

Claire Lovett: National champion and international competitor.

Marjory Shedd: Semi-finalist at the prestigious England tournament.

Marjory Shedd

BADMINTON

Marjory Shedd was another athlete for whom badminton was one of many challenges met with considerable success. She first excelled in basketball, leading her team to the Canadian junior championships in 1945 and, by 1950, was a member of the Canadian senior champion Montgomery Maids.

She then turned her attention to volleyball, contributing to the University of Toronto winning five national titles. Badminton was a pastime until 1949, when she decided to put more energy into that game and she was rewarded quickly, advancing to the finals at the 1951 and '52 national championships and winning the event in 1953. In her career she would win the national event six times, in addition to taking four mixed and 11 women's doubles titles.

She, too, made a foray to the All-England event, going as far as the semi-finals. She was also named to Canada's Uber Cup team six times.

Jane Youngberg & Wendy Clarkson Carter BADMINTON

Jane Youngberg and Wendy Clarkson Carter were to become both rivals and friends as Canada's top women badminton players through the 1970s. Edmonton's Clarkson won five national singles titles and was a quarter-finalist at All-England in 1976 and at the world badminton championships in 1977. She was a semi-finalist at the 1978 All-England event, where she defeated top seed Lene Koppen of Denmark 11-8, 6-11, 11-8 in the quarter-finals.

Clarkson also earned a bronze medal in singles at the 1978 Commonwealth Games in addition to contributing to Canada's team taking silver.

Jane Youngberg didn't take badminton seriously until she earned her university degree in 1971, although she was a winner in singles and doubles at the national junior championships. She decided to enter an open competition in Vancouver and, unheralded and unseeded, she won. That same year she was chosen to Canada's Uber Cup team and was named to the Canadian squad which toured China — an unusual and prestigious opportunity for the times.

Youngberg won her first national championship in 1974 and two years later joined teammate Wendy Clarkson in what was an extraordinary badminton story at the time. Both Canadians advanced to the quarter-finals at the All-England that year. In 1978 Youngberg and Claire Backhouse teamed to play in doubles semi-finals at the All-England event, for a time ranking the twosome in the top five in the world.

Youngberg continued as Canada's top-ranked female badminton player through the early '80s, winning national titles even as she began raising two small children.

Jane Youngberg: Success in singles and doubles.

Wendy Clarkson Carter: Five national titles.

Denyse Julien

BADMINTON

Denyse Julien is another all-around athlete who opted to make badminton her sport, even though with a career best score of 76 on the golf course it is surprising the LPGA (Ladies Professional Golf Association) never came calling. She began playing at age twelve and took up the game seriously at age fourteen. She began representing Canada internationally in 1981 and, as a member of Canada's Commonwealth Games team in 1994 at age thirty-four, remained one of the top three women badminton players in Canada.

Julien's laurels include victories in Canadian, U.S., German and Welsh Open competitions in addition to twice sweeping medals in singles, doubles and mixed doubles at the Pan-American championships. She also accumulated several Commonwealth Games medals, including team silver in 1982 and '86, doubles silver in 1986 and a silver in singles from the 1990 Games in Auckland.

She continued her winning ways in 1995, taking singles and doubles gold medals at the Pan-American Games in Mar del Plata, Argentina. (Photo on page 196)

Claire Sharpe

BADMINTON

"Follow your heart" is a worn but worthy adage that is often easier to advise than to carry out. Claire Sharpe has followed her heart ever since she found herself tugged in

several directions when it became clear she had a promising future as a badminton player. As much as she loved her sport she had personal aspirations — education, career, family. She found out those aspirations didn't jibe with what others were advising.

"They said you'll never make it unless you're a full-time athlete," she said. "I always felt it was important to get my education. I didn't want just a one-track life. I said: 'Okay, I'll do the best I can.' So I got my degree.

"Then, I got a full-time job after I got my degree and they said: 'No way you can carry on at your level and have a full-time job.' I said: 'That may be fine but I live in Vancouver and I can't afford not to work if I ever want to have a home. So I said: That's fine, I'll do the best I can, and got a job.

"Then, I started a family…"

It is easy for outsiders to wonder what Sharpe might have accomplished had she put on the blinkers and devoted herself solely to badminton. But a peek at her resumé shows she did very well for an athlete holding down a full-time job with Consumer and Corporate Affairs Canada and eventually combining international competition with the basic daily rigours of raising three children.

From 1978, where she and doubles partner Jane Youngberg advanced to the All-England semi-finals and status as one of the top women's doubles teams in the world, through to competing in her fifth Commonwealth Games

in 1994, Sharpe was an integral member of Canada's national badminton team. In addition to earning many B.C. titles, she was Canadian singles champion in 1985, doubles champion in 1978, '79, '80, '83, '84, '87 and '91 and won the mixed doubles title in 1980, '84 and '87. She also earned six medals, including gold in 1982, in Commonwealth Games competition.

Sharpe's badminton story began when one of the parents in her neighbourhood took time to organize a badminton league for the area's children.

"I got started by my neighbour, Lars Anderson," she said. "He gathered up all the kids in the neighbourhood and took us down to the school and got us playing badminton. That was my first experience with it."

At the time she was just another twelve-year-old who enjoyed many sports — volleyball, field hockey, tennis. By age seventeen, at Anderson's urging, Sharpe joined a club to further what was clearly a burgeoning talent. She went on to win national junior titles in women's and mixed doubles and would gain a reputation as an outstanding doubles player although she could hold her own in singles as well.

By 1978, then twenty, she made her first impact internationally by joining with Jane Youngberg to reach the semi-

Claire Sharpe: Took home six Commonwealth Games medals in a long international career.

finals at the All-England tournament, the most prestigious competition in badminton. The duo would also take the silver medal at the 1978 Commonwealth Games in Edmonton.

"I never really was one to set goals for myself," stressed Sharpe. "Saying I want to be champion of this or that. We'd get these questionnaires from Sport Canada or Badminton Canada asking what are your short-term goals, long-term goals. I used to write the same vague thing every time, something like improve Canada's standing internationally.

"My philosophy is you go out and do the best with what you've got on the day. It's the process, not the result."

Sharpe's philosophy toward competition may have been best illustrated by her reaction to events following the conclusion of women's doubles at the 1982 Commonwealth Games. She and partner Johanne Falardeau upset highly favoured Gillian Clark and Karen Beckhman of England to win the gold medal.

"I remember being somewhat shocked that people came rushing down to the court to give us hugs after we won," she said. "I thought, come on guys, it's just a game. It was an exciting match because we were behind but I have other memories that are just as satisfying. I think back on some of my big wins and they're nice, but there are other matches or games that I have enjoyed just as much but may not have won."

Sharpe's commitment to her sport goes beyond her work on the court, to acting as a coach, athletes' representative and speaker. In 1990 she was one of several women athletes who protested Sport Canada's policy of reducing or eliminating funding to pregnant women athletes. Her personal recommendations were utilized in what would ultimately be a change in the organization's policy.

Sharpe retired from national team competition in 1991 when she was expecting her third child. She and her family moved to Victoria, but in 1994 Sharpe came out of retirement to play in her fifth Commonwealth Games, with the badminton venue within walking distance of her home. She didn't add to her medal collection there, but was one of Canada's most celebrated athletes at the event because of her longtime commitment to excellence in the sport combined with her determination to have a life outside the court.

In 1995 she continued that commitment, serving as B.C. badminton team manager for the Canada Winter Games in Grande Prairie, Alberta.

Denyse Julien: Double gold medallist at 1995 Pan-Am Games.

FIELDS & GREENS

Golf

Golf — that pastoral pursuit — is beloved by people of all walks of life as much for its social quality as its status as an outdoor activity. Although weather precludes Canadian golfers in many regions from taking part in the sport year-round, Canada has produced many outstanding male and female golfers who have achieved success in amateur and professional play.

Ada MacKenzie

Ada MacKenzie: Promoted the game of golf for women.

Canadian women golfers who achieve success today owe much to the pioneering efforts of Ada MacKenzie, who not only emerged as Canada's first outstanding female golfer but also went on to promote and develop the game for women players in Canada.

She was born in Toronto in 1891 and was reported to have had her first taste of the links at about age ten, when her father sat her on the handlebars of his bicycle and took her to the Highlands Golf Club. Golf would be one of many of MacKenzie's passions, however, as she was also an outstanding basketball, ice hockey and tennis player, and excelled in swimming and diving.

In 1914 she won her first competition, the Toronto Golf Club championship, and for nearly three decades was a contender in every tournament she entered, winning the Canadian Ladies' Open championship four times and the Close championship six times in addition to nine Ontario championships and many district and regional honours. In international play she was twice a semi-finalist at the U.S. Women's Amateur Championship and won two Bermuda championships.

Living proof that golf is a lifelong game, MacKenzie went on to excel as a senior's player, winning the national senior title nine times and in 1963 she won the U.S. North-South Seniors title.

While her play offered one source of inspiration to young women golfers, her work off the green also contributed to opportunities enjoyed by women golfers. Frustrated with what she knew from experience to be uncomfortable and awkward golf clothes for women, she launched her own line of practical and comfortable golfwear. She was particularly keen to promote junior players and in 1928 was responsible for organizing the first Ontario junior championship.

A golfing vacation to England, where women seemed to enjoy far more playing opportunities than their counterparts in Canada, prompted MacKenzie to do something about giving women a place to play. Her work and energy resulted in the 1924 opening of the Ladies' Golf and Tennis Club of Toronto.

"She was a pretty good athlete," noted Marlene Stewart Streit, one of many young golfers who benefited from MacKenzie's encouragement. At 17, Streit outplayed MacKenzie to win the Canadian Ladies' Open. Said Streit about MacKenzie: "She was very determined and was a great competitor. She fought to the bitter end. That's a great competitor. But she was also a very nice lady, encouraging to everyone. She wanted you to go out and try to beat her."

Jocelyne Bourassa

Jocelyne Bourassa began playing golf at age thirteen and from 1965 to 1979 enjoyed a playing career that included her winning three Quebec junior championships, four senior amateur championships and two national senior amateur titles. She also was a member of Canada's team to the 1970 women's world amateur team championship and to the Commonwealth championship in New Zealand.

But her name in Canadian golf will forever be associated with events that unfolded in June of 1973 at the Montreal Municipal Golf Course. The event was La Canadienne, the only Canadian stop on the Ladies' Professional Golf Association tour. At the end of the requisite three rounds, Shawinigan-born Bourassa and American stars Judy Rankin and Sandra Haynie were tied, forcing a sudden death playoff.

That Bourassa maintained her composure under the close scrutiny of the partisan and boisterous Quebec gallery was remarkable. The threesome remained tied through the extra hole at the sixteenth tee. On the next hole Rankin three-putted and was dropped from the fray, while Haynie and Bourassa remained tied. At the eighteenth, Haynie cracked,

Jocelyne Bourassa: Kept her composure during La Canadienne playoff.

sending her ball into the water and eliciting an explosion of cheers from the crowd — not exactly proper golf etiquette but understandable given that short of Bourassa completely unravelling she was about to win her first LPGA title. Bourassa's nerve held and she won the event.

A year earlier she had opted to go professional with some support from Montreal businessman Jean-Louis Levesque. And at the end of the 1972 season she was voted the LPGA's rookie of the year and Canada's top woman athlete for that year.

Bourassa went on to become a popular player on the tour, delighting galleries with her outgoing personality. At one tournament stop in Atlantic City she drew double takes from supporters in the clubhouse when she came in sporting a Montreal Canadiens' team jersey.

But she was also plagued by a knee injury suffered playing basketball and by 1979 she was forced to leave the Tour. She didn't leave golf, however. La Canadienne event would eventually be renamed the du Maurier Classic after the tobacco company which took up sponsorship of the event. In a fitting twist of fate Bourassa went on to become executive director of the LPGA event.

Sandra Post

Sandra Post was five years old when she put a club to a golf ball, already forming in her mind an intent to become one of the best in the game which fascinated her. But she was a competent figure skater too, and what Canadian female skater didn't harbour some fantasy of becoming the next Barbara Ann Scott?

Golf? Or figure skating? The issue finally came to a head when one year Post decided she might want to stay at home

and skate instead of going to Florida for the family's annual stint in the sun, which included plenty of golf and taking in the LPGA events. Her father, no slouch on the links himself, discussed the dilemma with his daughter and put forward his philosophy. Would she want to compete knowing that her smile or the colour of her hair or costume might have an impact on the judges? Would she want to compete knowing that whatever she did as an unknown skater might

Sandra Post: Twice won the Dinah Shore Open.

not be judged the same as it might if she were more established?

"In golf, even if you go out and nobody likes you, if you have the lowest score you win; and nobody can take that away from you," reflected Post. "I said: 'I'm going to Florida.' You know, all sport at the top can be heartwrenching. Everybody has cried. You're going to lose more than you're going to win. But it would be awful to have another person take something away from you."

Post didn't lose much sleep over the decision. In a professional golf career that began in 1968 and ended in early 1984 she would win more LPGA tournaments than any Canadian woman to date, twice be awarded the Bobbie Rosenfeld trophy as Canada's top woman athlete, and would pave the way on the professional tour for other Canadian women to follow.

Constant practice and scrutiny of the points that made the top women golfers so successful quickly translated into success for Post, who by age fourteen enjoyed a six stroke handicap. She won the first of three Ontario junior championships when she was fifteen and at sixteen won the Ontario Ladies' championship and the first of three national junior championships.

In January 1968, at age nineteen, Post announced she was turning professional. She finished twentieth in her first pro tournament in Florida, earning enough money to get to the next stop. In her third event she shot a hole-in-one, and in June 1968 she astounded the golf world by taking venerable Kathy Whitworth into an eighteen-hole playoff at the LPGA Championship in Sutton, Massachusetts. The Canadian rookie from Oakville, Ontario, was expected to crack under pressure. Instead, she won by seven strokes with a five-under-par 68.

The victory earned Post Rookie of the Year honours from both the LPGA and *Golf Digest*.

She earned a reputation as a competitor who wasn't afraid to speak her mind.

"I think most golfers have their opinions, and voice them," she said. "I think that's why they make good interviews — they don't hedge. It's the nature of the sport. Golfers are going to fail more than they win and they've got to look in the mirror and know it wasn't the caddie — it was you didn't make the shot. You are continually soul searching. But you have to because you don't have a guaranteed paycheque every week."

Post's early success was followed by less outstanding years, her next victory coming in 1974 in the Colgate Far East Open in Australia. In the mid-1970s, the public was made much more aware of the ending of her marriage than of her golf scores, as Post experienced the downside of the media's attention to sports celebrities.

But the best times were still ahead. In 1978 and '79, Post won the Dinah Shore Open, a feat which would become the most cherished legacy of her pro years.

"For a time, a lot of people thought I was just a flash in the pan, and I had to fall down the ladder and climb back up," she mused. "I think in the first Dinah I was getting back up on that ladder again after going through all the other stuff in my life. To win back-to-back is really difficult to do. And it was THE tournament to win back then because it was so far out in front of everybody."

The tour rigours finally got to Post and she retired from play in early 1984 with eight LPGA victories to her credit. A decade later, she was content with teaching the game, and golf remained as much a part of her life and her dreams as it had when she was a young girl imagining making the big putt for a championship.

"Golf can be solitary or social and it shows someone's true personality," declared Post. "That's why a lot of executives, when they don't know who to hire, they take all these potential people out to play golf. The guy or gal who tends to lose temper, that all comes through on the golf course. It shows so much about a person."

Marlene Stewart Streit

GOLF

Forty-five years after first learning how to wield a driver, Marlene Stewart Streit put on a golf display that was characteristic of the form that secured her tenure as Canada's outstanding amateur woman golfer. At the 1994 U.S. Golf Association Senior Women's Amateur Championship at Sea Island, Georgia, sixty-year-old Streit birdied the final hole of an eighteen-hole playoff against American rival Nancy Fitzgerald for a two-stroke victory and her second win in the tournament. The first came in 1985.

"I came from behind a bit," she acknowledged of the playoff round which saw Fitzgerald leading 38-39 after nine holes. "I had a great round the last day, I played quite well in the playoff. Winning those USGA (U.S. Golf Association) tournaments, they have such great fields, they're so well-run. It's a great honour to win those and they're tough to win. Any tournament is tough to win."

Anyone who played against Streit from the time she won her first of two Ontario junior girls' titles in 1951 would add that any tournament Streit is in is tough to win.

Statistics? Consider these numbers: eleven-time Ontario Ladies Amateur champion from 1951 to 1977, plus seven second-place finishes; eleven-time Canadian Ladies' Golf Association champion from 1951 to 1973, plus five second-place finishes; nine-time Canadian Close Champion.

That's just in Canada. Streit's international résumé includes the titles British Women's Amateur Champion (1953) and Australian Women's Amateur Champion (1963).

Barely five feet tall, Marlene Stewart Streit is a giant in Canadian women's amateur golf.

"I don't think I was a natural," she insisted in 1995. "I practised a lot. I loved to practise and I would rather practise than play. I still do. I have probably hit more golf balls than most people. A lot of people don't like to practise, they'd much rather play. I was always in a game, in my own mind. I never got bored with it."

Marlene Stewart's playing career began in 1947 when she took up caddying at Lookout Country Club in Fonthill, Ontario, and started playing two years later. Her enthusiasm for the game caught the attention of club pro Gordon McInnis and it was he who helped her develop her game.

"He taught me everything," she said. "He taught me how to think going around a golf course. He believed in me, encouraged me and helped me get into golf tournaments."

He also helped her diffuse a hot temper, learning instead to channel that energy into concentration so that she displayed a mental toughness and ability to focus that was

Marlene Stewart Streit: Developed a professional attitude to become Canada's top woman amateur golfer.

uncharacteristic of most teens. That ability to detach from the distraction of tournament surroundings made her tough to beat, particularly in pressure situations.

"Being able to finish off matches was so important," she said. "The game was never over until it was absolutely over. I'm sure there were other girls who played equally as well as I did, but maybe, it was the concentration. I was gifted in that I was able to concentrate, I don't think I ever thought of negatives. That was Gordon too. He was never negative."

At age seventeen she astounded the Canadian golf world by defeating venerable Ada MacKenzie in the Canadian Ladies' Open. At nineteen she won the British Amateur title and representing Canada proved to be a career highlight and a major factor in her decision not to turn professional.

"I met my husband and was married after college and I could play all the amateur golf I wanted," she explained. "That was fulfilling enough. And representing Canada, I liked that. It was a big honour. And winning the U.S. Amateur, I don't think you can get much bigger than that."

Streit twice won the Lou Marsh Award as Canada's outstanding athlete in addition to earning the Bobbie Rosenfeld award as Canada's top female athlete in 1951, '53, '56, '60 and '63. She was named an officer of the Order of Canada on July 7, 1967.

At the age of sixty, her laurels had not abated. Streit's victory in the USGA senior event earned her *Golf World* magazine's award as 1994 Senior Woman amateur player of the year.

Dawn Coe-Jones GOLF

Dawn Coe-Jones: Former high school basketball star from Lake Cowichan makes good on the LPGA circuit.

Dawn Coe-Jones was just discovering the joys of golf when Jocelyne Bourassa was making headlines winning the 1973 LPGA La Canadienne tournament in Montreal. Coe took up golf at age nine while growing up in Lake Cowichan, B.C. By age twelve she not only broke eighty, but defeated her father in the process. A natural athlete, she also excelled in basketball, playing guard for the Lake Cowichan Secondary Lakers, the 1977 B.C. high school champions.

After high school, having won two B.C. junior titles and been ranked as one of the top junior women golfers in Canada, she explored the possibility of earning a golf scholarship to a U.S. school. Coe attended Lamar University in Texas and upon graduation in 1983 was named a first-team All-American. She turned professional after winning the 1983 Canadian Amateur championship.

She eventually made Florida her living and training base. Her first LPGA victory came at the 1992 Kemper Open in Hawaii. Two years later Coe-Jones took her second LPGA tour event, defeating Lauri Merten by one stroke at the LPGA Palm Beach Classic.

She began 1995 with an impressive victory in the LPGA Tournament of Champions, defeating a field that included five LPGA Hall of Famers.

Soccer

Sylvie Beliveau SOCCER

Sylvie Beliveau remembered just how far she was able to go as an avid soccer player in her teens.

"When I was playing there were no provincial teams and only championships for select teams. That was from 1978 to '82," said Beliveau, who also honed her skills as a varsity player at the University of Sherbrooke. "There was nothing for me. I was eighteen. A lot of people encouraged talented women to go into other sports. I'm sure soccer lost a great many athletes to other sports."

In 1991 Beliveau was appointed head coach of the Canadian women's soccer team after serving as an assistant coach with the squad since 1986. During that time she has seen the opportunities for women in soccer grow around the world. The women's game will be added to the program for the 1996 Olympics in Atlanta. A women's World Cup was organized on a quadrennial basis beginning in 1991 in China and a second tournament was held in Stockholm, Sweden, in June 1995.

Canada failed to advance out of its zone in qualifying for the 1991 World Cup, losing to the United States who went on and won the inaugural women's World Cup of soccer. But with the United States earning automatic entry as defending champion, Canada advanced to become one of the teams competing in Sweden by qualifying through CONCACAF (Confederation of North, Central American and Caribbean Football) zone competition in the summer of 1994.

The 1995 World Cup would serve to decide the field for the Summer Olympics in Atlanta, with the top seven plus the host team United States gaining an Olympic berth. Going into the World Cup Beliveau said Canada likely ranked about sixth in the fray. Earning a spot in the 1996 Olympics would do wonders for the profile of the women's game in Canada, she said.

"From a player's perspective, it's very important because of the recognition they get," she said. "Soccer, on the men's side, has the World Cup as its premier event but I think being included in the Olympic Games will help women to be more recognized just because of the exposure that comes with being part of the Olympics.

"There are such limited professional opportunities for women players while guys have opportunities all over the world."

Sylvie Beliveau: National women's team coach.

Carrie Serwetnyk: Found a career in Japan.

Carrie Serwetnyk

Carrie Serwetnyk is one of the few women athletes in Canada who can say she makes a good living from her sport, and she doesn't play tennis or golf. Serwetnyk is a longtime member of the Canadian women's soccer team. She managed to parlay a love of the game that developed in her early teens into a scholarship at the University of North Carolina. She then took the prowess she gained in NCAA (National Collegiate Athletic Association) competition, where she was the team's top scorer, into professional playing opportunities first in France and then in Japan.

"My whole life — well most of it since I was sixteen — has revolved around soccer," said Serwetnyk, who joined Canada's national team in 1985. "I've just lived from moment to moment, playing the game at the highest level I can."

In 1992 the twenty-six-year-old player from Mississauga, Ontario, signed a one-year deal worth $100,000 US to play on the Fujita Corporation team in Japan. The deal made headlines as the salary was worth more than many professional football players were making in the Canadian Football League.

Serwetnyk scored fourteen goals for the team that season and went on to sign the next year with the Yomiuri Club where, hampered by illness and injury, she scored two goals to help lead her club to the league championship. In 1995 Serwetnyk was living just outside Tokyo, nursing a knee injury while conducting clinics for a private company trying to promote the sport in Japan in general, and for Japanese women in particular. By then another Canadian national team member, Charmaine Hooper, had

also signed contracts to play in Japan which, in addition to Norway, was virtually the only country in the world where women could hope to earn a living as professional soccer players.

In 1991 Serwetnyk travelled to the first World Cup in Beijing as a freelance journalist after Canada failed to advance from the qualifying round. She watched the United States capture the inaugural women's World Cup — the squad included many of her teammates from North Carolina.

"There were sixty thousand people watching that game," she enthused. "Step by step it's going to go farther, get better for women. In ten years there are going to be more professional leagues around the world, more players will become known. This is a time when everyone who has played, who put their whole lives into something because they loved it, are able to see things happening. They had this idealistic image, hoping one day there would be a future and it is finally coming true. I'm just glad to be a part of it and to be able to make a living at something I truly love to do. In sport, not many women can say that."

Baseball & Softball

Sometimes called the ultimate team game, initially baseball was played by American men and watched by American women. All that changed when the men marched off to the second world war and women, including many Canadians, were recruited to the baseball diamond.

All-American Girls Professional Baseball League

In 1992 one of the most popular films of the time was Penny Marshall's *A League of Their Own*, a story about women who played in the All-American Girls Professional Baseball League from 1943 to 1954. The league was formed to satisfy the insatiable American hunger for baseball, and with the country's young men off doing duty in World War II, chewing gum magnate Philip K. Wrigley filled that void by forming a women's baseball league with rosters featuring players from the United States and Canada.

Indeed, more than fifty Canadian players donned uniforms and played in the league. Some played for a brief period while others, such as Mary "Bonnie" Baker of Regina, Saskatchewan, would become league stars and be featured in *Life* magazine.

"I held every game so dear because I loved the sport so much," said Baker, who played for much of her career with

the South Bend Blue Sox. Early in her career a sportswriter described her as a bonnie lass and the nickname Bonnie stuck.

Baker worked in a department store at the time the league was being formed and she learned about the league while reading a coffee shop newspaper during a break from her job. At the time she was an outstanding player in Saskatchewan and the thought of playing baseball at such a high level was appealing.

"There was a picture of Mrs. Wrigley and a model wearing one of the uniforms and I thought: 'Oh my God, if I could just get there,' she said. "That afternoon I got a call from Hub Bishop, who was a hockey scout on the lookout for the league for women players from the prairies. He said: 'I need your help, we need some good players.' That's where it all started. I went down to play and didn't tell my husband, who was in the RCAF, until I got down there."

Baker played from 1943 to 1951, making her name as a catcher although she at times played other positions. While dubbed "stylish" off the field she was all business behind the mound and was never afraid to speak her mind if an umpire's call didn't go the way it should.

"I had arguments with the umpires and did get thrown out of one game," she said. "My manager came to argue for me and he got thrown out, too. I wasn't afraid at all to speak my mind but I was smart about it. I never faced the umpire and said it. I just called him a lot of things while I was in my crouch, but he heard every word of it. You can't make all the calls right, I appreciate that, but I had to remind them once in a while."

Marge and Helen Callaghan came to the league via Vancouver after their play caught the eye of some scouts at the women's world softball championships in Detroit. Helen was a powerful hitter while Marge was a versatile third-base player who was often called to bat after her sister, moving hard-hitting Helen around the bases.

"When they approached us I initially wasn't too interested," Marge Callaghan Maxwell recalled some fifty years later. "I didn't really want to leave home and I didn't think anything would come of it anyway. But my dad talked me into going because he wasn't keen on Helen going down there by herself."

The initial reticence gave way to zeal and Marge Callaghan spent eight seasons in the league, primarily with the Fort Wayne Daisies.

"It was one of the most enjoyable times of my life," she said. "I met a lot of wonderful people. The fans were fantastic. It was a very good experience."

Many years later Maxwell took part in an exhibition game that celebrated some of the Canadian women who played in the league while recognizing some of the Canadian women national team members likely going on to compete at the 1996 Summer Olympics in Atlanta, where women's softball would make its debut. It had been a while since she chased a fly ball in earnest.

Mary 'Bonnie' Baker: Travelled from Saskatchewan to become one of the most popular and recognized players in the All-American Girls Professional Baseball League.

"A little pop went over the pitcher's head and I thought I'd better start running for it," she said. "I went flat on my face trying to catch the ball. Then my son yelled out: 'Way to go, Mom, way to shake the ground up!'"

Alpha Sports

SOFTBALL

In 1978 Canada enjoyed its best result in international women's softball when New Westminster-based Doc's Blues, in later years known as Alpha Sports, advanced to the final of the world women's softball championships in El Salvador. The Canadian squad allowed four runs in the first inning and couldn't get them back, losing to the United States 4-0 but the achievement marked the last time a club team would represent Canada at the event and the last time a Canadian women's team of any description would make the world final.

Through the 1970s and '80s, Doc's Blues/Alpha Sports became a dynasty in Canadian women's softball, winning eleven national and nineteen provincial championships,

Celebration Time: Alpha Sports' Tracey Huclack hugs Debbie Ross as the other teammates gather to congratulate Ross for hitting a home run.

overseen by manager and mentor Adrian Lavigne who demanded dedication and discipline as much as talent on the part of his players. While the team's crisp and powerful play made a statement on the field, they also made a statement away from the diamond, serious in the job of representing their country by often appearing and travelling in crisp white skirts and blazers.

Names that appeared on the team's roster over the years would represent the very best in Canadian softball. Rosemary Fuller, Janice Robinson, Patty Polych, Tracey Hucklack, Maureen McCarthy and Joanne Mick were just some of the outstanding players who donned the Blues' blue and white or the red and white of Alpha Sports.

Catcher Mick, who played fourteen years with the squad, was often called the team general by Lavigne because of her ability to organize strategy from her vantage point behind the plate.

Mick noted that many teams of talented individuals have come together only to fail as a team because of an inability to work together, a strong point evident in her squad's success through the years and sparked by Lavigne's insistence on work ethic and discipline.

"I've often said it was like being an orchestra leader," she said. "At times it might have been a bad band, but for the most part it was like a symphony, everyone playing their part and all of it coming together in harmony."

Archery

Initially a means of survival more than a sport, the practice of using a bow to shoot an arrow at a target has been around for thousands of years. Modern archery competition requires the competitor to shoot at a round target, which features a round, gold "bull's-eye" surrounded by circles of red, blue, black and white. Points are awarded depending on where the arrow strikes.

Lucille Lessard

ARCHERY

Peer pressure can be one of the most powerful factors in determining what a young person does in terms of physical activity. A teen who has friends playing basketball will likely become involved in the game while another, whose friends scorn athletics, may feel pressure to conform and give up sporting aspirations.

Many years later, Lucille Lessard Hutchinson still recalled how difficult it was being thirteen years old and the only female taking part in the school archery program.

"The boys started to tell me that the sport wasn't for girls, that I shouldn't be there," she said. "All I could think was: Someday I'll show you. If people put me down or tell me I can't do something, they've just said the right thing because it makes me want to go out and do it."

Lessard, born in Loretteville, Quebec, had joined the club at the urging of her Grade 9 teacher, Leonard Brisson, who also happened to be one of the country's top archery coaches. His tutelage and support paid off as a year after Lessard took up archery she finished second in the Quebec Games and a year later became provincial champion.

Her burgeoning interest in archery conflicted with other interests, notably swimming and figure skating. When she dislocated a shoulder in an attempt to land a double flip on the ice she was forced to make a choice between sports. Archery won.

"I've always been an individual," she declared, noting her interest in sports that were not team-oriented. "I played team sports in school but I always liked the idea that if I succeeded, it was me. If I blew it, it was me, it wasn't anyone else's fault."

Lucille Lessard: Made believers out of classmates.

Lessard was seventeen in 1974 when she travelled to Zagreb, Yugoslavia to compete at the world field championships. A two-time Canadian champion, she had no idea what to expect from her international rivals, although back in Quebec her coach had made a prediction to newspaper reporters that she would win the world title.

"I'm glad I didn't read about that," she said. "It was so hard to get news over there, I had no idea. He's a wonderful coach and wasn't one to put pressure on, but I'm glad it never got back to me until I came home."

Lessard suffered a slow start at the world event but rallied to take the world championship.

She felt pressure later, however, as the 1976 Olympics loomed in Montreal. Not only was Lessard a world champion in the field event, but she also finished fifth in the 1975 target world championships. Lessard finished third in the Canadian Olympic team trials and didn't make the team to the Montreal Games.

She carried on for several more years, however, and Lessard would be a five-time national champion and a Pan-American Games silver medallist before she retired in 1983. The jitters didn't ruin her Olympic aspirations in 1980 but politics did. Lessard was named to the Canadian team to Moscow but didn't compete because of Canada's boycott of those games.

In 1995, with a child and a management job at a trust company, she hasn't ruled out returning to the sport in the future. Even in taking time out to do other things she hadn't lost the mental toughness that allowed her to weather the taunts of her male classmates and go on to become a world champion.

"I've always believed in the three D's," she said. "Desire, discipline and the dream to do something. Whatever you do in life, go for it. Give yourself a goal and do it. I was young but I had a lot of discipline and that's why I was successful."

Dorothy Lidstone

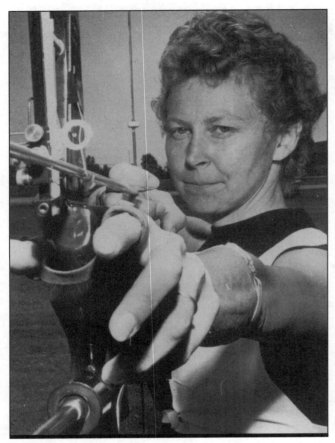

Dorothy Lidstone: Led Canada to best-ever results in archery.

Dorothy Lidstone knew she had come a long way from the one-room schoolhouse when she got a call to appear on Garry Moore's television variety show in New York.

When you're a world champion attention naturally follows, even if you're more comfortable out of the limelight in a sport that involves a human being, a bow and a target.

"When I was young I was very shy, very backward," said Lidstone, who was born in Wetaskiwin, Alberta. "So I wouldn't stick my nose out unless I really, really had to. I wasn't born to sing the national anthem on stage or anything like that. Sport was my thing."

Her thing, in particular, became archery. At the 1969 world championships in Valley Forge, Pennsylvania, Lidstone smashed the world record and her own expectations en route to winning the world target championship. The win was a triumph not only over forty rivals and extreme heat and humidity, but also over her own nerves, which tended to get the better of Lidstone at major competitions.

Winning a world championship was the farthest thing from her mind in 1962 when her then-husband received a bow as a gift and Lidstone, intrigued with the atmosphere and people she met at a Vancouver-area archery club, decided to get a bow as well. She had grown up in rural Alberta and developed a competitive streak playing basketball, tennis, badminton and, particularly, softball. Lidstone continued to play softball and shot rifle after she moved to Vancouver, but once she became enamored with archery it took up most of her free time.

The hand-eye coordination gleaned from playing other sports and her ability to shoot a rifle made Lidstone a quick study in her new sport and she began to have success in club and regional competitions as stepping stones to victories in B.C. and Pacific Northwest events.

She made Canada's team to the 1965 world championships which became, like many an athlete's first major international competition, a valuable learning experience.

"I did absolutely crummy," Lidstone said, laughing ruefully. "I don't know where I finished but it was a lot closer to last than first. I decided that since it was me who put me in near last place nobody else was going to put me in first place.

"That's when I got really serious. I quit drinking coffee. I quit drinking Coke. I ran every night. It became my life."

Four years later Lidstone won the Canadian championship in Victoria to earn a berth on the team to Pennsylvania but she wasn't optimistic about her chances as her scores didn't compare with what was being registered by competitors in meets around the world.

The conditions in Pennsylvania proved severe, with high temperatures and humidity causing some competitors to faint. From the first day Lidstone was among the leaders but fate initially gave her nerves a break. After the first day her excellent score was listed among the day's best but the scorekeepers had inadvertently put another Canadian team member's name next to the mark, allowing Lidstone to avoid the pressure that often accompanies the early leaders.

"I wasn't always that great when it came to the big shoot," she said. "I could lose ten pounds in a weekend, no problem. But in Pennsylvania, I don't know why, I was quite relaxed at that shoot. The whole time I was calm and relaxed."

Among the leaders through four days, Lidstone parlayed that relaxed attitude and consistency into a world championship win that weekend with 2,361 points, 100 better than the previous record and just 60 shy of the men's mark.

That was when the Garry Moore folks called. Winning the world championship proved far less stressful than that subsequent appearance in New York.

"It was a highlight for sure," she said. "But it was nerve-wracking, harder than shooting the Worlds. I had to get up and shoot when the cameras were on."

Lidstone opted not to try out for Canada's team to the 1972 Olympics in Munich and, after continuing to compete locally and regionally for a time, retired from competition in 1975. Archery remained a pivotal part of her life, however, as she started a business manufacturing bows.

The world championship victory remained special for Lidstone some twenty-five years later, although with the memory she welcomed the absence of the nerves that at times had plagued her concentration. She conceded that at times she has allowed her thoughts to drift back to those times in Pennsylvania, particularly when life threw in one of those bad days everyone experiences. More often than not, though, she would gain a sense of peace and satisfaction at the side of a river instead of facing a target.

"Now, I bring back a good feeling with a big fish," she said. "You have your moment in the sun and move on. Some of it just comes in different forms, like catching a fish when the guys on either side of you haven't caught anything."

Shooting

Shooting festivals were documented as far back as the sixteenth century and target shooting was among the events included in the first modern Olympic Games in 1896. Competition is divided into individual events dictated by the type of pistol or rifle used; moving target competitions such as skeet or trap shooting add another element of challenge.

Susan Nattrass

Some people collect hats, others china figurines. Over the years Susan Nattrass has amassed a collection of trap shooting world championships that most competitors only dream of attaining.

World champion — 1974, 1975, 1977, 1978, 1979, 1981; winner of more than twenty Canadian national titles; the first woman to compete against men in Olympic trap shooting — it is an impressive resumé, one that Nattrass never imagined she would create growing up in Calgary, then Edmonton, where her sporting passion through school was volleyball.

"My first trophy was in bowling. When I was thirteen years old I won the city championship," she said in a conspiratorial tone. "Actually, the truth is, the very, very first prize I won was in art. It was for the Calgary Stampede and I still have it — it was potato art. You know, you take a potato and cut it up and make a stamp and make some kind of artistic design.

"But I loved volleyball. My dream was to be on the national volleyball team. I played at university but I was never a star."

Nattrass exhibited prowess and interest in many sports, including swimming, canoeing and horseback riding which were an integral part of her summers spent at camp. She also came by her aim naturally. Her father had competed in three world championships and had taught Nattrass and her two brothers how to shoot. For a time her passion for the summer outdoor life at camp seemed at odds with what was clearly a burgeoning talent in shooting.

"I remember writing my Grade 12 final exams and my high school volleyball coach took me to the airport because my family had already gone out to Vancouver for the Canadian championships. I hopped on a plane, went to the Canadian championships and beat them all, which was really a shock. On the Sunday, I flew back to Edmonton and spent July and August at Pioneer Ranch Camp. Then, I went to university and was too old to go to camp."

At age eighteen Nattrass began to make her mark and get serious about the sport, her first big breakthrough coming by defeating some twelve hundred rivals at a major com-

Susan Nattrass: Eagle eye and steady nerves made her a sure fire world champion.

petition in Reno, Nevada. By 1972 she had established herself as one of the best by finishing second at the world championships. Two years later, in Switzerland, she won her first of six world championships even though her plans to take part in the event were threatened by sudden and necessary surgery to remove a large ovarian cyst.

"My doctor said the last thing I said before they put me out was: 'I'm going to the world championships,'" she said. "And the first thing I said when I got out of it was: 'I'm still going to the world championships.'"

Resolve mastering fatigue, Nattrass came into the final day of competition needing to shoot 24 out of 25 to establish a world record. She missed on her first shot and proceeded to shoot 24 straight for a 143 world record score and her first world championship. By 1976, with the 1975 world championship to her credit, Nattrass arrived at the Summer Olympics in Montreal as the first, and only, woman competing in the Olympic trap shooting event.

She became the focus of much media attention. After the first day she stood a credible fifth, then everything unravelled and she finished twenty-fifth. Some observers felt the attention might have caused too much pressure, but

Nattrass observed she had done just fine the first day despite the media swarm. Years later she conceded a mix-up had occurred and team officials didn't arrive with her gun until just before the competition. By then her nerves were on overdrive when she should have been well practised and focused.

"I missed six of the first ten and that was it," she lamented. "I thought I was out of it. As it turned out, the winner had the lowest score to ever win the Olympics, a 190. If I had just kept my motivation level up I could have done better. Believe me, I didn't do it again. In 1977, '78, '79 and '81, I still remembered what happened in '76."

Indeed, Nattrass emerged from that Olympic debacle and never looked back, setting a world record to win the 1977 world championship then returning a year later to rewrite her record for another world victory, her 1978 effort also being good enough to have earned her a bronze medal in the men's event.

There is nothing like the feeling of competing at one's peak.

"My mother says when I'm performing at my best it's like watching a ballet," said Nattrass. "I'm like a dancer and when everything is going right there is just a flow, and the gun is part of me just like the clay pigeon is part of me. When it's happening, when everything is flowing and everything is going right it's just incredible.

"When I finish a round of twenty-five, I'm exhausted because it takes a lot of mental energy. You've got to concentrate, but you can't force it."

Nattrass has juxtaposed her shooting with a variety of academic and career pursuits. She could, if she so decided, call herself Dr. Nattrass for her 1980s Ph.D. thesis work and research on sport and the media. She has worked as a teacher, a journalist, and an administrator, and in 1995 was planning her summer of competition around her job as athletic director at St. Mary's University in Nova Scotia.

Nattrass was also continuing a fight she began after the 1992 Summer Olympics in Barcelona, where she finished twenty-first. A move was afoot to prevent women from shooting trap at world championships or Olympics, with international officials deciding that double trap would be the women's event. After some twenty-six years as a trap shooter Nattrass was incensed, as were other international women competitors, that their event had been suddenly designated a "men's event."

Retire from competition? Not yet.

"I have had more highs than lows. Finances are always a problem," she said. "I don't do it for the glory and I don't do it for the money — God knows there isn't any. I do it because I love the challenge. And I'm still good at it."

Linda Thom

A decade later Linda Thom remembered the moment with distinct clarity.

"It sank in that night," she said of lying awake into the early hours, allowing the emotional energy she had held in check all day to wash over like a flooding stream.

"In this sport you have to have tremendous control, you have to have it in spades and have it for a long period of time. You're not moving, like a skier or a sprinter, where you can put that extra energy into movement and muscles. You have to be stock still and you have to channel it down the barrel of your gun. It's like being on a tightrope. You have to have control to give that wonderful performance, but if you have too much you go off the edge."

Earlier in the day Ottawa's Thom walked that emotional tightrope to the top of the 1984 Olympic podium, winning the gold medal in women's pistol shooting at the Summer Olympic Games in Los Angeles. Her victory was captivating from both a historical and personal interest perspective. Prior to the Los Angeles Games Canada had not won a Summer Olympic gold medal since the Canadian equestrian team took the show jumping event at the 1968 Games in Mexico City. Thom was the first Canadian woman to win an individual Summer Olympic event since Ethel Catherwood won the high jump at the 1928 Games in Amsterdam.

Her gold medal also marked the first Canadian shooting victory at the Olympics since 1956, where in Melbourne Gerald Ouellette won gold in the prone rifle competition.

But perhaps the most striking element in the gold medal story was the athlete herself — Thom was forty years old,

Linda Thom: Became a celebrity in Los Angeles.

married and a mother of two children, a caterer and cooking instructor who retired from shooting in 1975, then returned to the sport seven years later. Years after, she conceded she didn't fit the image of the twenty-something athlete most folk would associate with competing at an Olympic Games. Yet it was precisely this deviance from expectation that made her victory, the first Canadian gold medal earned on the first day of the two weeks of Olympic competition, one of the most memorable of those Games.

Most Canadians had never heard of Linda Thom prior to July 29, 1984. Shooting did not enjoy a high profile in the sports media. It was a sport that intrigued her as a young girl growing up in what she would later call "rural Scarborough. It's all paved over now." Her father had competed in shooting events in the United Kingdom but she never saw him compete, or even hunt, in Canada. Her penchant for the sport surfaced at age four when she badgered her parents to give her toy pistols for Christmas. She received a set for her sixth birthday and by age eight she exhibited surprisingly good aim in handling her elder brother's BB gun.

"I didn't care for the female figures in the comic books or cartoons," said Thom, adding that as a youngster she had excelled in track and field, baseball and volleyball, and was a "champion tree climber."

"My heroes were Roy Rogers and Gene Autry, the Lone Ranger and Tarzan. My parents exposed me to things and expected me to grow up like any other little girl but I didn't."

Her fascination with marksmanship continued into adulthood, where she shot rifles for a time before concentrating on the pistol. She became one of Canada's best shooters but remained largely anonymous outside the sport. When her husband was transferred to Paris in 1972, Thom used the time to compete at shooting competitions in Europe and to attend the Paris Cordon Bleu cooking school.

When they returned to Canada she gave up the sport to start a family. In 1982, hearing that women's pistol shooting would be contested in Los Angeles, she looked up national coach Joe Liota and told him she was interested in returning to the sport. Initially she just wanted to see if she could make the national team, but she had greater aspirations in her heart. The pivotal point came at a team meeting, which Thom left midway through as frustration overflowed from her.

"I walked outside and around the back, and was sobbing a bit. It was crunch time. I might have quit at that point because my performance wasn't very good and I didn't regard myself as worthy of being on the national team," she said. "Joe told me he was delighted to see me come back. I said: 'I'm really frustrated because on the one hand I'm saying to myself: I'm not good enough, I'm wasting people's time.' Then I said: 'My goal at the Olympics is to win a gold medal — isn't that a laugh?' But he didn't laugh at all. He said: 'I'm here to help you make it happen, because I think you can do it.'"

Later that year Thom took silver and bronze medals in match and air pistol respectively at the Pan-American Games, and a year later earned silver medals in both disciplines at the Cuban Invitational and won at the Zurich International.

In Los Angeles, when teammate Tom Guinn heard Thom was in fifth place half-way through the Olympic pistol event he told reporters they'd best stop chasing the story of Canadian weightlifters sent home for positive steroid tests and run out to the shooting venue because Thom would certainly get a medal. After six rounds of shooting Thom and American Ruby Fox were tied for first place, forcing a three-round shoot-off. Thom prevailed in the third round to take her historic gold medal.

A decade later she described the difference between a good performance and a bad one as keeping the energy in check and allowing instinct and experience to take over.

"The good shot always goes too soon," she explained. "If the shot breaks a split second too early then it's a really good shot, you didn't interfere with it, you subconsciously didn't interfere with it."

Thom's victory put her and her sport on the front pages of Canada's newspapers. In remembering the day, she said she was surprised how excited and moved people were by her effort. She became a celebrity of sorts after the Games, in demand for speaking engagements and motivational seminars, although she didn't garner the sponsorship and promotional contracts that gold medal swimmer Alex Baumann and diver Sylvie Bernier had attained.

Ten years after her gold medal victory found Thom working as a real estate agent and serving as a director for the Shooting Federation of Canada, speaking strongly on behalf of her sport in the wake of public and political calls against guns.

The memory of the gold medal day remained as clear as her task at the time. Thom recalled it wasn't until after the television cameras left the family motel room that she was able to finally relax and begin to appreciate what she had done.

"We had a modest little dinner at a family restaurant then we went to bed and everybody fell asleep but me," she laughed. "That is when the control started to leave me. It generates a lot of excitement, meeting your lifetime goal and having your family there. It was a dream of a lifetime come true. I was awake until two-thirty in the morning, beaming at the ceiling."

TRAILBLAZERS

Trailblazing

Some of the most significant contributions to Canadian sport came not with the winning of a gold medal or a world record. Over the years, the achievements of Canadian women as administrators, judges, and community role models have done much to further the opportunities for women and girls in sport while also serving as examples of what is possible when mind is put faithfully and fervently to task. Through their work, their tenacity and their courage, they have blazed a trail of opportunity for others to follow where prejudice and fear once flourished.

Abby Hoffman

Abby Hoffman: A lifetime of involvement in sport.

When the Canadian Association for the Advancement of Women and Sport and Physical Activity (CAAWS) presented Abby Hoffman with the 1992 Herstorical Award for her work in breaking down gender barriers in sport it might also have been considered a lifetime achievement award.

Hoffman made her athletic name as a middle distance runner, but from the start her athletic career was intertwined with a commitment to fight for greater opportunities for women in sport, not only during her tenure as an athlete but also as an administrator, author, and role model.

At age nine, frustrated that there were no opportunities for her to play hockey in a girls' league, Hoffman cut her hair and pretended to be a boy in order to play the game. She went on to be picked for an all-star team until someone noticed the name on her birth certificate did not fit in with the masculine names presented on the certificates of her teammates. A girl playing hockey on a boys' team? The situation sparked headlines.

After her elder brothers took up distance running, Hoffman decided that anything they could do she might do better, so at age fourteen she joined a track club. Her passion for sport had already given her a good fitness base and it wasn't long before Hoffman made her mark as a runner. In 1962, at age fifteen, she won the national 880-yard title and earned a spot on Canada's team to the Commonwealth Games in Perth, Scotland, finishing seventh in the 880-yard event. A year later she earned her first international gold medal by winning the 800 metres at the 1963 Pan-American Games in Sao Paulo, Brazil.

What followed was a long athletic career that would end in 1976 with Hoffman having competed in four Olympic Games, four Pan-American Games and two Commonwealth Games. In 1966 she won the 880-yard final at the British Empire-Commonwealth Games in Jamaica and in 1971 she added a second Pan-Am gold to her collection, winning the 800 metres in Cali, Colombia. In between, she finished seventh in the 800 metres at the 1968 Olympics in Mexico City.

For years she ranked in the world's top ten for the two-lap event. It could be said Hoffman had the best meet of her career at the 1972 Olympics, even though a quick look at the final results will reveal she finished eighth. In the heats Hoffman lowered the Canadian record she set in 1971 to 2:01.57. In the semi-finals she lowered it again to 2:01.37 and in the final she bettered the mark again with a 2:00.17.

Hoffman went on to compete at the 1976 Olympics in Montreal where she served as the Canadian team flagbearer at the opening ceremonies. She didn't make the 800-metre final in Montreal but was in good company on the sidelines as the world record holder, the European champion, the Commonwealth champion and the Olympic champion from 1968 were also eliminated.

Hoffman later took a job in sports administration with the Ontario government. In 1981 she was named director general of Sport Canada and for the next decade she would oversee the Canadian amateur sport system and grapple with some of the tumultuous issues that arose during that

time, from funding to Ben Johnson's steroid scandal at the 1988 Seoul Olympics.

In 1991 Hoffman was transferred — some would say demoted or at least moved sideways — out of Sport Canada and into the health and welfare ministry in a shift that was considered by many in the media and in the sport community to be the result of conflicting philosophies between herself and the assistant deputy minister of Fitness and Amateur Sport at the time.

But while her responsibilities may have changed, Hoffman's commitment to sport did not. In her new position as director general of the Women's Health Bureau in the department of health, Hoffman remains a sought-after speaker and a committed champion of the rights of all individuals to enjoy opportunities in sport and physical activity.

Jo-Anne Polak

TRAILBLAZER

Jo-Anne Polak learned early "not to sweat the small stuff." As general manager of the Canadian Football League's Ottawa Rough Riders, she had more pressing problems to deal with than those arising from her status as the first female general manager in league history. When she took the job in late 1988 the team's dismal win-loss record was matched by its equally dismal financial state. Working to issue paycheques and pay bills took precedence over getting worked up over gender-related insults that came her way.

"You just got tough," she said. "One guy called, he was screaming at the receptionist about not getting his money, so I got on the phone and ripped a piece of paper. I said: 'That was your cheque, it was going in the mail but now, because you're rude, you're not going to get paid yet. And you know something? Your invoice is going to the bottom of the pile.'

"Those were the fights I had. If you have a couple of problems on your plate, and one of them is whether a guy calls you "toots" and sends you for coffee, and the other one is if you're able to issue paycheques, when you have problems that big the other one seems so minor. It's just an irritant, that's all."

Insiders in the Canadian Football League, and many football fans around the country, were shocked in December 1988 when the twenty-seven-member community partnership, which had purchased the Ottawa Rough Riders from Allan Waters for one dollar a year earlier, announced that

Jo-Anne Polak: Marketing savvy and enthusiasm were her trademarks as first woman general manager in the CFL.

twenty-nine-year-old Jo-Anne Polak would succeed Paul Robson as the Riders' general manager. The move was labelled as a desperate publicity stunt to engender some interest in the floundering franchise.

"The first day, when the media found out it was: 'Oh my God, what have they done in Ottawa, they have completely lost their minds,'" laughed Polak.

Polak brought marketing, organizational and communications experience to the job — traits that have become increasingly valuable in professional sports, where the notion of running a sport as a business has become popular, if not imperative.

Polak honed her unique brand of leadership early in life, serving as her school's first female student council president in Barrie, Ontario, while also developing organizational skills as a member of the Young Progressive Conservatives. At eighteen she helped organize a party convention. At twenty-three she was an integral member of the committee devising the Ontario portion of John Crosbie's national campaign for leadership of the party.

She didn't attend her first football game until 1982, a Toronto Argonaut-Edmonton Eskimos tilt, but became a fan in 1984 when she moved to Ottawa. She worked for an international communications firm and for two seasons served as a marketing consultant to the Riders. She developed a keen interest in the finer points of the game, but Polak was astounded when, after organizing the 1988 Miss Grey Cup pageant, she was approached to take on the general manager's job. She knew they were looking for someone with a business and marketing background but in her mind she always wondered: Who is *he* going to be?

"I was stunned when they approached me," she said. Being a woman was one of the lesser things that concerned her as she pondered the offer. The major consideration was how to deal with a team that had just gone 2-16 in the 1988 season and had enormous financial problems.

"I knew the team, in essence, was bankrupt. They had no money in the bank and all money from season's tickets was being spent on previous years' bills. I knew there was no television contract per se and I thought the chances of actually succeeding and getting through the first year were probably about 10 per cent. The reason I did it was thinking: 'Could I live with myself five years from now, would I look back and wonder what if?'"

Polak's marketing savvy and enthusiasm swept through the franchise and the league. She could be relied upon for a quotable quip for the media and a strong opinion in the boardrooms and backrooms, although she left coach Steve Goldman alone to handle the workings of the team. Her first marketing coup occurred in the first game of the 1989 season, the same week Toronto Argonauts celebrated the opening of that city's SkyDome. She engineered a plan to create Ottawa's own domed stadium by encouraging fans to bring umbrellas, putting them up whenever the Riders scored. The plan proved popular beyond all expectation, with some five thousand people gaining free admission because the gate employees couldn't handle the crush of fans.

Polak also incurred the wrath of all Saskatchewan in changing the name of that province's Roughriders to the Prairie Dogs in promoting her team's game against the Saskatchewan squad. Toronto was not amused when Ottawa fans were given baby rattles in a Polak promotion prompted by Argonaut protests when Ottawa signed former Argo free agent Glenn Kulka. Her half-time shows were just as innovative, with the sumo wrestling demonstration being one of the most memorable.

Then there was the other stuff, the money problems that sometimes kept Polak awake well into the night.

"That dominated the job," recalled Polak of the financial woes she inherited, woes made worse by a nationwide recession. "It was brutal, to have to keep the players in a meeting for two extra hours while you scrounge up the payroll. To me, my greatest achievement was that I never missed a payroll."

One of the most difficult decisions of her three-year tenure with Ottawa was having to fire coach Goldman part way through the 1991 season. By then the remaining members of the community partnership had walked, leaving her in charge of finding ownership for the struggling club while maintaining operations in conjunction with the Canadian Football League. The team was off to a dismal start and the fans were restless.

"It got to the stage where we had to sell the team but it had gone 0-4," she said. "You have to think of the survival of the organization. He had gone 0-4 and the fans were beside themselves. They didn't see any improvement happening."

American Bernard Glieberman bought the team in October 1991 and Polak, worn out and looking for a new challenge, tendered her resignation soon after. She took a job as morning co-host for an Ottawa country music station where she put her gregarious nature to further good use.

But by the summer of 1994, she had quit her radio job and was back in promotions and marketing.

Looking back, she remembered her time with the Rough Riders as being both invigorating and draining. As for being the first woman to hold a position of power in the CFL, there was contentment knowing she was the first and some excitement that she won't be the last.

"The one thing I found very encouraging was that the

guys who were sixty or seventy years old had a real problem with me being there but the guys thirty-five to forty were pretty open-minded," she said. "The guys who were twenty-one to twenty-five were completely supportive. They thought it was the greatest thing. You could see a change in

attitude. It was inspiring and encouraging. But, you know, you can't sit back and expect someone who had never done business with a woman to automatically think it's fine. You have to go in, work with them for a bit, and they'll forget about it."

Donalda Smith

It's a long way from Dauphin, Manitoba, to the sunny climes of Spain and Cuba, to the grand societies of Switzerland and Scandinavia, to the pomp and athletic grandeur of an Olympic Summer Games.

Donalda Smith saw them all in her more than thirty years as a judge and builder in the sport of synchronized swimming, a career that culminated in her serving as a Canadian judge at the first Olympic synchronized swimming competition at the 1984 Summer Games in Los Angeles. It was fitting that the woman who helped build the sport, not only in Canada but around the world, should be a part of the sport's debut in the biggest international athletic event of all.

Smith was born in 1906. Synchronized swimming was far from Donalda Smith's mind when she was growing up on the prairies. Her interests included reading and she delighted in the adventures of the Tarzan series by Edgar Rice Burroughs. Her career options were limited — fancying a career as a doctor, she ended up becoming a teacher because there was available training nearby. Her other option was to take business courses but teaching appeared the most interesting of the two roads.

"The only place to swim was Lake Dauphin about ten miles east. I always liked to swim but I could only manage the dog paddle," she recalled. "I remember reading in the paper a description of the Australian crawl, which I tried, but it wasn't until I was married and moved to Regina that I improved my swimming and took lifesaving courses at the Y."

She came to Vancouver in 1934, the result of her husband's company transfer. Smith taught lifesaving and swimming as part of the Provincial Recreation Program. From time to time she heard about an activity dubbed "fancy swimming" and knew there were some clubs in the area. But she didn't become involved directly in synchronized swimming until her daughter, Margaret, a proficient competitive swimmer, decided to try the new discipline, which had made its official debut in Montreal in 1925 with the world's first compulsory figures competition.

"One day, they needed someone on deck. I was quali-

Donalda Smith: Helped develop synchronized swimming throughout Canada and internationally.

fied because I had my Red Cross lifesaving," said Smith. "But almost immediately I became interested. About all I could tell was if they had their legs straight. There wasn't much information or reference."

Smith went on to rectify that situation, becoming involved with the writing and organizing of the Canadian Amateur Synchronized Swimming Association handbook while also helping to develop the Star Awards used to gauge and reward a young swimmer's proficiency in figures.

Smith also travelled to the United States, taking the American judges' test while studying that country's approach and development in the sport. She became national technical chair for synchro in 1966 and two years later was appointed secretary to the sport's international committee, leading the group that would organize the first international conference on synchronized swimming in 1974.

On the judging side she presided at just about every synchronized swim meet going, from B.C. and national championships to Expo '70 in Japan, five Pan-Pacific Championships, two Pan-Am Games, the Spanish, French, Swiss and Berlin Open competitions and three World Aquatic Championships, including the 1982 event where she served as head judge. On the international development side she organized and conducted three South American judges' seminars.

Her work didn't go unrecognized. She received Synchro Canada's first Distinguished Service Award in 1971 and the Order of Canada in 1983.

Smith said she just about "burst with pride" when she served as judge at the 1984 Olympics, where Canadians Carolyn Waldo (solo) and Kelly Kryczka and Sharon Hambrook (duet) earned silver medals in the first Olympic synchronized swimming competition.

Who would have thought that when she went for a summer dip at Lake Dauphin she would end up being a major player in the early development of what is now a major international aquatic sport?

"I am a very small part," she said. "I tend to look at the overall picture and synchronized swimming has been very important to me. But when you look at the universe it's a very small part."

Sharon Wood

It is called a moment of truth, an instance forcing an individual to deal with something that is particularly difficult or horrifying.

Sharon Wood's moment came as she negotiated a face of rock and ice near the summit of Mount Everest, where she and climbing partner Dwayne Congdon were tackling a crucial section in their bid to make the top. Wood saw the face of fear and discovered it was her own.

"It happened about a third of the way up. The wind was bad, it was late in the day and we moved very slowly," she recalled. "It was the technical crux of the day and I was leading through the section. I was very apprehensive, I just wanted to get the hell out of there. Three moves into the lead I was at a place where you couldn't afford to think about anything but making the move that helps you maintain a place for your feet with the ground ten thousand feet below.

"I had this revelation that this battle isn't with the mountain, it's with myself and getting through my own fears and that I've got enough strength to do it. It was exhilarating. I just punched through into that 90 per cent potential that we have but never use."

Several hours later, at 9:00 p.m. on May 20, 1986, Wood and Congdon reached the 8,848-metre summit of Everest, the world's highest mountain. In doing so, Wood became the first North American woman, and one of a handful of women worldwide beginning with Japan's Junko Tabei in 1975, to stand on the summit.

Sharon Wood was born May 18, 1957, in Halifax. The youngest of four children, Wood and her family moved to Burnaby, B.C., in 1964 when her navy pilot father was trans-ferred west. The coast mountains awakened something in Wood, who by admission was an outsider in her peer group and "one of those kids parents hate to see their own kids hanging around with."

At age twelve Wood scaled her first coast summit — Sky Pilot — and found, in addition to a knack for securing a foothold in rock, a niche for her life:

"It felt like I was in the heart of an adventure where I could embrace the challenge completely. I wasn't afraid of it, I just wanted more. During the whole day I had this feeling of anticipation and excitement for the next step."

The next step was an Outward Bound wilderness course in the B.C. interior, which further whetted her appetite for adventure in general and mountaineering in particular. In 1974 Wood moved to Alberta, drawn by the mountains and the people in small communities and began honing her mountaineering skills while working as a guide in Jasper National Park. By 1982 she had developed into a competent climber, having conquered Canada's tallest peak, Mount Logan, as part of an all-female team, plus several tough climbs in the Rockies and ascents in California's Yosemite. But it was the death of climbing mentor John Lauchlan that caused her to intensify her approach, to "stop dabbling and do it."

Four years later Wood joined the thirteen-member Canadian team slated to tackle Mount Everest. She had already become the first North American woman to climb the south face of Aconcagua, the tallest mountain in the Western Hemisphere. Living in the Rocky Mountain community of Canmore, she also worked as a mountain guide and taught mountaineering courses, some of which she designed specifically for women. Also on the Jim Elzinga-led Everest expedition was Laurie Skreslit, a member of the 1982 Canadian Everest expedition, Congdon, Abdi Sole, Chris Shank, Dr. Bob Lee, Barry Blanchard, Dave McNab, Kevin Doyle, James Blench, Dan Griffith and climber/cook Jane Fearing.

Unlike the 1982 Canadian Everest expedition, the 1986 contingent opted for a more streamlined plan and adopted the name Everest Light. They had no Sherpas to help carry supplies, and despite the high altitude, they planned to climb without oxygen tanks, a plan that was altered on the final two days when bad weather made the physical effort even more difficult.

Wood's presence on the team also sparked media interest because

Sharon Wood: On her way to the top of the world – the summit of Mount Everest.

it was apparent she had the skill and strength to be considered for a summit bid. A parallel interest developed in the United States as an American team, which included climber Annie Whitehouse, was also planning an Everest assault at the same time via a different route. Who would be the first North American woman to reach the top?

Throughout her preparation Wood also experienced an unfounded but niggling dread that if she made it to the top, she would make her descent into the eerie and inhospitable darkness of Everest night.

The team began its assault on March 20, 1986. For several weeks they established camps located progressively higher and closer to the Everest peak, their progress hampered by severe snowstorms. By early May it was clear four climbers still had the physical and mental strength for a summit attempt — Wood, Sole, Blanchard and Congdon. There are several accounts of how the choice for the first summit duo was made. Wood recalled Elzinga proposed she and Congdon make the first summit attempt even though she had been climbing with Sole. Wood chose to support Congdon and Blanchard going first.

"I went back to my tent and had this awful feeling in my stomach like: My God, What have I done? I have just thrown the opportunity of a lifetime away. I had an intuition that said: Go Now! Jim came over and talked to me and asked

what I was doing, what was I throwing away? So I went to Barry and said I wanted to go first — if the opportunity exists then I'd like to do it."

Wood celebrated her twenty-ninth birthday on May 18, some 7,800 metres up Everest. By then, bad weather had forced the American team to abandon its attempt. On May 20, at 9:00 a.m., Wood and Congdon departed from their final camp at the 8,170-metre level and made their summit bid, a twelve-hour test up rock and ice, blasted at times by 100-kilometre-per-hour winds, to the top of the world.

They spent twenty minutes at the summit.

"The last few hundred feet were not particularly exciting, certainly not as exciting as that point a third of the way up," mused Wood. "I remember surrendering totally to the idea that I would keep putting one foot in front of the other until we reached the highest point. Breathing, you take three breaths for every step. It was windy, the sun was setting. What I remember most were valleys that were very dark below, and that we could be on another planet, we seemed so far away. Curving horizons. Pink sky. It was very, very windy. Then, it was: Here we are on the highest point on the earth and the sun is setting. Let's get out of here."

The descent proved to be the dark nightmare Wood had feared. Slow, painfully slow, with a lamp on her helmet showing the way a scant six feet ahead, she made her way down. Congdon suffered problems with his oxygen on the descent and after waiting for him for some time and beginning to hallucinate in her exhausted state, Wood decided she must forge ahead to the camp below and melt snow to give them water that was crucial for their survival. Congdon followed ninety minutes later. During the process of melting snow their gas stove exploded but they persevered through the night and made their way back to the next camp below. Poor weather ended the second summit attempt by Blanchard and Sole.

Wood returned to Canada a national hero, a situation she found uncomfortable because of the lack of attention given to her Everest Light teammates.

In the years following her successful climb Wood stood atop more speakers' podiums than mountains. In 1994 she

gave more than forty speeches to various business and community groups across North America in addition to parenting two boys. In regaling her Everest adventure she encouraged people to climb their mountains and face their own fears.

"I think we acquire special abilities. I don't think we necessarily start out as special people," said Wood. "The biggest challenge is dealing with the physical discomfort and altering your perspective of what discomfort is. It's the recognition of who your real enemies are, what your real obstacles are, and they're not on the outside, they're preconceived fears and limitations. I can't tell you how exhilarating it is to be up where it's really cold and windy and scary, and you feel like you are the master of your entire world, that you don't have to let all that stuff get to you."

Carol Anne Letheren

TRAILBLAZER

Carol Anne Letheren: Became one of a very few women presidents of a national Olympic committee.

In the early days of the 1988 Summer Olympics in Seoul, South Korea, Canadian team chef de mission Carol Anne Letheren was making a positive impression on the world sport community.

Calm yet forthright, pleasant yet exuding an air of toughness that lingered just below her diplomatic demeanour, the forty-two-year-old Canadian was everything a competent chef de mission should be. Yet, being the first woman chef de mission in the history of the Olympic Games meant her every move would be scrutinized and analyzed by a curious sporting fraternity. Consensus was that Letheren was faring well.

Any doubts about her ability to do the job were quelled in a series of events beginning September 24, 1988, when Canadian sprinter Ben Johnson won the men's 100-metre final and, two hours later, submitted a urine sample for dope testing. A day later Johnson's Sample A showed positive for the anabolic steroid stanozolol. On September 26, Letheren was handed a letter from the International Olympic Committee confirming the positive test and noting Johnson and/or Canadian team officials were to be present at the testing of Sample B, which also turned up positive.

On September 27, at about 3:30 a.m., Letheren met with Johnson and asked him to return his Olympic gold medal, informing him that he was disqualified from the Games. For all the grace under pressure she would exhibit in the following days she would be remembered most as the individual who had the uncomfortable task of retrieving the medal from Johnson.

"It wasn't so much the actual taking back of the medal

but the realization of what all of that represented. That was probably one of the tougher times of my life," Letheren noted years later.

"There's no question it was a great awakening for me personally, in two ways: I think it was an instance that teaches you your own inner strength, which is not an opportunity we always get; but the more important thing is what it really did teach sport and what we've done with it. It took the lid off the can of worms and said this is not about Ben Johnson, this is not about sport, this is about a system that has succumbed to the greed of the '80s and has lost its way, lost its value system. Now, the opportunity is to get it all back."

In April 1990, Letheren, who was a vice-president of the Canadian Olympic Association (COA) when the organization's executive committee appointed her to the volunteer chef de mission position to Seoul, was acclaimed the tenth president of the COA, succeeding Roger Jackson. Again she was blazing a trail in a man's domain, becoming one of a handful of women presidents of a national Olympic committee and the only woman who did not come to the position enjoying royalty status or privilege.

Letheren brought to the COA presidency what would be two increasingly necessary skills for administrating sport in the '90s — experience in operating a business combined with a passion for, and experience in, sport. In the 1980s Letheren had served as senior partner in a Toronto marketing and consulting firm. And the sport side?

"Sport has been a way of life for me," laughed Letheren, who in 1994 counted running, skiing, cycling and tennis as favourite activities. "I would classify it as my first love. It's so much a part of my life that if I don't run or exercise, or if I miss a couple of days because I've been travelling, I feel it. I think it's become part of my chemical make-up."

Letheren was born in Toronto and grew up in Guelph, Ontario. She made her first athletic mark as a capable gymnast, competing at the local level when she was in high school and going on to compete in university. As a youngster she was also an Ontario badminton champion. In addition to studying physical education and, later, earning an M.B.A. at York University, Letheren served as a gymnastics judge at many international events, including two Olympics, two Commonwealth Games and six world championships.

Interestingly, the administrative and leadership skills that

would help her through those difficult days in Seoul surfaced much earlier in life. Letheren was her school's first female student council president.

"I don't know what they were," she laughed when asked about capabilities that put her into leadership roles. "Maybe it was just the stupidity to jump into the fray."

In the fall of 1994 Letheren jumped into a new fray, stepping down as COA president to take up new duties as the organization's chief executive officer.

"The president's duties are a little more like chairman of the board whereas the CEO is truly the person responsible for the operation of the organization," she explained. "I just decided the timing was right in my own life, that it would give me a chance to complete some of the things in a much more comprehensive fashion than I was trying to do as president."

At the time of taking on her new position as CEO, Letheren conceded drugs in sport had continued to be a major issue since Seoul. That Canada opted to address the issue in the Dubin Inquiry into drug use in sport, and subsequently adopted out-of-competition, unannounced testing, reveals the country's commitment to attacking the problem. Since Seoul there have been other Canadian athletes test positive for drug use as have other athletes around the world. Rather than wring her hands at the thought that the message isn't getting through to Canadian athletes, Letheren saw the positive tests in a different light:

"I suggest it's our system of random, out-of-competition testing at work. So it's demonstrating these kids are getting caught. The ones you're seeing internationally in some instances are demonstration there are some countries that have not been as dedicated to cleaning it up as we have."

Letheren is equally forthright about her situation as one of a few women to hold a position of power in a national Olympic committee. She laments there are still few women in that role, yet it is not her style to climb onto a soapbox. A more effective way to make a statement is the action of doing a job well, setting an example and encouraging others to follow.

"Definitely I'd love to see more women moving into these positions because I quite enjoy working with them and I find women approach situations differently and bring a wonderful balance to any decision-making room," she said.

"People say to me you don't appear to be a feminist, you're irresponsible in that sense. Well, maybe I'm a quiet feminist as opposed to a noisy one."

Christine Nordhagen

Christine Nordhagen was in trouble. With one minute remaining in the women's world championship 70-kilo final, the twenty-three-year-old Canadian was down 0-6 to Russian rival Elmira Kurbanova, who appeared set to take the weight class title at the 1994 women's world wrestling championships at Sofia, Bulgaria.

"My plan had been to do a certain move on her (an arm drag to a trip) because it had been successful throughout the tournament with my other opponents," said Nordhagen of that final match.

"I think her coach must have scouted me because she kept blocking me, anticipating when I would try it. I had this tunnel vision to do this move and that's when she did her attacks and that cost me for a while. I finally realized I had to switch to something else so I went to another trip. I had nothing to lose. I went full out and it worked."

Nordhagen reduced the deficit by earning three points with an inside leg trip and seconds later pinned her opponent for a remarkable comeback win, becoming the first Canadian woman to win a gold medal at a women's wrestling world championship.

Freestyle wrestling is one of the oldest Olympic sports but, until recently, it was largely closed to women because of traditional barriers and notions that deemed combative sports unacceptable for women. Now, freestyle wrestling is becoming more popular for women worldwide as a test of technique, fitness, agility and ability to react quickly and intelligently in difficult situations. As a world champion Nordhagen has become a leading figure and role model in the sport not only in Canada but internationally. Hers is a story of a dedicated yet unspectacular athlete who took part in many "traditional" sports for women yet was unable to find her competitive niche.

"I finally found a sport I could excel at," she said. "I was always involved in athletics. I competed in badminton, volleyball, slo-pitch, curling. I'd be on all the team sports but I never was the best. I was a hard worker but I didn't seem to have natural ability to be really good. I loved volleyball but I just didn't have what it takes to be good enough to make a university team."

Christine Nordhagen grew up in Valhalla Centre, a Norwegian community near Grande Prairie, Alberta. Living with two brothers and two sisters and an enthusiastic family attitude toward sport provided the base for an active young life. Looking back on her youth she realized that even then she had a knack for winning in neighbourhood rough-and-

tumble rough-housing and wrestling with her younger brother and friends. While not necessarily stronger, she exhibited good balance and an understanding of the mechanics of pushing or pulling at the right time. Above all, she discovered she had a mind for tactics.

In 1991, during her stint as an education student at the University of Alberta in Edmonton, Nordhagen took a class in wrestling because it might be something she would be required to teach as a high school physical education teacher. She excelled immediately and the instructor, who also coached wrestling, encouraged her to try the sport.

"I remember my first tournament. It was an exhibition match," she laughed. "I had never even watched wrestling. I'd been training but I hadn't actually seen a match. I was confused about shaking the official's hand. Which corner do I go to? I had a hard time at first. I was aggressive but I didn't want to hurt the other person. I'd throw her, she'd land on her back, and I'd say: 'Sorry, are you okay?' My coach would yell at me: 'Christine, stop saying sorry!'"

In 1993 Nordhagen, by then a two-time Canadian champion, with Vancouver's Janna Penny and Erica Sharp of Whitehorse, became the first Canadian women to compete at a women's world wrestling championship. Nordhagen earned the silver medal in the 70-kilo category at the world event in Larvik, Norway while Penny took bronze in the 65-kilo division.

Taking silver not only buoyed Nordhagen's confidence, it also sparked what already was a powerful work ethic to improve. She had, indeed, found her niche.

"Wrestling is different from any other sport," she observed. "For volleyball, you need to have the height and vertical jump; in basketball you need endurance and speed. Wrestling requires so many elements, plus an ability to make decisions quickly. A lot of it is technique and body awareness. It's great because it allows a girl who is forty-four kilos, who maybe couldn't be competitive in swimming or basketball, or a girl who is eighty kilos and might automatically be thought of as a shot putter, another sporting option. That's what I like about it."

At the 1994 championships in Sofia, Nordhagen sailed through her first three matches. In her first bout she defeated two-time world champion Mikoci Musaka of Japan 10-1, then went on to pin Evan Angola of Greece. Later, she defeated Ukraine's Tiania Tamarlitzkaia 9-1. Initially, her goal had been to get to the final. Once there, she could have given up — a six-point deficit

Christine Nordhagen (left): Tactics and tenacity are crucial to success in freestyle wrestling.

in wrestling is difficult to reverse.

"It was the most exciting feeling I ever had in my life," she said of her win. "It was so emotional because I was losing and came back, I didn't give up. It would have been so easy to give up, to think maybe I'll do it next year, but I stuck with it.

"When we stood on the podium it was amazing. I'd been athletic as a child but not the best, and I never thought I'd be the best in my province, let alone the world. At our training camp in New York I remember doing visualization about being in the final and winning and going up to the podium. I almost started crying thinking about it. I didn't realize I wanted to do it so bad."

By the end of 1994 Nordhagen had made a move south,

training at the University of Calgary. Winning the world championship didn't affect her wallet at all — receiving no funding meant taking on part-time work at an out-of-school care program for children. In between she continued her regime of weight training, practising technique and improving cardiovascular fitness. She had also become a popular guest speaker at high schools, not only as a world champion but as an ambassador for her sport.

"I've played a lot of sports and out of all of them, wrestling is the toughest," she said. "I would love for people to come out and try it, to wrestle for four minutes straight. They'd be dead-dog tired. You just don't realize how tough it is unless you actually do it."

Ann Peel

Ann Peel learned how to make a case long before she became a lawyer, just as she learned how to compete long before she became an athlete.

Both skills were honed in the safest, most innocent setting — at the family dinner table.

"In our family, dinner table discussions were often philosophical and political," she said. "We were very close. My father was in the foreign service so the focus was always on the family as the one stable thing when I was growing up.

"I grew up with a love of argument and debate. Around our dinner table there were always discussions — other people might call it arguing but we called it debating. We all loved to find an issue and talk it to death."

Peel took her competitive nature and found a spot for it in athletics, becoming for many years Canada's top female racewalker. She also took her interest in debate to the Uni-

Ann Peel: Athlete and advocate.

versity of Toronto, where she studied to become a lawyer. She melded both as she took on national and international sport establishments in areas where she saw inequity and unfairness, particularly regarding women and sport.

"My realization that women and men weren't treated equally started in 1984 when I should, by rights, have been on the Olympic team but I wasn't because the women's racewalk was not yet an Olympic event," she said. "That was when I started learning about women and sport. I took my usual approach — I read the history books, I talked to academics and I discovered this is not just about women's racewalking, but a social issue."

Peel was one of the most vocal voices in the battle to have women's racewalking included on the Olympic program, which finally occurred at the 1992 Summer Olympics in Barcelona, Spain. Yet she is perhaps best known for her 1991 work in gaining changes to Sport Canada's funding system which called for a 40 per cent reduction in funding to women athletes in their first pregnancy, and a 60 per cent cut in a second pregnancy. Peel was personally affected by the policy in 1991 when she took part in the national indoor championships in Saskatoon one month after giving birth to her son in order to have her funding restored.

She argued that the system, which continued full funding to injured athletes, was based on the assumption that pregnancy marked the end of a woman's athletic career even though many international calibre athletes, including Canadian high jumper Debbie Brill, had returned to compete after childbirth and often performed even better after maternity leave.

In 1994, as chair and one of the founders of the Canadian Athletes Association, Peel served as the athletes' advocate for the Canadian team at the Commonwealth Games in Victoria. Her role was to act as a liaison between an athlete and team officials if any problems arose between the two — an innovative move in Canadian sport that aroused the interest of other national teams competing at the Games.

As a competitor, Peel was Canada's top female racewalker for nearly a decade, winning some eighteen national championships and earning bronze medals in the 3,000-metre racewalk at the 1985 and '87 world indoor championships.

"My ideal is that every single Canadian would play sports, not necessarily organized sport but be involved in physical activity every single day," she said.

"I don't know how I would separate myself from sport, it's such an integral part of who I am."

Ivy Granstrom

Ivy Granstrom leaned forward slightly, sharing the secret like a conspirator whispering a plot to a new recruit.

"You take a big, deep breath," she said, inhaling lustily as an example. "Then slowly let it out and don't take a breath again until you're in. You don't scream 'Aaaagh.' You hit the water and you don't feel so bad. A lot of people go in screaming."

Most Vancouver residents consider the annual New Year's Day Polar Bear Swim in English Bay something they must certainly do once in their years of living on B.C.'s west coast. A hale and hardy few opt to take the plunge more than once, some deciding to make it an annual activity to start off a new year.

On January 1, 1995, at age eighty-three, Ivy Granstrom endured the New Year's waters again, just as she had every year since she took her first Polar Bear dip in 1928. As every year, her presence was an anticipated and expected addition to the shivering mob that lined the beach. Reporters covering the event know documenting Granstrom's

participation is standard story fare.

"I never smoked, I never drank, I never ran around," is Granstrom's happy reply to queries about how she attained her octagenarian vigour.

But Ivy Granstrom is more than just a character with the steel constitution to endure January ocean water. She is a runner and, although she doesn't like to stress the point, a blind runner. She didn't begin running until 1976 and went on to become one of the best and beloved masters athletes and an inspiration to others who might have equated getting older with slowing down. A veteran of international masters track and field competition, it seemed as soon as she entered a new masters age category Granstrom could be relied upon to improve on the existing record. She was named B.C.'s master athlete of the year for 1982 and in 1989 received the Order of Canada from then-Governor General Jeanne Sauvé.

Granstrom competes against sighted masters athletes. Her vision had never been good, but by the time she estab-

Ivy Granstrom: Masters athlete takes an invigorating dip in the waters of Vancouver's English Bay.

lished herself as a masters runner her vision had waned to where she could see only shadows. Paul Hoeberigs of Vancouver, another master athlete, serves as her guide in training and races.

Ivy Granstrom was born September 28, 1911, in Glace Bay, Nova Scotia, the youngest of fourteen children and one of seven to survive. She started to go blind soon after birth when an infection set in. No one noticed at the time because there was more concern about her mother, who went into a coma after the delivery.

The family made several attempts to improve her sight, even sending her to an infirmary in Leeds, but little could be done. She proved a quick learner as a student despite her poor vision.

The family eventually moved to Fernie, B.C. and then to Vancouver in 1926 where Granstrom worked at the YWCA and took up acrobatic dancing. She would marry and become a widow twice, bearing two children of her own and raising an additional four foster children. During the Second World War she was part of the Red Cross nursing contingent and joined the air raid patrol.

"I could see a little bit then — I didn't tell them I was registered blind," she said. "If I did I wouldn't have a chance. I wanted them to see I could do it properly. Then I didn't care if they found out."

Granstrom took up running after suffering a major back injury in an auto accident. She started running around the block of her Vancouver home, determined not to give in or slow down. She initially took part in blind sports events but later opted to compete against sighted competitors in masters competitions, with Hoeberigs guiding her via voice with each holding an end of a cloth band. In 1993, competing as an eighty-two-year-old in the 80-84 age group, she won seven gold medals at the World Senior Games in Utah and took home two silver and three bronze medals from the World Veterans championships in Japan.

In 1994 Granstrom's laurels included rewriting age world records over 5,000 metres and 15 kilometres at the Pan-Am Masters championships. A week later she defeated longtime rival Pearl Mehl of the United States at the U.S. Masters championship and at the World Masters Games in Brisbane, Australia, she rewrote three world records for eighty-three-year-olds. She ended the season being named Queen of the Huntsman World Senior Games in St. George, Utah.

"She has her own will, a very strong, independent will," observed Hoeberigs. "When she wants to do something, she does it."

Granstrom's determination has taken her around the world, allowed her to be introduced to royalty and has enabled her to inspire many people who might find lesser excuses than age and blindness to give up on life.

"I just love life, I really do," she smiled. "I always try to be straightforward, and I tell children never lie when you can tell the truth, always be honest with people. My Mamma always said it takes a lifetime to build a character and five minutes to knock it down."

STATISTICS
ROSTERS
MEDALLISTS
& AWARDS

World Alpine Ski Championships

1993 Morioka
Gold: Kate Pace (downhill)

1989 Vail
Silver: Karen Percy (downhill)

1982 Haus
Gold: Gerry Sorensen (downhill)
Bronze: Laurie Graham (downhill)

1974 St. Moritz
Silver: Betsy Clifford (downhill)

1970 Val Gardena
Gold: Betsy Clifford (giant slalom)

1968 Grenoble
Gold: Nancy Greene (combined — non-Olympic event)

1960 Squaw Valley
Gold: Anne Heggtveit (combined — non-Olympic event)

1958 Badgastein
Gold: Lucile Wheeler (downhill)
Gold: Lucile Wheeler (giant slalom)
Silver: Lucile Wheeler (combined)

World Cup Race Winners
Nancy Greene:
Downhill (3): 1968 — Aspen, Chamonix; 1967 — Grindelwald
Giant slalom (6): 1968 — Rossland, Aspen, Grenoble, Grindelwald; 1967 — Jackson Hole, Vail; 1966 — Oberstaufen.
Slalom (3): 1968 — Aspen; 1967 — Jackson Hole; 1966 — Oberstaufen
Betsy Clifford:
Giant slalom (1): 1970 — Val Gardena
Slalom (2): 1971 — Schruns; 1970 — Val d'Isere
Kathy Kreiner:
Giant slalom (1): 1974 — Pfronten
Gerry Sorensen:
Downhill (4): 1984 — Puy St. Vincent; 1982 — Grindelwald, Grindelwald (double downhill); 1981 — Haus
Combined (1): 1984 — Puy St. Vincent
Laurie Graham:
Downhill (5): 1986 — Val d'Isere, Crans Montana; 1985 — Val d'Isere, Sunshine; 1983 — Mont Tremblant
Super giant slalom (1): 1984 — Puy St. Vincent
Liisa Savijarvi:
Super giant slalom (1): 1986 — Furano

Canadian Women's Curling Champions
1995 Manitoba: Connie Laliberte, Cathy Overton, Cathy Gauthier, Janet Arnott
1994 Saskatchewan: Sandra Peterson, Jan Betker, Joan McCusker, Marcia Gudereit
1993 Saskatchewan: Sandra Peterson, Jan Betker, Joan McCusker, Marcia Gudereit
1992 Manitoba: Connie Laliberte, Laurie Allen, Cathy Gauthier, Janet Arnott
1991 B.C.: Julie Sutton, Jodie Sutton, Melissa Soligo, Karri Willms
1990 Ontario: Alison Goring, Kristin Turcotte, Andrea Lawes, Cheryl McPherson
1989 Team Canada: Heather Houston, Lorraine Lang, Diane Adams, Tracy Kennedy
1988 Ontario: Heather Houston, Lorraine Lang, Diane Adams, Tracy Kennedy
1987 B.C.: Pat Sanders, Georgina Hawkes, Louise Herlinveaux, Deb Massullo
1986 Ontario: Marilyn Darte, Kathy McEdwards, Chris Jurgenson, Jan Augustyn

1985 B.C.: Linda Moore, Lindsay Sparkes, Debbie Jones, Laurie Carney
1984 Manitoba: Connie Laliberte, Chris More, Corinne Peters, Janet Arnott
1983 Nova Scotia: Penny LaRocque, Sharon Horne, Cathy Caudle, Pam Sanford
1982 Nova Scotia: Colleen Jones, Kay Smith, Monica Jones, Barbara Jones-Gordon
1981 Alberta: Susan Seitz, Judy Erickson, Myrna McKay, Betty McCracken
1980 Saskatchewan: Marj Mitchell, Nancy Kerr, Shirley McKendry, Wendy Leach
1979 B.C.: Lindsay Sparkes, Dawn Knowles, Robin Wilson, Lorraine Bowles
1978 Manitoba: Cathy Pidzarko, Chris Pidzarko, Iris Armstrong, Patty Vanderkerckhove
1977 Alberta: Myrna McQuarrie, Rita Tarnava, Barb Davis, Jane Rempel
1976 B.C.: Lindsay Davie, Dawn Knowles, Robin Klassen, Lorraine Bowles
1975 Quebec: Lee Tobin, Marilyn McNeil, Michelle Garneau, Laurie Ross
1974 Saskatchewan: Emily Farnham, Linda Saunders, Pat McBeath, Donna Collins
1973 Saskatchewan: Vera Pezer, Sheila Rowan, Joyce McKee, Lenore Morrison
1972 Saskatchewan: Vera Pezer, Sheila Rowan, Joyce McKee, Lenore Morrison
1971 Saskatchewan: Vera Pezer, Sheila Rowan, Joyce McKee, Lenore Morrison
1970 Saskatchewan: Dorenda Schoenhals, Cheryl Stirton, Linda Burnham, Joan Anderson
1969 Saskatchewan: Joyce McKee, Vera Pezer, Lenore Morrison, Jennifer Falk
1968 Alberta: Hazel Jamieson, Gail Lee, Jackie Spencer, June Coyle
1967 Manitoba: Betty Duguid, Joan Ingram, Laurie Bradawaski, Dot Rose
1966 Alberta: Gail Lee, Hazel Jamieson, Sharon Harrington, June Coyle
1965 Manitoba: Peggy Casselman, Val Taylor, Pat MacDonald, Pat Scott
1964 B.C.: Ina Hansen, Ada Callas, Isabel Leith, May Shaw
1963 New Brunswick: Mabel DeWare, Harriet Stratton, Forbis Stevenson, Marjorie Fraser
1962 B.C.: Ina Hansen, Ada Callas, Isabel Leith, May Shaw
1961 Saskatchewan: Joyce McKee, Sylvia Fedoruk, Barbara MacNevin, Rosa McFee

Canadian Winners of World Women's Curling Championships
1994: Sandra Peterson, Jan Betker, Joan McCusker, Marcia Gudereit
1993: Sandra Peterson, Jan Betker, Joan McCusker, Marcia Gudereit
1989: Heather Houston, Lorraine Lang, Diane Adams, Tracy Kennedy
1987: Pat Sanders, Georgina Hawkes, Louise Herlinveaux, Deb Massullo
1986: Marilyn Darte, Kathy McEdwards, Chris Jurgenson, Jan Augustyn
1985: Linda Moore, Lindsay Sparkes, Debbie Jones, Laurie Carney
1984: Connie Laliberte, Chris More, Corinne Peters, Janet Arnott
1980: Marj Mitchell, Nancy Kerr, Shirley McKendry, Wendy Leach

Canadian Winners of Women's Junior World Curling Championships
1994: Kim Gelland, Corie Beveridge, Lisa Savage, Sandy Graham
1989: LaDawn Funk, Sandy Symyrozum, Cindy Larsen, Laurelle Funk
1988: Julie Sutton, Judy Wood, Susan Auty, Marla Geiger

Canadian Medallists at World Figure Skating Championships

1994 Chiba
Silver: Isabelle Brasseur with Lloyd Eisler (pair)

1993 Prague
Gold: Isabelle Brasseur with Lloyd Eisler (pair)

1992 Oakland
Bronze: Isabelle Brasseur with Lloyd Eisler (pair)

1991 Munich
Silver: Isabelle Brasseur with Lloyd Eisler (pair)

1990 Halifax
Silver: Isabelle Brasseur with Lloyd Eisler (pair)

1989 Paris
Silver: Cindy Landry wih Lyndon Johnston (pair)

1988 Budapest
Silver: Elizabeth Manley (ladies)
Bronze: Tracy Wilson with Robert McCall (dance)

1987 Cincinnati
Bronze: Tracy Wilson with Robert McCall (dance)

1986 Geneva
Bronze: Cynthia Coull with Mark Rowsom (pair)
Bronze: Tracy Wilson with Robert McCall (dance)

1985 Tokyo
Bronze: Katherina Mathousek with Lloyd Eisler (pair)

1984 Ottawa
Gold: Barbara Underhill with Paul Martini (pair)

1983 Helsinki
Bronze: Barbara Underhill with Paul Martini (pair)

1973 Bratislava
Gold: Karen Magnussen (ladies)

1972 Calgary
Silver: Karen Magnussen (ladies)

1971 Lyon
Bronze: Karen Magnussen (ladies)

1966 Davos
Bronze: Petra Burka (ladies)

1965 Colorado Springs
Gold: Petra Burka (ladies)

1964 Dortmund
Silver: Paulette Doan with Kenneth Ormsby (dance)
Bronze: Petra Burka (ladies)
Bronze: Debbi Wilkes with Guy Revell (pair)

1963 Cortina d'Ampezzo
Bronze: Paulette Doan with Kenneth Ormsby (dance)

1962 Prague
Gold: Maria Jelinek with Otto Jelinek (pair)
Silver: Wendy Griner (ladies)
Bronze: Virginia Thompson with William McLachlan (dance)

1960 Vancouver
Gold: Barbara Wagner and Robert Paul (pair)
Silver: Maria Jelinek and Otto Jelinek (pair)
Silver: Virginia Thompson with William McLachlan (dance)

1959 Colorado Springs
Gold: Barbara Wagner with Robert Paul (pair)
Bronze: Geraldine Fenton with William McLachlan (dance)

1958 Paris
Gold: Barbara Wagner with Robert Paul (pair)
Silver: Geraldine Fenton with William McLachlan (dance)
Bronze: Maria Jelinek with Otto Jelinek (pair)

1957 Colorado Springs
Gold: Barbara Wagner with Robert Paul (dance)
Silver: Geraldine Fenton with William McLachlan (dance)
Bronze: Maria Jelinek with Otto Jelinek (pair)

1956 Garmisch-Partenkirchen
Silver: Frances Dafoe with Norris Bowden (pair)

1955 Vienna
Gold: Frances Dafoe with Norris Bowden (pair)

1954 Oslo
Gold: Frances Dafoe with Norris Bowden (pair)

1953 Davos
Silver: Frances Dafoe with Norris Bowden (pair)

1948 Davos
Gold: Barbara Ann Scott (ladies)
Bronze: Suzanne Morrow with Wallace Distelmeyer (pair)

1947 Stockholm
Gold: Barbara Ann Scott (ladies)

1932 Montreal
Bronze: Constance Samuel (ladies)

1930 New York
Silver: Cecil Smith (ladies)

World Speedskating Championships — Long Track

1989 Lake Placid
Silver: Ariane Loignon (500 metres)

1978 The Hague
Bronze: Sylvia Burka (Overall)
Bronze: Sylvia Burka (1,000)
Bronze: Sylvia Burka (1,500)

1977 Keystone
Silver: Sylvia Burka (1,000)
Silver: Sylvia Burka (1,500)

1976 Gjovik
Gold: Sylvia Burka (Overall)
Gold: Sylvia Burka (1,500)
Bronze: Sylvia Burka (1,000)

1973 Stromsund
Silver: Sylvia Burka (500)

World Long Track Sprint (Speedskating) Championships
Races are run on different days, allowing one skater to win more than one medal in each event

1995 West Allis
Silver: Susan Auch (500 metres)
Bronze: Susan Auch (500)

1994 Calgary
Silver: Susan Auch (500)

1979 Inzell
Silver: Sylvia Burka (1,000)

1977 Alkmaar
Gold: Sylvia Burka (Overall)
Gold: Sylvia Burka (1,000)
Gold: Sylvia Burka (1,000)
Silver: Sylvia Burka (500)
Bronze: Sylvia Burka (500)

1976 Berlin
Bronze: Sylvia Burka (Overall)
Bronze: Sylvia Burka (500)

Bronze: Sylvia Burka (1,000)
Bronze: Sylvia Burka (500)
Silver: Sylvia Burka (1,000)

1975 Gotheburg
Bronze: Cathy Priestner (Overall)
Gold: Cathy Priestner (500)

1974 Innsbruck
Bronze: Cathy Priestner (500)

1973 Oslo
Silver: Sylvia Burka (500)
Bronze: Sylvia Burka (1,000)
Silver: Cathy Priestner (500)

World Junior Speedskating Championships

1979 Grenoble
Silver: Kathy Vogt (1,000 metres)

1976 Madonna di Campiglio
Gold: Elizabeth Appleby (Overall)
Silver: Elizabeth Appleby (1,000)
Silver: Elizabeth Appleby (1,500)
Silver: Elizabeth Appleby (3,000)
Gold: Kathy Vogt (500)
Bronze: Kathy Vogt (1,000)

1975 Stromsund
Silver: Cathy Priestner (500)
Silver: Cathy Priestner (500)

1974 Cortina d'Ampezzo
Silver: Sylvia Burka (500)
Bronze: Sylvia Burka (1,500)

1973 Assen
Gold: Sylvia Burka (Overall)
Gold: Sylvia Burka (500)
Gold: Sylvia Burka (1,000)
Gold: Sylvia Burka (1,500)

World Speedskating Championships — Short Track

1995 Gjovik
Bronze - Canadian women's team (relay)

1994 Guildford
Gold: Nathalie Lambert (overall)
Gold: Nathalie Lambert (1,000 metres)
Gold: Nathalie Lambert (3,000)
Gold: Canadian women's team (relay)
Silver: Nathalie Lambert (500)
Silver: Nathalie Lambert (1,500)

1993 Beijing
Gold: Canadian women's team (relay)
Gold: Nathalie Lambert (1,000)
Gold: Nathalie Lambert (1,500)
Gold: Nathalie Lambert (3,000)
Gold: Nathalie Lambert (overall)
Silver: Isabelle Charest (500)
Bronze: Angela Cutrone (500)

1992 Denver
Gold: Canadian women's team (relay)

1991 Sydney
Gold: Canadian women's team (relay)
Gold: Nathalie Lambert (1,500)
Gold: Nathalie Lambert (3,000)
Gold: Nathalie Lambert (overall)
Gold: Sylvie Daigle (1,000)

Silver: Nathalie Lambert (1,000)
Silver: Sylvie Daigle (1,500)
Silver: Sylvie Daigle (3,000)
Silver: Sylvie Daigle (overall)

1990 Amsterdam
Gold: Canadian women's team (relay)
Gold: Nathalie Lambert (1,500)
Gold: Sylvie Daigle (1,000)
Gold: Sylvie Daigle (500)
Gold: Sylvie Daigle (overall)
Silver: Eden Donatelli (500)
Silver: Sylvie Daigle (3,000)
Bronze: Eden Donatelli (1,500)
Bronze: Eden Donatelli (3,000)
Bronze: Eden Donatelli (overall)

1989 Solihull
Gold: Canadian women's team (relay)
Gold: Maryse Perrault (1,000)
Gold: Sylvie Daigle (1,500)
Gold: Sylvie Daigle (overall)
Silver: Maryse Perrault (overall)
Silver: Nathalie Lambert (3,000)
Silver: Sylvie Daigle (1,000)
Silver: Sylvie Daigle (500)
Bronze: Maryse Perrault (1,500)
Bronze: Maryse Perrault (500)

1988 St. Louis
Gold: Canadian women's team (relay)
Gold: Sylvie Daigle (1,500)
Gold: Sylvie Daigle (overall)
Silver: Sylvie Daigle (500)
Bronze: Eden Donatelli (1,000)

1987 Montreal
Gold: Canadian women's team (relay)
Gold: Eden Donatelli (500)
Gold: Nathalie Lambert (3,000)
Silver: Nathalie Lambert (1,500)
Silver: Nathalie Lambert (overall)
Bronze: Maryse Perrault (1,000)

1986 Chamonix
Gold: Canadian women's team (relay)
Silver: Maryse Perrault (500 - tie)
Silver: Maryse Perrault (overall - tie)
Silver: Nathalie Lambert (1,000)
Silver: Nathalie Lambert (1,500)
Silver: Nathalie Lambert (overall - tie)
Bronze: Maryse Perrault (3,000)

1985 Amsterdam
Gold: Canadian women's team (relay)
Silver: Nathalie Lambert (3,000)
Bronze: Maryse Perrault (3,000)
Bronze: Maryse Perrault (500)
Bronze: Nathalie Lambert (overall)

1984 Peterborough
Gold: Canadian women's team (relay)
Gold: Marie-Josee Martin (1,000)
Gold: Sylvie Daigle (3,000)
Silver: Nathalie Lambert (3,000)
Silver: Sylvie Daigle (500)
Silver: Sylvie Daigle (overall)
Bronze: Nathalie Lambert (1,000)

1983 Tokyo
Gold: Canadian women's team (relay)
Gold: Sylvie Daigle (1,000)
Gold: Sylvie Daigle (1,500)
Gold: Sylvie Daigle (3,000)

Gold: Sylvie Daigle (500)
Gold: Sylvie Daigle (overall)
Bronze: Maryse Perrault (3,000)
Bronze: Maryse Perrault (500)
Bronze: Maryse Perrault (overall)

1982 Moncton
Gold: Canadian women's team (relay)
Gold: Maryse Perrault (1,000)
Gold: Maryse Perrault (1,500)
Gold: Maryse Perrault (overall)
Gold: Sylvie Daigle (500)
Silver: Maryse Perrault (3,000)
Silver: Maryse Perrault (500)
Silver: Sylvie Daigle (1,000)
Bronze: Sylvie Daigle (overall)

1981 Meudon La Foret
Gold: Canadian women's team (relay)
Bronze: Nathalie Grondin (1,000)

1980 Milan
Silver: Cathy Turnbull (3,000)
Bronze: Cathy Turnbull (1,000)
Bronze: Cathy Turnbull (1,500)
Bronze: Cathy Turnbull (500)
Bronze: Cathy Turnbull (overall)

1979 Quebec City
Gold: Canadian women's team (relay)
Gold: Cathy Turnbull (overall)
Gold: Sylvie Daigle (500)
Gold: Sylvie Daigle (overall)
Silver: Cathy Turnbull (1,500)
Silver: Cathy Turnbull (500)
Silver: Cathy Turnbull (overall)
Silver: Sylvie Daigle (1,000)
Silver: Sylvie Daigle (3,000)
Bronze: Brenda Webster (1,000)
Bronze: Cathy Turnbull (3,000)
Bronze: Sylvie Daigle (1,500)

1978 Solihull
Silver: Brenda Webster (500)
Silver: Brenda Webster (1,500)
Silver: Canadian women's team (relay)

1977 Grenoble
Gold: Brenda Webster (1,500)
Gold: Brenda Webster (500)
Gold: Brenda Webster (overall)
Gold: Kathy Vogt (1,000)
Silver: Canadian women's team (relay)
Silver: Kathy Vogt (500)
Silver: Kathy Vogt (overall)
Bronze: Nancy Durnin (500)

Canadian Long Course Swimming Records
As of March, 1995

Freestyle
50 metres .... 0:26.01 Kristin Topham, PEPSI, 1991
0:26.01 Andrea Nugent, UCSC, 1987
100 .... 0:56.29 Marianne Limpert, NYAC, 1993
200 .... 2:00.61 Patricia Noall, CNMN, 1988
400 .... 4:12.83 Julie Daignault, PCSC, 1983
800 .... 8:36.24 Debbie Wurzburger, LAC, 1988
1,500 .... 16:40.60 Elissa Purvis, CDSC, 1986

Backstroke
100 .... 1:03.28 Nancy Garapick, HTAC, 1976
200 .... 2:14.23 Cheryl Gibson, ETOB, 1978

Breaststroke
100 .... 1:08.86 Allison Higson, EPS, 1988
200 .... 2:27.27 Allison Higson, EPS, 1988
Butterfly
100 .... 1:01.18 Kristin Topham, PEPSI, 1991
200 .... 2:11.48 Jill Horstead, ESC, 1985
Individual Medley
200 .... 2:15.15 Marianne Limpert, NYAC, 1992
400 .... 4:43.64 Joanne Malar, HWAC, March 1995

National Swim Team Relay Records
4x50 medley: 1:55.16 Lori Melien, Keltie Duggan, Debbie Gaudin, Kristin Topham (Pan Pacific team) 1989

4x100 medley: 4:09.26 Nikki Dryden, Guylaine Cloutier, Kristin Topham, Andrea Nugent (Olympic team) 1992

4x100 freestyle: 3:45.89 Marianne Limpert, Shannon Shakespeare, Jessica Amey, Joanne Malar (National team) 1994

4x200 freestyle: 8:08.25 Katie Brambley, Marianne Limpert, Shannon Shakespeare, Joanne Malar (Pan-American Games team) 1995

World Aquatic Championships — Canadian Synchronized Swimming Team Winners
1986: Carolyn Waldo, Sylvie Frechette, Michelle Cameron, Nathalie Audet, Traci Meades, Chantal Laviolette, Karin Larsen, Missy Morlock, Norma McBurney, Kathy Glen

1982: Carolyn Waldo, Penny Vilagos, Vicky Vilagos, Sharon Hambrook, Kelly Kryczka, Janet Arnold, Chantal Laviolette, Susan Clarke (Wendy Barber, Renee Paradis — alternates)

Canadian Outdoor Track and Field Records
As of March 1995
100 metres: .... 0:10.98 Angela Bailey, 1987
200: .... 0:22.62 Marita Payne, 1983
400: .... 0:49.91 Jillian Richardson, 1988
0:49.91 Marita Payne, 1984;
800: .... 1:58.52 Charmaine Crooks, 1990
1,000: .... 2:38:00 Sarah Howell, 1993
1,500: .... 4:00.27 Lynn Williams, 1985
Mile: .... 4:24.61 Lynn Williams, 1985
2,000: .... 5:39.96 Debbie Bowker, 1986
3,000: .... 8:32.17 Angela Chalmers, 1994
5,000: .... 15:01.30 Lynn Williams, 1988
10,000: .... 31:50.51 Sue Lee, 1988
Marathon: .... 2:28:36 Sylvia Ruegger, 1985
100-metre hurdles: .... 0:12.78 Julie Rocheleau, 1988
400-metre hurdles: .... 0:54.53 Rosey Edeh, 1993

High Jump: .... 1.98 metres Debbie Brill, 1984
Long Jump: .... 6.61 metres Donna Smellie, 1985
Triple Jump: .... 13.40 metres Sharon Clarke, 1986
Javelin: .... 59.76 metres Celine Chartrand, 1987
Shot Put: .... 17.17 metres Carmen Ionesco, 1979
Discus: .... 62.74 metres Carmen Ionesco, 1979
Hammer: .... 56.26 metres Theresa Brick, 1993
Pole vault: .... 3.30 metres Rebecca Chambers, 1994

Heptathlon: .... 6193 points Catherine Bond-Mills, 1994

5K Walk (road): .... 21:34 Alison Baker, 1992

10K Walk (road):	44:44 Alison Baker, 1992
20K Walk (road):	1:37:32 Janice McCaffrey, 1994

5,000-metre Walk (track): 21:52.95 Pascale Grand, 1990
10,000-metre Walk (track): 44:30.1 Alison Baker, 1992

Relays
4x100: .... 0:43.17 Margaret Howe, Patty Loverock,
Joanne McTaggart, Marjorie Bailey, 1976
4x200: .... 1:35.35 Jill McDermid, Esmie Lawrence,
Gwen Wall, Jillian Richardson, 1988
4x400: .... 3:21.21 Charmaine Crooks, Jillian
Richardson, Molly Killingbeck, Marita Payne, 1984

Women's World Hockey Championships — Team Rosters

1994 World Championship Team

Lesley Reddon
Manon Rheaume
Therese Brisson
Cassie Campbell
Judy Diduck
Geraldine Heaney
Nathalie Picard
Cheryl Pounder
Nancy Drolet
Danielle Goyette
Marianne Grnak
Andria Hunter
Angela James
Laura Leslie
Karen Nystrom
Margot Page
Jane Robinson
France St-Louis
Hayley Wickenheiser
Stacy Wilson

1992 World Championship Team

Manon Rheaume
Marie Claude Roy
Danielle Goyette
Andria Hunter
France St-Louis
Nancy Drolet
Angela James
France Montour
Geraldine Heaney
Karen Nystrom
Heather Ginzel
Margot Verlaan (Page)
Nathalie Picard
Laura Schuler
Diane Michaud
Stacy Wilson
Nathalie Rivard
Sue Scherer
Dawn McGuire
Judy Diduck

1990 World Championship Team

Denise Caron
Cathy Phillips
Angela James
Heather Ginzel
Susana Yuen
Shirley Cameron
Stacy Wilson
Vicky Sunohara

France Montour
Geraldine Heaney
Dawn McGuire
Sue Scherer
Margot Verlaan (Page)
Diane Michaud
Laura Schuler
Brenda Richard
Kim Ratushny
Teresa Hutchinson
Judy Diduck

Women's World Hockey Championships — Statistics

1994 Women's World Hockey Championships
Final: Canada 6 USA 3

Tournament Scoring Leaders:	G	A	PTS
1. Rikka Nieminen, Finland	4	9	13
2. DANIELLE GOYETTE, CANADA	9	3	12
3. Karyn Bye, USA	6	6	12
4. Cammi Granato, USA	5	7	12
5. Liu Hongmei, China	8	3	11
6. Tiia Reima, Finland	7	4	11
7. Sari Krooks, Finland	3	7	10
8. S. O'Sullivan, USA	3	7	10
9. Hanna Teerijoki, Finland	5	4	9
10.Gretchen Ulion, USA	5	4	9

Canadian Goaltenders:	G	GPI	Min	GA	SOG	S%	GAA
Manon Rheaume	6	4	209	6	44	86.36	.72
Lesley Reddon	6	2	91	1	15	93.33	0.66

1992 Women's World Hockey Championships
Final: Canada 8 USA 0

Tournament Scoring Leaders:	G	A	PTS
1. Cammi Granato, USA	8	2	10
2. DANIELLE GOYETTE, CANADA	3	7	10
3. ANDRIA HUNTER, CANADA	5	4	9
4. Lisa Brown, USA	2	7	9
5. Shelley Looney, USA	1	8	9
6. Rikka Nieminen, Finland	6	2	8
7. FRANCE ST. LOUIS, CANADA	5	3	8
8. NANCY DROLET, CANADA	4	4	8
9. Jeanine Sobek, USA	3	5	8
10.Karyn Bye, USA	3	5	8

Canadian Goaltenders:	GP	GPI	Min	GA	SOG	S%	GAA
Manon Rheaume	5	3	180	2	47	95.74	0.67
Marie Claude Roy	5	2	120	1	24	95.83	0.50

1990 Women's World Hockey Championships
Final: Canada 5 USA 2

Tournament Scoring Leaders:	G	A	PTS
1. Cindy Curley, USA	11	12	23
2. Tina Cardinale, USA	5	10	15
3. Cammi Granato, USA	9	5	14
4. Kim Urech, Switzerland	8	6	14
5. ANGELA JAMES, CANADA	11	2	13
6. HEATHER GINZEL, CANADA	7	5	12
7. SUSANA YUEN, CANADA	5	7	12
8. Kelly O'Leary, USA	6	5	11
9. SHIRLEY CAMERON, CANADA	5	6	11
10. STACY WILSON, CANADA	3	8	11

Canadian Goaltenders:	GP	GPI	Min	GA	SOG	S%	GAA
Denise Caron	5	3	144	5	32	84.38	2.08
Cathy Phillips	5	4	156	3	32	90.63	1.15

Canadian Women's Wheelchair Basketball — Team Rosters

1994 World Championship Gold Medal Team

Jennifer Krempien
Joanne Kelly
Kendra Ohama
Renee LeDrew
Lori Radke
Judie Millard
Tammy Cunningon
Linda Kutrowski
Chantal Benoit
Kelly Krywa
Marni Abbott
Tracey Ferguson

Tim Frick — Head Coach
Barb Griffin — Assistant Coach
Paul Zachau — Team Manager
Kristine Godziuk — Team Physio

1992 Paralympic Gold Medal Team

Marni Abbott
Chantal Benoit
Tracey Ferguson
Judy Goodrich
Patti Jones
Jennifer Krempien
Linda Kutrowski
Judie Millard
Kendra Ohama
Diane Rakiecki
Helene Simard
Irene Wownuk

Tim Frick — Head Coach
Barb Griffin — Assistant Coach
Joe Higgins — Assistant Coach

Canadian Players in the All-American Girls Professional Baseball League

Velma Abbott	Daisy Junor
Betty Betryna Allen	Dorothy Ferguson Key
Mary "Bonnie" Baker	Muriel Kohn
Barbara Barbaze	Olive Bend Little
Doris Barr	Mildred Warwick McAuley
Chris Jewett Beckett	Colleen Smith McCulloch
Eleanor Callow	Key Heim McDaniel
Betty Carveth	Gene George McFaul
Dorothy Cook	Martha Rommelaere Manning
Penny O'Brian Cooke	Ruby Knezovich Martz
Audrey Haines Daniels	Marge Callaghan Maxwell
Gladys Davis	Ev Wawryshn Moroz
Marguerite Jones Davis	Arlene Johnson Noga
Lena Surkowski Del Monico	Vickie Panos
Ann Surkowski Deyotte	Janet Anderson Perkins
Terry Donahue	Lucella McLean Ross
Julie Dusanko	Helen Callaghan St. Aubin
Elsie Wingrove Earl	Helen Nelson Sanderford
June Emerson	Yolanda Teillett Schick
Helen Nicol Fox	June Schofield
Ruth Middleton Gentry	Mary Kustra Shastal
Ethel McCreary Gould	Marion Watson Stanton
Olga Grant	Anne Jay Thompson
Marjorie Hanna	Thelma Walmsley
Agnes Zurkowski Homes	Betty Berthiaume Wickin
Thelma Grambo Hundeby	Hazel Measner Wildfong
Dorothy Hunter	Doris Shero Witiuk

Summer Olympic Games — Canadian Women Medallists

1992 Barcelona

Rowing
Gold: Kirsten Barnes and Kathleen Heddle (pair)
Gold: Kirsten Barnes, Brenda Taylor, Kay Worthington, Jessica Monroe (fours)
Gold: Kirsten Barnes, Brenda Taylor, Megan Delehanty, Shannon Crawford, Marnie McBean, Kay Worthington, Jessica Monroe, Kathleen Heddle, Lesley Thompson (eights with coxswain)
Bronze: Silken Laumann (single sculls)

Synchronized Swimming
Silver: Sylvie Frechette (solo)
Silver: Penny and Vicky Vilagos (duet)

Track and Field
Bronze: Angela Chalmers (3,000 metres)

Tae Kwon Do (demonstration event)
Silver: Marcia King (middleweight)
Bronze: Shelley Vettese-Baert (welterweight)

1988 Seoul

Synchronized Swimming
Gold: Carolyn Waldo (solo)
Gold: Carolyn Waldo and Michelle Cameron (duet)

Swimming
Bronze: Lori Melien, Allison Higson, Jane Kerr, Andrea Nugent (4x100-medley relay)

Equestrian
Bronze: Cindy Ishoy, Eva-Maria Pracht, Gina Smith, Ashley Nicoll (team dressage)

1984 Los Angeles

Diving
Gold: Sylvie Bernier (three-metre)

Rhythmic Gymnastics
Gold: Lori Fung (all-around)

Shooting
Gold: Linda Thom (sport pistol)

Swimming
Gold: Anne Ottenbrite (200 breaststroke)
Silver: Anne Ottenbrite (100 breaststroke)
Bronze: Reema Abdo, Michelle MacPherson, Anne Ottenbrite, Pam Rai (4x100 medley relay)

Track and Field
Silver: Angela Bailey, France Gareau, Marita Payne, Angella Taylor (4x100 relay)
Silver: Charmaine Crooks, Molly Killingbeck, Marita Payne, Jillian Richardson (4x100 relay)
Bronze: Lynn Williams (3,000 metres)

Rowing
Silver: Betty Craig and Tricia Smith (pair without cox)
Silver: Barbara Armbrust, Marilyn Brain, Angela Schneider, Jane Tregunno, Lesley Thompson (coxed four)
Bronze: Daniele Laumann, Silken Laumann (double sculls)

Synchronized Swimming
Silver: Carolyn Waldo (solo)
Silver: Sharon Hambrook, Kelly Kryczka (duet)

Canoeing
Bronze: Alexandra Barre, Lucie Guay, Sue Holloway, Barb Olmsted (K4 - 500 metres)

1976 Montreal

Swimming
Silver: Cheryl Gibson (400 individual medley)
Bronze: Nancy Garapick (100 backstroke)
Bronze: Nancy Garapick (200 backstroke)
Bronze: Shannon Smith (400 freestyle)
Bronze: Becky Smith (400 individual medley)
Bronze: Robin Corsiglia, Wendy Hogg, Anne Jardin, Susan Sloan (4x100 medley relay)

Bronze: Gail Amundrud, Barbara Clark, Anne Jardin, Becky Smith
(4x100 freestyle relay)

1972 Munich
Swimming
Silver: Leslie Cliff (400 individual medley)
Bronze: Donna-Marie Gurr (200 backstroke)

1968 Mexico City
Swimming
Silver: Elaine Tanner (100 backstroke)
Silver: Elaine Tanner (200 backstroke)
Bronze: Angela Coughlan, Marilyn Corson, Marion Lay, Elaine Tanner
(4x100 freestyle relay)

1956 Melbourne
Diving
Bronze: Irene MacDonald (three-metre)

1948 London
Track and Field
Bronze: Dianne Foster, Patricia Jones, Nancy MacKay, Viola Myers
(4x100 relay)

1936 Berlin
Track and Field
Bronze: Dorothy Brookshaw, Hilda Cameron, Jeanette Dolson,
Aileen Meagher (4x100 relay)
Bronze: Betty Taylor (80-metre hurdles)

1932 Los Angeles
Track and Field
Silver: Hilda Strike (100 metres)
Silver: Mary Frizzell, Mildred Frizzell, Lillian Palmer, Hilda Strike
(4x100 relay)
Bronze: Eva Dawes (high jump)

1928 Amsterdam
Track and Field
Gold: Ethel Catherwood (high jump)
Gold: Florence Bell, Myrtle Cook, Bobbie Rosenfeld, Ethel Smith
(4x100 relay)
Silver: Bobby Rosenfeld (100 metres)
Bronze: Ethel Smith (100 metres)

Winter Olympic Games — Canadian Women Medallists

1994 Lillehammer
Biathlon
Gold: Myriam Bedard (7.5K)
Gold: Myriam Bedard (15K)
Figure Skating
Bronze: Isabelle Brasseur with Lloyd Eisler (pairs)
Speedskating — Long Track
Silver: Susan Auch (500 metres)
Speedskating — Short Track
Silver: Nathalie Lambert (1,000)
Silver: Christine Boudrias, Nathalie Lambert, Sylvie Daigle, Isabelle
Charest (3,000 relay)

1992 Albertville
Alpine Skiing
Gold: Kerrin Lee-Gartner (downhill)
Speedskating — Short Track
Gold: Angela Cutrone, Sylvie Daigle, Nathalie Lambert, Annie
Perrault (3,000 relay)
Biathlon
Bronze: Myriam Bedard (15K)
Figure Skating
Bronze: Isabelle Brasseur with Lloyd Eisler (pairs)
Curling (demonstration event)
Bronze: Julie Sutton, Jodie Sutton, Melisa Soligo, Karri Willms
(alternate: Elaine Dagg-Jackson)

1988 Calgary
Alpine Skiing
Bronze: Karen Percy (downhill)
Bronze: Karen Percy (super giant slalom)
Curling (demonstration event)
Gold: Linda Moore, Lindsay Sparkes, Debbie Jones, Penny Ryan
(alternate: Patti Vande)
Figure Skating
Silver: Elizabeth Manley (singles)
Bronze: Tracy Wilson with Rob McCall (ice dance)
Speedskating — Short Track (demonstration event)
Gold: Sylvie Daigle (1,500)
Silver: Sylvie Daigle (1,000)
Silver: Sylvie Daigle (3,000)
Silver: Eden Donatelli (500)

1976 Innsbruck
Alpine Skiing
Gold: Kathy Kreiner (giant slalom)
Speedskating
Silver: Cathy Priestner (500)

1972 Sapporo
Figure Skating
Silver: Karen Magnussen (singles)

1968 Grenoble
Alpine Skiing
Gold: Nancy Greene (giant slalom)
Silver: Nancy Greene (slalom)

1964 Innsbruck
Figure Skating
Bronze: Petra Burka (singles)
Bronze: Debbi Wilkes with Guy Revell (pairs)

1960 Squaw Valley
Alpine Skiing
Gold: Anne Heggtveit (slalom)
Figure Skating
Gold: Barbara Wagner with Robert Paul (pairs)

1956 Cortino D'Ampezzo
Figure Skating
Silver: Francis Dafoe with Norris Bowden (pairs)
Alpine Skiing
Bronze: Lucile Wheeler (downhill)

1948 St. Moritz
Figure Skating
Gold: Barbara Ann Scott (singles)
Bronze: Suzanne Morrow with Wallace Distelmeyer (pairs)

Winter Paralympic Games — Canadian Women Medallists

1994 Lillehammer
Alpine Skiing
Silver: Ramona Hoh (slalom)
Silver: Lana Spreeman (slalom)
Bronze: Ramona Hoh (downhill)
Bronze: Lana Spreeman (super-G)
Bronze: Lana Spreeman (downhill)
Bronze: Lana Spreeman (giant slalom)

1992 Albertville
Alpine Skiing
Gold: Caroline Viau (super giant slalom)
Silver: Sandra Lynes (giant slalom)
Silver: Sandra Lynes (downhill)
Silver: Lana Spreeman (super giant slalom)
Silver: Lana Spreeman (slalom)

Bronze: Lana Spreeman (giant slalom)
Bronze: Lana Spreeman (downhill)
Bronze: Caroline Viau (giant slalom)
Bronze: Caroline Viau (downhill)

1988 Innsbruck
Nordic Skiing
Gold: Sandra Lecour, Francine Lemire (5K Nordic)
Silver: Sandra Lecour, Francine Lemire (10K Nordic)
Bronze: Sandra Lecour, Tricia Lovegrove, Kim Umbach (3x5 Nordic relay)
Alpine Skiing
Silver: Lana Spreeman (slalom)
Bronze: Lana Spreeman (downhill)

1984 Innsbruck
Alpine Skiing
Silver: Lynda Chyzyk, Lana Spreeman (giant slalom)
Silver: Lana Spreeman (downhill)
Bronze: Lynda Chyzyk (downhill)
Bronze: Lynda Chyzyk (combined)

1980 Geilo
Alpine Skiing
Gold: Lana Spreeman (giant slalom)
Gold: Lorna Manzer (slalom)
Bronze: Lorna Manzer (giant slalom)
Nordic Skiing
Bronze: Janet Schuster, Judy Shaw, Mary Brunner, Dawn Coyle
(4x5K Nordic relay)

Summer Paralympic Games — Canadian Women Medallists

1992 Barcelona
Track and Field
Gold: Joanne Bouw (shot put)
Gold: Joanne Bouw (discus)
Gold: Joanne Bouw (javelin)
Gold: Ljiljana Ljubisic (shot put)
Gold: Kristine Harder (400 metres)
Gold: Kristine Harder (discus)
Silver: Kristine Harder (200 sprint)
Silver: Ljiljana Ljubisic (shot put)
Bronze: Colette Bourgonje (100 sprint)
Bronze: Colette Bourgonje (800)
Bronze: Chantal Petitclerc (200)
Bronze: Chantal Petitclerc (800)
Swimming
Gold: Joanne Mucz (100 freestyle)
Gold: Joanne Mucz (100 breaststroke)
Gold: Joanne Mucz (100 individual medley)
Gold: Joanne Mucz (400 freestyle)
Gold: Joanne Mucz (100 butterfly)
Silver: Yvette Weicker (50 freestyle)
Silver: Marie-Claire Ross (100 breaststroke)
Bronze: Nora Bednarski (50 butterfly)
Bronze: Rebeccah Bornemann (100 freestyle)
Bronze: Rebeccah Bornemann (400 freestyle)
Bronze: Marie-Claire Ross (50 freestyle)
Bronze: Nancy Irvine, Carla Qualtrough, Marie-Claire Ross, Yvette
Weicker (4x100 freestyle relay)
Bronze: Nancy Irvine, Carla Qualtrough, Marie-Claire Ross, Yvette
Weicker (4x100 medley relay)
Basketball
Gold: Wheelchair Basketball Team
Cycling
Silver: Monique Glasgow (5,000 metres - cycling)
Bronze: Agnes Meszaros (5,000 metres - cycling)
Goalball
Bronze: Patricia Campion, Nathalie Chartrand, Eva Gill-Sager,
Anne Jarry, Teresa Loy, Helena Rooyakkers

Shooting
Bronze: Heather Kuttai (air pistol)

1988 Seoul
Track and Field
Gold: Joanne Bouw (discus)
Gold: Joanne Bouw (javelin)
Gold: Joanne Bouw (shot put)
Silver: Linda Hamilton (800)
Silver: Linda Hamilton (400)
Silver: Sylvie Bergeron (400)
Silver: Sonja Atkins (200)
Silver: Norma Lorincz (800)
Silver: Debbie Kostelyk (100)
Bronze: Trish Lovegrove (shot put)
Bronze: Ljiljana Ljubisic (shot put)
Bronze: Jacquie Toews (discus)
Bronze: Linda Hamilton (100)
Bronze: Linda Hamilton (400)
Bronze: Linda Hamilton (1,500)
Bronze: Lynette Wildeman (100)
Bronze: Lynette Wildeman (200)
Bronze: Sylvie Sauve (100)
Bronze: Sylvie Bergeron (200)
Bronze: Sonja Atkins (200)
Bronze: Racquel Head (800)
Bronze: Marjorie Lynch (shot put)
Swimming
Gold: Joanne Mucz (400 freestyle)
Gold: Yvette Weicker (100 backstroke)
Gold: Tammy Barker (100 freestyle)
Gold: Tammy Barker (200 freestyle)
Silver: Tammy Barker (100 backstroke)
Silver: Joanne Mucz (100 freestyle)
Silver: Yvette Weicker (100 freestyle)
Silver: Judy Goodrich (100 backstroke)
Bronze: Joanne Mucz (100 backstroke)
Bronze: Yvette Weicker (50 freestyle)
Bronze: Yvette Weicker (50 breaststroke)
Bronze: Yvette Weicker (100 breaststroke)
Bronze: Yvette Weicker (200 individual medley)
Bronze: Tami Boccaccio (200 breaststroke)
Bronze: Michelle Arnold (400 freestyle)
Bronze: Michelle Arnold (100 backstroke)
Bronze: Michelle Arnold (200 individual medley)
Bronze: Michelle Arnold (400 individual medley)
Bronze: Susie Chick (100 freestyle)
Bronze: Judy Goodrich (100 freestyle)
Bronze: YvetteWeicker,MichelleArnold, Tami Boccaccio, Carla
Qualtrough (4x100 medley relay)
Shooting
Silver: Heather Kuttai (team shooting)
Silver: Heather Kuttai (air pistol)
Goalball
Bronze: Patricia Campion, Lucy Greco, Danielle Lessard, Diane
Robitaille, Helena Rooyakkers, Lisa Wade

1984 New York
Track and Field
Gold: Christine Nicholas (1,500 metres)
Gold: Cheryl Hurd (3,000)
Gold: Christine Nicholas (3,000)
Gold: Norah Good (3,000)
Gold: Joanne Bouw (javelin)
Gold: Joanne Bouw (shot put)
Gold: Judy Goodrich (javelin)
Gold: Laura Misciagna (100)
Gold: Laura Misciagna (200)
Gold: Laura Misciagna (slalom)

Gold: Stephania Balta (discus)
Gold: Stephania Balta (shot put)
Gold: Anne Farrell (javelin)
Gold: M. Gustafson (discus)
Gold: M. Gustafson (100)
Gold: M. Gustafson (200)
Gold: M. Gustafson (400)
Gold: M. Gustafson (800)
Gold: T. Simpson (100)
Gold: Debbie Kostelyk (100)
Gold: Debbie Kostelyk (400)
Gold: T. Simpson (200)
Gold: T. Simpson (400)
Gold: T. Simpson (800)
Gold: A. Ieretti (800)
Gold: A. Ieretti (1,500)
Gold: A. Ieretti (5,000)
Silver: D. Willows (precision throw)
Silver: Rene Larochere (100)
Silver: Stephania Balta (javelin)
Silver: J. Zellman (shot put)
Silver: Debbie Kostelyk (200)
Silver: A. Ieretti (400)
Silver: Diane Rakiecki (800)
Silver: Cheryl Hurd (1,500)
Silver: Norah Good (1,500)
Bronze: D. Willows (boccia)
Bronze: Susan Smith (discus)
Bronze: D. Willows (distance throw)
Bronze: H. Lahman (distance throw)
Bronze: Susan Smith (javelin)
Bronze: Martha Johnson (shot put)
Bronze: Sandy Morgan (100)
Bronze: Elaine Hewitt (200)
Bronze: Cheryl Barrer (long jump)
Bronze: Anne Farrell (100)
Bronze: J. Zellman (javelin)
Bronze: J. Zellman (400)
Swimming
Gold: Yvette Michel (100 freestyle)
Gold: Yvette Michel (100 backstroke)
Gold: Yvette Michel (200 individual medley)
Gold: Andrea Rossi (400 individual medley)
Gold: Judy Goodrich (100 freestyle)
Gold: Judy Goodrich (50 backstroke)
Gold: Judy Goodrich (50 freestyle)
Gold: Susie Chick (50 freestyle)
Gold: D. Willows (25 freestyle)
Gold: Josee Lake (100 freestyle)
Gold: Josee Lake (50 backstroke)
Gold: Josee Lake (50 breaststroke)
Gold: Josee Lake (150 individual medley)
Gold: J. Fauche (200 freestyle)
Gold: J. Fauche (50 freestyle)
Gold: J. Fauche (25 butterfly)
Gold: M. Gustafson (25 freestyle)
Silver: Yvette Michel (400 freestyle)
Silver: T. Boccaccio (50 freestyle)
Silver: Yvette Michel (100 breaststroke)
Silver: Andrea Rossi (200 individual medley)
Silver: Patricia Hemm (200 freestyle)
Silver: Patricia Hemm (50 freestyle)
Silver: Judy Goodrich (100 backstroke)
Silver: Susan Smith (50 breaststroke)
Silver: J. Fauche (50 backstroke)
Silver: M. Gustafson (25 backstroke)
Silver: S. Voth (100 breaststroke)
Silver: S. Voth (100 backstroke)
Silver: S. Voth (400 freestyle)

Bronze: Andrea Rossi (400 freestyle)
Bronze: Andrea Rossi (400 breaststroke)
Bronze: Andrea Rossi (100 butterfly)
Bronze: T. Boccaccio (50 breaststroke)
Bronze: Patricia Hemm (100 freestyle)
Bronze: Susie Chick (25 backstroke)
Bronze: Jennifer Veenboer (50 breaststroke)
Bronze: Jennifer Veenboer (150 individual medley)
Bronze: S. Voth (100 freestyle)
Cycling
Gold: Leslie Lord (1,000)

Commonwealth Games — Canadian Women Medallists

1994 Victoria
Track and Field
Gold: Angela Chalmers (3,000)
Gold: Carole Rouillard (marathon)
Silver: Charmaine Crooks (800)
Silver: Paula Schnurr (1,500)
Silver: Robyn Meagher (3,000)
Silver: Lizanne Bussieres (marathon)
Bronze: Alanna Yakiwchuk, Stacy Bowen, Donalda Duprey, Charmaine Crooks (4x400 relay)
Bronze: Janice McCaffrey (10K racewalk)
Bronze: Catherine Bond-Mills (heptathlon)
Swimming
Silver: Andrea Nugent (50 freestyle)
Silver: Marianne Limpert (200 individual medley)
Silver: Nancy Sweetnam (400 individual medley)
Bronze: Shannon Shakespeare (50 freestyle)
Bronze: Marianne Limpert (100 freestyle)
Bronze: Nikki Dryden (800 freestyle)
Bronze: Lisa Flood (200 breaststroke)
Bronze: Nancy Sweetnam (200 individual medley)
Bronze: Marianne Limpert, Shannon Shakespeare, Jessica Amey, Glencora Maughan (4x100 freestyle)
Bronze: Beth Hazel, Lisa Flood, Jessica Amey, Marianne Limpert (4x100 medley relay)

Diving
Gold: Annie Pelletier (one-metre)
Gold: Annie Pelletier (three-metre)
Gold: Anne Montminy (platform)
Silver: Paige Gordon (three metre)
Silver: Paige Gordon (platform)
Bronze: Mary DePiero (one-metre)
Bronze: Myriam Boileau (platform)
Synchronized Swimming
Gold: Lisa Alexander (solo)
Gold: Lisa Alexander and Erin Woodley (duet)
Cycling
Gold: Tanya Dubnicoff (women's sprint)
Silver: Linda Jackson (road race)
Silver: Clara Hughes, Anne Samplonius, Alison Sydor, Lesley Tomlinson (team time trial)
Badminton
Silver: Sian Deng (women's singles)
Bronze: Denyse Julien, Sian Deng (women's doubles)
Artistic Gymnastics
Gold: Stella Umeh (all-around)
Gold: Stella Umeh (vault)
Silver: Stella Umeh (uneven bars)
Silver: Stacey Galloway, Jaime Hill, Lisa Simes, Stella Umeh (team competition)
Bronze: Lisa Simes (vault)
Bronze: Lisa Simes (floor)

Rhythmic Gymnastics
Gold: Lindsay Richards, Camille Martens, Gretchen McLennan (team)
Silver: Camille Martens (all-around)
Silver: Camille Martens (ball)
Silver: Camille Martens (clubs)
Silver: Camille Martens (ribbon)
Silver: Lindsay Richards (hoop)
Bronze: Gretchen McLennan (ball)
Bronze: Gretchen McLennan (ribbon)

Shooting
Gold: Sharon Bowes and Christina Ashcroft (women's pairs
    smallbore rifle, three position)
Gold: Helen Smith (air pistol)
Gold: Sharon Bowes (women's individual smallbore rifle, three position)
Silver: Sharon Cozzarin and Helen Smith (women's pairs sport pistol)
Bronze: Christina Ashcroft and Sharon Bowes (women's pairs air rifle)
Bronze: Christina Ashcroft and Linda Szulga (women's pairs
    smallbore rifle, prone)
Bronze: Sharon Cozzarin (women's air pistol)
Bronze: Sharon Bowes (women's individual air rifle)
Bronze: Christina Ashcroft (women's individual smallbore rifle, three
    position)

1990 Auckland
Swimming
Gold: Keltie Duggan (100 breaststroke)
Gold: Nathalie Giguere (200 breaststroke)
Gold: Nancy Sweetnam (200 individual medley)
Silver: Guylaine Cloutier (100 breaststroke)
Silver: Guylaine Cloutier (200 breaststroke)
Silver: Allison Higson, Erin Murphy, Patricia Noall, Kim Patton
    (4x100 freestyle relay)
Bronze: Andrea Nugent (50 freestyle)
Bronze: Patricia Noall (100 freestyle)
Bronze: Patricia Noall (200 freestyle)
Bronze: Keltie Duggan, Lori Melien, Patricia Noall, Nancy Sweetnam
    (4x100 medley relay)

Synchronized Swimming
Gold: Sylvie Frechette
Gold: Christine Larsen and Kathy Glen (duet)

Track and Field
Gold: Angela Chalmers (1,500)
Gold: Angela Chalmers (3,000)
Bronze: Rosey Edeh, France Gareau, Cheryl Allen, Gail Harris
    (4x400 relay)

Artistic Gymnastics
Gold: Larissa Lowing, Janet Morin, Lori Strong, Stella Umeh (team)
Gold: Lori Strong (all-around)
Gold: Lori Strong (balance beam)
Gold: Lori Strong (floor exercise)
Silver: Larissa Lowing (balance beam)
Silver: Larissa Lowing (floor exercise)
Silver: Lori Strong (uneven bars)
Silver: Lori Strong (vault)

Rhythmic Gymnastics
Gold: Mary Fuzesi (all-around)
Gold: Mary Fuzesi (hoop)
Gold: Mary Fuzesi (ribbon)
Gold: Madonna Gimotea (ball)
Silver: Madonna Gimotea (all-around)
Silver: Madonna Gimotea (hoop)
Silver: Madonna Gimotea (ribbon)
Silver: Madonna Gimotea (rope)
Silver: Mary Fuzesi (ball)
Bronze: Mary Fuzesi (rope)

Judo
Silver: Karen Hyde (66 kilos)
Silver: Alison Webb (72 kilos)
Silver: Jane Patterson (open)

Bronze: Mandy Clayton (61 kilos)
Diving
Gold: Mary DePiero (one-metre)
Gold: Anna Dacyshyn (platform)
Silver: Barb Bush (three-metre)
Bronze: Paige Gordon (platform)

Badminton
Silver: Denyse Julien (singles)
Silver: Johanne Falardeau, Denyse Julien, Claire Sharpe, Doris Piche,
    Linda Cloutier (women members of Canadian team)
Bronze: Johanne Falardeau and Denyse Julien (doubles)

Cycling
Bronze: Kelly-Ann Way (3,000-metre individual pursuit)

1986 Edinburgh
Track and Field
Gold: Angella Issajenko (200)
Gold: Lynn Williams (3,000)
Gold: Charmaine Crooks, Molly Killingbeck, Marita Payne, Jillian
    Richardson (4x400 relay)
Silver: Jillian Richardson (400)
Silver: Debbie Bowker (1,500)
Silver: Debbie Bowker (3,000)
Silver: Donalda Duprey (400-metre hurdles)
Silver: Angela Bailey, Angella Issajenko, Esmie Lawrence, Angela
    Phipps (4x100 relay)
Bronze: Angella Issajenko (100)
Bronze: Lynn Williams (1,500)
Bronze: Odette LaPierre (marathon)

Swimming
Gold: Jane Kerr (100 freestyle)
Gold: Allison Higson (100 breaststroke)
Gold: Allison Higson (200 breaststroke)
Gold: Donna McGinnis (200 butterfly)
Gold: Jane Kerr, Patricia Noall, Andrea Nugent, Pam Rai (4x100
    freestyle relay)
Silver: Jane Kerr (200 freestyle)
Silver: Cindy Ounpuu (200 breaststroke)
Silver: Allison Higson, Jane Kerr, Barb McBain, Donna McGinnis
    (4x100 medley relay)
Bronze: Jill Horstead (200 butterfly)
Bronze: Jane Kerr (200 individual medley)

Synchronized Swimming
Gold: Sylvie Frechette (solo)
Gold: Michelle Cameron and Carolyn Waldo (duet)

Diving
Gold: Debbie Fuller (three-metre)
Gold: Debbie Fuller (platform)
Bronze: Kathy Kelemen (three-metre)

Rowing
Gold: Kathryn Barr and Andrea Schreiner (pair)
Gold: Tina Clarke, Tricia Smith, Jane Tregunno, Jennifer Walinga,
    Lesley Thompson (coxed four)
Silver: Heather Clarke, Lisa Robertson (double sculls)
Silver: Lisa Wright (single sculls)
Bronze: Heather Hattin (lightweight single sculls)
Bronze: Anne Drost, Marni Hamilton, Marlene Van der Horst,
    Wendy Wiebe (four without cox)

Badminton
Silver: Denyse Julien and Johanne Falardeau (doubles)
Silver: Denyse Julien, Johanne Falardeau, Claire Sharpe, Linda
    Cloutier, Sandra Skillings (women members of Canadian team)

1982 Brisbane
Track and Field
Gold: Angella Taylor (100)
Gold: Debbie Brill (high jump)
Gold: Charmaine Crooks, Jillian Richardson, Molly Killingbeck,
    Angella Taylor (4x400 relay)

Silver: Angela Bailey, Marita Payne, Angella Taylor, Molly
   Killingbeck (4x100 relay)
Bronze: Angella Taylor (200)
Bronze: Susan Kameli (100-metre hurdles)
Bronze: Rosemarie Hauch (shot put)
Bronze: Jill Ross (heptathlon)
Swimming
Gold: Kathy Bald (100 breaststroke)
Gold: Anne Ottenbrite (200 breaststroke)
Gold: Cheryl Gibson, Anne Ottenbrite, Michelle MacPherson,
   Maureen New (4x100 medley relay)
Silver: Anne Ottenbrite (100 breaststroke)
Silver: Kathy Bald (200 breaststroke)
Silver: Cheryl Gibson (200 individual medley)
Bronze: Kathy Richardson (200 breaststroke)
Bronze: Cheryl Gibson (200 backstroke)
Bronze: Michelle MacPherson (400 individual medley)
Bronze: Michelle MacPherson (100 butterfly)
Diving
Silver: Sylvie Bernier (three-metre)
Silver: Jennifer McArton (platform)
Bronze: Kathy Kelemen (platform)
Badminton
Gold: Claire Backhouse and Johanne Falardeau (doubles)
Silver: Claire Backhouse, Johanne Falardeau, Denyse Julien, Sandra
   Skillings, Jane Youngberg (women members of Canadian team)

1978 Edmonton
Track and Field
Gold: Diane Jones Konihowski (pentathlon)
Gold: Carmen Ionesco (discus)
Silver: Carmen Ionesco (discus)
Silver: Debbie Brill (high jump)
Silver: Alison Hayward (javelin)
Silver: Angela Bailey, Margaret Howe, Patty Loverock, Marjorie
   Bailey (4x100 relay)
Bronze: Lucette Moreau (discus)
Bronze: Julie White (high jump)
Bronze: Penny Werthner (1,500)
Bronze: Laurie Kern (javelin)
Bronze: Margaret Stride, Debbie Campbell, Anne Mackie-Morelli,
   Rochelle Campbell (4x400 relay)
Swimming
Gold: Robin Corsiglia (100 breaststroke)
Gold: Lisa Borsholt (200 breaststroke)
Gold: Wendy Quirk (100 butterfly)
Gold: Carol Klimpel (100 freestyle)
Gold: Cheryl Gibson (200 backstroke)
Gold: Gail Amundrud, Carol Klimpel, Susan Sloan, Wendy Quirk
   (4x100 freestyle relay)
Gold: Helen Boivin, Marian Stuart, Wendy Quirk, Carol Klimpel
   (4x100 medley relay)
Silver: Wendy Quirk (200 butterfly)
Silver: Helen Boivin (100 backstroke)
Silver: Becky Smith (400 individual medley)
Bronze: Wendy Quirk (100 freestyle)
Bronze: Cheryl Gibson (100 backstroke)
Bronze: Marian Stuart (100 breaststroke)
Bronze: Becky Smith (200 individual medley)
Diving
Gold: Janet Nutter (three-metre)
Gold: Linda Cuthbert (10-metre platform)
Silver: Beverley Boys (three-metre)
Bronze: Enike Kiefer (three-metre)
Bronze: Janet Nutter (10-metre platform)
Gymnastics
Gold: Elfi Schlegel (individual)
Gold: Karen Kelsall, Elfi Schlegel, Monica Goermann, Sherry Hawko (team)
Silver: Sherry Hawko (individual)

Silver: Monica Goermann (individual)
Badminton
Silver: Wendy Clarkson, Jane Youngberg, Johanne Falardeau, Claire
   Backhouse, Sharon Crawford (women members of Canadian team)
Silver: Jane Youngberg and Claire Backhouse (doubles)
Bronze: Wendy Clarkson (singles)

1974 Christchurch
Track and Field
Gold: Yvonne Saunders (400)
Gold: Glenda Reiser (1,500)
Gold: Jane Haist (shot put)
Gold: Jane Haist (discus)
Silver: Louise Hanna (high jump)
Silver: Brenda Eisler (long jump)
Bronze: Thelma Wright (1,500)
Bronze: Brigitte Bittner (high jump)
Bronze: Carol Martin (discus)
Bronze: Maureen Crowley, Brenda Walsh, Margaret MacGowan,
   Yvonne Saunders (4x400 relay)
Swimming
Gold: Wendy Cook (100 backstroke)
Gold: Wendy Cook (200 backstroke)
Gold: Patti Stenhouse (100 butterfly)
Gold: Leslie Cliff (200 individual medley)
Gold: Leslie Cliff (400 individual medley)
Gold: Gail Amundrud, Becky Smith, Anne Jardin, Judith Wright
   (4x100 freestyle relay)
Gold: Wendy Cook, Marian Stuart, Patti Stenhouse, Gail Amundrud
   (4x100 medley relay)
Silver: Gail Amundrud (100 freestyle)
Silver: Donna-Marie Gurr (100 backstroke)
Silver: Wendy Quirk (400 freestyle)
Silver: Marian Stuart (100 breaststroke)
Silver: Patti Stenhouse (200 butterfly)
Silver: Becky Smith (200 individual medley)
Silver: Becky Smith (400 individual medley)
Bronze: Judy Wright (100 freestyle)
Bronze: Gail Amundrud (200 freestyle)
Bronze: Donna-Marie Gurr (200 backstroke)
Diving
Gold: Cindy Shatto (three-metre)
Gold: Beverley Boys (10-metre)
Silver: Beverley Boys (three-metre)
Bronze: Teri York (three-metre)

1970 Edinburgh
Track and Field
Gold: Debbie Brill (high jump)
Bronze: Thelma Fynn (1,500 metres)
Bronze: Joanne Hendry, Joyce Sadowick, Patty Loverock, Stephanie
   Berto (4x100 relay)
Bronze: Carol Martin (discus)
Bronze: Judith Dahlgren (javelin)
Bronze: Jenny Meldrum (pentathlon)
Swimming
Gold: Angela Coughlan (100 freestyle)
Silver: Angela Coughlan (200 freestyle)
Silver: Susan Smith (100 butterfly)
Silver: Donna-Marie Gurr (200 backstroke)
Silver: Susan Smith, Linda Hall, Karen James, Angela Coughlan
   (4x100 freestyle relay)
Bronze: Donna-Marie Gurr (100 backstroke)
Bronze: Donna-Marie Gurr, Sylvia Dockerill, Susan Smith, Angela
   Coughlan (4x100 medley relay)
Diving
Gold: Beverley Boys (three-metre)
Gold: Beverley Boys (10-metre)
Silver: Liz Carruthers (three-metre)
Silver: Nancy Robertson (10-metre)

1966 Kingston
Track and Field
Gold: Abby Hoffman (880 yards)
Silver: Irene Piotrowski (100 yards)
Bronze: Nancy McCredie (shot put)
Bronze: Irene Piotrowski (220 yards)
Bronze: Jennifer Wingerson (80-metre hurdles)
Bronze: Carol Martin (discus)
Bronze: Judith Dahlgren (javelin)
Swimming
Gold: Elaine Tanner (110-yard butterfly)
Gold: Elaine Tanner (220-yard butterfly)
Gold: Elaine Tanner (440-yard individual medley)
Gold: Marion Lay (100-yard freestyle)
Gold: 4x110-yard freestyle relay (Elaine Tanner, Jane Hughes, H. Louise Kennedy, Marion Lay)
Silver: Elaine Tanner (110-yard backstroke)
Silver: Elaine Tanner (220-yard backstroke)
Silver: Marilyn Corson (220-yard butterfly)
Silver: H. Louise Kennedy, Donna Ross, Elaine Tanner, Marion Lay (4x110-yard medley relay)
Bronze: Jane Hughes (440-yard individual medley)
Diving
Silver: Beverley Boys (three-metre)
Bronze: Beverley Boys (10-metre)
Badminton
Silver: Sharon Whittaker (singles)

1962 Perth
Swimming
Gold: Mary Stewart (110-yard butterfly)
Silver: Patricia Thompson, Sara Barber, Madeleine Sevigny, Mary Stewart (4x110-yard freestyle relay)
Bronze: Mary Stewart (110-yard freestyle)
Bronze: Sara Barber, Alison Glendenning, Mary Stewart, Patricia Thompson (4x110-yard medley relay)

1958 Cardiff
Diving
Silver: Irene MacDonald (three-metre)
Swimming
Silver: Sara Barber, Margaret Iwasaki, Gladys Priestley, Susan Sangster (4x110-yard freestyle relay)
Bronze: Margaret Iwasaki (110-yard butterfly)
Bronze: Sara Barber, Irene Service, Margaret Iwasaki, Gladys Priestley (4x110-yard medley relay)
Track and Field
Bronze: Jacqueline Gelling (shot put)
Bronze: Diane Matheson, Eleanor Haslam, Maureen Rever, Freyda Berman (4x110-yard relay)

1954 Vancouver
Track and Field
Silver: Jacqueline MacDonald (shot put)
Silver: Gwendolyn Hobbins (80-metre hurdles)
Bronze: Alice Whitty (high jump)
Bronze: Marie Dupree (discus)
Bronze: Shirley Couzens (javelin)
Bronze: Margery Squires, Dorothy Kozak, Annabelle Murray, Geraldine Bemister (4x110-yard relay)
Swimming
Silver: Virginia Grant (110-yard freestyle)
Silver: Gladys Priestley (440-yard freestyle)
Silver: Virginia Grant, Gladys Priestley, Helen Stewart, Elizabeth Whittall (4x110-yard freestyle relay)
Diving
Bronze: Irene MacDonald (three-metre)

1950 Auckland
Diving
Bronze: Lynda Hunt (three-metre)
Track and Field
Bronze: Eleanor McKenzie, Geraldine Bemister, Pat Jones, Elaine Silburn (660-yard relay)

1938 Sydney
Track and Field
Gold: Robina Higgins (javelin)
Silver: Aileen Meagher, M. Jeanette Dolson, Barbara Howard (440-yard relay)
Bronze: M. Jeanette Dolson (100 yards)
Bronze: Violet Montgomery, Barbara Howard, Aileen Meagher, M. Jeanette Dolson (660-yard relay)
Swimming
Gold: Florence Humble, Dorothy Lyon, Noel Oxenbury, Phyllis Dewar (4x110-yard freestyle relay)
Bronze: Dorothy Lyon (110-yard freestyle)
Bronze: Joan Langdon (220-yard breaststroke)
Diving
Silver: Lynda Adams (three-metre)
Silver: Lynda Adams (tower)
Bronze: Marie Sharkey (three-metre)

1934 London
Track and Field
Silver: Hilda Strike (100 yards)
Silver: Aileen Meagher (220-yards)
Silver: Betty Taylor (80-metre hurdles)
Silver: Eva Dawes (high jump)
Silver: Evelyn Goshawk (long jump)
Silver: Audrey Dearnley, Aileen Meagher, Hilda Strike (440-yard relay)
Bronze: Margaret Bell (high jump)
Swimming
Gold: Phyllis Dewar (100-yard freestyle)
Gold: Phyllis Dewar (440-yard freestyle)
Gold: Margaret Hutton, Phyllis Haslam, Phyllis Dewar (3x100-yard medley relay)
Gold: Phyllis Dewar, Florence Humble, Irene Pirie, Margaret Hutton (4x100-yard freestyle relay)
Silver: Irene Pirie (100-yard freestyle)
Silver: Phyllis Haslam (200-yard breaststroke)
Bronze: Irene Pirie (440-yard freestyle)
Diving
Gold: Judith Moss (three-metre)
Bronze: Doris Ogilvie (three-metre)

1930 Hamilton
Diving
Gold: Pearl Stoneham (10-metre)
Silver: Helen McCormack (10-metre)
Silver: Doris Ogilvie (three-metre)
Bronze: H. Mollie Bailey (three-metre)
Swimming
Silver: Irene Pirie, Betty Edwards, Marjorie Linton, Peggy Bailey (4x100-yard freestyle relay)

Pan-American Games — Canadian Women Medallists
1995 Mar del Plata
Track and Field
Silver: Sarah Howell (1,500)
Silver: Carol Montgomery (10,000)
Silver: Donalda Duprey (100-metre hurdles)
Bronze: Valerie Tulloch (javelin)
Bronze: Carol Montgomery (5,000)

Swimming
Gold: Joanne Malar (200 individual medley)
Gold: Joanne Malar (400 individual medley)
Gold: Lisa Flood (100 breaststroke)
Gold: Lisa Flood (200 breaststroke)
Silver: Shannon Shakespeare (50 freestyle)
Silver: Guylaine Cloutier (100 breaststroke)
Silver: Guylaine Cloutier (200 breaststroke)
Silver: Marianne Limpert (200 freestyle)
Silver: Joanne Malar, Shannon Shakespeare, Marianne Limpert, Lisa Flood (4x100 freestyle relay)
Silver: Joanne Malar, Marianne Limpert, Katie Brambley, Shannon Shakespeare (4x200 freestyle relay)
Bronze: Andrea Moody (50 freestyle)
Bronze: Katie Brambley (400 freestyle)
Bronze: Marianne Limpert (100 freestyle)
Cycling
Gold: Tanya Dubnicoff (sprint)
Gold: Alison Sydor (mountain-cross-country)
Silver: Clara Hughes (road race)
Bronze: Clara Hughes (individual time trial)
Rowing
Gold: Silken Laumann (single sculls)
Gold: Marnie McBean and Diane O'Grady (double sculls)
Silver: Wendy Wiebe (lightweight single sculls)
Badminton
Gold: Denyse Julien (women's singles)
Gold: Denyse Julien and Sian Deng (women's doubles)
Gold: Denyse Julien (mixed doubles)
Silver: Sian Deng (women's singles)
Silver: Milaine Cloutier and Robyn Hermitage (women's doubles)
Silver: Sian Deng (mixed doubles)
Fencing
Bronze: Sherraine Schalm, Marie-Francois Hervieu, Maureen Griffin and Heather Landymoore (team épée)
Racquetball
Silver: Vicki Shanks and Debbie Ward (women's doubles)
Silver: Carol McFetridge, Josee Grand-Maitre, Christie Van Hees, Vicki Shanks and Debbie Ward (women's team)
Bronze: Carol McFetridge (women's singles)
Sailing
Gold: Caroll-Ann Alie (Mistral)
Gold: Penny Davis and Leigh Pearson (470 class)
Synchronized Swimming
Silver: Karen Clark (solo)
Silver: Lisa Alexander and Erin Woodley (duet)
Silver: Canadian team
Diving
Gold: Annie Pelletier (three-metre)
Gold: Anne Montminy (platform)
Silver: Annie Pelletier (one-metre)
Bronze: Bobbi-Anne MacPherson (three-metre)
Equestrian
Bronze: Nancy MacLachlan, Louise Miechowsky, Victoria Winter (team dressage)
Bronze: Victoria Winter (individual dressage)
Shooting
Silver: Sharon Bowes (standard 3x20 rifle)
Bronze: Susan Nattrass (double trap)
Archery
Bronze: Veronic Dufour, Caroline Labrecque, Sylvie Plante (team)
Squash
Gold: Heather Wallace (women's singles)
Gold: Melanie Jans, Heather Wallace, Kelsey Souchereau, Anita Soni (women's team)
Gold: Canadian team (overall)
Table Tennis
Gold: Lijuan Geng (singles)

Gold: Petra Cada, Barbara Chiu, Lijuan Geng, Chris Hong Ngo (team)
Gold: Lijuan Geng (mixed doubles)
Gold: Lijuan Geng and Barbara Chiu (doubles)
Bronze: Barbara Chiu (mixed doubles)
Bronze: Barbara Chiu (singles)
Bowling
Gold: Sandra Lowe, Anne Saasto, Deborah Ship, Catharine Willis (team)
Gold: Catharine Willis (singles)
Volleyball
Bronze: Canadian team
Field Hockey
Bronze: Canadian team
Tae Kwon Do
Silver: Roxanne Forget (54 kilos)
Bronze: Miranda Hall (47 kilos)
Bronze: Marcia King (70 kilos)
Bronze: Dominique Bosshart (70 kilos)
Kayaking
Gold: Catherine Breckenridge, Jessica Ferguson, Marie-Josee Gibeau, Danica Rice (500 fours)
Silver: Marie-Josee Gibeau and Kelly O'Leary (500 doubles)
Judo
Silver: Michelle Buckingham (61 kilos)
Silver: Carolyne LePage (48 kilos)
Bronze: Nancy-Jewitt Filteau (72-plus kilos)
Bronze: Michelle Buckingham (61 kilos)
Bronze: Renee Hock (52 kilos)
Bronze: Nathalie Gosselin (56 kilos)
Karate
Gold: Nicole Poirier (52-plus kilos)
Water Skiing
Gold: Susi Graham, Kim DeMacedo (team)
Silver: Susi Graham (slalom)
Silver: Kim DeMacedo (tricks)
Silver: Kim DeMacedo (jumps)
Bronze: Kim DeMacedo (slalom)
Triathlon
Gold: Kirstie Otto, Fiona Cribb, Lisa Bentley (team)
Silver: Kirstie Otto
Bronze: Fiona Cribb
Team Handball
Silver: Canadian women's team

1991 Havana
Track and Field
Silver: Lisa Harvey (10,000 metres)
Bronze: Sarah Howell (1,500 metres)
Canoeing
Gold: Corinna Kennedy (K1-500 metres)
Gold: Tessa Desouza and Corinna Kennedy (K2-500 metres)
Silver: Tessa Desouza, Corinna Kennedy, Lucy Slade, Leslie-Anne Young (K4-500 metres)
Cycling
Gold: Tanya Dubnicoff (sprint)
Silver: Clara Hughes (3,000-metre pursuit)
Bronze: Edie Fisher, Clara Hughes, Denise Kelly, Sharon Keogh (team time trial)
Diving
Silver: Paige Gordon (three-metre)
Equestrian
Gold: Lorraine Stubbs (individual dressage)
Gold: Lorraine Stubbs, Ashley Monroe, Leslie Reid, Gina Smith (team dressage)
Silver: Ashley Monroe (individual dressage)
Silver: Beth Underhill (individual jumping)
Silver: Beth Underhill, Sandra Anderson (team jumping)
Field Hockey
Silver: Canadian women's team (Bernadette Bowyer, Joel Brough,

Michelle Conn, Deb Covey, Sharon Creelman, Tammy Holt, Heather Jones, Sandra Levy, Rochelle Low, Gaye Porteous, Candy Thompson, Debbie Whitten

Gymnastics
Silver: Mylene Fleury (uneven bars)
Bronze: Jennifer Wood (vault)
Bronze: Canadian team (Mylene Fleury, Colleen Johnson, Meghan McCurdy, Tara Sherwood, Jennifer Wood)

Judo
Silver: Brigitte Lastrade (48 kilos)
Bronze: Alison Webb (72 kilos)
Bronze: Jane Patterson (72-plus kilos)
Bronze: Jane Patterson (open)

Rhythmic Gymnastics
Gold: Canadian team (Mary Fuzesi, Madonna Gimotea, Susie Cushman)
Gold: Mary Fuzesi (hoop)
Silver: Mary Fuzesi (rope)
Silver: Mary Fuzesi (ball)
Silver: Mary Fuzesi (all around)
Bronze: Madonna Gimotea (ball)

Rowing
Gold: Nori Doobenen, Laurie Feathersone (lightweight pairs without cox)
Gold: Danita Sepp, Shannon Crawford, Julie Jespersen, Andrea Walsh (fours without cox)
Silver: Shannon Crawford, Julie Jespersen (pairs without cox)

Shooting
Gold: Sharon Cozzarin (air pistol)
Silver: Sharon Cozzarin, Claudine Tanguay, Helen Smith (team air pistol)
Silver: Christina Ashcroft (standard rifle)
Silver: Sharon Bowes, Christina Ashcroft, Therese Lander
Bronze: Sharon Bowes (air rifle)

Softball
Silver: Sandie Beasley, Jodie Biggan, Shannah Biggan, Juanita Clayton, Karen Doell, Nancy Drolet, Carrie Flemmer, Lisa Jubinville, Pati-Lou King, Pauline Maurice, Kara McGaw, Christine Parris, Lori Sippel, Karen Snelgrove, Wendy Sofiak, Alecia Stephenson, Marina Watson (team)

Swimming
Gold: Kristin Topham (50 freestyle)
Gold: Kristin Topham (100 butterfly)
Silver: Joanne Malar (200 individual medley)
Silver: Joanne Malar (400 individual medley)
Silver: Nikki Dryden (100 backstroke)
Silver: Nikki Dryden (200 backstroke)
Silver: Chantal Dubois (200 breaststroke)
Silver: Sharon Turner, Kristin Topham, Joanne Malar, Kim Paton (4x100 freestyle relay)
Silver: Kim Paton, Joanne Malar, Nikki Dryden, Tara Seymour (4x200 freestyle relay)
Bronze: Kristin Topham (100 freestyle)
Bronze: Kim Paton (200 freestyle)
Bronze: Tara-Lynn Seymour (400 freestyle)
Bronze: Tara-Lynn Seymour (800 freestyle)
Bronze: Lisa Flood (100 breaststroke)
Bronze: Lisa Flood (200 breaststroke)
Bronze: Joanne Malar (200 backstroke)
Bronze: Beth Hazel (200 butterfly)

Synchronized Swimming
Silver: Kelsey Corbitt, Carrie DeGuerre, Nancy Dore, Marie-France Lemieux, Chantal Vallieres, Erin Woodley, Susan Crews (team)
Bronze: Corinne Keddie, Julie Bibby (duet)

Table Tennis
Bronze: Julie Barton, Caroline Sylvestre (doubles)
Bronze: Julie Barton (mixed doubles)

Yachting
Gold: Shona Moss (Laser)

Silver: Edithe Trepanier (sailboard)

1987 Indianapolis

Track and Field
Silver: Jillian Richardson (400)
Silver: Debbie Bowker (1,500)
Silver: Angela Chalmers (3,000)
Silver: Nancy Tinari (10,000)
Silver: Charmaine Crooks, Molly Killingbeck, Marita Payne, Jillian Richardson (4x400 relay)
Silver: Ann Peel (10K racewalk)
Silver: Connie Polman-Tuin (heptathlon)
Bronze: Brit McRoberts (1,500)

Basketball
Bronze: Andrea Blackwell, Alice Cochran, Sandra Espeseth, Janet Fowler, Carol Hamilton, Debbie Huband, Karla Karch, Angela Orton, Anna Pendergast, Lynn Polson, Bev Smith, Misty Thomas

Canoeing
Silver: Erika Revesz (K1-500 metres)
Silver: Louise Hine, Cynthia Leonard (K2-500 metres)
Silver: Erika Revesz, Cynthia Leonard, Louise Hine, Alexandra Rubinger (K4-500 metres)

Cycling
Silver: Kelly Anne Carter (individual pursuit)
Bronze: Sara Neil (road race)

Diving
Silver: Wendy Fuller (10-metre)
Bronze: Debbie Fuller (springboard)

Equestrian
Gold: Lisa Carlsen, Laura Balisky (team jumping)
Gold: Christilot Boylen (individual dressage)
Gold: Christilot Boylen, Diana Biles, Eva-Maria Pracht, Martina Pracht (team dressage)
Silver: Martina Pracht (individual dressage)
Silver: Moira Tone (team: three-day event)

Fencing
Silver: Madeleine Philion (foil)

Gymnastics
Bronze: Andrea Conway, Yanic Giguere, Ildiko Hattayer, Theresa McKenzie, Amelie Major, Daphne Vallieres (team)

Team Handball
Silver: Julie Audette, Judith Begin, Caroline Benoit, France Brunet, Marie Gibert, Louise Gratton, Suzie Houle, Mirjana Jurcic, Monique Lamy, Johanne Legault, Lucie Lemire, Michele Levasseur, Marie-Claude Pesant, Manon Rouleau, Evelyne Seguin

Field Hockey
Bronze: Danielle Audet, Wendy Baker, Sara Ballantyne, Sharon Bayes, Jody Blaxland, Laura Branchaud, Nancy Charlton, Maureen Conn, Mary Conn, Deb Covey, Sharon Creelman, Elizabeth Scenczek, Sandra Levy, Lisa Lyn, Kathryn MacDougall, Shona Schleppe

Judo
Gold: Sandra Greaves (66 kilos)
Silver: Alison Webb (72 kilos)
Bronze: Lyne Poirier (48 kilos)
Bronze: Kathy Hubble (52 kilos)
Bronze: Nathalie Gosselin (56 kilos)
Bronze: Mandy Clayton (61 kilos)

Rhythmic Gymnastics
Silver: Mary Fuzesi (clubs)
Bronze: Mary Fuzesi (all-around)
Bronze: Mary Fuzesi (hoop)
Bronze: Mary Fuzesi (ribbon)

Rowing
Gold: Silken Laumann (single sculls)
Gold: Kirsten Barnes and Kathleen Heddle (coxless pairs)

Gold: Michele Murphy (lightweight single sculls)
Silver: Siobhan Herron and Marlene Van der Horst (lightweight double sculls)
Silver: Diane Sinnige and Karen Smyte (lightweight coxless pairs)
Bronze: Karen Ashford and Connie Delisle (double sculls)

Shooting
Gold: Sharon Bowes (air rifle)
Bronze: Joele Fefer (standard rifle: prone)

Softball
Bronze: Jolayne Anderson, Claudette Bergeron, Shanna Biggan, Janis Cookson, Kathy Fisher, Tracy Gelsinger, Tracey Hucklak, Kelly Kelland, Morgan Kyule, Sandy Leroux, Marie-Claude Routhier, Susan Scherer, Lori Sippel, Debbie Smallwood, Brenda Staniforth, Debbie Tidy, Donna Veale, Mary-Anne Walz

Swimming
Gold: Keltie Duggan (100 breaststroke)
Silver: Denise Gereghty, Cheryl McArton, Robin Ruggiero, Manon Simard (4x100 freestyle relay)
Silver: Keltie Duggan, Cheryl McArton, Robin Ruggiero, Manon Simard (4x100 medley relay)
Bronze: Megan Holliday (400 freestyle)
Bronze: Megan Holliday (800 freestyle)
Bronze: Robin Ruggiero (100 butterfly)
Bronze: Shay McNicol (200 butterfly)
Bronze: Karin Helmstaedt (200 individual medley)
Bronze: Karin Helmstaedt (400 individual medley)
Bronze: Anne-Marie Anderson, Denise Gereghty, Sally Gilbert, Cheryl McArton (4x200 freestyle relay)

Synchronized Swimming
Silver: Sylvie Frechette (solo)
Silver: Karen Fonteyne and Karen Sribney (duet)
Silver: Lisa Alexander, Karen Fonteyne, Nathalie Guay, Colleen Harvey, Heather Johnston, Andrea Manning, Helene Normand, Karen Sribney (Canadian team)

Table Tennis
Silver: Mariann Domonkos (singles)
Silver: Mariann Domonkos and Thanh Mach (doubles)
Bronze: Mariann Domonkos, Thanh Mach, Helene Bedard (team)
Bronze: Marianne Domonkos (mixed doubles)

Yachting
Silver: Caroll-Ann Alie (sailboard)

Roller Skating
Bronze: Heather Patterson (pairs free dance)

1983 Caracas
Track and Field
Gold: Charmaine Crooks (400)
Gold: Ranza Clarke (1,500)
Silver: Charmaine Crooks, Christine Slythe, Gwen Wall, Jillian Richardson (4x400 relay)
Bronze: Gwen Wall (400-metre hurdles)
Bronze: Tanya Brothers, Charmaine Crooks, Karen Nelson, Jillian Richardson (4x100 relay)

Archery
Silver: Roberta Barker, Linda Kazienko, Lucille Lemay, Lucille Lessard (team)
Bronze: Linda Kazienko (individual)

Diving
Bronze: Sylvie Bernier (three-metre)

Judo
Silver: Mandy Clayton (52 kilos)
Silver: Lorraine Methot (66 kilos)
Silver: Nancy Jewitt (72 kilos)
Bronze: Tina Takahashi (48 kilos)
Bronze: Diane Amyot (61 kilos)
Bronze: Sara Riives (open)

Rowing
Silver: Marie-Claude Gaudet and Heather Hattin (double sculls)
Bronze: Maureen Grace (single sculls)

Shooting
Silver: Linda Thom (match pistol)
Silver: Joelle Fefer, Christine Schulze, Jackie Terry (smallbore, three position rifle, team)
Silver: Joelle Fefer, Christine Schulze, Jackie Terry (air rifle team)
Bronze: Linda Thom (air pistol)
Bronze: Sheila MacQuarrie, Christine Schulze, Jackie Terry (prone rifle team)
Bronze: Christina Schulze (smallbore rifle, three position)

Softball
Gold: Claudette Bergeron, Nancy Brentnell, Nancy Bulmer, Janis Cookson, Lucie Foucault, Shawna Hicks, Laura Houle, Kathleen McCune, Treshan McDonald, Rose McEachern, Kathy McGuire, Claire Reed, Sue Scherer, Lori Sippel, Darlene Solie, Brenda Staniforth, Ann Tkachuk, Donna Veale

Swimming
Gold: Anne Ottenbrite (100 breaststroke)
Gold: Kathy Bald (200 breaststroke)
Silver: Jane Kerr (100 freestyle)
Silver: Michelle MacPherson (200 individual medley)
Silver: Michelle MacPherson (100 butterfly)
Silver: Kathy Bald (100 breaststroke)
Silver: Kathy Bald, Jane Kerr, Carol Klimpel, Pam Rai (4x100 freestyle relay)
Silver: Jane Kerr, Michelle MacPherson, Barb McBain, Anne Ottenbrite (4x100 medley relay)
Bronze: Kathy Bald (100 freestyle)
Bronze: Julie Daigneault (200 freestyle)
Bronze: Julie Daignault (400 freestyle)
Bronze: Julie Daignault (800 freestyle)
Bronze: Michelle MacPherson (400 individual medley)
Bronze: Barb McBain (100 backstroke)
Bronze: Barb McBain (200 backstroke)
Bronze: Marie Moore (200 butterfly)

Synchronized Swimming
Gold: Nathalie Audet, Sharon Hambrook, Kelly Kryczka, Chantal Laviolette, Penny Vilagos, Vicky Vilagos, Renee Paradis, Carolyn Waldo (Canadian team)
Silver: Penny Vilagos and Vicky Vilagos (duet)
Silver: Sharon Hambrook (solo)

Table Tennis
Silver: Mariann Domonkos (mixed doubles)
Bronze: Mariann Domonkos, Gloria Hsu, Thanh Mach (team)
Bronze: Mariann Domonkos, Thanh Mach (doubles)

1979 San Juan
Track and Field
Gold: Diane Jones Konihowski (pentathlon)
Silver: Angella Taylor (200)
Silver: Sharon Lane (100 hurdles)
Bronze: Angella Taylor (100)
Bronze: Penny Werthner (1,500)
Bronze: Geri Fitch (3,000)
Bronze: Micheline Racette, Marita Payne, Janet Wood, Anne Mackie-Morelli (4x400 relay)
Bronze: Debbie Brill (high jump)
Bronze: Carmen Ionesco (shot put)
Bronze: Carmen Ionesco (discus)
Bronze: Jillian Ross (pentathlon)

Gymnastics
Gold: Monica Goermann (overall)
Gold: Sherry Hawco (beam)
Gold: Monica Goermann (uneven bars)
Gold: Canadian women's team (team all-around)
Silver: Monica Goermann (floor exercises)
Silver: Elfi Schlegel (uneven bars)
Silver: Elfi Schlegel (vault)
Bronze: Elfi Schlegel (overall)

Swimming
Gold: Anne Gagnon (200 breaststroke)
Silver: Patricia Bedard (200 breaststroke)
Silver: Cheryl Gibson (100 backstroke)
Silver: Cheryl Gibson (200 backstroke)
Silver: Nancy Garapick (200 individual medley)
Silver: Gail Amundrud, Carol Klimpel, Anne Jardin, Wendy Quirk (4x100 freestyle relay)
Silver: Cheryl Gibson, Anne Gagnon, Nancy Garapick, Gail Amundrud (4x100 medley relay)
Bronze: Gail Amundrud (100 freestyle)
Bronze: Gail Amundrud (200 freestyle)
Bronze: Wendy Quirk (400 freestyle)
Bronze: Barbara Shockey (800 freestyle)
Bronze: Anne Gagnon (100 breaststroke)
Bronze: Nancy Garapick (100 butterfly)
Bronze: Nancy Garapick (400 individual medley)
Diving
Bronze: Janet Nutter (three-metre)
Bronze: Linda Cuthbert (10-metre)
Synchronized Swimming
Gold: Helen Vanderburg (solo)
Gold: Kelly Kryczka, Helen Vanderburg (duet)
Silver: Sharon Hambrook, Janet Arnold, Beth Irwin, Kim Binnie, Raphaela Jablonca, Leslie Ringrose, Kelly Kryczka, Helen Vanderburg (team)
Basketball
Bronze: Canadian women's team
Equestrian
Silver: Terry Leibel (team jumping)
Fencing
Silver: Chantal Payer, Lousie LeBlanc, Patricia Balz, Jacynthe Poirie (team foil)
Roller Skating
Bronze: Sylvie Gingras (long program)
Bronze: Sylvia Gingras (pairs long program)
Bronze: Lori Beal (free dance)
Archery
Silver: Linda Kazienko (70 metres)
Silver: Joan McDonald, Linda Kazienko, Marie Pietrie (team)
Bronze: Joan McDonald (50 metres)

1975 Mexico City
Track and Field
Gold: Joyce Yakubowich (400)
Gold: Diane Jones (pentathlon)
Gold: Margaret McGowan, Joanne McTaggert, Rachelle Campbell, Joyce Yakubowich (4x400 relay)
Silver: Patty Loverock (100)
Silver: Abby Hoffman (800)
Silver: Thelma Wright (1,500)
Silver: Louise Walker (high jump)
Bronze: Marjorie Bailey (100)
Bronze: Abby Hoffman (1,500)
Bronze: Marjorie Bailey, Patty Loverock, Joanne McTaggart, Joyce Yakubowich (4x100 relay)
Bronze: Lucette Moreau (shot put)
Bronze: Jane Haist (discus)
Swimming
Gold: Lyne Chenard (100 backstroke)
Silver: Gail Amundrud (200 freestyle)
Silver: Lyne Chenard (200 backstroke)
Silver: Joann Baker (200 breaststroke)
Silver: Cheryl Gibson (400 individual medley)
Silver: Gail Amundrud, Jill Quirk, Janice Stenhouse, Anne Jardin (4x100 freestyle relay)
Silver: Lyne Chenard, Joann Baker, Wendy Quirk, Jill Quirk (4x100 medley relay)
Bronze: Wendy Quirk (100 butterfly)

Bronze: Marian Stuart (100 breaststroke)
Bronze: Jill Quirk (100 freestyle)
Bronze: Anne Jardin (200 freestyle)
Bronze: Michele Oliver (400 freestyle)
Bronze: Janice Stenhouse (800 freestyle)
Bronze: Cheryl Gibson (200 backstroke)
Bronze: Cheryl Gibson (200 individual medley)
Diving
Gold: Janet Nutter (10-metre)
Silver: Elizabeth Carruthers (three-metre)
Bronze: Linda Cuthbert (10-metre)
Synchronized Swimming
Silver: Sylvie Fortier (solo)
Silver: Laura Wilkin and Carol Stuart (duet)
Silver: Laura Wilkin, Carol Stuart, Frances Hambrook, Kim Birnie, Michelle Calkins, Nancy Good, Helen Vanderburg, Raphaela Jablonca (team)
Equestrian
Gold: Christilot Boylen (individual dressage)
Silver: Christilot Boylen, Barbara Stracey, Lorraine Stubbs (team dressage)
Silver: Liz Ashton (three-day event, team)
Bronze: Norma Chornawka-Myers (team jumping)
Fencing
Silver: Donna Hennyey, Susan Stewart, Louise LeBlanc, Chantal Gilbert-Payer (team foil)

1971 Cali
Track and Field
Gold: Stephanie Berto (200)
Gold: Abby Hoffman (800)
Gold: Debbie Brill (high jump)
Gold: Brenda Eisler (long jump)
Gold: Debbie Van Kiekebelt (pentathlon)
Silver: Stephanie Berto (100)
Silver: Penny May (pentathlon)
Bronze: Penny Werthner (800)
Bronze: Penny May (80-metre hurdles)
Bronze: Carol Martin (discus)
Swimming
Gold: Donna-Marie Gurr (100 backstroke)
Gold: Donna-Marie Gurr (200 backstroke)
Gold: Sylvie Dockerill (100 breaststroke)
Gold: Janie Wright (200 breaststroke)
Gold: Leslie Cliff (200 individual medley)
Gold: Leslie Cliff (400 individual medley)
Gold: Donna-Marie Gurr, Janie Wright, Leslie Cliff, Angela Coughlan (4x100 medley relay)
Silver: Angela Coughlan (100 freestyle)
Silver: Angela Coughlan (200 freestyle)
Silver: Janie Wright (200 breaststroke)
Silver: Leslie Cliff (100 butterfly)
Silver: Leslie Cliff, Donna-Marie Gurr, Diane Gate, Angela Coughlan (4x100 freestyle relay)
Bronze: Karen James (100 freestyle)
Bronze: Angela Coughlan (400 freestyle)
Diving
Gold: Elizabeth Carruthers (three-metre)
Gold: Nancy Robertson (10-metre)
Silver: Beverley Boys (10-metre)
Bronze: Beverley Boys (three-metre)
Synchronized Swimming
Silver: Jocelyne Carrier (solo)
Silver: Mado Ramsay and Jocelyne Carrier (duet)
Silver: Linda Bedard, Sylvie Fortier, Gail Bedard , Deborah Humphrey, Susan Thomas, Laura Wilkin, Lorraine Nicholl (team)
Equestrian
Gold: Christilot Hanson (individual dressage)
Gold: Christilot Hanson, Cynthia Neale (team dressage)

Gold: Wendy Irving, Cathy Wedge (team three-day event)
Gold: Barbara Simpson (team jumping)
Gymnastics
Bronze: Canadian women's team (team all-around)
Bronze: Lisa Arsenault (floor exercises)
Bronze: Jennifer Diachun (floor exercises)

1967 Winnipeg
Swimming
Gold: Elaine Tanner (100 backstroke)
Gold: Elaine Tanner (200 backstroke)
Silver: Marion Lay (100 freestyle)
Silver: Marion Lay (200 freestyle)
Silver: Elaine Tanner (100 butterfly)
Silver: Sandra Dowler, Angela Coughlan, Elaine Tanner, Marion Lay (4x100 freestyle relay)
Silver: Elaine Tanner, Donna Ross, Marilyn Corson, Marion Lay (4x100 medley relay)
Bronze: Angela Coughlan (200 freestyle)
Bronze: Angela Coughlan (400 freestyle)
Bronze: Angela Coughlan (800 freestyle)
Bronze: Shirley Cazalet (100 backstroke)
Bronze: Marilyn Corson (100 butterfly)
Bronze: Sandra Dowler (200 individual medley)
Bronze: Marilyn Corson (400 individual medley)
Track and Field
Gold: Nancy McCredie (shot put)
Silver: Carol Martin (discus)
Silver: Jenny Meldrum (pentathlon)
Bronze: Jay Dahlgren (javelin)
Bronze: Irene Piotrowski (100 metres)
Bronze: Abby Hoffman (800 metres)
Bronze: Susan Nigh (high jump)
Bronze: Maureen Dowds (shot put)
Gymnastics
Gold: Susan McDonnell (uneven bars)
Silver: Canadian women's team (team all-around)
Diving
Silver: Kathy McDonald (three-metre)
Silver: Beverley Boys (10-metre)
Basketball
Bronze: Canadian women's team
Equestrian
Bronze: Inez Fischer-Credo, Christilot Hanson, Jean McKenzie (team dressage)
Fencing
Bronze: Pacita Wiedel (foil)
Bronze: Pacita Wiedel, Donna Hennyey, Sigred Chatel (team foil)
Tennis
Bronze: Vicki Berner, Faye Urban (doubles)

1963 Sao Paulo
Track and Field
Gold: Abby Hoffman (800)
Gold: Nancy McCredie (discus)
Gold: Nancy McCredie (shot put)
Silver: Jennifer Wingerson (80-metre hurdles)
Silver: Diane Gerace (high jump)
Bronze: Noreen Deuling (800)
Swimming
Silver: Mary Stewart (100 freestyle)
Silver: Mary Stewart (100 butterfly)
Silver: Mary Stewart, Sharon Pierce, Eileen Weir, Lynne Pomfret (4x100 freestyle relay)
Silver: Mary Sewart, Madeleine Sevigny, Sharon Pierce, Lynne Pomfret (4x100 medley relay)
Bronze: Lynn Pomfret (200 freestyle)
Bronze: Lynn Pomfret (400 freestyle)
Bronze: Eileen Weir (100 backstroke)

Bronze: Marjon Wilmink (200 breaststroke)
Diving
Silver: Judy Stewart (three-metre)
Synchronized Swimming
Bronze: Sandra Marks (solo)
Bronze: Marilyn Malenfant and Sandra Marks (duet)
Gymnastics
Silver: Canadian women's team (team all-around)
Silver: Susan McDonnell (floor exercises)

1959 Chicago
Track and Field
Bronze: Sally McCallum (200)
Bronze: Marian Monroe (80-metre hurdles)
Bronze: Alice Whitty (high jump)
Gymnastics
Gold: Ernestine Russell (individual)
Gold: Ernestine Russell (beam)
Gold: Ernestine Russell (uneven bars)
Gold: Ernestine Russell (vault)
Silver: Ernestine Russell (floor exercise)
Silver: Canadian women's team (all-around)
Bronze: Marie-Claire Larsen (all-around)
Bronze: Marie-Claire Larsen (uneven bars)
Bronze: Louise Parker (vault)
Swimming
Silver: Sara Barber (100 backstroke)
Silver: Margaret Iwasaki, Sara Barber, Helen Hunt, Lynn Scott (4x100 freestyle relay)
Silver: Sara Barber, Janice Schepp, Margaret Iwasaki, Lynn Scott (4x100 medley relay)

1955 Mexico City
Swimming
Gold: Helen Stewart (100 freestyle)
Gold: Beth Whittall (400 freestyle)
Gold: Lenore Fisher (100 backstroke)
Gold: Beth Whittall (100 butterfly)
Silver: Helen Stewart, Beth Whittall, Gladys Priestly, Virginia Grant (4x100 freestyle relay)
Silver: Helen Stewart, Beth Whittall, Virginia Grant, Lenore Fisher (4x100 medley relay)
Bronze: Virginia Grant (100 freestyle)
Synchronized Swimming
Silver: Canadian team
Bronze: Diana Baker and Beverly McKnight (duet)
Track and Field
Bronze: Heather Campbell, Maureen Rever, Sally McCallum, Valerie Jerome (4x100 relay)

1951 Buenos Aires - *Canada did not compete*

Velma Springstead Award
Presented annually to Canada's outstanding female athlete of the year.

1994: Myriam Bedard (Biathlon)
1993: Kate Pace (Alpine Skiing)
1992: Kerrin Lee-Gartner (Alpine Skiing)
1991: Silken Laumann (Rowing)
1990: Sylvie Daigle (Speedskating)
1989: Heather Houston (Curling)
1988: Carolyn Waldo (Synchronized Swimming)
1987: Carolyn Waldo (Synchronized Swimming)
1986: Carolyn Waldo (Synchronized Swimming)
1985: Carolyn Waldo (Synchronized Swimming)
1984: Linda Thom (Shooting)
1983: Lynn Chornobrwy (Modern Pentathlon)
1982: Angella Taylor (Track and Field)
1981: Susan Nattrass (Shooting)
1980: Angella Taylor (Track and Field)

1979: Helen Vanderburg (Synchronized Swimming)
1978: Diane Jones Konihowski (Track and Field) / Cathy Sherk (Golf)
1977: Sylvia Burka (Speedskating) / Susan Nattrass (Trap Shooting)
1976: Cheryl Gibson (Swimming)
1975: Nancy Garapick (Swimming) / Diane Jones (Track and Field)
1974: Wendy Cook (Swimming)
1973: Karen Magnussen (Figure Skating)
1972: Karen Magnussen (Figure Skating)
1971: Karen Magnussen (Figure Skating)
1970: Angela Coughlan (Swimming)
1969: Linda Crutchfield (Luge)
1968: Nancy Greene (Alpine Skiing)
1967: Nancy Greene (Alpine Skiing)
1966: Elaine Tanner (Swimming)
1965: Petra Burka (Figure Skating)
1964: Gail Daley (Gymnastics)
1963: Nancy McCredie (Track and Field)
1962: Mary Stewart (Swimming)
1961: Mary Stewart (Swimming)
1960: Anne Heggtveit (Alpine Skiing)
1959: Anne Heggtveit (Alpine Skiing)
1958: Lucile Wheeler (Alpine Skiing)
1957: Irene MacDonald (Diving)
1956: Marlene Stewart (Golf)
1955: Ernestine Russell (Gymnastics)
1954: Ernestine Russell (Gymnastics)
1953: Ernestine Russell (Gymnastics)
1952: Luella Law (Track and Field)
1951: Betty Hamilton (Fencing)
1950: Rosella Thorne (Track and Field)
1949: Eleanor McKenzie (Track and Field)
1948: Viola Myers (Track and Field)
1947: Barbara Ann Scott (Figure Skating)
1946: Irene Strong (Swimming)
1945: Barbara Ann Scott (Figure Skating)
1944: Rhoda and Rhona Wurtele (Alpine Skiing)
1943: Joan Langdon (Swimming)
1942: Joan Langdon (Swimming)
1941: Rose Mary Thacker (Figure Skating)
1940: Dorothy Walton (Badminton)
1939: Jannette Dolson (Track)
1938: Noel MacDonald (Basketball)
1937: Robina Higgins (Track and Field)
1936: Betty Taylor (Track and Field)
1935: Aileen Meagher (Track and Field)
1934: Phyllis Dewar (Swimming)

Elaine Tanner Award
Presented annually to Canada's top junior female athlete.

1994: Melanie Turgeon (Alpine Skiing)
1993: Anne Montminy (Diving)
1992: Nancy Drolet (Hockey)
1991: Paige Gordon (Diving)
1990: Stacy Singer (Baton Twirling)
1989: Stacy Singer (Baton Twirling)
1988: Mary Fuzesi (Rhythmic Gymnastics)
1987: Lori Strong (Gymnastics)
1986: Sylvie Frechette (Synchronized Swimming)
1985: Stacy Singer (Baton Twirling)
1984: Sylvie Bernier (Diving)
1983: Sylvie Daigle (Speedskating)
1982: Marie-Claude Asselin (Freestyle skiing)
1981: Angela Bailey (Track and Field)
1980: Becky McKnight (Table Tennis)
1979: Sylvie Daigle (Speedskating)
1978: Helen Vanderburg (Synchronized Swimming)
1977: Michelle Calkins (Synchronized Swimming) / Helen
      Vanderburg (Synchronized Swimming)

1976: Shannon Smith (Swimming)
1975: Sylvie Fortier (Synchronized Swimming)
1973: Glenda Reiser (Track and Field)
1972: Leslie Cliff (Swimming)

Canadian Press Award
Presented annually to the top woman athlete of the year in voting by Canadian sport journalists; since 1978 the award recipient has received the Bobbie Rosenfeld Trophy, honouring Canada's woman athlete of the half-century.

1994: Myriam Bedard (Biathlon)
1993: Kate Pace (Alpine Skiing)
1992: Silken Laumann (Rowing)
1991: Silken Laumann (Rowing)
1990: Helen Kelesi (Tennis)
1989: Helen Kelesi (Tennis)
1988: Carolyn Waldo (Synchronized Swimming)
1987: Carolyn Waldo (Synchronized Swimming)
1986: Laurie Graham (Alpine Skiing)
1985: Carling Bassett (Tennis)
1984: Sylvie Bernier (Diving)
1983: Carling Basset (Tennis)
1982: Gerry Sorenson (Alpine Skiing)
1981: Tracey Wainman (Figure Skating)
1980: Sandra Post (Golf)
1979: Sandra Post (Golf)
1978: Diane Jones Konihowski (Track and Field)
1977: Cindy Nicholas (Swimming)
1976: Kathy Kreiner (Alpine Skiing)
1975: Nancy Garapick (Swimming)
1974: Wendy Cook (Swimming)
1973: Karen Magnussen (Figure Skating)
1972: Jocelyne Bourassa (Golf)
1971: Debbie Van Kiekebelt (Track and Field) / Debbie Brill (Track
      and Field)
1970: Beverley Boys (Diving)
1969: Beverley Boys (Diving)
1968: Nancy Greene (Alpine Skiing)
1967: Nancy Greene (Alpine Skiing)
1966: Elaine Tanner (Swimming)
1965: Petra Burka (Figure Skating)
1964: Petra Burka (Figure Skating)
1963: Marlene Stewart Streit (Golf)
1962: Mary Stewart (Swimming)
1961: Mary Stewart (Swimming)
1960: Anne Heggtveit (Alpine Skiing)
1959: Anne Heggtveit (Alpine Skiing)
1958: Lucile Wheeler (Alpine Skiing)
1957: Marlene Stewart (Golf)
1956: Marlene Stewart (Golf)
1955: Marilyn Bell (Swimming)
1954: Marilyn Bell (Swimming)
1953: Marlene Stewart (Golf)
1952: Marlene Stewart (Golf)
1951: No Award Presented
1950: No Athlete of the Year selected: Bobbie Rosenfeld named
      Canada's female athlete of the half century.
1949: Irene Strong (Swimming)
1948: Barbara Ann Scott (Figure Skating)
1947: Barbara Ann Scott (Figure Skating)
1946: Barbara Ann Scott (Figure Skating)
1942-1945: No award presented due to World War II
1941: Mary Rose Thacker (Figure Skating)
1940: Dorothy Walton (Badminton)
1939: Mary Rose Thacker (Figure Skating)
1938: Noel MacDonald (Basketball)
1937: Robina Higgins (Track and Field)
1936: Betty Ann Taylor (Track and Field)

1935: Aileen Meagher (Track and Field)
1934: Phyllis Dewar (Swimming)
1933: Ada McKenzie (Golf)

Lou Marsh Award — Women Winners
Presented annually by the Toronto Star to Canada's Athlete of the Year.

1994: Myriam Bedard (Biathlon)
1991: Silken Laumann (Rowing)
1988: Carolyn Waldo (Synchronized Swimming)
1981: Susan Nattrass (Shooting)
1979: Sandra Post (Golf)
1968: Nancy Greene (Alpine Skiing)
1967: Nancy Greene (Alpine Skiing)
1966: Elaine Tanner (Swimming)
1965: Petra Burka (Figure Skating)
1960: Anne Heggtveit (Alpine Skiing)
1959: Barbara Wagner (with Rob Paul - Figure Skating)
1958: Lucile Wheeler (Alpine Skiing)
1956: Marlene Stewart Streit (Golf)
1955: Beth Whittall (Swimming)
1954: Marilyn Bell (Swimming)
1951: Marlene Stewart (Golf)
1948: Barbara Ann Scott (Figure Skating)
1947: Barbara Ann Scott (Figure Skating)
1945: Barbara Ann Scott (Figure Skating)

HALLS OF FAME INDUCTEES
(Through 1994)

Canada's Sports Hall of Fame
Florence Bell (Track and Field), 1955
Marilyn Bell (Marathon Swimming), 1958
Sylvie Bernier (Diving), 1987
Beverley Boys (Diving), 1979
Lela Brooks (Speedskating), 1972
Petra Burka (Figure Skating), 1965
Michelle Cameron (Synchronized Swimming), 1991
Ethel Catherwood (Track and Field), 1955
Leslie Cliff (Swimming), 1984
Betsy Clifford (Alpine Skiing), 1970
Myrtle Cook (Track and Field), 1955
Frances Dafoe (Figure Skating), 1955
Phyllis Dewar (Swimming), 1971
Sylvie Fortier (Synchronized Swimming), 1977
Laurie Graham (Alpine Skiing), 1993
Nancy Greene (Alpine Skiing), 1967
Anne Heggtveit (Alpine Skiing), 1960
Maria Jelinek (Figure Skating), 1962
Kathy Kreiner (Alpine Skiing), 1960
Lucille Lessard (Archery), 1977
Dorothy Lidstone (Archery), 1977
Irene MacDonald (Diving), 1981
Noel MacDonald (Basketball), 1971
Ada MacKenzie (Golf), 1955
Karen Magnussen (Figure Skating), 1973
Susan Nattrass (Shooting), 1977
Cindy Nicholas (Marathon Swimming), 1993
Anne Ottenbrite (Swimming), 1994
Karen Percy (Alpine Skiing), 1994
Sandra Post (Golf), 1988
Pat Ramage (Skiing — Builder), 1984
Bobbie Rosenfeld (Track/Multi-Sport), 1955
Barbara Ann Scott (Figure Skating), 1955
Peggy Seller (Synchronized Swimming), 1966
Marjory Shedd (Badminton), 1970

Ethel Smith (Track and Field), 1955
Gerry Sorenson (Alpine Skiing), 1989
Marlene Stewart (Golf), 1962
Hilda Strike (Track and Field), 1972
Elaine Tanner (Swimming), 1971
Linda Thom (Shooting), 1992
Cathy Townsend (Bowling), 1977
Barbara Underhill (Figure Skating), 1988
Helen Vanderburg (Synchronized Swimming), 1983
Barbara Wagner (Figure Skating), 1957
Carolyn Waldo (Synchronized Swimming), 1991
Dorothy Walton (Badminton), 1961
Lucile Wheeler (Alpine Skiing), 1958
Jean Wilson (Speedskating), 1955

British Columbia Sports Hall of Fame and Museum
Lillian (Palmer) Alderson (Track and Field), 1969
Rita (Panasis) Bell (Basketball), 1975
Stephanie Berto-Berkun (Track and Field), 1989
Carole Bishop (Volleyball), 1988
Debbie Brill (Track and Field), 1989
B.C. Members, 1992 Olympic rowing team (Rowing), 1994
Karen (Magnussen) Cella (Figure Skating), 1972
Leslie Cliff (Swimming), 1978
Moira Colborne (Field Hockey), 1985
Patricia (Jones) Dalziel (Track and Field), 1991
Faye (Burnham) Eccleston (All-Around), 1966
1954-55 Vancouver Eilers (Basketball), 1991
Rosemary Fuller (Softball), 1991
Lori Fung (Rhythmic Gymnastics), 1985
Donna-Marie Gurr (Swimming), 1987
1944-45 Hedlunds (Basketball), 1989
Wendy (Cook) Hogg (Swimming), 1990
Helen (Stewart) Hunt (Swimming), 1968
Lynda (Adams) Hunt (Diving), 1970
Audrey (Griffin) Kieran (Swimming), 1971
Kerrin Lee-Gartner (Alpine Skiing), 1994
Marjorie Leeming (Tennis), 1977
Dorothy Lidstone (Archery), 1981
Claire Lovett (Badminton), 1975
Irene Macdonald (Diving), 1972
Mary (Stewart) McIlwaine (Swimming), 1966
Joan (Langdon) McLagan (Swimming), 1988
Ann (Mundigal) Meraw (Swimming), 1985
1985 Linda Moore Rink (Curling), 1985
Irene Piotrowski (Track and Field), 1993
Pamela Rai (Swimming), 1993
Nancy (Greene) Raine (Alpine Skiing), 1969
Donalda Smith (Synchronized Swimming), 1992
Shannon Smith (Swimming), 1983
Tricia Smith (Rowing), 1992
Louise Soper (Figure Skating), 1979
Gerry Sorensen-Lenihan (Alpine Skiing), 1986
Violet (Pooley) Sweeny (Golf), 1974
Elaine Tanner (Swimming), 1969
Margaret (Sutcliffe) Todd (Golf) 1973
Margaret (Taylor) Turner (Badminton), 1967
Eileen (George) Underhill (Badminton), 1970
1930 UBC Women's Team (Basketball), 1981
Eleanor (Cave) Whyte (All-Around), 1987
Ruth Wilson (Basketball), 1966
Tracy Wilson (Figure Skating), 1991

Alberta Sports Hall of Fame and Museum

Elsie Barlow (Softball), 1966
Pamela Barnard (Table Tennis - Disabled), 1978
Margaret Berezowski (Figure Skating), 1983
Nancy Brawley (Diving), 1985
Michelle Calkins (Synchronized Swimming), 1980
Michelle Cameron (Synchronized Swimming), 1991
Elizabeth Carruthers (Diving), 1974
Betty Stanhope Cole (Golf, Curling), 1980
June Cox (Multi-Sport), 1984
Thelma Crowe (Speedskating), 1976
Mary Currie (Bowling), 1978
Thelma Dean (Track and Field), 1976
Dianne Earl (Track and Field), 1976
Elaine Ell (Wheelchair Sports), 1976
Marjorie Eustance (Tennis), 1980
Cheryl Gibson (Swimming), 1986
Gail Greenough (Equestrian), 1994
Susan Halak (Swimming), 1978
Sharon Hambrook (Synchronized Swimming), 1988
Vera Holdsworth (Trapshooting), 1989
Hazel Jamieson (Golf, Curling), 1980
Barbara Kerr (Equestrian), 1987
Rose Kohn (Community Sports), 1970
Kelly Kryczka (Synchronized Swimming), 1980
Juanita Lawrence (Track and Field), 1958
Phyllis Loewen (Speedskating), 1992
Anne Mackie-Morelli (Track and Field), 1987
Joan Maclagan (Figure Skating, Swimming), 1985
Annabelle McLean (Track and Field), 1960
Lisa Miller (Broadcast), 1990
Debbie Muir (Synchronized Swimming), 1994
Susan Nattrass (Shooting), 1994
Sandra Osborne (Swimming), 1978
Enid Dowdle Pepper (Multi-Sport), 1982
Dorothy Pogue (Track and Field), 1982
Cathy Priestner (Speedskating), 1976
Mary Ann Reeves (Synchronized Swimming), 1993
Winnie Reid (Multi-Sport), 1989
Gail Ross (Equestrian), 1982
Jean Ross (Synchronized Swimming), 1968
Doreen Ryan (Speedskating), 1974
Margaret Scott (Synchronized Swimming), 1976
Dianne Sharkey (Swimming - Disabled), 1976
Gwen Smith (Swimming), 1988
Rebecca Smith (Swimming), 1974
Marg Southern (Equestrian), 1992
Pat Underhill (Speedskating), 1970
Helen Vanderburg (Synchronized Swimming), 1980
Carolyn Waldo (Synchronized Swimming), 1980

Edmonton Grads Basketball Teams - 1915-1949   1974

Marguerite Bailey	Frances Gordon	Helen McIntosh
Betty Bawden	Hattie Hopkins	Eleanor Mountifield
Babe Belanger	Jessie Innis	Mabel Munton
Elsie Bennie	Daisy Johnson	Doris Neale
Mae Brown	Dot Johnson	Helen Northrup
Sophie Brown	Joan Johnston	Nellie Perry
Evelyn Caulson	Margaret Kinney	Betty Ross
Babe Daniel	Winnie Martin	Abbie Scott
Etta Dann	Kate MacCrae	Connie Smith
Mary Dunn	Noel MacDonald	Edith Stone
Elizabeth Elrick	Kay MacRitchie	Helen Stone
Gladys Fry	Margaret McBurney	Jean Williamson
Winnie Gallen	Mildred McCormick	

Canada West Ringette Teams 1990 and 1992, 1994

George Buzak (staff)	Anne Gillespie
Frances Willis (staff)	Stacey Hanny
Reg Wood (staff)	Tami Ironside
Cheryl Goenlock (captain)	Diana Kondrosky
Karen White (captain)	Tamara McKernan
Tamara Anderson	Deb Marek
Cindy Annla	Susan Olson
Cara Brown	Tanya Orr
Lisa Brown	Holly Reeves
Nicole Chapdelaine	Shelley Reynolds
Shauna Chomik	Jackie Richards
Jenny Cook	Jennifer Rogers
Susan Curran	Lyndsay Wheelans
Sandy Fenton	Janine Wood
Shauna Flath	Krisal Zwarych

Saskatchewan Sports Hall of Fame and Museum

Mary (Bonnie) Baker (Softball), 1985
Gail Bakker (Gymnastics), 1993
Bonnie Ballantine (Bowling), 1975
Jean Black (Lawn Bowling - Builder), 1983
Ethel Catherwood (Track and Field), 1966
Muriel Coben (Softball), 1979
Betty Lou Dean (Swimming - Builder), 1991
Phyllis Dewar (Swimming), 1967
Maureen (Rever) Duwors (Track and Field), 1977
Joanne Goulet (Golf), 1980
Martha (Nelson) Grant (Swimming), 1981
Phyllis Haslam (Swimming), 1975
Eleanor (Haslam) Jensen (Track and Field), 1974
Nancy Jewett-Filteau (Judo), 1992
Daisy Junor (Baseball), 1989
Sadie Caulder Knight (Synchronized Swimming-Builder), 1981
Diane Jones Konihowski (Track and Field), 1980
Patricia A. Lawson (Multi-Sport), 1985
Wendy Lee (Swimming), 1986
Claire (Ehman) Lovett (Badminton), 1977
Laura Malesh (Softball), 1987
Mille (Warwick) McAuley (Softball), 1986
Arleene (Johnson) Noga (Baseball), 1989
Sandra Roberts (Synchronized Swimming-Builder), 1992
Kelly (Rollo) Seaman (Diving), 1989
Barbara Shockey-Milanese (Swimming), 1990
Geraldine Street (Golf), 1988
Annie Thompson (Tennis), 1981
Margaret (George) Tosh (Track and Field), 1978
Barbara Turnbull (Golf), 1973
Audrey Turner (Diving), 1971
Eleanor (Powley) Van Impe (Speedskating), 1984
Dorothy Walton (Badminton), 1966
Brenda Webster (Speedskating), 1991
Cathy Wedge (Equestrian), 1982
Lynn (Kanuka) Williams (Track and Field), 1994
Doreen (Dredge) Wolff (Track and Field), 1990
Muriel Youngson (Curling - Builder), 1980

Teams:

Saskatoon Aces Ladies Basketball Team, 1974
Saskatoon Adilman Aces Ladies Basketball Team, 1974
Saskatoon Ladies Bowling Team, 1974
Evelyn Krahn Curling Rink, 1988
Larry McGrath Mixed Curling Rink (Darlene Hill, Marlene Dorsett), 1981
Larry McGrath Mixed Curling Rink (Darlene Hill, Audrey St. John), 1981
McKee Curling Team (Saskatoon): Joyce McKee, Syl Fedoruk, Donna Belding, Muriel Coben, 1973
McKee Curling Team (Saskatoon): Joyce McKee, Syl Fedoruk, Rosa McFee, Barbara McNevin, 1973

Marj Mitchell Curling Rink (Regina): Marj Mitchell, Nancy Kerr,
   Shirley McKendry, Wendy Leach, 1981
Vera Pezer Curling Rink (Saskatoon): Vera Pezer, Joyce McKee,
   Sheila Rowan, Lee Morrison, 1982
Dorenda Shoenhals Curling Rink: Dorenda Shoenhals, Cheryl
   (Stirton) Zipper, Linda (Burnham) Seaman, Joan Anderson, 1989
Saskatoon Imperials Senior Women's Fastball Team, 1970
University of Saskatchewan Huskiette Volleyball Team, 1981
University of Saskatchewan Huskiette Volleyball Team, 1980
University of Saskatchewan Huskiette Volleyball Team, 1979

Manitoba Sports Hall of Fame
Pat Ball (Figure Skating), 1994
Ethel Bieber (Swimming), 1991
Sylvia Burka (Speedskating), 1983
Peggy Colonello (Golf - Builder), 1994
1965 CUAC Blues (Softball), 1992
Maureen Dowds (Track and Field), 1988
Marj Edey (Golf), 1984
Elfride Goermann (Gymnastics - Builder), 1987
Monica Goermann (Gymnastics), 1991
Robina Higgins (Track and Field), 1984
Ollie Hynduik (Bowling), 1990
Catherine Kerr (Swimming), 1985
Vivian King (Swimming), 1984
Connie Laliberte Rink (Curling), 1984
Elizabeth Levin (Speedskating), 1986
Olive Little (Softball/Baseball), 1985
Kay Minions (Lawn Bowling), 1993
Evelyn Moroz (Baseball), 1992
Judy Moss (Diving), 1980
Jane Maddin Neale (Track and Field), 1987
Janet Nutter (Diving), 1986
Betty (Mitchell) Olson (Speedskating), 1989
Zlatica Stauder (Rhythmic Gymnastics), 1988
Anne Tachan (Golf), 1994
Mary Rose Thacker (Figure Skating), 1984
Dodie Wardle (Figure Skating - Builder), 1991
Joan Whalley (Curling - Builder), 1981
Bonnie Wittmeier (Gymnastics), 1992

Northwestern Ontario Sports Hall of Fame
Joann Baker-Anderson (Swimming), 1994
Ruth Black (All-Around), 1985
Winnie (Harpell) Bocking (Figure Skating, Tennis), 1987
Beryl Campbell (Figure Skating - Builder), 1992
Hilda (Fiori) Donati (Hockey - Builder), 1988
Barbara Hutcheon (Figure Skating), 1994
Kathy Kangas (Parachuting), 1989
Helen (Gerry) Reith (Curling), 1988
Lorraine Sharpe (Bowling), 1983
June Shaw (Curling), 1989
Ella Wilson (Tennis), 1986
Teams:
Heather Houston Curling Rink - Canadian and World Champions,
   1988 and 1989 (Heather Houston, Lorraine Lang, Diane Adams,
   Tracy Kennedy, Gloria Taylor)
Lang Curling Rink - Canadian Mixed Champions, 1981
   (Rick Lang, Anne Provo, Bert Provo, Lorraine Edwards Lang)
Lund Curling Rink - Canadian Mixed Champions, 1979
   (Roy Lund, Nancy Lund, Ron Apland, Marsha Kerr Apland)
Northern Ontario Open Mixed 5-Pin Bowling Champions, 1975
   (Elvira Dustin, Ovide Duguay, Lucille Harris and Bev McCool)

Quebec Sports Hall of Fame / Pantheon des Sports du Québec
Sylvie Bernier (Diving), 1991

Jocelyne Bourassa (Golf), 1992
Linda Crutchfield (Luge, Alpine and Water Skiing), 1993
Myrtle Cook McGowan (Track and Field), 1974
Lucile Wheeler Vaughan (Alpine Skiing), 1974
Carolyn Waldo (Synchronized Swimming), 1994

New Brunswick Sports Hall of Fame
Millicent Anderson (Curling), 1989
Lesley Armstrong (Figure Skating-Builder), 1987
Ethel Babbi (Tennis), 1971
Sybil Beatteay (Speedskating), 1983
Dorothy Brockway (Track and Field), 1980
Diane Clement (Track and Field), 1979
Della Cody (Synchronized Swimming), 1990
Sandra DeVenney (Wheelchair Sports), 1987
Mabel DeWare Rink (Curling), 1976
Jean Dickeson (Golf), 1995
Mary Ellen Driscoll (Golf), 1988
Carole Keyes (Luge), 1995
Gems Moncton (Bowling), 1990
Margaret Purdy (All-Around), 1979
Joyce Slipp (Basketball/Field Hockey), 1992
Mabel Thomson (Golf), 1975

Nova Scotia Sports Hall of Fame
Marjorie Bailey (Track and Field), 1984
Edith Bauld (Golf), 1981
Elizabeth Connor (Golf), 1993
Anne Marie Dodge (Paddling), 1994
Nancy Garapick (Swimming), 1986
Dorothy Holmes (Golf), 1980
Maisie Howard (Golf), 1982
Vida Large (Tennis), 1980
Rita Lohnes (Golf), 1982
Annie Longard (Builder), 1988
Gladys Longard (Builder), 1988
Karin Maessen (Volleyball), 1994
Susan Mason (Swimming), 1985
Aileen Meagher (Track and Field), 1964
Janet Merry (Builder), 1987
Miriam Penney (Golf), 1993
Gertrude Phinney (Track and Field), 1964
Freda Wales (Builder), 1981
Teams:
Acadia Women's Swim Team, 1977-78
Liverpool Jets Senior Women's Softball, 1965-67
Truro Slugs Girls Softball, 1945-46, 1950

Prince Edward Island Sports Hall of Fame
Evelyn Henry Brown (Marathon Swimming), 1973
Adele Marchbank Gillis (Track and Field), 1976
Blanche Hogg (Golf), 1976
Mary McLennan Lea (Shooting), 1970
Gertie Doyle Martin (Bowling), 1992
Barbara McNeill (Marathon Swimming), 1990
Nancy White (Speedskating), 1980

Newfoundland Sports Hall of Fame
Caroline Ball (Curling, Golf), 1987
Margaret Davis (Softball, Field Hockey, Soccer, Ice Hockey, Ball
Hockey), 1994
Paula (Kelly) Dowey (Swimming), 1993
Gillian Grant (Race Walking, Nordic Skiing), 1994
Margaret Hitchens (Tennis), 1992
Joanne MacDonald (Basketball, Slalom, Track, Table Tennis), 1993
Violet Pike (Curling, Golf), 1986
Elizabeth Swan (Figure Skating), 1986

Bibliography & Credits

Bibliography and reading of further interest:

Brill, Debbie with Lawton, James. *Jump*. Vancouver: Douglas & McIntyre, 1986.

Browne, Lois. *Girls of Summer*. Toronto: Harper Collins, 1992.

Bryden, Wendy. *Canada at the Winter Olympic Games*. Edmonton: Hurtig Publishers, 1987.

Chapman, Currie with Starkman, Randy. *On the Edge: The Inside Story of the Canadian Women's Ski Team*. Toronto: McGraw-Hill Ryerson, 1988.

Cobley, John. *Winning Canadian Runners*. Victoria: Quail Run Publishing, 1994.

Cochrane, Jean; Hoffman, Abby; Kincaid, Pat. *Women in Canadian Sports*. Toronto: Fitzhenry and Whiteside, 1977.

Colombo, John Robert (general editor). *The 1995 Canadian Global Almanac*. Toronto: Macmillan, 1994.

Dheenshaw, Cleve. *The Commonwealth Games: The First 60 Years — 1930-1990*. Victoria: Orca Book Publishers, 1994.

Frayne, Trent. *The Best of Times: Fifty Years of Canadian Sport*. Toronto: Key Porter Books Ltd., 1988.

Frayne, Trent and Gzowski, Peter. *Great Canadian Sports Stories: A Century of Competition*. Toronto: The Canadian Centennial Publishing Company Limited, 1965.

Frechette, Sylvie with Lacroix, Lilianne. *Gold at Last*. Toronto: Stoddart Publishing Co. Ltd., 1994.

Ferguson, Bob. *Who's Who in Canadian Sport*. Scarborough: Prentice-Hall of Canada, Ltd. 1977.

Hurdis, John. *Speed Skating in Canada, 1854-1981: A Chronological History*. Montreal and Toronto: Canadian Printing Ltd., 1980.

Irwin, Petra (editor). Svoboda, Chuck and Grant, Gordon — Sports consultants. *The Canadian Sports Almanac and Directory*. Toronto: Copp Clark Publishing, 1974.

Kearney, Jim with Sport B.C.. *Champions: A British Columbia Sports Album*. Vancouver: Douglas & McIntyre, 1985.

Kelso, J.G. *Canadian Swimming Medalists/Finalists - Olympic Games 1912-1992*. School of Human Kinetics, University of B.C.

McDonald, David and Drewery, Lauren. *For the Record: Canada's Greatest Women Athletes*. Toronto: Mesa Associates, John Wiley & Sons, Distributors, 1981.

McFarlane, Brian. *Proud Past, Bright Future: One Hundred Years of Canadian Women's Hockey*. Toronto: Stoddart Publishing Co. Ltd., 1994.

McNulty, Bill and Radcliffe, Ted. *Canadian Athletics 1839-1992*: Vancouver, 1992.

May, Zita Barbara. *Canada's International Equestrians*. Toronto: Burns and MacEachern, 1975.

Mott, Morris (editor). *Sports in Canada: Historical Readings*. Toronto: Copp Clark Pitman Ltd., 1989.

Pan-American Sports Organization (PASO). *Compendium of the Results of the Pan-American Games from Buenos Aires 1951 to Indianapolis 1987. Mexico City*: PASO, 1989.

Patterson, Bruce. *Canadians on Everest*. Calgary: Detselig Enterprises, 1990.

Rheaume, Manon (with Chantal Gilbert). *Manon: Alone in Front of the Net*. Toronto: Harper Collins, 1993.

Smith, Beverly. Diamond, Dan (editor). *Figure Skating: A Celebration*. Toronto: McClelland and Stewart, 1994.

Stewart, Barbara. *She Shoots...She Scores: A Complete Guide to Women's Hockey*. Toronto: Doubleday Canada Ltd., 1993.

Wallechinsky, David. *The Complete Book of the Olympics*. New York: Viking Penguin Inc., 1988.

Wallechinsky, David. *The Complete Book of the Winter Olympics: 1994 Edition*. Toronto: Little, Brown & Company (Canada) Ltd, 1993.

Wise, S.F. and Fisher, Douglas for Canada's Sports Hall of Fame. *Canada's Sporting Heroes*. Don Mills: General Publishing Company Limited, 1974.

Young, David. *The Golden Age of Canadian Figure Skating*. Toronto: Summerhill Press, 1984.

Credits:

Many thanks to the following Provincial and National sport organizations for supplying background, results and all manner of important information upon request, and for conveying information in the past that wound up in background files that were integral to the creation of this book.

Alpine Canada
Athlete Information Bureau
Athletics Canada
B.C. Athletics
Badminton Canada
Basketball Canada
Biathlon Canada
Canadian Amateur Diving Association
Canadian Amateur Hockey Association
Canadian Amateur Speed Skating Association
Canadian Amateur Wrestling Association
Canadian Association for the Advancement of Women and
    Sport and Physical Activity
Canadian Curling Association
Canadian Cycling Association
Canadian Equestrian Federation
Canadian Figure Skating Association
Canadian Gymnastics Federation
Canadian Ladies' Golf Association
Canadian Olympic Association
Canadian Paralympic Committee
Canadian Rhythmic Sportive Gymnastic Federation
Canadian Ski Association - Freestyle
Canadian Soccer Association
Canadian Yachting Association
Commonwealth Games Association of Canada
Curl B.C.
Federation of Canadian Archers
Manitoba Ladies' Curling Association
Promotion Plus
Ringette Canada
Rowing Canada
Royal Canadian Golf Association
Saskatchewan Ladies' Curling Association
Shooting Federation of Canada
Softball B.C.
Softball Canada
Sport B.C.
Sport Information Resource Centre
Swim B.C.
Swimming Canada
Synchro Canada
Tennis Canada
Water Ski Canada

. . . .

Credit also goes to the following sports halls of fame for providing background information and aid in tracking down athletes.

Alberta Sports Hall of Fame and Museum
B.C. Sports Hall of Fame and Museum
Canada's Sports Hall of Fame
Manitoba Sports Hall of Fame
New Brunswick Sports Hall of Fame
Newfoundland and Labrador Sports Hall of Fame
Northwestern Ontario Sports Hall of Fame
Nova Scotia Sports Hall of Fame
Prince Edward Island Sports Hall of Fame
Quebec Sports Hall of Fame/Pantheon des Sports du Quebec
Saskatchewan Sports Hall of Fame

. . . .

Newspapers and magazines that were essential in my research:

Alberta Report
Athletics
Calgary Herald
Canadian Rowing
Canadian Yachting
Champion Magazine
Curl Canada
Edmonton Journal
Horse Sport
Maclean's
Montreal Gazette
Ottawa Citizen
Sports Illustrated
Swim Magazine
The Blood Horse
Toronto Globe and Mail
Toronto Star
Track and Field News
Vancouver Sun
Victoria Times-Colonist
Winnipeg Free Press

Photo Credits:

<u>LEGEND:</u>

ASHF = Alberta Sports Hall of Fame & Museum
BCSHFM = British Columbia Sports Hall of Fame and Museum
CP = Canapress Photo Services
CSHF = Canada's Sports Hall of Fame
CSI = Canadian Sports Images
SSHF = Saskatchewan Sports Hall of Fame and Museum

FRONT COVER, (clockwise from top):

Gail Greenough and Jappeloup de Luze: Pennington Galleries
Chantal Petitclerc: F. Scott Grant, CSI
Anne Ottenbrite: Swim Canada
Charmaine Crooks: Denise Howard, Vancouver Sun
Kate Pace: Claus Andersen, CSI
Silken Laumann: Ted Grant, CSI

. . . .

<u>PAGE</u> <u>PHOTOGRAPHER, SOURCE</u>

16	Chris Relke
17	CSHF
19	CSHF
20	CSHF
22	Michael Burns, CSHF
23	CSHF
25	Jacques Boissinot, CP
26	Claus Andersen, CSI
29	Chris Relke
30	Chuck Stoody, CP
31	upper: CSI
31	lower: Carmichael Photography
32	Don Weixl Photography
34	Paul Morrison Photography
35	Lauralee Bowie collection
36	Marie Claude Asselin collection
37	F. Scott Grant, CSI
38	W.P. McElligott
40	Chris Relke
42	Claus Andersen, CSI
45	Barbara Ann Scott collection
46	Giuseppe Ghedina, Petra Burka collection
48	Brian Kent, Vancouver Sun
49	CSI
50	Ted Grant, CSI
51	F. Scott Grant, CSI
52	CSHF
53	CSHF
54	upper: CSHF
54	lower: CSI
55	F. Scott Grant, CSI
57	left: CSHF
57	right: CSHF
58	left: F. Scott Grant, CSI
58	right: Paquin, CP
60	ASHF
63	Victoire/Desjardins Bibeau Inc.
65	ASHF
67	Ryan Remiorz, CP
68	Sandy Grant, CSI
70	left: F. Scott Grant, CSI

70	right: F. Scott Grant, CSI
72	F. Scott Grant, CSI
73	left: F. Scott Grant, CSI
73	right: Veronica Milne. Toronto Sun/Photo-Canada Wide
76	left: SSHOF
76	right: Dave Buston, CP
78	Steve Bosch, Vancouver Sun
79	BCSHFM
80	A. Stawicki, Toronto Star
81	Michael Burns
82	Michael Burns
84	Scott Gardner, CP
85	Dave Buston, CP
89	Bill Cunningham, BCSHFM
91	Swim Canada
92	BCSHFM/Health Canada
93	CSHF
94	Jeff Vinnick, Vancouver Sun
95	left: BCSHFM
95	Athlete Information Bureau/Canadian Olympic Association
96	Swim Canada
97	upper: Nova Scotia Sport Heritiage
97	lower: BCSHFM
98	upper: Swim Canada
98	lower: Swim Canada
99	C. Chew, CSI
101	Toronto Star
102	CSHF
103	left: CSHF
103	right: Ian MacAlpine, CP
105	ASHF
106	L.T. Webser/Libra Photographic, ASHF
107	CSI
109	upper left: ASHF
109	upper right: ASHF
109	lower: Ted Grant, CSI
110	L.T. Webster/Libra Photographic, ASHF
111	BCSHFM
112	CSHF
113	CSI
114	Frank Gunn, CP

115	upper: Chris Relke		181	Chris Relke
115	lower: Frank Gunn, CP		183	ASHF
116	Dave Buston, CP		184	Canadian Wheelchair Basketball Association
118	Ron Poling, CP		185	Canadian Wheelchair Basketball Association
121	Ted Grant, CSI		186	Eileen Langsley, CSI
123	F. Scott Grant, CSI		187	left: J. Merrithew, CSI
125	Ted Grant, CSI		187	right: C. McNeill, CSI
126	Greg Kinch, CSI		188	University of Winnipeg
128	F. Scott Grant, CSI		189	Gary Hershorn, CP
129	F. Scott Grant, CSI		190	Mark Van Manen, Vancouver Sun
131	Canadian Yachting Association		191	left: Nick Didlick, Vancouver Sun
132	left: Canadian Yachting Association		191	right: John Mahoney, CP
132	right: Canadian Yachting Association		193	left: Ellen Saenger, BC Report/SSHF
133	Bill Marsh		193	right: CSHF
134	Ross Outerbridge		194	left: J. Goode, Toronto Star
135	Ross Outerbridge		194	right: R. Bull, Toronto Star
136	Ross Outerbridge		195	Chris Relke
138	J. Merrithew, CSI		196	Chris Relke
139	left: CSI		198	CSHF
139	right: Chris Relke		199	CP
141	Chris Relke		200	Hans Deryk, CP
143	Calgary Herald/Gail Greenough collection		201	CSHF
145	upper left: Claus Andersen, CSI		202	Brian Kent, Vancouver Sun
145	upper right: Claus Andersen, CSI		203	left: CP
145	lower left: Claus Andersen, CSI		203	right: Canadian Soccer Association
145	lower right: Claus Andersen, CSI		205	SSHF
146	Claus Andersen, CSI		206	Vancouver Sun
147	Liz Ashton collection		207	CSHF
148	Michael Burns, Toronto Star/Photo Canada Wide		208	Bill Cunningham, BCSHFM
150	B. Spremo, Toronto Star		210	CSHF
152	CSHF		211	CSI
153	left: Turofsky, CSHF		214	CP/Toronto Star
153	right: CSHF		215	John Hryniuk Photography
154	BCSHFM		217	BCSHFM
155	Chris Relke		219	CP
156	Bob Warren, CSHF		220	Canadian Olympic Association
158	Denise Howard, Vancouver Sun		223	Leigh Bierling
160	BCSHFM/Health Canada		224	Photo Canada Wide
161	SSHF		225	Chris Relke
163	Chris Relke			
165	F. Scott Grant, CSI			
167	upper: C. Chew, CSI			
167	lower: Vancouver Sun			
169	left: CSI			
169	right: Chris Relke			
171	Chris Relke			
173	Lynn Chornobrywy collection			
177	left: Dinsmore, Toronto Star			
177	right: Ray Smith, CP			
178	Chris Relke			
179	CP			
180	left: F. Scott Grant			
180	right: CSI			

Chris Relke was the photo editor for **Celebrating Excellence**. Much recognition is due for his skill, patience and perseverance in tracking down sources and aquiring photographs, and for his professional eye in selecting the right images.

A special thank you to Sandy Grant of Canadian Sports Images, Allan Stewart of Canada's Sports Hall of Fame, and Laurie J. Taylor of Canapress Photo Service for their help in tracking down photographs, and to individual athletes who allowed us access to their personal photo collections.

An attempt was made to correctly credit all photographers and sources. If information contained herein is incorrect or insufficient, we will be pleased to correct it in subsequent editions.

Index of Athletes

DATE DUE

MAR 0 3 1997	APR 3 2004		
MAR 0 6 1997	FEB 5 2005		
MAR 2 7 1997	FEB 0 3 2005		
MAR 3 1 1997	OCT 1 3 2005		
APR 2 2 1998	NOV 1 5 2007		
APR 1 5 1998	FEB 0 9 2009		
MAR 1 4 2001			
FEB 2 2 2001			
MAR 2 8 2001			
APR 0 9 2001			
APR 0 1 2001			
OCT 3 0 2001			
NOV 2 6			
APR 1 2 2003			
APR 1 0 2003			
NOV 0 6 2003			Printed in USA
APR 2 3 2004			